Civilians in the Path of War

Edited by Mark Grimsley and Clifford J. Rogers

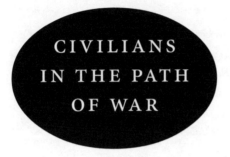

CIVILIANS
IN THE PATH
OF WAR

University of Nebraska Press

Lincoln and London

© 2002 by the University of Nebraska Press

All rights reserved

Manufactured in the United States of America ⊗

Library of Congress Cataloging-in-Publication Data

Civilians in the path of war / edited by Mark Grimsley
and Clifford J. Rogers.

p.   cm. – (Studies in war, society, and the military)

Includes bibliographical references and index.

ISBN 0-8032-2182-7 (cloth : alkaline paper)

1. Military art and science – History. 2. Military history. 3. War – Protection of civilians. I. Grimsley,
Mark. II. Rogers, Clifford J. III. Series.

U27 .C56 2002   355.4 – dc21   2001043075

CONTENTS

MAPS

ACKNOWLEDGMENTS

Most of the essays in this collection originated as papers given at the Fourth Midwest Military History Consortium Conference, Columbus, Ohio, in autumn 1993. We would like to express our appreciation to the Mershon Center, whose financial assistance underwrote the cost of the conference and many of the expenses involved in preparing this volume. Stephen Stein was indispensable in organizing the conference. William B. Feis gave the project invaluable help at an early stage of the editorial process. Paul Bodine of The Operative Word ably copyedited the final manuscript, while cartographer Ron McLean supplied the numerous maps. Last, but hardly least, we would like to thank our contributors for their great patience and good cheer during the volume's lengthy gestation process.

Mark Grimsley
Clifford J. Rogers

Introduction

Mark Grimsley and Clifford J. Rogers

If war is the scourge of humanity, the killing of the helpless is its worst manifestation. The deaths of thousands, even millions, of young servicemen are mourned but accepted. But the deaths of even a few women, children, or elderly people can provoke outrage when they die at the hands of soldiers. The cry from time immemorial has been that such killings are pointless, vicious, immoral, atrocious. Ethical prescription and international law alike have condemned the evil and sought to restrict it if they could not eliminate it altogether. And yet the killing of the helpless has been a hallmark of warfare throughout the centuries, and never more so than during the one just ended.

"Helpless" is a term chosen with care. Although the title of this book employs a more common word whose current meaning seems clear, "civilians" is arguably ambiguous and, in any case, altogether anachronistic when applied much earlier than the late Middle Ages. Another expression, "innocent," is even less satisfactory. Who is innocent? In the bitter annals of atrocity even infants have been denied this quality. John Chivington, the colonel responsible for the Sand Creek Massacre, is reported to have authorized the killing of Cheyenne and Arapaho babies with the curt observation, "Nits make lice."[1]

A third possibility, "noncombatant," comes closer to the mark, but like civilian and innocent it can be contested. Is a worker in a munitions factory truly a noncombatant? A farmer whose grain fields help feed an army? An educator whose teachings legitimize and help to perpetuate a hated regime? Then too, strictly speaking, the term "noncombatant" also encompasses military personnel (e.g., chaplains and prisoners of war) whose exemption from violent harm derives mainly from military convention, not moral imperative.

The language of war is inherently politicized, and no portion more than the language used to refer to its victims. In this respect, a recent mass killing of American men, women, and children is instructive. In the hours after an explosion shattered the Alfred P. Murrah federal office building in Oklahoma City in April 1994, no one knew the perpetrator's identity. It was quickly established that a massive car bomb had detonated at curbside, but who had planted it? Early speculation centered on Islamic resistance groups, which would have made the bombing an act of terrorism. In such a case, by American standards, the bombing would have been a criminal act with political overtones. By the standards of many in the Middle East, it would have been a military strike against an aggressive, imperialistic, and intolerable American regime. Eventually, it transpired that the perpetrator was a disturbed ex-soldier whose motive appeared to be revenge against a despised "big government."

In each case, the victims were helpless. They had scant ability to protect themselves; indeed, they died without even knowing what had killed them. But were they innocent, or civilians, or noncombatants? Middle America regarded them as innocent victims as a matter of course. Surely these fathers, wives, and toddlers were *murdered*. A terrorist organization, on the other hand, might well have regarded them as "civilians," a term that does not necessarily connote inviolability but does strongly imply recognition that their killing was an act of war, not criminal homicide. And within the tortured mind of Timothy McVeigh, most of the dead were not innocent, civilians, or noncombatants but rather agents of an enemy government.

In such moral terrain the truth gets slippery. Who shall make distinctions concerning who may legitimately be butchered and who may not? Perhaps such distinctions should not even be made. "Kill them all, let God sort them out," is not merely a callous T-shirt logo. All too often, it has been the way in which soldiers and governments have actually operated.[2]

This book is about occasions in which soldiers and governments have deliberately attacked the helpless. It is concerned less with the legitimacy of such attacks than the reasons they occurred, the objectives sought, and the measures taken or eschewed. The shelves of libraries groan beneath the weight of works that address the legal or ethical aspects of such attacks. But in such works the attacks themselves are usually treated in general terms or viewed so thoroughly through the lens of morality that their actual motives and conduct escape close examination. We hope that a sustained appraisal of several specific attacks will contribute to a better understanding of a phenomenon that is melancholy to contemplate but unlikely to disappear.

In popular imagination, perceptions about the history of attacks upon civilians—we will use the word for the sake of convenience, despite its pitfalls—fall into three patterns. Some employ a whiggish interpretation that depicts a gradual journey toward enlightenment. Defeated populations were once killed or enslaved as a matter of course, the argument runs; today such treatment is rare and widely condemned. Others, taking their cue from the killing fields of Babi Yar, Cambodia, and Bosnia, see instead a descent into darkness. War was once a contest between chivalrous, brightly uniformed soldiers; now the killing of civilians is routine. (And, in truth, it was common for twentieth-century warfare to kill more civilians than soldiers.) Still others see war as a constant: always savage, always merciless. They nod agreement with William T. Sherman's famous dictum, "War is cruelty, and you cannot refine it."[3]

But none of these broad-brush characterizations can survive much scrutiny. The whiggish interpretation holds well enough when one contemplates the 1991 Gulf War, with its much-ballyhooed barrage of U.S. smart munitions that scrupulously avoided civilian killing. It fares more poorly when one turns to American search-and-destroy missions in Vietnam, and of course collapses altogether when one considers the atomic immolations of Hiroshima and Nagasaki. The reverse of the whig interpretation is similarly flawed. The twentieth century has seen the most vicious atrocities that mass politics, ideological fervor, and perverted technologies can offer, but it has also seen the most impressive steps to codify restraints on war. The notion of war as uniform horror, for its part, is simply absurd. Some wars kill many civilians, others almost none. Often the killing of civilians is regretted and minimized where possible. At other times the killing of civilians is in fact the principal objective.

Are historians then condemned merely to comment on attacks upon civilians? Could it be that discerning and articulating patterns is impossible? We think not. When the essays in this volume were originally presented at the Ohio State University in November 1993, presenters and audience were repeatedly struck by intriguing parallels and contrasts. The patterns were not simple, nor did they repeat themselves in each case study, but they were nevertheless evident.

The first pattern is that forbearance toward the helpless has always been instrumental rather than absolute. The crude version of noncombatant immunity in biblical times stemmed mainly from what might be called the "plunder principle." Conquerors viewed the noncombatant component of the enemy as valuable booty. The war code of the ancient Hebrews required that an enemy city that refused to surrender be besieged. Once captured, the males were to be killed, but "the women, and the little ones, and the cattle, and all that is in the city, even all the spoil thereof," were to be taken and used.[4] In the eighteenth century, a desire for maximal control over one's army, coupled with an interest in extracting supplies from an enemy countryside as smoothly as possible, contributed to comparatively mild treatment of enemy noncombatants. Armies on the march found it easier to eat if the local population cooperated by bringing them food. Indiscriminate violence against the common people only jeopardized that cooperation: as Marshal Villars explained to the army he led into Germany in 1707, "[M]y friends . . . if you burn, if you make the people run away, you will starve."[5] The risk of retaliation too has often encouraged the fighters of one side to spare the enemy's population so as to encourage equal restraint on the other side.

The second pattern emerges from the first. If the decision to spare civilians is generally instrumental, the decision to attack them is equally so. Such a recourse tends to occur when direct military action against the enemy regime seems unavailing. The conditions may vary. Sometimes the attacking army lacks the ability to achieve victory exclusively on the battlefield, as the Union army discovered during the American Civil War. Sometimes the enemy refuses to cooperate. In the early stages of the Peloponnesian War, for example, the Athenians took refuge behind their walls, relied on their naval superiority to carry the war to Sparta, and refused to face the stronger Spartan army in open combat. This strategy prompted the Spartans to turn their violence against the Attic countryside, devastating the land, burning houses, and chopping down olive trees in an attempt to force the Athenian phalanx into battle.

Sometimes in order to reach the enemy army on advantageous terms, an attacker cannot rely on its own supplies and must extract them from the countryside, with greater or less brutality depending on the discipline of its soldiers and the political costs it is willing to pay. This introduces a third pattern. As with other aspects of war, attacks on civilians can be usefully seen as negotiations, albeit of a rather nasty kind. "The power to hurt is bargaining power," political scientist Thomas Schelling has observed. "To exploit it is diplomacy—vicious diplomacy, but diplomacy."[6] These implicit negotiations are not merely with the enemy regime but also with the enemy people, with "bystanders" who will be influenced by what is done or avoided, and often with one's own soldiers.

The stance toward the enemy regime is obvious: see, we have hurt you, and we will hurt you more if you do not change your policies to accommodate us. In that respect, although the medium is different, the message is similar to what is communicated through action against the regime's military forces.

Toward the civilians under attack the message is slightly more subtle but easy to discern: see, your regime cannot protect you, so accept our rule. This is the classic rationale for attacks on civilians in areas under revolt. It was also evident in the *chevauchées* of the Hundred Years' War, when the English kings coerced the peasants of the contested French provinces to accept their claim to rule. A variant of this has become more prevalent since the rise of mass politics: see, your regime cannot protect you, so pressure your regime to accept our terms. General Sherman made this statement explicitly (though not altogether seriously) when he expelled the population of Atlanta. British planners employed it as a rationale for the area bombing of Germany during the World War II.[7]

Attacks on civilians are often conducted with an eye to their effect not only upon the enemy regime and people but also upon "bystander" regimes and peoples likely to be influenced by it. The most extreme cases of violence against noncombatants have often revolved around such considerations as strategic precedent, especially when applied to siege warfare. Until quite recently, it was permissible under the laws of war to put a besieged city to the sack if the garrison prolonged resistance until its defenses were stormed. The avowed objective was to encourage other besieged cities to abandon their defense before a final, expensive assault became necessary. Yet even here attackers have chosen to modulate the violence against civilians, depending on how they wished to influence "bystander" communities.

Two examples from the Peloponnesian War will serve to illustrate. During that conflict, the Athenians threatened the complete destruction of Melos if its people dared to resist the army that besieged it. When the city resisted anyway and was at last overcome, every Melian adult male was executed. The women and children for their part were sold into slavery. The objective, however, was less to punish Melos than to instruct those who were watching. The policy of frightfulness (as the Greek historian Thucydides has the ambassadors explain to the Melians) would serve to terrify other *poleis* that might consider rebellion against the Athenian Empire. A more moderate policy can be equally calculated for effect. In the case of Mytilene, a genuine rebel against Athenian authority (rather than a would-be neutral like Melos), the Athenian assembly initially decreed a genocidal punishment but then reconsidered, electing to execute "only" some one thousand men who had led the rebellion. In this case, it was argued that a harsher treatment would only encourage other rebellious cities to resist to the last.

Attacks on civilians can indeed backfire in just such a fashion. Especially in modern times, they may exert a powerful effect on the climate of opinion within the community of nations (though not, alas, as powerful as one might wish). During the Gulf War, therefore, the United States scrupulously avoided killing civilians for fear it would jeopardize the fragile Arab coalition and probably undercut support for the war at home. Ruthless dictatorships deny or soft-pedal their own killings for much the same reasons. For regimes that do resort to attacks on civilians the consequences can be serious. The massacres committed by Ottoman troops in Bulgaria in 1876, eloquently documented by a London journalist who saw the grisly aftermath, caused the British government to reverse its contention that the Ottoman suppression of the Bulgarian uprising was justified, and indeed forced it to abandon temporarily its long-held commitment to the preservation of the Ottoman Empire.[8] Similarly, American opinion toward imperial Germany grew more negative as a result of Germany's callous adoption of unrestricted submarine warfare in 1915 and 1917, with fateful consequences.

Implicit negotiations may also occur between the attacking regime

xiv

and its own soldiers. From medieval times through the early eighteenth century, European monarchs often could not pay or supply their troops on a sustained basis. To obtain their continued service, they were obliged to permit these troops to make up for shortfalls by pillaging the civilians around them — not just enemy civilians but also the monarch's own subjects — through what historian John A. Lynn has termed a "tax of violence."[9] The greater risks entailed in the storming of a city rather than protracted siege operations resulted in a tacit bargain by which troops enjoyed the right, in such cases, to sack the city once captured. Even in instances where a given regime has no policy interest in harming civilians, its attitude toward soldiers who assault or steal from civilians sends a powerful signal concerning what behaviors will be permitted or punished. During the American Civil War, Union commanders often indulged acts of petty theft but reacted strongly to reports of rape or murder, with the result that such acts were rare. During the Vietnam War, by contrast, official injunctions to observe the laws of war and respect Vietnamese civilians were usually sandwiched between other routine information given to arriving soldiers by a bored lieutenant temporarily detailed for such duty. The unofficial message thus communicated eclipsed the official policy and, coupled with the American "search-and-destroy" tactic, helped set the stage for atrocities like My Lai.

Finally, attacks on civilians are strongly conditioned by cultural and ideological assumptions. The most obvious cultural assumption is that such attacks are morally dubious at best. Within the Western tradition, this belief is one of long standing, albeit replete with exceptions and qualifications. This is not the place for a history of noncombatant immunity, but a few general points should be made. First, the basic concept flows from the notion that noncombatant enemies, by definition, are enemies who make no resistance; therefore, it is pointless to kill them. Second, historically this proscription has applied mainly to the subjects of a sovereign state. Subjects of an area in rebellion have enjoyed no such immunity. Unless they actively distance themselves from the rebellion (and sometimes not even then), they are often killed and not infrequently killed in as fiercely gruesome a fashion as possible. Such treatment was and is justified by its deterrent effect. As Sir John Fastolf wrote in the fifteenth century, "traitors and rebels must needs [be subjected to] another manner of war, a sharper and more cruel type of war" than that directed against a "natural" enemy; otherwise, rebellion would become endemic.[10] In other words, hard treatment of rebels—like the harsh penalties directed at recalcitrant defenders of a fortified place captured by assault—is intended at least as much to deter as to punish.[11] The belief that more rigorous measures are permissible to suppress rebellion than to fight an external war has remained important down to this day.

The principal qualification to the rule against killing civilians occurs in the context of military necessity. In some instances, if military operations are to be conducted effectively some civilian deaths are unavoidable. Even a "surgical" air strike against a military installation may well result in bombs missing the target and striking women and children instead. If a massive, sustained aerial campaign against an enemy's economic base or transportation net seems required, civilian casualties can easily climb into the thousands. How can military necessity be squared with the prohibition against killing noncombatants? Some would argue that, for all practical purposes, the effort is seldom made, that noncombatant immunity contracts as perceptions of military necessity expand. "It is patently obvious," one critic declared during the renewed Cold War atmosphere of the early Reagan years, "that military necessity has been elevated to an end to itself. How else can one explain the 'scenarios' of defense analysts who describe the way in which millions will die if the superpowers resort to nuclear warfare, while they ignore the condition of the human race in the aftermath?"[12]

But this is a rather despairing view. It is more accurate to suggest that at least some of the world's armed forces recognize and respect the tension between military necessity and noncombatant immunity. Their solution, imperfect but surely far better than nothing, is to achieve the military objective through the most discriminating, proportional use of force possible, even (ideally) at the acceptance of greater risks than required by a purely military calculation. Thus, a strategic bridge may be bombed in a fashion that requires greater danger to the attacking pilots in order to reduce the chance of injury to civilians on the ground. An enemy machine gun nest may be reduced by infantry assault rather than artillery bombardment because of the proximity of civilians.

The immediate reason such costs are accepted may vary. Often the political price of a more callous policy seems too high. Somewhat more rarely, it is judged too dishonorable, too damaging to morale, or too dangerous to the psychological well-being of servicemen to permit them to kill civilians when it is avoidable. But ultimately, the reason flows from a strong cultural perception that the killing of civilians is wrong, a perception embraced by the community of nations or by the people back home if not universally by the servicemen in combat.

The proscription against the killing of civilians is strongest, of course, when their full humanity is evident. It erodes rapidly when that humanity is denied. Usually, the denial occurs on religious, ideological, or racial grounds. Within the Christian tradition, the Crusades are the best-known example of a denial of full humanity made on religious grounds, but there are many others. The heretical Albigensian "Cathars," for example, were ruthlessly exterminated despite the fact that they were pacifists.[13] The sectarian strife between Catholics and Protestants during the Wars of Religion and the Thirty Years' War sparked atrocities of legendary proportions. Ideology, the modern secular variant of religion, can produce similar results. Ideological fury guided revolutionary France in its brutal suppression of the Vendée; it spurred Nazi Germany not only to an aggressive war in western Europe but to a far more horrific, anti-Bolshevik crusade in the Soviet Union. And it underlay the shocking "autogenocide" of the Pol Pot regime against its own people. Racial prejudice, for its part, produces a mindset in which it becomes easy to see one's adversaries as little better than animals.

In each of these cases, the implicit argument is not only that these "others" do not deserve mercy but also that they pose a threat so elemental that mercy is foolish. If heresy is permitted to survive, the argument runs, it will inevitably spread, ultimately overwhelming orthodoxy. The danger from an ideological foe is similar: his mind contains a bacillus; left alone, it can infect others. Forbearance to savages, for its part, will be interpreted as weakness and only spur further acts of barbarity—and in any event, savages are beyond redemption. Still worse, the survival of a racial enemy—except on terms the victor utterly controls—leaves open the possibility of racial pollution. It is no accident that the rhetoric of race hatred is strongly laced with fears of seduction and rape.

The instrumental nature of civilian immunity, the equally instrumental nature of resort to civilian attack, the reality of such attacks as a negotiation on multiple levels, and the role of belief systems in inhibiting or encouraging such attacks: such are the basic patterns that shape the fate of civilians in the path of war. As is perhaps evident by now, these four patterns are interwoven, not discrete. How they have influenced and reacted upon one another at various times and places is the central subject of this book. Each essay takes a certain slice of history, from the Peloponnesian War to Operation Desert Storm; examines how prevalent the use of military force against civilians was at that time; and then proceeds to weigh the various elements that encouraged or limited violence directed against noncombatants and their property.

Paul A. Rahe opens the discussion with a penetrating analysis of attacks on noncombatants during the Peloponnesian War (431 to 404 B.C.) and the way in which the great historian of that conflict, Thucydides, depicted the moral calculus involved. Debunking the superficial view that Thucydides was a "realist" contemptuous of ethics in war, Rahe demonstrates the richness and complexity of his extended treatments of the arguments deployed by the belligerents to justify harshness or forbearance toward the peoples under their power. The desire to gain support by magnanimity as well as deter by ruthlessness is evident in the debates on Mytilene, Melos, and many others. Considerations of justice, necessity, and honor were debated and weighed. Thucydides represents such concerns as authentic: human beings are indeed capable of governing themselves in rational and enlightened ways. But, as Rahe observes, Thucydides also finds that such conduct is rare, especially under the stress of war. Justice and calculated statecraft all too often collapse in the face of haste, unreason, and shortsightedness.

Underscoring this point is Clifford J. Rogers's appraisal of the English *chevauchées* during the Hundred Years' War (1337–1453). That conflict, so extended and so ruthlessly fought on both sides, affords countless examples of the employment of violence against civilians as an instrument of political intercourse. The *chevauchées*—army-sized mounted raids inaugurated by King Edward III—were intended as messages to both the French monarch and the peasantry. To the king, the message was in essence an ultimatum: give the English what they want or suffer the consequences. To the French peasantry, it was a demonstration of their king's inability to perform the first duty of a monarch, the protection of his subjects, and was thus a goad for them to repudiate his authority. These messages were conveyed at the strategic level, where military actions and political goals were directly related, but similar negotiations took place at much lower levels as well, in the context of individual sieges, campaigns, or garrisoning operations. As at Melos in the Peloponnesian War, in the Hundred Years' War the threat of total destruction was often employed to persuade a besieged town or fortress to surrender quickly. Similarly, garrisons, *routiers*, and armies on campaign alike used it to compel the local population to purchase safety with contributions of cash or supplies.

Most of the case studies in this book concentrate on war against noncombatants as, at one level or another, a particularly harsh form of politics, where the goal of the action is persuasion or coercion. John A. Lynn's essay on the devastation of the Palatinate (1688–1689) reminds us that such destruction has material as well as psychological objectives, and sometimes the former are more desired than the latter. By systematically razing the cities and towns of the Palatine region (present-day western Germany), Louis XIV and his advisers hoped not to instill terror but to impede invasion by creating an artificial desert along the eastern frontier of France. In the short term, the tactic may have worked. In the long run, however, its psychological impact outweighed the purely military advantage gained. Rather than forestalling war, the ruined cities of the Palatinate confirmed European fears of the Sun King's hegemonic designs and pushed his rivals into fighting, and fighting hard, to contain him.

The Palatinate and neighboring German territory witnessed additional depredations in the 1790s. Despite a sincere wish to liberate Europe from the weight of absolute monarchy, the armies of revolutionary France probably did more harm to the people of Germany than the troops of Louis XIV had done in the preceding century. Certainly, they were responsible for more pillage and abuse—though fortunately not outright murder—than even the ferocious *chevaucheurs* of Edward III. Yet, as T. C. W. Blanning explains in "Liberation or Occupation?", this magnified level of depredation was not due to any principle of revolutionary strategy. On the contrary, the new French regime began its campaigns intent on waging war in a new style explicitly aimed at sparing the enemy population, whom it regarded as prospective allies in the crusade for *liberté, egalité, fraternité.* This luminous hope collapsed for one simple reason: like the armies of the Hundred

Years' War, the soldiers of the Revolution relied heavily on local provisionment for their food supplies. Further, the French armies of the 1790s were huge—far larger than even the Sun King's impressive hosts. Though commanders often tried to keep coercion to a minimum, the imbalance between the supplies required by famished soldiers and the available surplus meant that the requisitioners demanded more than civilians would willingly sell. Instead, they resisted and that in turn brought retribution.

Material circumstances thus imposed a dissonance between revolutionary ideals and actions. Since the army's material needs could not be met without coercion, enlightened ideology gave way to expedience. The "Edict of Fraternity," which contemplated cordial relations between the armies and the civilians in their midst, was revoked. The erstwhile "brothers in liberty" were denigrated, even dehumanized, until they seemed wretches who deserved their miserable fate. But the material gains of this harsh policy came at a high cost to French aspirations of carrying revolutionary fervor into other lands. As in the Palatinate, the heavy hand on the civilian population created unwelcome consequences.

At the outset of the American Civil War, the Union army held the same friendly intentions toward the Southern white population as had the French revolutionary armies toward the common people of western Europe. Believing that most Southern whites had been hoodwinked into secession by a slaveholding political elite, many Northern public officials thought that a program of forbearance would reassure the wayward Southerners and detach them from the Confederate government. This "conciliatory policy" remained the dominant Union stance for the first fifteen months of the conflict. Even during its heyday, however, it came under significant pressure because of the inability of some Federal commanders to feed their troops via regular supply lines. Moreover, foraging operations—both authorized and freelance—partly eclipsed the message of conciliation, as did Union military interference (much of it unintended) with the institution of slavery. Eventually, the logistical imperative to secure supplies from the countryside, and the corollary need to deny those supplies to the enemy, led to a "hard war" policy in which Union forces systematically attacked the Confederate war economy, including railroads, factories, crops, and livestock. These attacks, argues Mark Grimsley, inaugurated a new *chevauchée*. However, unlike the English version during the Hundred Years' War, this one did not degenerate into unrestrained murder, rape, and devastation. Rather, the Union hard war was characterized by a striking mixture of severity and restraint, discriminating and roughly proportionate in both intent and practice.

In this respect, Grimsley continues, U.S. military policy toward Southern whites bore little resemblance to white America's final wars with Native America. Although many Civil War commanders commanded forces on the western plains, they did not simply transfer tactics learned in 1861–1865 to those Indians who refused to accept life on the reservations. The measures used against Native Americans were far more sweeping, indiscriminate, and brutal—a war of cultural if not literal annihilation born of racism and expedience. White Americans largely embraced the common Anglo-Saxon notion of the era that they were the highest expression of civilization and therefore had a claim to hegemony over the other peoples of the world.

Appalling as it was, however, the United States's subjugation of the American Indian was not without moments of decency, pathos, and regret. Not so the less sentimental strain of "social Darwinism" that emerged in Germany. Warriors from the classical Greeks onward had recognized claims of morality, however imperfectly observed. As Holger Herwig argues, from 1871 onward the Germans increasingly did not.

The twentieth century has witnessed the most horrific attacks on civilians, attacks made possible by new technologies of mass destruction, by exterminationist ideologies, and—as Herwig demonstrates in his essay—by a sheer willingness to divorce military operations from any political or ethical context. Simply put, the German military from the late nineteenth century onward exalted a "blinkered professionalism" that consistently overlooked the political illogic and strategic impracticality of what it was asked to do. They plunged into both World Wars I and II with a fanatical belief in the ability of operational art to overcome all difficulties. As the seriousness of their strategic predicament became more evident, they readily took up any cudgel—the use of poison gas, unrestricted submarine warfare, or terror bombing—that seemed in the short run militarily efficacious, however questionable from a moral perspective. They dealt with moral questions by simply ignoring them.

Worse, the German officer corps eagerly embraced the aggressive, expansionist policies of their political masters in *both* world wars. This was not an officer corps honorably defending the German state and waging a "clean war," whatever the darker aspirations of a Kaiser Wilhelm II or a Hitler. It was an officer corps all too ready to accept an ideological program of conquest and extermination, all too ready to embrace a *Weltanschauung* based on the inevitability of struggle and the false dichotomy of world power or decline. World War I both deepened existing ideological trends and added new dimensions. Beginning with the cavalier sacrifice of Belgian neutrality on the altar of military expedience, it ended with German plans to annex or control European Russia. World War II continued and extended this pattern. The German military not only made no protest against Hitler's war of aggression, it actively supported its racial war against the "Jewish-Bolshevik bacilli" in the Soviet Union and played a substantial role in the execution or enslavement of Jews, Soviet civilians, and prisoners of war. "Barbarossa," Herwig writes, "perhaps the greatest *chevauchée* in history, ended in senseless and meaningless destruction as ends in themselves."

It is all too easy for the sheer scale of violence against civilians on the Eastern Front—an estimated ten million Soviet civilians perished during the war—to overwhelm its nuances and complexities.[14] Truman O. Anderson rectifies this tendency with a close analysis of the destruction of the Ukrainian village of Yeline in the winter of 1942, as German and Hungarian forces fought to eradicate partisan activity in its vicinity. Anderson makes two main observations. First, although three hundred civilians likely perished during the Yeline operation, the German program was actually somewhat less severe than in other areas like Belarus, probably because Nazi ideology deemed Ukrainians a slightly more advanced form of *Untermenschen* than their Russian counterparts. Second, he reminds us how easily civilians in the path of war may be caught between two fires: the villagers of Yeline paid the price for partisan resistance whether they supported it or not.

If the Third Reich was responsible for "the greatest *chevauchée* in history," it is fair to add that World War II witnessed an aerial *chevauchée* as well. Proponents of airpower actually championed destruction of population centers as a virtue, arguing that it would break an enemy society's will to fight more quickly and, in the long run, less bloodily than a protracted ground struggle like that on the Western Front during World War I. Moreover, unlike previous epochs, in which killing on a massive scale required more effort rather than less, it was actually easier to employ strategic bombers indiscriminately than to attempt precision methods. Britain's Royal Air Force yielded to this view in early 1941, after a review of its bombing effectiveness revealed that most of the tonnage dropped on Germany to date had not landed within five miles of its intended target. But Americans resisted this conclusion, doggedly adhering to a doctrine of daylight precision bombing as not only the most effective but also, in the words of air commander James Doolittle, "the most ethical way to go." Like the Union armies during the Civil War, the U.S. Army Air Forces sought to channel their destructive energies against the enemy's war resources and to avoid indiscriminate strikes against his civilian population.

Such a policy, as Conrad C. Crane ably points out, not only required a pinpoint accuracy difficult to achieve, but also existed in tension with a harsher program that championed the efficacy of a sweeping aerial assault that would shatter military and civilian morale. Although a number of American air planners resisted the concept—a staff officer dismissed one such proposal as "the same old baby-killing plan dressed up in a new kimono"—in the closing months of World War II the United States flirted ever more seriously with it and finally, for all practical purposes, embraced it. Although after the war the U.S. Air Force preferred to recall its precision-bombing campaign over Europe, the fire bombing of Tokyo and the atomic immolation of Hiroshima and Nagasaki (as well as complicity in the Dresden raid) left a much more disturbing legacy.

Even so, precision bombing remained an American ideal during the post-1945 era. The so-called surgical air strike became a cherished means to punish an enemy regime without harming the innocent. This goal became even more important in the politically charged atmosphere of the Cold War, when concerns loomed large not only about the disapproval of other countries but also of one's own people. At its worst, this bomber-as-scalpel brand of warfare could generate such absurdities as the rules of engagement during the Vietnam War. Yet even with the most exacting restrictions on airmen, for an air force equipped with "iron bombs" this degree of accuracy was tough to achieve. The advent of precision-guided munitions in 1972 offered the prospect of finally realizing this long-beloved dream, and the 1991 Gulf War—Operation Desert Storm—delivered the chance to make it reality.

In some respects, argues Williamson Murray, the American air campaign against Iraq exhibited a sophistication in operational planning unmatched in previous conflicts. Armed with a new generation of stealth fighter-bombers, "smart" bombs, and cruise missiles that could see terrain as accurately as the human eye, the U.S. Air Force (and its coalition counterparts) destroyed Iraq's air defense capability practically overnight and inflicted severe damage to key command and communications targets, including the Iraqi electric power grid. The objective of the campaign was almost identical to that of the *chevauchée*—a demonstration of the Baʿthist regime's inability to protect its population that would, in turn, promote a coup d'état removing Saddam Hussein from power (assuming the air strikes did not, by happy "chance," kill the Iraqi dictator outright). At the same time, however, American planners perceived a powerful need to avoid significant civilian casualties that might explode the fragile coalition and dissolve domestic political support for Desert Storm. Precision-guided munitions offered the hope of squaring the circle, but, as events would demonstrate, aerial bombardment was still more butcher knife than scalpel.

That reality struck home on 13 February 1991, when an estimated 314 civilians perished after two laser-guided "smart bombs" found the Al Firdos bunker in downtown Baghdad.[15] Here was just the sort of public relations disaster that planners feared, and the coalition promptly suspended further attacks on command and communications facilities in the Iraqi capital. Ironically, Murray notes, those who died in the bunker were not ordinary Iraqi citizens, who had little or no access to air raid shelters, but rather family members of high-ranking Baʿthist officials. If a coup against Saddam Hussein were to materialize anywhere, it would have to come from this quarter. Yet coalition air commanders shied from further strikes against this elite segment of the population, even as B-52s rained devastation on thousands of hapless conscripts in the Kuwaiti desert.

The nine essays that follow are far from providing a continuous narrative history of attacks on noncombatants as an instrument of policy, for that is not the purpose of this book. We hope instead that the in-depth case studies presented here will allow the reader to develop a sounder comprehension of the issue's complexities than would be possible from a survey approach. If this volume demonstrates anything it is that resort to such attacks proceeds from different motives, has varying purposes, and is encouraged or inhibited by a number of factors. Ethical concerns are seldom controlling, but they are rarely absent altogether. And the fact that the claims of morality have persisted, even in the melancholy episodes explored herein, is one of the few hopes available to civilians in the path of war.

Notes

1. Quoted in Dee Brown, *Bury My Heart at Wounded Knee* (New York, 1970), 90.

2. The roots of this phrase go back to a famous statement by the papal legate Armold Amalric in 1209. Just before the besieged city of Beziers was to be stormed and sacked, Almaric was asked how soldiers might distinguish between the heretics who had prompted the attack and the orthodox believers who might be within the walls. "Kill them all! God will know his own!" Amalric is said to have responded. See Richard Shelly Hartigan, *The Forgotten Victim: A History of the Civilian* (Chicago, 1982), 112.

3. William T. Sherman, *Memoirs*, 2 vols. (reprint ed.; Westport CT, 1972 [1875]), 2:126.

4. Deuteronomy, 20:13–14. However, even the limited mercy described in this passage was not allowed to the Hittites, Amorites, and other peoples living in the lands the Hebrews were to inhabit themselves.

5. Claude Villars, *Mémoires du Maréchal de Villars*, ed. Charles de Vogüé; 6 vols. (Paris, 1887), 2:229–30. Cf. Christopher Duffy, *The Military Experience in the Age of Reason* (New York, 1988), 13.

6. Thomas C. Schelling, *Arms and Influence* (New Haven, 1966), 2.

7. Sherman, *Memoirs*, 2:126; Barrie Paskins and Michael Dockrill, *The Ethics of War* (London, 1979), 35–36.

8. Misha Glenny, "Why the Balkans Are So Violent," *New York Review of Books* (19 September 1996), 34–36.

9. "How War Fed War: The Tax of Violence and Contributions during the *Grand Siècle*," *Journal of Modern History* 65, no. 2 (June 1993): 286–310.

10. John Fastolf, in *Letters and Papers Illustrative of the Wars of the English in France: During the Reign of Henry the Sixth*, ed. Joseph Stevenson, 2 vols. in 3 (London, 1861–64), 2:580: "traitours and rebellis must nedis have anothere manere of werre, and more sharpe and more cruelle werre than a naturelle and anoien ennemye; or els be liklines in proces of tyme no manere of man,

ner tounes, ner countries shalle rekenene shame to be traitours nere to rebelle causeles ayens theire souveryen lorde and ligeaunce at alle tymes aftere theire owne wilfulle [disob]ediens."

11. Cf. the Earl of Salisbury's letter excerpted in Rogers's article, this volume.

12. Hartigan, *The Forgotten Victim*, 9.

13. This was often the result of a siege pressed to the assault stage, where for reasons of strategic precedent one might expect this result regardless of heresy. However, the need to deter long defense of fortified places does not explain the burning of four hundred Cathars after the fall of Lavaur or the massacre of all the townspeople at Marmande *after the towns had surrendered.* J. R. Strayer, *The Albigensian Crusade* (New York, 1971), 79–80, 118.

14. The estimate of Soviet civilian loss is drawn from J. M. Winter, "Demography of the War," in *The Oxford Companion to World War II*, ed. I. C. B. Dear and M. R. D. Foot (Oxford, 1995), 290.

15. Lawrence Freedman and Efraim Karsh, *The Gulf Conflict, 1990–1991* (Princeton NJ, 1993), 326.

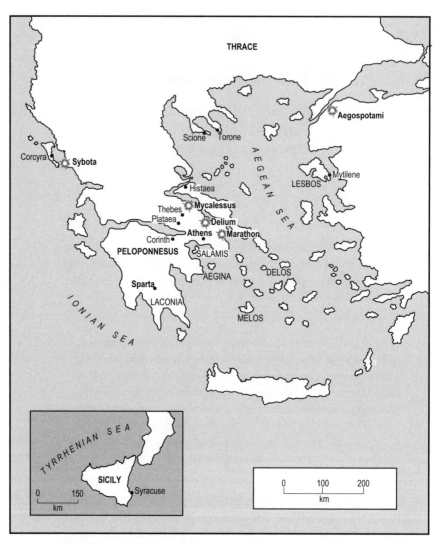

Map 1.1. The Peloponnesian War

Justice and Necessity

The Conduct of the Spartans and the Athenians in the Peloponnesian War

Paul A. Rahe

Few passages in the surviving works of the ancient historians are more plaintive than Xenophon's terse description of the reaction of his countrymen to the appearance at Peiraeus of a dispatch-trireme bearing news of the defeat and annihilation of the Athenian fleet at Aegospotami:

> Word of the disaster reached Athens the night the Paralus arrived, and a sound of lamentation reached from Peiraeus along the long walls to the town, one man reporting the news to another—so that during that night no one rested, and all mourned, not just for the dead, but much more for themselves, thinking that they would suffer the very fate that they had inflicted on Sparta's colonists the Melians, when they had taken them by siege, and on the Histiaeans and Scionaeans and Toronaeans and Aeginetans and many other Greek peoples.[1]

The Lacedaemonian admiral Lysander's decisive victory marked the climax of the long and bitter struggle between the Athenians and their Peloponnesian opponents, and everyone in Greece recognized the fact (see map 1.1). In the event, Athens held out against the Spartan siege for a few months after receiving the report. But resistance at this stage was an act of desperation. Barring divine intervention, the city's surrender was foreordained once it was cut off both by land and by sea, for it was deprived thereby both of the territory that it farmed and of access to the grain that it imported each year from the regions around the Black Sea and from other places abroad.

It is not surprising that a people soon to be in the hands of their enemies should fear that they would be made to suffer as they had themselves made citizens and resident aliens from conquered communities suffer in the past. Violent deeds of the sort that are generally recognized as war crimes may pass almost unremarked in the first flush of victory. But they have a way of returning to haunt a people when the time comes for their own defeat. The ancient Greeks may not have distinguished soldiers from civilians in the manner in which we do; they may not have subscribed to any formal notion of noncombatant immunity; but, at least in their wars with one another, they did concede to bystanders a moral claim.

To discover precisely what it was that the Athenians did to the Histiaeans, the Scionaeans, the Toronaeans, the Aeginetans, and the Melians, one must turn to the contemporary historian Thucydides and to his account of the Peloponnesian War.[2] One would not ordinarily think of this failed Athenian general as a humanitarian especially eager to understand just why communities at war so often commit atrocities against defenseless women, children, and captured enemy soldiers. He has long had a reputation, among political scientists, historians, and many classicists, as the first great proponent of "realism" in foreign policy, and there is a powerful case to be made for such a characterization. But there is another side to Thucydides—one, until recently, less often remarked.[3] For the historian's chief theme is neither the acquisition and retention of power nor the causes of anarchy in the international realm: Thucydides is, in fact, much more interested in exploring the conditions essential for, the circumstances conducive to, and the fragile character of what we would now call civilized life.[4] And in examining these questions, he pays close attention to the manner in which the Spartans, the Athenians, and their various allies treated noncombatants during the Peloponnesian War.

Thucydides' brief but poignant discussion of the disaster at Mycalessus illustrates his concern. As he explains, in 413 B.C., some Thracian mercenaries, sought by Demosthenes, had reached Athens too late to accompany that general on the relief expedition to Sicily. The Athenians at the time were under financial pressure and appointed a commander to conduct the Thracians back home. En route, they were to do whatever damage they could do to those of Athens's enemies living near the coast. It was this that occasioned their landing in Boeotia near the town of Mycalessus, whose inhabitants they caught completely off guard:

> The Thracians burst into Mycalessus, sacked the houses and temples, and butchered the inhabitants, sparing neither the young nor the old, but methodically killing everyone they met, women and children alike, and even the farm animals and every living thing they saw. For the Thracian race, like the most bloodthirsty of the barbarians, is at its most murderous when most caught up in audacity. So now there was confusion on all sides and death in every shape and form. Among other things, they broke into a boys' school, the largest in the place, into which the children had just entered, and killed every one of them. Thus disaster fell upon the entire city, a disaster more complete than any, more sudden and more horrible.

Thucydides does go on to discuss the Theban counterassault on the retreating Thracians, and in characteristic fashion, he takes care to remark on the effectiveness of the tactics used by these light-armed troops against the Theban cavalry, for we are clearly meant to recognize that they would have been useful against the horsemen of Syracuse. But the historian returns at the end of his account to the losses at Mycalessus: "It was a small city, but in the disaster just described its people suffered calamities as pitiable as any that took place during the war" (7.29–30). It is only after reading an account such as this that one can appreciate the significance of Thucydides' concluding his proof for the claim that the Peloponnesian War was "the greatest movement" or "commotion" in the history of the Greeks by noting that it produced "sufferings without precedent."[5] The renowned historian is not only our chief source of information concerning the fate meted out to noncombatants in the course of the Peloponnesian War. His history is also, among other things, an extended meditation on the disasters that befell the Mytilenians, the Plataeans, the Histiaeans, the Scionaeans, the Toronaeans, the Aeginetans, the Melians, and the young boys of Mycalessus. In pondering the fate of noncombatants in the Peloponnesian War, we cannot do better than to follow his lead.

Thucydides sets the stage for his consideration of these disasters in his summary of what was said by the Corcyraeans and the Corinthians at Athens in 433 B.C. when they disputed as to whether the Athenians should take the former into alliance and protect them against the latter. The speeches themselves are more or less what we would expect. The Corcyraeans have little in the way of a moral claim to make on the Athenians: they had remained on the sidelines during the Persian Wars, and they had done nothing since to earn either admiration or gratitude. They can only assert that a war between the Athenians and the Peloponnesians is inevitable and that a defeat of the second most powerful maritime power in Hellas would so strengthen the Corinthians as to make them a threat to Athens (1.32–36).

The Corinthians are in the opposite situation. They can deny that war is inevitable, and they can present themselves as the friends of the Athenians, but the evidence that they cite in their support casts doubt on both claims.[6] Their most powerful argument is an appeal to sentiment, for they fought alongside the Athenians in the Persian Wars, and there were times in the distant past when they were the genuine benefactors of the Athenians (1.37–43). It is impossible to be confident whether, to what degree, and just where Thucydides, in his account, departs from what was actually said on this occasion. In composing the speeches included in his narrative, his aim was twofold—to summarize the most important arguments made at that time and to throw light on events. In pursuing the latter aim, he was perfectly willing to elaborate on the incomplete reports available to him.[7] In this case, we can almost certainly detect his intervention in at least one particular. The first speech, which asserts that the Athenians have no rational choice in this matter but to attend first and foremost to their own self-preservation, begins with the word *díkaion*: "it is just." The second speech, which demands that the Athenians honor the obligations they have incurred and attend to justice, begins with the word *anagkaîon*: "it is necessary." In ironically juxtaposing the two speeches in this way, Thucydides invites his readers to join him in pondering the relationship in human affairs between justice and the moral necessity constituted by the human concern with self-preservation. Moreover, in indicating that the Athenians held two assemblies on two successive days to discuss the issue; that they were at first inclined to reject the Corcyraean alliance; and that ultimately, after sleeping on the matter, they voted to make a defensive alliance with Corcyra (1.44), he draws our attention to the manner in which justice tends to be subordinated to necessity in the conduct of foreign affairs.

Thucydides returns to the tension between justice and necessity repeatedly in the remainder of his work, notably in the chapters of his third book.[8] There, on two separate occasions he explores the question with regard to the treatment of those who have surrendered and are at the mercy of their captors. The first set of events concerns the Mytilenians, islanders from Lesbos who had been allied to the Athenians since the end of the Persian Wars and who had been treated with respect throughout and left undisturbed in full control of their own affairs. Thucydides devotes most of the early chapters of the book (3.1–19, 25–35) to the circumstances of their revolt and to the fecklessness of the Lacedaemonians and their allies in failing to take advantage of the opportunity that it afforded them. He then turns to the debate that took place in the Athenian assembly after the revolt's collapse as to the final disposition of the Mytilenians.[9] In anger, he explains, the Athenians voted to execute the entire adult male population of Mytilene and to enslave the women and children and sent off a dispatch-trireme to see that this was done (3.36.1–3). We have been led to expect the Athenians to be harsh: three years earlier, they had censured their generals for allowing the rebellious Potidaeans to surrender on terms and go into exile, taking with them clothing and a fixed sum of money (2.70). But a day after their initial determination in the Mytilenian case, after having slept on the matter, the Athenians met again, for they had undergone a change of mind. As a result, they reconsidered their original decision judged it "savage [ōmón] and excessive . . . to destroy an entire city and not just those responsible" for its misdeeds (3.36.4–5).

The debate on the second day, as reported, consists of two speeches —one was delivered by the demagogue Cleon (3.37–40), who commands the confidence of the Athenian people and who had originally proposed executing the adult male citizens of Mytilene (3.36.6); and another delivered by Diodotus, a figure otherwise unknown (3.41–48).[10] Cleon prefaces his argument with a critique of Athenian propensities, intimating that his compatriots are too generous and trusting, that their instinct for compassion is dangerous, that their empire is a tyranny and must be administered ruthlessly, that the city is better off with bad laws that remain fixed than with good laws constantly undergoing change, that ordinary folk who do not think themselves more intelligent than the laws make better citizens than the clever, that imperial cities should respond to injury by venting their anger, and that the characteristic Athenian love of novelty renders the citizens the means of *húbris* and pride, wealth will nourish greed. "Hope (*elpís*) and the lust for all (*érōs epì pantí*), . . . being invisible, are more powerful than terrors that can be observed," and this is especially true in the case of "cities" concerned "with the greatest of things, freedom and rule over others," in which "each citizen, acting in concert with all," is inclined to overestimate his capacities "*alogístōs*"—"in a manner devoid of calculation and impervious to speech" (3.45).

Athens can profit from magnanimity. So Diodotus contends. For if rebellions cannot be deterred, they can be subverted. When the initial hopes of the rebels are disappointed, the prospect of generous treatment is an irresistible invitation to surrender and that of annihilation is a powerful encouragement to further resistance: only those most responsible for the revolt should lose their lives (3.46). Indeed, Diodotus asserts, the common people everywhere are well disposed to the Athenians. They never join the oligarchs in revolting except when under extreme duress. "If you destroy the common people of Mytilene, who never participated in the revolt and who, as soon as they were in command of arms, voluntarily handed over the city to you, you will first of all have unjustly murdered your benefactors, and, secondly, you will be doing exactly what the powerful most want" by driving the innocent multitude into the arms of the guilty few (3.47). Diodotus concludes by denying that he is making an appeal to "pity" and "decency." His intention is simply to inform his compatriots concerning their interests (3.48).

Here, as elsewhere, Thucydides is reticent. Nonetheless, that he disapproved of the proposal to execute the Mytilenians is relatively easy to discern. To begin with, he prejudices the discussion by introducing Cleon as "the most violent of the citizens" (3.36.6); at the end, he describes at some length the process by which the dispatch-trireme sent to Mytilene to call off the execution managed to get there just in time to prevent the event, remarking that "the first ship did not in haste make its way to accomplish its monstrous task" (3.49). What Thucydides thought concerning the two speeches and the arguments that they advance is more difficult to determine. It would, for example, be tempting to conclude that he judged atrocities less likely where policy is directed by self-interest and a concern with self-preservation than where it is dictated by a desire for justice. To this conclusion, however, there are insuperable objections. First, Thucydides nowhere suggests that Diodotus's appeal to self-interest was effective. He traces the Athenian change of heart to the very sense of decency that both speakers expressly abjure (3.36.4–5), and he makes it clear that the rowers of the first dispatch-trireme shared their compatriots' sense of dismay at what had initially been decided (3.49.4). Moreover, Diodotus's speech contains an oblique but unmistakable appeal to this very sense of decency: in suggesting that the Mytilenians were "aiming at the greatest of objects, their own liberty or rule over others," he encourages the Athenians to see in the rebels an image of themselves (3.45.6); and in representing the common people of Mytilene as innocent and in describing them as the "benefactors" of the Athenians (3.47), he intimates that their execution would be unjust. That, in the process, he misrepresents what happened on Mytilene, ascribing to the common people of that city opinions that they never expressed and attributing to them deeds that the oligarchs were, in fact, responsible for, simply reinforces the point.[11] To secure the goal he sought, Diodotus had to achieve what Cleon had attempted. He had to persuade the Athenians that justice and self-interest were in accord; and to accomplish this worthy end, he had to do what he had warned at the outset the bitterness of the political struggle at Athens required: he had to lie.[12] As Diodotus demonstrates, the appeal to justice need not always be an appeal to moral indignation: compassion and decency play at least as large a role.

To see what can happen when the dictates of justice are genuinely ignored and when self-interest and a concern with self-preservation alone determine events, one need only turn from the debate concerning Mytilene to that concerning Plataea. Here, the Spartans sit in judgment. The war between the Peloponnesians and the Athenians had actually begun in 431 B.C. when the Thebans launched a surprise attack on Athens's long-time ally Plataea with the help of a small group of conspirators from within that city. When the assault proved ineffective, they withdrew, and the Plataeans executed those whom they had captured (2.2–6). Two years later, the Peloponnesians invested the city (2.71–78). When the situation became desperate, about half of the town's defenders made a successful attempt to break out (3.20–24). Some months later, in the same summer in which Mytilene fell, those who remained surrendered the town to the Lacedaemonians on condition that they receive a fair trial (3.52.1–2). It is this event that Thucydides juxtaposes with the Mytilenian debate. As he tells the story, there were in fact two exchanges. When the Peloponnesians came to besiege the city, the Plataeans had objected to their intentions on moral grounds, alluding to the special role their forebears had played in the Persian Wars and to the promise made by Pausanias, the Spartan commander at the battle of Plataea, that the Plataeans would henceforth be guaranteed forever against unprovoked attack and foreign domination (2.71). To these objections, the Spartan king Archidamus had replied that the Peloponnesians would honor Pausanias's pledge if the Plataeans abandoned their Athenian alliance, which committed them to aid the Athenians in subjugating other Hellenes (2.72). The second debate, which presupposes the Plataeans' refusal to give up their ancient alliance with Athens, took place in 427 B.C., after the arrival of five judges sent from Lacedaemon.[13]

Initially, the judges posed to the surviving Plataeans a single question: "Have you done anything to help the Lacedaemonians and their allies in the present war" (3.52.3–4)? The Plataeans responded by asking to speak at length and appointed two citizens to do so on their behalf. The latter of the two was the Spartan *próxenos* at Plataea (3.52.5), the vice consul responsible for taking care of Lacedaemonian interests there.[14] The man's father had not only led the Plataean contingent half a century before at the battle of Plataea. He had personally vanquished and killed the Persian commander Mardonius, and he had later died in Messenia along with three hundred Plataeans sent to help the Spartans suppress a helot revolt.[15] Thucydides tells us none of this, but he can hardly have been unaware of the man's ancestry, and in the course of the speech he plays on the meaning of the man's name: Lakon ("Laconian"), the son of Aieimnestus ("Always-remembered"). No one could have been better placed to appeal to the sensibilities of the Spartans, who resided in Laconia. And that is what the two spokesmen try to do, objecting to the question posed, demanding the fair trial promised, spelling out in detail what the Plataeans had done for Greece in the Persian Wars and what they had done for Sparta at the time of the helot revolt, noting that Athens had long protected them against Theban aggression and reminding the Lacedaemonians that the Thebans had fought alongside the Persians at Plataea. "If you are going to take as indicative of justice the hostility of the Thebans toward us and that which is immediately useful to you," they observe, "you will present yourselves not as true judges of what is right but rather as

9

men enslaved to advantage." At stake, as they put it, is Spartan "faith
and honor." They are themselves suppliants, "and Hellenic law forbids
killing in these circumstances."[16] All in all, it is a powerful speech (3.53–
59), and it was recognized as such in antiquity.[17]

Fearful that the Plataean address might have an effect on the Lacedaemonians, the Thebans then requested the right to reply (3.60).
They, too, appeal to justice, contending that they had founded the city
of Plataea, objecting to that community's long separation under Athenian protection from the rest of Boeotia, excusing the Medism of their
fathers on the grounds that this was the work of a small coterie of dominant aristocrats, alluding to the period in which Athens ruled Boeotia
and to the battle of Coronea by which they and the other Boeotians
had recovered their freedom, charging the Plataeans with responsibility for Athens's crimes against the Greeks, justifying their surprise
attack on Plataea on the grounds that they had been invited in by the
city's most distinguished men, and objecting to the Plataean execution of the Thebans captured in the course of fending off that assault
(3.61–67).[18]

The fair trial promised the Plataeans who surrendered never really materializes: the actual proceedings travesty the judicial process.
After listening to the two speeches, the Spartan judges resolutely ignored them both, concluding that the question originally posed was
the proper question to ask and that the Plataeans' refusal to abandon
the Athenian alliance had released the Peloponnesians from the oaths
taken after the battle of Plataea. The original question was then posed
to each of the surviving Plataeans; and when each answered "no," he
was taken out and killed (3.68.1–3). "It was largely, or entirely," Thucydides concludes, "for the sake of the Thebans that the Lacedaemonians
were so averse to the Plataeans; they considered that with regard to
the war then underway the Thebans would be useful to them" (3.68.4).
There is evidently much to be said for the suspicions voiced by the
Plataeans concerning the motives of their Spartan captors as well as
for an observation that Thucydides later attributes to the Athenians:
that, when dealing with foreigners, the Lacedaemonians are "of those
whom we know the most conspicuous for thinking that the pleasant
is noble and that the advantageous is just" (5.105.4). Abroad, at least,
Spartan policy was dictated by self-interest and a devotion to utility
unmitigated by magnanimity.

There was, in this particular, a genuine difference between the Athenians and the Spartans. On the eve of the outbreak of the war, an Athenian delegation at Sparta found itself called upon to reply to charges lodged against Athens by the Spartans' Corinthian allies.[19] The Athenian defense was a calculated offense, aimed less at apology, Thucydides notes, than at "providing an indication of the power of their city—at reminding those older of what they knew, and at informing those younger with regard to matters of which they had no experience" (1.72.1). In order to alarm the Spartans, the Corinthians had suggested that the Athenians were "daring beyond their strength" (1.70.3). In making their response, the Athenian delegates seek to deter the Spartans from war and to encourage them to remain at rest by embracing the charge (1.72.1). They remind the Lacedaemonians of the risks that their compatriots had taken when they fought alone against the Mede at Marathon and of the fact that, at the time of Salamis, they had contributed the most ships to the common cause and had provided in Themistocles the most intelligent commander. "We displayed a zeal most daring by much," they observe in reference to their remarkable decision to evacuate Attica and to take to the sea. "Had we not been daring" in this extreme manner, they contend, the battle of Salamis would never have taken place, and events would have progressed "in a restful manner"—as the Persians wished (1.73–74).[20]

After reminding the Spartans of the daring that the Athenians had displayed at the time of the Persian Wars, the delegates demonstrate, in their defense of Athens' subsequent acquisition of a maritime empire, a species of intellectual daring suggesting that, when Themistocles had persuaded their ancestors to uproot their families from the land and to become men of the sea they had become deracinated in more ways than one. In the process, they had opened themselves up to radically new ways of thinking about the relationship between justice and necessity.[21] At the outset, the delegates note that their allies had voluntarily sought Athenian hegemony and that the Athenians had been compelled to increase their power above all by fear, then by a love of honor, and later by a legitimate concern for their own interests (1.75). The Spartans, they observe, have certainly paid attention to their own interests in their disposition of affairs within the Peloponnesus (1.76.1). "We have done nothing wondrous," they insist, "nothing contrary to human ways, in accepting an empire given to us and in not yielding it

11

up, having been conquered by the three greatest things—honor, fear, and self-interest. Nor were we the first such, for it has always been the case that the weaker are subject to those more powerful. In any case, we think that we are worthy. Indeed, we seemed so to you—at least until now when, after calculating your advantage, you resort to the argument from justice." When one has weighed the realities, they assert, one must conclude that "those are worthy of praise who, while following human nature in ruling over others, nonetheless are more just than is required by a concern for retaining power. We certainly think that others, taking our place, would show very clearly whether we are measured [metriázomen] in our conduct of affairs" (1.76.2–4). The delegates concede that Athens's allies are restless, but they attribute this to their failure to appreciate the only viable alternatives to Athenian rule (1.77.1–5). "At any rate," they remark, "if you were to overcome us and to take up an empire, you would swiftly lose all the goodwill that you have secured because of the fear we inspire—that is, if you hold to the pattern of behavior that you evidenced in the brief span when you were the leaders against the Mede. You have institutions, customs, and laws that do not mix well with those of others; and, in addition, when one of you goes abroad he follows neither his own customs and laws nor those employed in the rest of Hellas" (1.77.6).

There is a boldness and baldness evident in the Athenian speech for which there is no Spartan counterpart. It is hard to imagine a Lacedaemonian statesman openly acknowledging that it is a law of nature that the strong rule the weak. And yet, if the outcome of the Mytilenian and Plataean debates is taken into account, there is clearly much to be said for the Athenian claim that their city's policy is dictated by a concern for honor as much as by fear and self-interest and that they are consequently "more just" in their treatment of their allies than the Spartans would be in their stead.

One can discern the source of the Athenian claim to superiority in this regard in Pericles' Funeral Oration (2.34–46), in which he celebrates the Athenian constitution and the Athenian way of life.[22] He does so by stressing his compatriots' trust in the capacity of rational speech (lógoi) to do justice to events and their ability to yoke daring with calculation (eklogízesthai) while emphasizing that the audacity they display in battle is rooted not in "ignorance" but in a strength of soul that enables them to take risks in clear knowledge as to "what is pleasant" in life and "what is terrible."[23] Taken as a whole, Pericles asserts, Athens is "the school of Hellas"; considered as individuals, its citizens demonstrate an astonishing self-sufficiency, versatility, and grace in the face of the most varied circumstances (2.37–41). In this connection, he boasts, "We love the beautiful with frugality, and we love wisdom [*philosophoûmen*] without softness [*malakía*]" (2.40.1). According to Pericles, one consequence of the spirit of daring that informs the Athenians' love of beauty and nobility is their magnanimity. "In matters respecting the practice of virtue, we are opposed to the many: it is not by receiving benefits but by conferring them on others that we come to possess friends." So he reminds his fellow citizens. "The one doing the gracious act is the firmer friend, aiming to preserve a sense of obligation on the part of those in his debt by demonstrating continued goodwill; the one fulfilling an obligation is less keen because he knows that he is returning the virtuous deed not as a gracious act but because of a debt owed. We alone come to another's aid without the guidance from fear—not so much from a calculation of advantage as from a trusting liberality."[24]

By contrast, the Spartans are bereft of daring (*átolmoi*), and they are inclined to treat outsiders in an exceedingly brutal fashion.[25] It was evidently something worthy of note that the Athenians should execute without trial captured enemy agents and deny them a proper burial (2.67.4). But this is what the Spartans did as a matter of course. Indeed, early in the war, when they seized merchant ships on the high seas, they killed the individuals captured and hurled their bodies into ravines, taking no notice whether these voyagers were Athenians, citizens of communities allied or subjected to Athens, or neutrals completely uninvolved in the war (2.67.4). The behavior of Alcidas, the Spartan commander sent with a fleet to come to the aid of the rebellious Mytilenians, is even more striking. When he learned that he had reached the Aegean too late to be of much use to the Mytilenians, he unthinkingly dispatched most of the prisoners captured in the course of his journey. It had to be explained to him by a deputation of Samian rebels that killing noncombatants was no way for Sparta to make plausible its claim to be the liberator of Hellas from Athenian domination and that massacring innocents subjected to Athens was a recipe for turning potential friends and allies into genuine enemies.[26] As Thucydides makes clear in describing Brasidas, the one

13

Lacedaemonian commander who proved effective in the early years of the war, it was exceedingly rare for a Spartan to be "just and measured" in his treatment of outsiders (4.81.2–3, 108.2–7). Instinctively liberal and generous the Spartans were not.

Sparta was, however, famous for being "well-ordered." At the end of the Peloponnesian War, Thucydides tells us, the Lacedaemonians could boast that they had never been ruled by tyrants; their strength in dealings abroad he traced to the fact that they had managed to sustain themselves in good order (*eunomía*) for some four hundred years under the same regime (1.18.1). Such was evidently the explanation for their victory in the great struggle with Athens: they possessed *eunomía*, and so they never succumbed to lawlessness (*anomía*) and never fell prey to civil strife. Even the Athenians concede that "the Lacedaemonians display virtue very much both in their dealings with one another and in holding to the established laws and customs of the land" (5.105.4).

To fathom just why this should be so, one must consider what it was that distinguished the Spartans from the Athenians.[27] On the eve of the war, the Corinthians compare the Lacedaemonians unfavorably with the Athenians, charging them with a lack of the daring and enterprise that Pericles will subsequently celebrate in his Funeral Oration. This characterization of the two antagonists deserves careful attention, for the thrust of what the Corinthians have to say is confirmed by Thucydides (1.118.2, 4.55.2–4, 8.96) and borne out by the subsequent narrative.[28]

> The Athenians are innovators, keen in forming plans, and quick to accomplish in deed what they have contrived in thought. You Spartans are intent on saving what you now possess; you are always indecisive, and you leave even what is needed undone. They are daring beyond their strength, they are risk-takers against all judgment, and in the midst of terrors they remain of good hope — while you accomplish less than is in your power, mistrust your judgment in matters most firm, and think not how to release yourselves from the terrors you face. In addition, they are unhesitant where you are inclined to delay, and they are always out and about in the larger world while you stay at home. For they think to acquire something by being away while you think that by proceeding abroad you will harm what lies ready to hand. In victory over the enemy, they sally farthest forth; in

defeat, they give the least ground. For their city's sake, they use their bodies as if they were not their own; their intelligence they dedicate to political action on her behalf. And if they fail to accomplish what they have resolved to do, they suppose themselves deprived of that which is their own—while what they have accomplished and have now acquired they judge to be little in comparison with what they will do in the time to come. If they trip up in an endeavor, they are soon full of hope with regard to yet another goal. For they alone possess something at the moment at which they come to hope for it: so swiftly do they contrive to attempt what has been resolved. And on all these things they exert themselves in toil and danger through all the days of their lives, enjoying least of all what they already possess because they are ever intent on further acquisition. They look on a holiday as nothing but an opportunity to do what needs doing, and they regard peace and quiet free from political business as a greater misfortune than a laborious want of leisure. So that, if someone were to sum them up by saying that they are by nature capable neither of being at rest nor of allowing other human beings to be so, he would speak the truth. (1.70).

Shortly after reporting this speech, Thucydides provides us with the means to infer what Spartan slowness and Athenian daring meant for political life in the two cities, respectively, by telling us, in an extended digression, of the fate meted out by the Spartans and the Athenians to the two great commanders of the Persian Wars. Pausanias of Lacedaemon and Themistocles of Athens were both ultimately convicted of treason, but the Spartans acted slowly against their fellow citizen, only after the discovery of incontrovertible proof, while the Athenians moved rapidly against their compatriot on what may well have been entirely specious grounds (1.128–38). As the Athenians' notorious and self-destructive penchant for fining, exiling, and even executing generals who met with failure or incomplete success confirms, at Athens, suspicion was all too often a sufficient demonstration of guilt.[29]

The reply made by Archidamus the Spartan king to the charges lodged against his fellow Lacedaemonians by the Corinthians deserves attention as well—for, in defending his city and its way of life, he makes two crucial claims. He attributes to his compatriots a "sensible moderation" (*sōphrosúnē*) and suggests that, because of their sense of shame and moderation, they alone "refrain from giving way to *húbris*" when events turn out well; and after emphasizing that they are both brave in battle and prudent in council, he traces this prudence to the fact that they are not educated to think themselves wiser than their laws and that they are trained to avoid being excessively knowledgeable and intelligent in matters that are of no use (1.84.2–3).

That both claims are true is evident.[30] Neither Thucydides nor Pericles ever attributes *sōphrosúnē* to the Athenians.[31] In fact, at Camarina the Athenian spokesman Euphemus rebuffs those who would presume to teach that virtue to his countrymen and embraces "meddlesomeness" in its stead (6.87.2–4).[32] In contrast, the Spartans are said to have been almost unique in managing to remain moderate while enjoying prosperity and flourishing (8.24.4). That the Lacedaemonians never made wisdom a pursuit is visible in their speeches, for they focus solely on what they deem of immediate use. Nowhere do they evidence an awareness of the distinction, introduced by the sophists and taken up and deployed in speech after speech by the Athenians, between the dictates of nature (*phúsis*) and those of law, custom, or convention (*nómos*). Nowhere do they demonstrate an interest in elaborating the logic of imperialism. Their lack of daring and enterprise in politics and war is accompanied by a lack of intellectual daring and enterprise and by a species of moral myopia that may in fact be necessary to communal well-being. Their lack of theoretical sophistication certainly helps explain why in dealing with outsiders the Spartans are so conspicuous for their all too convenient inability to distinguish "what is advantageous" to their community from "what is just"; it may account in part for the political and social solidarity that distinguished them from their rivals—for their intense loyalty to one another would appear to be rooted in a failure or refusal to recognize the artificial character of the distinctions separating one political community from another.

Thucydides does not tell us precisely why the Spartans possessed *sōphrosúnē*, lacked daring, concentrated their attention on the useful, shied away from intellectual speculation, and were law abiding and just in their dealings with one another. But he does encourage us to attend to the presence at Lacedaemon of a large servile class of helots ever ready for revolt. Indeed, he goes out of his way to enable us to discern that the Spartans' fierce loyalty to one another and their exaggerated dedication to the law is inextricably linked with the brutality that characterizes their relations with the helots at home and with strangers abroad.[33]

The relative generosity of the Athenians to outsiders would appear, then, to rest on their comparative freedom from the necessities that dictated or at least encouraged Spartan severity. There is, however, no sign of Periclean magnanimity in Cleon's mean-spirited contribution to the debate concerning Mytilene, and this fact should give us pause. Cleon takes evident care to ape his distinguished predecessor's style of speech, and he actually borrows a number of Pericles' more striking locutions, but his purpose is to urge his compatriots to adopt a policy similar in ethos to the one practiced by Sparta.[34] In doing so, he denounces as a sign of *malakía* the Periclean notion that by means of gracious acts an imperial power can somehow secure the goodwill of its subjects (3.37.2). The rise to prominence of the man whom Thucydides describes as "the most violent of the citizens," his near success in securing the execution of the Mytilenians, his subsequent victory in persuading the Athenians to execute all the adult male citizens of the rebellious city of Scione if and when it is recaptured (4.120–22, 129–31; 5.18.8, 32), and the matter-of-fact manner in which Thucydides reports his selling the women and children of Torone into slavery (4.110–16, 120–22, 129, 132; 5.2–3) — all of this suggests that Athenian magnanimity is exceedingly frail.[35]

To understand why, one must compare two crucial passages — Thucydides' discussion of the plague (2.47–54), and his account of the civil strife at Corcyra (3.69–85).[36] The first passage stands between the Funeral Oration, with its ethos of generosity, and Pericles' last oration, which though high-minded, is much less magnanimous in tone.[37] Thucydides takes great care to describe the epidemic that descended on Athens in the second year of the war. Above all else, however, his purpose is to examine its impact on "human nature" (2.50.1); to this end, he explores the manner in which the plague (2.51.4) instills in human beings a "spiritlessness" (*athumía*) that subverts the influence of honor and eliminates the capacity of convention—whether sanctioned solely by custom or by force of law—to restrain human conduct.

By his choice of words, Thucydides intimates a kinship between Cleon, "the most violent of the Athenians," and the plague. "Overpowered by the violence done by the evil and not knowing what would become of them," he writes, "human beings became neglectful of things alike sacred and profane." That neglect began with "the conventions [*nómoi*] that they had formerly observed with regard to burials," and it ended with a general "increase in lawlessness [*anomía*]." The situation unfolds inexorably. "Seeing the abrupt changes—the unforeseen demise of those who were flourishing and the manner in which the propertyless suddenly came to possess the substance of those who had died—the individual more readily dared to do what he had previously kept hidden and had done in a manner contrary to the dictates of pleasure. . . . No one was enthusiastic about persisting in what was deemed beautiful and noble since they thought it unclear whether they would die or not before achieving it. So whatever gave immediate pleasure or seemed conducive to it in any way was regarded as both noble and useful" (2.52–53). The collapse of morals and manners described in this remarkable passage, the emancipation of individual daring, and the attendant disappearance of all respect for *nómos* (whether human in origin or putatively divine) deserve attention because they cast light on the erosion of the more generous instincts of the Athenians and suggest that the disaster caused them to conduct their affairs at home as did the Spartans abroad: by identifying honor with pleasure. These developments merit notice also because Thucydides uses the same sort of language when describing the civil strife that engulfed Corcyra and the violence done to human nature by the war itself.[38]

The details need not concern us here. What deserves attention is what Thucydides (3.82.1) calls "the savage [*ōmḗ*] manner in which this revolution progressed" and its subversion of the conventions governing the relationship between words and deeds (3.82.1). "In light of what, in the circumstances, seemed justified, the evaluation customarily given particular deeds by names underwent a transformation. A daring devoid of calculation and impervious to speech (*tólma mèn alógistos*) was now regarded as the courage one would expect to find in a fellow member of one's club; forethought for the future was a fancy phrase for cowardice; moderation was a disguise for a lack of manliness; the ability to consider a question in all its aspects meant that one was incapable of doing anything" (3.82.4–5).[39] The linguistic lawlessness described in this passage is as disturbing as the more substantive *anomía* generated by the plague, for linguistic conventions are as crucial to the maintenance of civilization as are the customs and laws that

normally govern conduct. As a consequence of the inconstant signifi-
cation of words, speech and reason (*lógos*) lost their purchase on reality, and traditional communities collapsed: "Ties of kinship were less
close than those based on one's membership in a political club since
those in the latter were readier, without hesitation, to engage in daring action. Such associations were of use not within the context of the
established laws but for aggrandizement contrary to them. And their
members confirmed their trust in one another not by an appeal to the
divine law but by a common project of breaking the law" (3.82.6–7).
In one particular, the civil strife at Corcyra was quite different from
the plague at Athens. The *anomía* associated with the former was not
rooted in *athumía*. If anything, those who engaged in revolution evidenced an excess of spiritedness (*thumós*).[40] As Thucydides puts it,

> The cause of all these things was imperial rule pursued out of greed
> and the love of renown. From these prevailing passions arose as well
> a keen love for victory. The leading figures in the cities claimed to be
> serving the common good—with each of the two sides adopting an
> attractive slogan, the patrons of the multitude expressing a prefer-
> ence for political equality and their opponents expressing one for a
> moderate aristocracy—but they were in fact seeking prizes for them-
> selves. In their desire to prevail, they dared to conduct their struggle
> with one another with no holds barred and proceeded against one
> another in a terrible fashion and took a revenge greater still, not set-
> ting forth as a limit the dictates of justice and the city's advantage but
> limiting themselves always, on both sides, solely with an eye to their
> own pleasure. (3.82.8)

If this passage were merely an account of events at Corcyra, it would
matter little. But we have already been told (1.23.1–2) that civil strife
played a crucial role in the unprecedented suffering that made this the
greatest of wars, and Thucydides treats the revolution on that island as
an exemplum. It was merely "the first to break out." Later, virtually "the
entirety of Hellas was subject to commotion with rival parties in every
city—the patrons of the common people trying to bring in the Athenians, and the few trying to bring in the Spartans." In time of peace,
he insists, there would have been no opportunity for intervention: it
was the war that occasioned the plague of civil strife. "In peace and
when matters go well," Thucydides remarks, "cities and individuals are

better-minded because they have not fallen into the necessity of doing what they do not wish. But war is a violent teacher; in depriving them of the means for easily satisfying their daily wants, it assimilates the thinking of the many to their present circumstances" (3.82.1–3). It was this "violent teacher" and its equally violent cousin the plague that deprived the Athenians of their sense of measure and proportion and brought Cleon, "the most violent of the citizens," to the fore; it was "the greatest movement" or "commotion" in the history of the Greeks that produced such a "movement" or "commotion" within the cities. In the process, the sort of brutality that had once seemed "savage and excessive" to Athenians confronting rebellious subjects became the rule within communities — even, in the end, within Athens itself.

Thucydides' employment of the adjective *ōmós* deserves attention.[41] Literally, it means not "savage" but "raw." This is what the Athenians, upon reflection, think of their decision to execute the Mytilenians (3.36.4); this is what, Thucydides believes, characterized the civil strife that, as a consequence of the war, ran through Greece much as after the plague (3.82.1). Elsewhere (3.94.5), the historian uses a cognate only once — in describing an Aetolian tribe so uncivilized that, although technically Greek, its members "are said to be unintelligible when they use their tongues and to eat their meat raw [*ōmophágoi*]." It is a revealing passage, for the Greeks discerned a close connection between the inability to communicate in speech and the consumption of uncooked meat: these two characteristics distinguished animals from men. Consequently, one finds *ōmós* employed by a character in Euripides to denounce Sparta, where the citizens were notably taciturn and notoriously brutal in their treatment of outsiders.[42] The word is similarly used in a rhetorical treatise to single out human beings who resemble wild beasts in conducting their affairs in a manner contrary to the dictates of reasoned speech (*lógos*).[43] In short, Thucydides is intimating in his description of the revolution at Corcyra that this protracted war tended to reverse the process described in his "archaeology" (1.2–21) by which a world in constant motion came to enjoy a measure of rest — and peace emerged from war, civilization from chaos, and Hellenism from barbarism.[44] Put bluntly, the greatest movement or commotion (*kínēsis*) in history (1.1.2) subjected the cities of Hellas to a species of internal movement or commotion (3.82.1).[45] Moreover, by subverting the linguistic, social, and political conventions (*nómoi*) by which human beings articulate and sustain the sense of measure and proportion that distinguishes them from beasts, this commotion restored the Greeks from their exalted status as political animals to their primordial condition as barbarians—subhuman animals never at rest, subject to frenzy, and inclined to fall prey to a daring incompatible with magnanimity and grace. This sort of daring leads them to commit raw and savage deeds and renders them irrational and inarticulate (*alógistos*), incapable of forethought for the future, and unable to employ *lógos* in deliberating together as a community about the advantageous, the just, and the good.[46]

Nowhere are the results of this process more visible than in the Melian Dialogue (5.84–113), which took place at the halfway point in Thucydides' war and was apparently intended to serve as the centerpiece in his narrative of the whole.[47] On the face of it, that exchange takes the form of common deliberation about a practical question. In principle, the resort to dialogue should obviate the potential for deception widely recognized in Thucydides' day to be inherent in uninterrupted speech. In practice, however, the exchange travesties the forms of calm, cool, detached rationality so favored by the sophists, Socrates, and his disciples. For one is never allowed to forget that the Athenians are about to besiege their interlocutors. This exchange is no more a dialogue than the Plataean debate was a trial; nothing that the Melians can say will alter the outcome. Whatever illusions they may for the moment entertain, they have been invited to listen and not to speak.[48]

Of course, the Melians were foolish in the extreme. Their situation was hopeless, and they should have recognized the fact and acted as advised. They were victims, but they were also, in a sense, responsible for their own fate, as the Athenians (5.111.2–4) suggest: for they could and should have been more "moderate" in estimating their prospects, and they displayed so great an incapacity for clear thinking (*alogía*) that they justified a charge of mindlessness (*ánoia*). To be precise, the Melians allowed their policy to be dictated by a sense of shame unsuited to their situation and by the vain hope (*elpís*) that the gods or the Spartans would come to their rescue (5.102–13). There is certainly nothing in Thucydides' history to disprove the bald Athenian claim that, in the international arena, "the strong do what they can and the weak acquiesce" (5.89). Of course, there may seem to be force in the Melian suggestion that there is a "common good" uniting disparate

21

peoples and that the Athenians have an interest in conceding to those in great peril a claim to "fair treatment" since someday, after all, Athens, too, may succumb (5.90). As we have already seen, when the Athenians learned of their defeat at Aegospotami they dreaded the consequences of the terrible precedent they had set at Melos and elsewhere. But Thucydides refuses to allow us to credit this argument, for the Athenian response (5.91) to the Melians—implying that in the event of Athens's defeat the Spartans would consult their interests and nothing else in disposing of the city—was, in fact, borne out by events.[49] The tension between justice and the moral necessity constituted by the human concern with self-preservation and self-interest, which was first suggested by the exchange between the Corcyraeans and the Corinthians at Athens remains unresolved.

None of this serves, however, to eliminate the misgivings that grip the reader of the dialogue, for the magnanimity and generosity that the Athenians once boasted of and that they belatedly displayed in the Mytilenian case have now entirely disappeared. Once upon a time, the Athenians could justifiably pride themselves on being "measured" in their conduct of affairs (1.76.4); at Melos(5.111.4), they assert that they are offering reasonable and measured terms (*métria*), and they still espouse treating one's inferiors in a measured manner (*métrioi*). But these claims ring hollow, for they are anything but measured in their treatment of the Melians. They give no weight to the fact that the Melians are not a subject people in rebellion against Athens, that they have been independent all along. They seem almost to have forgotten that they themselves had once risked everything to defend their own liberty and that of their fellow Greeks against the Persians (5.89), and they are utterly unmoved by the Melians' appeal to the nobility of their struggle to retain their freedom (5.100). They institute and sustain a siege (5.114, 115.4). And when the city falls, they execute all the men of military age and sell the women and children into slavery (5.116.2–4), paying no attention to the fact, much emphasized at the beginning of the dialogue (5.84.3–85), that Melos was an oligarchy and that the ordinary citizens of that city played no role at all in deciding to resist Athens's assault. When, later in the narrative, one reads Thucydides' account of the fate of Mycalessus and his remark that "the Thracian race, like the most bloodthirsty of the barbarians, is at its most murderous when most caught up in audacity" (7.29–30), one cannot help recalling what the Athenians did to the Melians.

In a manner that invites one to wonder whether nemesis is at work, Thucydides juxtaposes the Melian Dialogue with the Sicilian campaign.[50] The sentence immediately following his account of the fate meted out to the Melians reports that "in the same winter the Athenians decided to sail against Sicily" (6.1.1).[51] There is more to this juxtaposition than a mere striving for dramatic effect, for the link between the two events can be found in the dialogue itself. Despite their disclaimers, the Athenians do attempt to justify their assault on Melos; and they do so, as one would by now expect, by an appeal to the necessity of the case. They have attacked neutral islanders, they suggest, because they have no other choice. The Athenians may not greatly fear what Sparta would do to them if they were defeated, but they do fear their own subjects, and they are persuaded that to allow islanders, such as the Melians, to remain independent is to risk having their subjects regard them as weak and vulnerable to rebellion. As a consequence, forgetting what had happened to their first expedition to Sicily just a few years before (4.58–65), they are quick to dismiss the Melians' retort that an attack on a neutral city is bound to alert and unite the other neutral communities in common defense (5.90–91, 94–99).[52]

This lame attempt to justify the expedition to Melos as a prerequisite for Athens's self-preservation deserves close attention because the implausible logic of the Athenian argument would necessitate an attack on Sicily as well, for it, too, is an island; this logic, in fact, reappears in the debate concerning the great expedition sent to Sicily in 415 B.C. In arguing for the venture, Alcibiades contends that the Athenians must forever be expanding their dominion if they are to retain what they hold and that "rest" would be fatal to their city (6.18.2–3, 6).[53] Ironically, however, it is "motion," not rest, that imperils Athens, for the Sicilian expedition does in fact alert the communities allied neither with Athens nor Sparta to the common danger they face, and its failure convinces the neutrals that Athens is now vulnerable to attack and persuades her subject cities that a rebellion on their part will be met with success (8.2).

To grasp why the Athenians fell prey to an illogic comparable to the *alogía* they had attributed to the Melians, one must consider Thucydides' description of the debate and its result. Alcibiades' speech (6.16–

18) was a response to a speech delivered at an assembly called, some five days after the decision to send an expedition to Sicily, for the purpose of considering the expedition's details (6.8.3–4). Nicias, one of the generals appointed to conduct the flotilla, had taken this as an occasion to try to dissuade his compatriots from undertaking the expedition (6.9–14). When it became clear that he had failed and that the assembly had rejected his claim (6.13.1) to "foresight" (*prónoia*) and preferred the advice of a much younger man who repeatedly boasted (6.16.3, 17.1) of the accomplishments that flowed from his "mindlessness" (*ánoia*), Nicias made one last desperate attempt at dissuasion (6.19–23), hoping that if he magnified the size, scope, and difficulty of the endeavor his compatriots would come to their senses, entertain second thoughts, and change their minds. The result was precisely the opposite of that intended. In his initial speech, Nicias had warned his compatriots against becoming "perversely lustful for that which is far afield" (6.13.1). As a consequence of the picture that Nicias painted in his second oration, Thucydides reports,

> A lust [*érōs*] for the enterprise fell upon everyone alike: to the older men it seemed that they would either subdue the places against which they were sailing or, with so great a force, trip up not at all; those in their prime felt a yearning for sights and spectacles far afield and were of good hope that they would be safe; the great mass of people and the soldiers presumed that they would secure silver in the short run and add to their possessions a power whence they would draw wages forever. Because of the excessive desire of the majority, if there was anyone not pleased at the prospect, he feared lest in voting against it he might seem hostile to the city and so remained at rest.

In the grips of this passion, Thucydides explains, the Athenians greatly expanded the armada (6.24–26).

What Diodotus once said in defending the Mytilenians (3.45) can evidently be applied to the Athenians as well. If all human beings really are "by nature" inclined to do wrong, if law is incapable of imposing restraint since "hope [*elpís*] and the lust for all [*érōs epì pantí*]" are more powerful than the fear of death, especially in the case of "cities" concerned "with the greatest of things, freedom and rule over others," in which "each citizen, acting in concert with all," is inclined to overestimate his capacities "in a manner devoid of calculation and impervious

24

to speech [*alogístōs*]," then it is in no way surprising that in Athens, as in Mytilene, the reasoned speech (*lógos*) defended against Cleon by Diodotus should give way to passions such as "haste and anger" and that there, in that imperial city, public deliberation concerning advantage should similarly fall prey to a daring devoid of calculation and impervious to speech (*tólma alógistos*), spawned by hope, and fueled by a lust for unlimited expansion. It is evident that the passionate pursuit of unbounded, undefinable ends is incompatible with prudent, measured deliberation concerning advantage, for one cannot proportion means to ends when the ends are indeterminate. But this is by no means all that Thucydides implies, for the juxtaposition of and interplay between the Melian Dialogue and the Sicilian expedition suggest that, in the absence of a sense of moral boundaries, human beings will pursue the unlimited. There would appear to be a connection between the civilized capacity to respond to the claims of human decency and the sense of measure, of limits, and of restraint necessary for a sober consideration of self-interest.[54] At least, when Athens loses the former, she loses the latter as well.

We are left to wonder whether success and the expectation of further success must always give rise to a daring and audacity that verge on *húbris* and to a maniacal lust for all (*érōs epì pantí*)—for Thucydides' account would appear to suggest that, in human nature, there is no reliable foundation at all for the magnanimity and measuredness preached by Pericles nor any for moderation other than fear and an absence of hope.[55] The Spartans are not an exception to this rule—for if they display *sōphrosúnē* and retain the sense of limits essential to a sober assessment of their own self-interest, it is, as we have seen, because they are acutely aware that at home a myriad of helots lie in wait for them to make a false step. It is striking that the one Athenian to make a case at Athens on behalf of moderation is Cleon: it is revealing that he links "moderation," in the Spartan fashion, with a lack of learning and intellectual sophistication, a strict and uncritical adherence to established law, and a ruthless treatment of outsiders; and it is noteworthy that he does so in a context in which he compares Athens's empire with a tyranny, warns his compatriots of the grave dangers that they face, hints that their much vaunted cleverness gives rise to indiscipline (*akolasía*), and charges them with softness (3.37–38).

Thucydides nowhere denies that mankind is capable of governing itself in accord with the dictates of *nómos, lógos,* and *prónoia.* But he evidently deems it exceedingly difficult and rare for them to do so. As a consequence, he resorts repeatedly to alpha-privatives to convey the fact that men are inclined to give way to *anomía, alogía,* and *ánoia* as well as *akolasía.* "Human beings judge more by indistinct wish than by secure foresight [*prónoia*]," he reports (4.108.4). "They are accustomed to give in to inconsiderate hope when contemplating that which they desire. It is when they look on that which has no attraction for them that they are inclined to push it away with a calculating reason to which they grant plenipotentiary power." Such is the harsh judgment formed by the most astute observer of the conduct of the Spartans and the Athenians in the Peloponnesian War. His verdict bodes ill for noncombatants who find themselves in the path of war.

Notes

This essay was first composed for presentation at a conference on "Civilians in the Path of War" held at the Mershon Center of Ohio State University in Columbus, Ohio, on 5–6 November 1993. It was later delivered as a public lecture at the Woodrow Wilson International Center for Scholars in Washington DC on 25 January 1994. I am indebted to the organizers of and the participants in the original conference and to Bernard M. W. Knox, Donald Kagan, James W. Muller, David Harris Sacks, and Philip Selznick for comments and suggestions. While working on this essay, I was a fellow of the National Endowment for the Humanities and of the Woodrow Wilson International Center for Scholars, and I profited from support awarded me by the Arts and Humanities Council of Tulsa. I am indebted to Professor Alexis Papadopoulos of DePaul University for the map of classical Greece.

1. Xen. *Hell.* 2.2.3. I cite classical texts by the divisions and subdivisions employed by the author or introduced by subsequent editors (that is, by book, part, chapter, section number, paragraph, act, scene, line, Stephanus page, or by page and line number), using throughout the standard abbreviations provided in *The Oxford Classical Dictionary*, 2d ed., ed. N. G. L. Hammond and H. H. Scullard (Oxford, 1970). The translations used here are my own.

2. Thuc. 1.114.3, 2.27.1–2, 4.57, 5.3.4, 32.1, 116.4.

3. This dimension of Thucydides' argument was never fully ignored: see, for example, Francis M. Cornford, *Thucydides Mythistoricus* (London, 1907), and David Grene, *Man in His Pride: A Study in the Political Philosophy of Thucydides and Plato* (Chicago, 1950), 3–92.

4. See Paul A. Rahe, "Thucydides' Critique of *Realpolitik*," *Security Studies* 5, no. 2 (winter 1995–96): 105–41.

5. Cf. Thuc. 1.1.2–3 with 23.1–3, and see Adam Parry, "Thucydides' Historical Perspective," *Yale Classical Studies* 22 (1972): 47–61.

6. Consider Thuc. 1.40.5–41.2 in light of A. H. M. Jones, "Two Synods of the Delian and Peloponnesian Leagues," *Proceedings of the Cambridge Philological Society*, n.s. 2 (1952–53): 43–46, and see G. E. M. de Ste. Croix, *The Origins of the Peloponnesian War* (London, 1972), 200–224.

7. On the scholarly debate concerning 1.22.1 and its import for our understanding of the speeches in Thucydides, see Clifford Orwin, "Thucydides' Contest: Thucydidean 'Methodology' in Context," *Review of Politics* 51 (1989): 345–64. Cf. Simon Hornblower, *Thucydides* (Baltimore, 1987), 45–72. In this connection, see also Richard Claverhouse Jebb, "The Speeches of Thucydides," in *Hellenica: A Collection of Essays on Greek Poetry, Philosophy, and Religion*, ed. Evelyn Abbott (London, 1880), 266–323, and *The Speeches in Thucydides: A Collection of Original Studies With a Bibliography*, ed. Philip A. Stadter (Chapel Hill, 1973).

8. For a thorough, careful, and remarkably subtle discussion of the pertinent issues, see Leo Strauss, "On Thucydides' War of the Peloponnesians and the Athenians," *The City and Man* (Chicago, 1964), 139–241. See also Clifford Orwin, *The Humanity of Thucydides* (Princeton, 1994).

9. The literature on this exchange is extensive. I have profited from perusing Felix Martin Wassermann, "Post-Periclean Democracy in Action: The Mytilenean Debate (Thuc. III 37–48)," *Transactions of the American Philological Association* 87 (1956): 27–41; Colin Macleod, "Reason and Necessity: Thucydides III 9–14, 37–48," *Journal of Hellenic Studies* 98 (1978): 64–78; Marc Cogan, "Mytilene, Plataea and Corcyra: Ideology and Policy in Thucydides, Book Three," *Phoenix* 35 (1981): 1–21, and *The Human Thing: The Speeches and Principles of Thucydides' History* (Chicago, 1981), 50–65; Clifford Orwin, "The Just and the Advantageous in Thucydides: The Case of the Mytilenaian Debate," *American Political Science Review* 78 (1984): 485–94, and "Democracy and Distrust: A Lesson from Thucydides," *American Scholar* 53 (1984): 313–25; W. Robert Connor, *Thucydides* (Princeton, 1984), 78–91; Steven Forde, *The Ambition to Rule: Alcibiades and the Politics of Imperialism in Thucydides* (Ithaca, 1989), 40–56; and Laurie M. Johnson, "Rethinking the Diodotean Argument," *Interpretation* 18 (1990): 53–62. The essay of Colin Macleod just cited and those that will be cited later in this chapter have all been reprinted in Colin Macleod, *Collected Essays* (Oxford, 1983).

10. For an attempt to identify the man, see Martin Ostwald, "Diodotus, Son of Eucrates," *Greek, Roman, and Byzantine Studies* 20 (1979): 5–13.

27

11. Cf. Thuc. 3.47 with 3.1–19, 25–35 (esp., 27–28). There is no evidence that the common people were pro-Athenian. They distrusted the city's oligarchic government; when armed, they demanded that the available food be brought out and distributed; and they threatened to surrender to the Athenians if (and only if) this were not done. But there apparently was no food being held in reserve, and in fear, the oligarchic leadership of the city made a preemptive surrender.

12. For those who see through his subterfuge, Diodotus adds a further re-mark to the effect that, even if the common people of Mytilene had been par-ticipants in the revolt and had done Athens an injustice, it would be appropri-ate "to feign" the contrary in order to keep as allies the only group not hostile to that city: Thuc. 3.47.4–5.

13. Here again, the secondary literature is considerable. I have profited from Colin Macleod, "Thucydides' Plataean Debate," *Greek, Roman, and Byzantine Studies* 18 (1977): 227–46; Peter R. Pouncey, *The Necessities of War: A Study of Thucydides' Pessimism* (New York, 1980), 17–19; and Connor, *Thucydides,* 91–95.

14. The institution of *proxenía* has been frequently an object of study: see Paul Monceaux, *Les proxénies grecques* (Paris, 1886); Shalom Perlman, "A Note on the Political Implications of Proxenia in the Fourth Century B.C.," *Classical Quarterly,* n.s. 8 (1958): 185–91; M. B. Wallace, "Early Greek *Proxenoi*," *Phoenix* 24 (1970): 189–208; D. J. Mosley, "Spartan Kings and Proxeny," *Athenaeum,* n.s. 49 (1971): 433–35; Christian Marek, *Die Proxenie* (Frankfurt, 1984); André Gerolymatos, *Espionage and Treason: A Study of the Proxenia in Political and Military Intelligence Gathering in Classical Greece* (Amsterdam, 1986). See also Gabriel Herman, *Ritualised Friendship and the Greek City* (Cambridge, 1987).

15. Consider Hdt. 9.64.2, 72; Plut. *Arist.* 11, 19; and Paus. 9.4.1 in light of George Huxley, "Two Notes on Herodotus," *Greek, Roman, and Byzantine Studies* 4 (1963): 5–7.

16. Here the Plataeans were certainly in the right. The killing of prisoners of war was not condoned: see Pierre Ducrey, *Le traitement des prisonniers de guerre dans la Grèce antique* (Paris, 1968), esp. 289–311. It was, however, not uncommon: see W. Kendrick Pritchett, *The Greek State at War* (Berkeley, 1971–), 5:203–312.

17. Dionysius of Halicarnassus (*Thuc.* 42) thought it the finest speech in the book.

18. It was disputed between the Plataeans and the Thebans whether the former had taken an oath to release the Theban prisoners if the latter withdrew from their territory and refrained from seizing hostages: Thuc. 2.5.5–6.

19. See Jacqueline de Romilly, *Thucydides and Athenian Imperialism,* trans.

Philip Thody (Oxford, 1963), 242–72; A. E. Raubitschek, "The Speech of the Athenians at Sparta," in *The Speeches in Thucydides*, 32–48; Christopher Bruell, "Thucydides' View of Athenian Imperialism," *American Political Science Review* 68 (1974): 11–17; and Clifford Orwin, "Justifying Empire: The Speech of the Athenians at Sparta and the Problem of Justice in Thucydides," *Journal of Politics* 48 (1986): 72–85.

20. Cf. Herodotus's claim (7.139) that the Athenians were "the saviors of Greece."

21. Consider 1.18.2 in light of 1.91.5, 93.3–8, and note 4.97–99 (esp. 98.6). In his first speech (1.144.4), Pericles similarly places emphasis on the daring that the Athenians exhibited in abandoning Attica. Thucydides (1.90.1, 91–92, 102.3) makes it clear that the Athenian display of *tólma* at the time of the Persian Wars and thereafter left the citizens of the other Greek cities and the Spartans in particular both fearful and shocked. For an extended and enlightening discussion of the role played by *tólma* in Thucydides' account of the political psychology of the Athenians, see Steven Forde, "Thucydides on the Causes of Athenian Imperialism," *American Political Science Review* 80 (1986): 433–48. I have profited also from Pierre Huart, *Le vocabulaire de l'analyse psychologique dans l'oeuvre de Thucydide* (Paris, 1968), 431–36.

22. On this speech, see John E. Ziolkowski, *Thucydides and the Tradition of Funeral Speeches at Athens* (New York, 1981), and Nicole Loraux, *The Invention of Athens: The Funeral Oration in the Classical City*, trans. Alan Sheridan (Cambridge MA, 1986).

23. For an extended discussion of the fragility of the ethos celebrated in Thuc. 2.40, see J. Peter Euben, "Creatures of a Day: Thought and Action in Thucydides," in *Political Theory and Praxis: New Perspectives*, ed. Terence Ball (Minneapolis, 1977), 28–56.

24. Thuc. 2.40.4. Cf. 1.9.3; note 1.32.1–33.2; and see 3.37.2. For an interpretation of this passage at odds with my own, see J. T. Hooker, "χάρις and ἀρετή in Thucydides," *Hermes* 102 (1974): 164–69.

25. Consider Thuc. 8.96.3–5 in light of 4.55.4. Elsewhere, Thucydides makes it clear that the Syracusans were capable of defeating the Athenians where the Spartans were not because they were of similar disposition (*homoiótropoi*) and possessed comparable *tólma*: 6.69.1, 7.21.2–4, 67.1, 8.96.5.

26. Consider Thuc. 3.29–33 in light of 1.124, 2.8.4–5, 4.85–87, 114.3–4, 120.3–121.1, 5.9.9–10.

27. In this connection, one may wish to consult Paul A. Rahe, *Republics Ancient and Modern: Classical Republicanism and the American Revolution* (Chapel Hill, 1992), 15–229 (esp. 136–218).

28. See Pouncey, *The Necessities of War*, 57–62. For an extended commen-

tary on the Corinthians' speech, see Lowell Edmunds, *Chance and Intelligence in Thucydides* (Cambridge MA, 1975), 7–142.

29. Consider Hdt. 6.132–36, Thuc. 2.65.3–4 (with Pl. *Grg.* 516a, Plut. *Per.* 35, and Diod. 12.45.4), 4.65, 5.26.5 (with 4.102–8), 6.26.1–32.2, 53–61 (with 74, 88.7–93.3, 7.18.1–2, 8.6–109; Xen. *Hell.* 1.4.10–20, 5.10–17), 7.47–49 (with Plut. *Nic.* 22); Xen. *Hell.* 1.6.19–7.35 (with Diod. 13.97.1–103.2), 2.1.20–32 (with Diod. 13.104.8–106.7); and Andoc. 3.33–35 (with Philochorus *FGrH* 328 F149a) in light of Machiavelli, *Discorsi sopra la prima deca di Tito Livio* 1.28, 31, 53, in Niccolò Machiavelli, *Tutte le opere*, ed. Mario Martelli (Florence, 1971), 110, 113–14, 134–36.

30. Among other things, they are borne out by the testimony of Herodotus: 4.77.

31. For Thucydides' sparing use of this term and its cognates, see Huart, *Le vocabulaire de l'analyse psychologique*, 468–73.

32. In considering the importance of the crucial term *polupragmosúnē*, cf. Thuc. 1.70.8, 2.40.2, and 63.2–3 with 6.18.6–7; see Victor Ehrenberg, "Polypragmosune: A Study in Greek Politics," *Journal of Hellenic Studies* 68 (1947): 46–67; and cf. Donald Lateiner, "'The Man Who Does Not Meddle in Politics': A Topos in Lysias," *Classical World* 76 (1982–83): 1–12, with L. B. Carter, *The Quiet Athenian* (Oxford, 1986), 26–130.

33. Cf. Thuc. 8.24.4 with 40.2, and see 4.80.

34. Forde, *The Ambition to Rule*, 45, aptly suggests a kinship between this species of civic morality and the "pious cruelty" later condemned by Niccolò Machiavelli: see *Il principe* 21, in Machiavelli, *Tutte le opere*, 291–93.

35. The fact that the men of this city were sent to Athens and held there is explained by their ultimate exchange for prisoners held by the Olynthians: Thuc. 5.3.4.

36. See Clifford Orwin, "Stasis and Plague: Thucydides on the Dissolution of Society," *Journal of Politics* 50 (1988): 831–47. Note also Charles Norris Cochrane, *Thucydides and the Science of History* (New York, 1965); Adam Parry, "The Language of Thucydides' Description of the Plague," *Bulletin of the Institute of Classical Studies* 16 (1969): 106–18; Lowell Edmunds, "Thucydides' Ethics as Reflected in the Description of Stasis (3.82–83)," *Harvard Studies in Classical Philology* 79 (1975): 73–92; Arlene Saxonhouse, "Nature and Convention in Thucydides' *History*," *Polity* 10 (1978): 461–87; Colin Macleod, "Thucydides on Faction (3.82–83)," *Proceedings of the Cambridge Philological Society* 205 (1979): 52–68; and Nicole Loraux, "Thucydide et la sédition dans les mots," *Quaderni di storia* 23 (1986): 95–134.

37. For a full discussion of Pericles' speeches, see Romilly, *Thucydides and Athenian Imperialism*, 110–55.

38. As Simon Hornblower, *A Commentary on Thucydides* (Oxford, 1991–), vol. 1, 480, points out, Thucydides' description is replete with language found in the Hippocratic medical texts.

39. For the problems this sentence poses for the translator, see John T. Hogan, "The ἀξίωσις of Words at Thucydides 3.82.4," *Greek, Roman, and Byzantine Studies* 21 (1980): 139–49, and John Wilson, "'The Customary Meanings of Words Were Changed'—Or Were They? A Note on Thucydides 3.82.4," *Classical Quarterly* 32 (1982): 18–20.

40. See, in this connection, Seth Benardete, "Achilles and the Iliad," *Hermes* 91 (1963): 1–16.

41. See Thomas S. Engeman, "Homeric Honor and Thucydidean Necessity," *Interpretation* 4, no. 2 (winter 1974): 65–78 (at 74 n. 21), and Connor, *Thucydides*, 82 n. 5.

42. Eur. *Supp.* 187.

43. Arist. [*Rh. Al.*] 1420a28–1421a24 (esp. 1420a28 b1).

44. Consider Thuc. 1.3, 5–6, 17–18 in light of 12.1.

45. Note Thucydides' use (5.25.1) of the cognate *diekínoun* in asserting a continuity between the movement or commotion that preceded and the one that followed the Peace of Nicias: 5.25–26. Cf. his use of the word *kínēsis* at 3.75.2 and 5.10.5 and of the verbal form at 4.55.4.

46. Consider Arist. *Pol.* 1252b27–1253a39 in light of Paul A. Rahe, "The Primacy of Politics in Classical Greece," *American Historical Review* 89 (1984): 265–93, and see Rahe, *Republics Ancient and Modern*, 15–229.

47. In considering why Thucydides reserved the place of honor (Sall. *Iug.* 11.3, Verg. *Aen.* 11.234–40, Plut. *Cic.* 2.2–3) for the dialogue, one should begin by consulting Hunter R. Rawlings III, *The Structure of Thucydides' History* (Princeton, 1981), esp. 243–49.

48. See Felix Martin Wassermann, "The Melian Dialogue," *Transactions of the American Philological Association* 78 (1947): 18–36; H. Ll. Hudson-Williams, "Conventional Forms of Debate and the Melian Dialogue," *American Journal of Philology* 71 (1950): 156–69; Romilly, *Thucydides and Athenian Imperialism*, 273–343; Colin Macleod, "Form and Meaning in the Melian Dialogue," *Historia* 23 (1974): 385–400; Pouncey, *The Necessities of War*, 83–104; and Connor, *Thucydides*, 147–57.

49. For the details, see Paul A. Rahe, "Lysander and the Spartan Settlement, 407–403 B.C." (Ph.D. diss., Yale University, 1977), 76–177.

50. Cf. Cornford, *Thucydides Mythistoricus*, 174–220, with Connor, *Thucydides*, 147–209.

51. That one sentence ends book five and the other begins book six means nothing. The division of the text into books was not the work of the author.

52. See Connor, *Thucydides*, 119–26.

53. See Colin Macleod, "Rhetoric and History (Thucydides, VI, 16–18)," *Quaderni di Storia* 2 (1975): 39–65. Note also Hans Peter Stahl, "Speeches and Course of Events in Books Six and Seven of Thucydides," in *The Speeches in Thucydides*, 60–77.

54. From a perspective differing from my own, James Boyd White, *When Words Lose Their Meaning: Constitutions and Reconstitutions of Language, Character, and Community* (Chicago, 1984), 59–92, makes a similar point.

55. With regard to Thucydides' use of the word *sophrosúnē*, see Huart, *Le vocabulaire de l'analyse psychologique*, 141–52.

By Fire and Sword

Bellum Hostile *and "Civilians"*
in the Hundred Years' War

Clifford J. Rogers

There is ful many a man that crieth "Werre! werre!" that wot ful litel
what werre amounteth

Geoffrey Chaucer

France, at the beginning of the fourteenth century, was "fat, sated and
strong, its people wealthy and rich in material goods; none of them
knew the first thing about war." The chronicler Jean de Venette described her as "before all the kingdoms and parts of the world . . . secure in glory and honor and the blessings of peace and renown, and
opulent in the affluence of every good thing." Godfrey de Harcourt's
depiction of Normandy as "the best country, the richest, fattest, and
best provided with all goods which there was in the world" could be
taken as representative of the realm as a whole.[1]

   Things were very different by the end of the Hundred Years' War — or
even by the time of the peace of Brétigny, which ended the first phase of
the conflict in 1360. The great Anglo-French war, which began in 1337,
ultimately left the fair land of France "completely messed up, deserted,
dissipated, laid waste and broken down."[2] Thomas Basin wrote how,
toward the end of the war, he personally had seen "the vast fields of
Champagne, of all Beauce, Brie, Gâtinais, Chartres, Dreux, Maine and
Perche, both the French and the Norman Vexin, Beauvaisis, Caux, from
the Seine up to Amiens and Abbeville, and Senlis, Soissonnais, and Valois all the way to Laon and even farther in the direction of Hainault,
absolutely deserted, uncultivated, abandoned, squalid, emptied of all
the country folk, [and] filled up with thickets and brambles." Petrarch,
who first traveled in France before the outbreak of the Hundred Years'

33

War, wrote after his return there around 1360 that the English had "reduced the entire kingdom of France by fire and sword to such an extent that I . . . had to force myself to believe that it was the same country I had seen before."[3] The realm of France as a whole, like Jean Juvenal des Ursins's bishopric of Beauvais, was "simply falling to bits."[4]

Or, at least, that was the state of the kingdom as it was presented by chroniclers, churchmen, and poets. Their testimony, however, cannot simply be accepted at face value without further examination. After all, some modern historians have argued that medieval wars "were, in fact, little better than caricature: petty gang-warfare flamboyantly decked out and caparisoned, but for the most part, mere swagger and bluster, clamour and rodomontade."[5] The Hundred Years' War, more particularly, has been characterized as merely "the greatest tourney of the middle ages"—which has a certain aptness when we consider that the conflict was launched by Edward III, founder of the Order of the Garter and chivalric monarch par excellence.[6] Henry V, the other great soldier-king of the war, was known for his piety and the strict discipline he imposed on his troops. Is there sufficient reason to believe that these chivalrous, Christian rulers, who considered themselves kings of France as well as of England, would have waged a war directed "against the poor laboring people and their goods" that left the countryside "desolate and deserted," the peasants living in dwellings that appeared more like the lairs of wild beasts than like human habitations, and the towns "in piteous devastation and total ruin"?[7] Would they have sought to win the loyalty of their "rebellious subjects" by pillaging them; would they have fought so hard to gain a kingdom that they themselves were responsible for reducing to cinders?

To understand, then, the impact of the Hundred Years' War on the civilians who came in the path of its armies, we have a number of questions to answer. How credible are the chroniclers' descriptions of a France left in a state of utter ruin? If their accounts are credible, how is it that the small armies of the day (often comprising ten thousand men or fewer) were able to have such a large effect? How did these "chivalrous" knights and kings justify the pillage and killing of helpless peasants, women and children, or churchmen—all of whom, the medieval legists agreed, should ideally have been spared from harm in war? And, perhaps most importantly, *why* did it all occur—was it just unavoidable "collateral damage," or perhaps a "tax of violence" to support military operations that, because of their scale and duration, were beyond the resources available to the fledgling royal states of France and England?[8] Or did the devastation, in fact, serve a deeper strategic purpose?

"And so he made his way forward . . . burning and destroying all the countryside around" is a phrase often repeated, in its many variations, in almost every chronicler's account of the campaigns of the Hundred Years' War. But the medieval chronicles mix together history and storytelling in a way that sometimes sacrifices accuracy for drama. The chroniclers liked to paint their canvases with bright colors and stark contrasts. So when Froissart writes that in the northeast of France in 1359 "the country had been so constantly ravaged, for the previous two or three years, that no one had cultivated the land," or when Thomas Basin claims that in the fifteenth century "from the river Loire to the Seine and from there up to the Somme, nearly all the agricultural lands remained uncultivated for a long time, many years, lacking people who could farm them, the peasants having been killed or put to flight," we are entitled to take their testimony with a grain of salt until we have found other evidence to support their statements.[9]

Petitions for exemption from taxation, either secular or papal, provide us with another major source of descriptions of French and English lands "burned and destroyed" or monasteries "totally destroyed, dilapidated, and demolished" because of the wars.[10] These documents, and similar ones seeking to justify the merging of parishes or the granting of extra lands for the better support of the local clergy, must also be considered critically since the authors had an obvious motive to exaggerate the extent of the damage. The same might be said of political tracts like *Tragicum argumentum de miserabili statu regni Francie*, which used descriptions of the miseries of France to spur the realm toward moral and martial reforms.[11] Similarly, when the Black Prince wrote back to England describing how much harm he had done to his enemies, he clearly had reasons to overstate the effects of his *chevauchée*.[12]

The testimony of biased sources, however, is not always false. Indeed, the consistency and the sheer volume of the narrative and archival records on the subject show that the destruction was unquestionably both widespread and severe. It is easy to believe the claims of the canons of Chapelle-Taillefertin that Bernard-Ezii, the sire d'Albret, killed and wounded many of their number, drove out the rest, seized some precious objects, appropriated the revenues of their church to himself, and then demanded that they obtain for him papal absolution for his acts.[13] After all, in the will he prepared the very next year, Albret himself admitted that he had "killed some peasants, destroyed some villages and hospices, molested churchmen, and held merchants for ransom."[14] But these actions were mild compared to the sufferings some other soldiers of the day inflicted on noncombatants. The Englishman Walter Strael, for example, made certain that the letter of pardon he received in 1368 excused him for having "committed and perpetrated many murders, larcenies, robberies, sacrileges, having assaulted towns and fortresses, killed men, women and children, set fires, raped women and violated maids, burned and destroyed churches, chapels, and monasteries, held men for ransom, ransomed towns and countryside, and done all other evils, crimes, wrongdoings and delicts which he could."[15]

The question is not *whether* such things occurred but rather how commonplace they were and how much of an impact they had on the scale of the whole kingdom of France. Is it mere dramatic overstatement when Philip the Good of Burgundy writes that the army of Liège so devastated and burned his county of Namur that "nearly all of our subjects of the county have been so harmed . . . that they suffer greatly, deprived of what they need to live"?[16] When Edward III says that his invasion of 1339 left the entire Cambrésis "quite completely destroyed," his men having devastated a swath of territory twelve to fourteen leagues wide, how literally should we take his words?[17]

The issue of the breadth of devastation is an important one. Jean le Bel, describing Edward III's advance in Normandy in 1346, says that the English devastated the countryside over the same area: for six to seven leagues on either side of the host.[18] Richard Wynkeley, who traveled with that army, gives essentially the same figure — twenty miles, or six and two-third leagues — while Michael Northburgh, another eyewitness, makes it "five or six leagues around."[19] Many other contemporary sources, describing a dozen other *chevauchées* of this period, also give similar figures — from four to seven leagues — as the radius of devastation.[20] In one extraordinary example, reliable sources indicate that while the Black Prince's main division marched north to Vierzon in 1356, his rear guard ranged typically some *forty miles* to his right, while his vanguard traveled some distance to his left. Cities in between the separate divisions, such as Bourges and Limoges, had their suburbs burned by Anglo-Gascon *coureurs*.[21] Thus, it seems reasonable to take the rather conservative, but commonly given, figure of five leagues (13.4 modern miles) as a typical "havoc radius."[22] Since we know the routes of all the major *chevauchées* of the fourteenth century, we can use this figure to make a good first cut at assessing how widely the damage they inflicted spread—without necessarily accepting the chroniclers' assertions that the *coureurs* were so effective in their work that "they did not leave town nor hamlet, abbey nor priory in the land, except for fortresses, which was not completely burned and wasted."[23]

Map 2.1, which shows the routes of the *chevauchées* of 1339, 1342, 1345, 1346, 1355, 1356, 1359–1360, 1369, 1370, 1373, and 1380 indicates the zones within five leagues of the lines of march. All of these were conducted by substantial forces and all were characterized by vigorous destruction of the surrounding countryside.

The English *chevauchées*, it should be noted, generally covered a substantial amount of ground in a relatively short period of time. The Black Prince, for example, traversed 675 miles in 68 days during the course of the 1355 Languedoc campaign.[24] If the soldiers who rode on this expedition did indeed scour the landscape for a breadth of ten leagues, they would have devastated a total of over 18,000 square miles—nearly 4 square miles for every man in the force. And each man obviously could not have acted on his own. If we assume that the standard raiding party comprised only thirty men, then each member would have had to have participated in the destruction of 120 square miles.[25] Assuming that only half the army was involved in the work of havoc at a time and that the raiders had to spend three hours a day making forward progress to keep up with the army, that would suggest that each band would have had only about five hours to lay waste nearly 4 square miles. This calculation, of course, is an extremely rough one built on a sequence of guesses, but it does give some idea of the haste with which the *coureurs* would have to act. Although it does not seem impossible that a raiding party could hit all the hamlets and villages of such an area within that time frame, they would certainly not have had much time to spend on each—making assaults on fortified buildings,

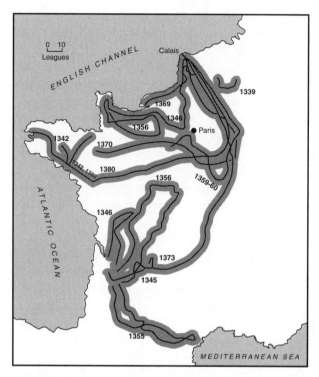

Map 2.1. Chevauchée Routes, 1339–1380

seeking out the hiding places of valuables, searching through woods for livestock driven out of their path, and so on.

Yet in the short time they had they could do much damage. Fire, far and away the most destructive weapon available to the warriors of the fourteenth century, could do great harm without requiring much time or effort. Henry V himself, it is said, observed that "war without fire is as worthless as sausages without mustard."[26] Houses, barns, windmills, water mills, churches, monasteries, even entire villages or towns, all could be reduced to cinders very quickly.[27] The other major stores of wealth for medieval peasant communities (in addition to wooden structures) were food supplies, casks of wine, and livestock. The wine and grain, too bulky to hide or carry out of harm's way easily, could be carted off to supply the invading forces—and what could not be taken away could be (and generally was) destroyed.[28] If the watchmen did not give the peasants enough warning to get their livestock to safety that too could be appropriated by the *coureurs* with only minimal effort or loss of time.[29] Philip VI's army, for example, managed to bring away twelve thousand sheep, one thousand pigs, and five hundred cattle from its brief raid on Chimay in 1340.[30]

Strong evidence for the severity of the destruction thus inflicted can be found in the records of official commissions sent to investigate claims of devastation. Sometimes these documents provide only minimal information, for example, that 128 vills in the North Riding of Yorkshire alone "had been so burned and devastated by the Scots that they had no goods which might be taxed."[31] Despite its lack of detail, such information is valuable for its reliability: medieval tax collectors were not known for their generosity in granting exemptions. If the county of Longueville was granted six years of remission from taxation, we can be sure that it was no great exaggeration to describe the area as "completely uninhabited, laid waste, and in a complete way of destruction."[32]

A small number of records from this period supply a far more detailed and intimate portrait of what a medieval *chevauchée* could do to a village or region that lay in its path. In the following pages, we will look at three such sources, which describe, respectively: the costs of a brief attack on a single village in the summer of 1298; the effects of Edward III's 1339 two-week *chevauchée* from the Cambrésis through the Vermandois and Thiérache; and the damage done in the war between Liège and Namur from June to September 1430.

The first of these documents, and by far the most detailed, describes individually the losses suffered by each of eighty-three households of the village of Cagnoncles in the Cambrésis during a raid led by a local seigneur, Gilles de Busigny.[33] "He burned two houses belonging to demoiselle Erme, which were worth 12 *livres tournois* (l.t.); seized and carried off one cow, five sheep, and other things of her possessions which were worth 6 l.t. . . . He took and carried off a coat belonging to Marget, Jehan Gobiert's granddaughter, worth 12 s.t.," and so on.

The raid was apparently quick and rather haphazard since only about half the village's houses were actually burned. Most, but not all, of these had been plundered before being put to the torch. Various households had goods to the value of as little as 20 deniers or as much as 35 *livres tournois* taken away.[34] In total, Gilles de Busigny's pillagers gained eleven horses, six cows, and about a hundred sheep.

These, along with the wool, cash, wheat, pieces of cloth, armor, and other miscellaneous items that they took, were worth a total of 431 l.t. The estimated value of the houses and other buildings destroyed amounted to just under 1,000 l.t.[35]

The losses could easily have been much worse, but the villagers were apparently given enough advance warning to escape before the arrival of de Busigny's men. Only one man, Simon de Lalent, was captured. He was put in prison and mistreated until he ransomed himself for the remarkable sum of 63 l.t., which was nearly eight times the value of his house! It is not clear whether he had that sum cached away or if his neighbors contributed to his ransom. If the former, it would indicate that the villagers had far more wealth hidden away than what the raiders got. It seems likely that most of the villagers succeeded in driving away their livestock before the enemy arrived; otherwise, the total lost, though the equivalent of over 200 l.t., would be very small indeed for a village that probably had over four hundred inhabitants. Aside from de Lalent, only two of the villagers reported losing cash, another sign that most of them fled the village before the raiders arrived.

The key point is that even a swift, almost careless attack on a single medium-sized village caused nearly 1,500 l.t. in damages. At current wage rates, that was the equivalent of over forty thousand man-hours of skilled labor destroyed in a fraction of a day.[36] If a single *chevauchée* could produce hundreds or even thousands of "Cagnon-cles" and there were half a dozen or more such campaigns of devastation all over France between 1339 and 1360, it is easy to see why France might, as Jean de Venette wrote, "put on confusion and mourning like a garment."[37]

How many villages like Cagnoncles, then, *would* be destroyed over the course of a campaign? That question can be answered with some precision for one representative case thanks to the detailed records left by a charitable relief operation organized by the Papacy. In 1340, Pope Benedict XII sent two commissioners to distribute 6,000 florins (8,900 l.t.) of alms in the areas devastated during Edward III's Cambrésis campaign the previous year.[38] The officials swore to seek out the poorest and most unfortunate victims of the war, determine their estate and condition (especially making certain that their poverty was not their own fault but due to the devastation of the enemy), and then disburse the relief money among them.[39] These alms, which were by no means intended or able to compensate the victims fully for their losses, were distributed among the inhabitants of a total of just over two hundred villages ruined by the war in the dioceses of Laon, Reims, Noyon, and Cambrai.[40] A full record was kept for each parish of every single recipient of the charity—his or her name, age, number of dependents, the amount of loss claimed to have been suffered, and amount of relief money received. The last figure bore virtually no relationship to the damages reported, so there was little or no motive for the recipients to perjure their oath to the Pope's representatives.[41]

The full record has been published for one of the 174 parishes in question, that of La Capelle-en-Thiérache. In that parish, listed simply as "burned," eighty-eight beneficiaries (each representing a household of from one to nine souls) received alms totaling just under 94 l.t.[42] This indicates that La Capelle was approximately the same size as Cagnoncles. Seventy-six of the recipients made sworn statements as to the losses they had suffered because of the war, the total amounting to 5,805 l.t., an average of 76 l.t. per household. This is roughly three times the per capita damage suffered by Cagnoncles, but the discrepancy can be accounted for by two factors. First, La Capelle was thoroughly burned, while Cagnoncles was less than half destroyed. Second, it seems that the parishioners of La Capelle had less advance warning of the enemy's arrival or were less willing to flee, since at least two villagers were killed by the English, and the old bailiff was captured.[43] A fair number of the plaintiffs at Cagnoncles reported only the loss of "small things" worth a single pound or less, but at La Capelle very few lost less than twenty pounds, and many lost over one hundred. When these considerations are taken into account, the two cases are close enough to be mutually supporting.[44]

The commissioners' report also allows us to see the broader picture of which the fate of La Capelle is only one detail. Map 2.2 shows the location of the places that received Benedict XII's alms as well as others reported in narrative sources as having been destroyed in relation to the main Anglo-German line of march.[45]

As the map shows, most of the villages devastated lay within about three leagues of the main line of march. Quite a few, however, were over five leagues distant. Some villages that Froissart reports as destroyed, such as Bruyères, are as much as nine leagues from Edward III's path. English raiding parties seem to have followed the local roads,

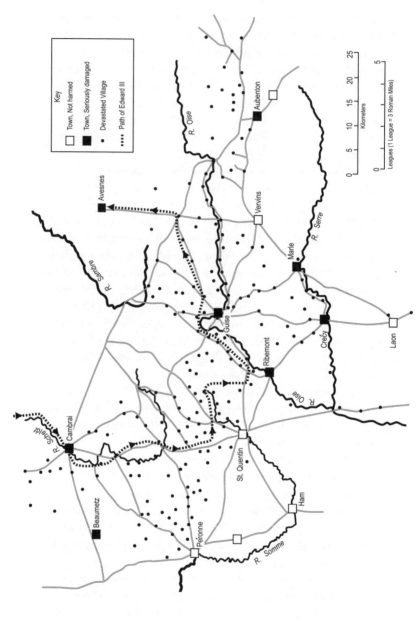

Map 2.2. The Devastation of Cambrai-Thiérache, 1339–1340

destroying villages on or visible from them. It is worth noting that while most of the places mentioned in the narrative sources as having been destroyed are also listed among the alms recipients, others (e.g., Bruyères near Laon, Iron, Moÿ, St.-Gobain, and Tupigny) are not. This fact indicates that the commissioners' list, extensive as it is, falls well short of being complete.[46] Furthermore, monasteries, convents, abbeys, and other ecclesiastical communities are often not shown, nor are a large number of villages in the Cambrésis proper (outside the realm of France), which the English also ravaged.[47]

Of course, as the contrast between Cagnoncles and La Capelle shows, a "devastated" village could be thoroughly destroyed or only partly ruined. The fact that La Capelle lay directly on the path of Edward's armies makes it unsurprising that it fell into the former category, but what about the villages further out, outside the center zone of destruction? A codicil to the main record of the Carit mission, dealing with the eleven villages listed as devastated in the deanery of Crécy-sur-Serre, suggests part of an answer to that question. All eleven are described as plundered, but only three are said to have been completely burned. Three more are rated "mostly" or "almost completely" burned, and the same number "half" or "partly" burned. The remaining two were not burned.[48] It is worth noting that some of the most severely damaged villages, like Parigny-les-Bois, which was "mostly burned," are over four leagues from the main army's march. It is also significant that all three of the villages that were completely destroyed lay directly on roads, while both of the two that entirely avoided burning were located some distance away from the roads.

So, to sum up the evidence from the various sources for the *chevauchée* of Edward III in 1339: over the course of two weeks, from the ninth to the twenty-second of October, the English army and its imperial allies did indeed, as Edward himself wrote, do all the destruction they could.[49] Edward's claim that his troops devastated the countryside over a breadth of twelve to fourteen leagues is passably accurate as an indication of the greatest distances at which his plunderers operated, but the most intense area of destruction extended only about half as far. The claim of one contemporary source that 2,117 villages and castles were destroyed on this campaign is further off the mark, but the actual figure was easily somewhere in the hundreds—substantial enough for two weeks' work.[50] The total damage inflicted by the Anglo-German armies could conceivably have reached one million *livres tournois*.[51] "Mere swagger and bluster" it was not.

Some of the contemporary sources for the 1339 *chevauchée* (the first major English campaign of the Hundred Years' War) point out that one of the reasons for its great destructiveness was that the inhabitants of the area had no experience of war; even some of the larger towns were not protected by walls. Le Bel comments that the English "found such a great abundance of cattle and other things that they didn't know what to do with it all" because "nothing had been hidden, or cleared away, or taken to safety." France, he adds, had never before seen such burning and devastation.[52] The chronicles and the documentary sources alike, however, are full of the precautions taken throughout France as the war went on—castles and town walls repaired, parish churches fortified, watches set, cattle so accustomed to the alarms of war that they would, of their own accord, run to safety when the warning bells sounded.[53] After a hundred years of such security measures, could war still be so devastating?

To answer that question, we can turn to our third source. Throughout the 1420s, hostility was building between the towns of the principality of Liège and those of the small county of Namur (which, since 1421, had been a possession of the dukes of Burgundy). On 10 June 1430, open war broke out. The conflict was sharp: according to the chronicler Jean Stavelot, the Liègeois burned three hundred villages, thirty-two fortresses and fortified houses, and seventeen mills.[54] All of this was done before the conclusion of a truce in September. One of the clauses of the treaty of peace that followed a year later required the Liègeois to pay an indemnity to cover the duke's costs and damages as well as the harm done to his subjects. The indemnity eventually amounted to the remarkable sum of 172,700 gold florins, about one third of which the duke distributed to his subjects who had suffered during the war. The recompense this provided was far from complete, however. Duke Philip also provided the inhabitants of the county with some free construction materials to help them rebuild and furthermore granted them exemption from taxation, rents, and other revenues due to him until March 1438.[55]

In preparation for the distribution of the indemnity money, a great inquest was made to gather information on the "loss and destruction" that had been suffered by the Namurois. Each group or individual

44

requesting a share of the indemnities filled out a "remonstrance," listing in detail any losses caused by the war with Liège. Unfortunately, these documents no longer exist; but a summary account does remain to us and has been published in full. This account lists 209 claimants, along with (in 187 cases) the amount of compensation they requested and the amount they received.[56]

The correlation between loss claimed and indemnity received was slight, so once again there was little incentive for the claimants to exaggerate their statements.[57] Even so, the reported damages for the 187 fully recorded claimants exceeded 450,000 gold florins—more than it would have cost to employ twenty-five hundred laborers for *five years*.[58] Since the army of Liège probably did not greatly exceed that number, yet managed to do that much harm in only three months, this is an excellent illustration of the principle already suggested by the analysis of the Cagnoncles raid[59]: damage could be inflicted infinitely more rapidly and easily than it could be repaired.

The warfare in Thiérache in 1339 and Namur in 1430, destructive though it was, diminishes into insignificance when compared to the great *chevauchées* of Edward III in 1346 and 1359–1360 or of Edward the Black Prince in 1355 and 1356. The entire county of Namur comprised only about six hundred square miles; the area within France devastated in 1339 was not much more than twice that. Thus, even if our earlier calculation overstated the average radius of destruction by 100 percent, the 1355 Languedoc *chevauchée* alone still laid waste *four times* as much land as the 1339 and 1430 operations combined. Furthermore, it was not only their great extent that made the *chevauchées* of the mid-fourteenth century so phenomenally destructive. By far the greatest concentrations of wealth in the medieval world were to be found in the towns and cities.[60] This was all the more true in wartime, when as much as possible would have been carried within town walls for safekeeping.[61] Since the siege of Cambrai in 1339 failed, no city, and only four substantial towns, suffered a sack during that campaign. Nor were any of the Namurois cities destroyed in the 1430 war. By contrast, the 1346 *chevauchée* in the north burned Barfleur, Cherbourg, and much of Carentan; thoroughly sacked and burned St.-Lô, Lisieux, Louviers, Pontoise, and Poix; plundered Caen (larger, according to a contemporary, than any town in England save London), Valognes, and Longueville; destroyed the suburbs of Pont-de-l'Arche, Beauvais, and Montreuil-sur-Mer; and burned Le Crotoy, to mention only some of the most considerable places.[62] "No man alive," wrote the contemporary chronicler Jean le Bel of the sack of St.-Lô, "could imagine or believe the riches which were there acquired and robbed, even if he were told of it."[63] The fact that the inhabitants of Carcassonne offered the Black Prince 250,000 gold *écus* to spare their *Bourg* from the flames reflects how much material damage each of these burnings did.[64] Béthune, a much smaller city, claimed to have suffered two hundred thousand *livres tournois* of damages when it was *unsuccessfully* besieged by the Flemings in 1346.[65] In 1359, the citizens of Auxerre were willing to offer Robert Knolles forty thousand gold florins and forty thousand pearls worth ten thousand florins more to refrain from burning their city, even *after* it had been plundered for eight days straight, until "there was nothing left to take." The value of the booty taken by the looters reportedly amounted to six hundred thousand florins, without counting the ransoms paid or promised by the bourgeois.[66]

Furthermore, it was in the towns that the worst loss of life occurred. As we have seen, raids on country villages relied much more on fire and pillage than on the sword: in the chroniclers' descriptions of the *chevauchées*, we only occasionally see "killing" beside "burning and destroying the countryside."[67] The peasants usually fled with their most valuable goods to the walled towns. Behind good fortifications, they had more motivation to fight (given that the possibility of further escape, especially with their valuables, was slight) and also more chance of success in driving off the raiders. But if they lost, the soldiers upon whom they had been dropping rocks and quicklime were likely to be more than a little irritable. Contemporary laws of war allowed virtually any excess in this case. In 1346 at Caen, which put up a stout resistance, the English archers "killed people without defense and without pity," though some of Edward's nobles tried to "forbid and break up the great killing which was carried on, and to preserve the women and maidens of the town from rape and villainy."[68] They were not very successful in this task: "a great number of knights, squires, and other townsmen were killed in the streets, houses, and gardens."[69] According to other eyewitnesses, some twenty-five hundred were killed and a like number taken prisoner to be held for ransom.[70] Similarly, after the sack of Sainte-Suzanne in 1423, "many of the inhabitants of the town were killed and mutilated, some were taken prisoner and others put to flight; and the outcome is that this town, which formerly was full of people and merchandise, now is in piteous desolation and total ruin."[71]

Between the sacking and destruction of the towns and the desolation of the countryside, the great *chevauchées* of 1346–1359 were indeed calamitous. But most of the country felt the effects of these operations only once, if ever. While rebuilding required incomparably more effort than did destroying, the men and women of France did have time to recover from the havoc caused by these great raids, the like of which was never seen during the fifteenth-century phase of the war. Yet even so, in the 1430s Jean Juvenal des Ursins, the bishop of Beauvais, painted the following picture of his diocese: "I have many fine lands and lordships which used to hold laborers and cattle: but the enemy, and those who claim to be the king [of France]'s men, have killed, taken prisoner, led off, pillaged, robbed, and tyrannized the peasants, and taken away all the cattle. The country is completely laid waste and desolate, and so are the churches, [and the] houses [are] burned down and fallen into ruins."[72]

What had reduced the Beauvaisis to such dire straits was not a *chevauchée*. It was, rather, the ravages of a large number of small garrison forces operating from bases in Lancastrian Normandy—and, as Juvenal des Ursins suggests, the damage done by the nominally "friendly" French forces that were supposed to be opposing the English. In other places in his writings, the bishop made it clear that the soldiers of the Valois were every bit as cruel in their treatment of the French peasantry as were the English garrisons (or even, indeed, "much more terrible")[73]:

> I certainly do not mean to say that these crimes are committed only by the enemy; for they have also been carried out by those who call themselves the king's men, who have, with the pretext of *appatis* [i.e., of compelling the payment of "contributions"] and otherwise, taken prisoner men, women, and small children, without distinction of age or sex; raped women and girls; captured husbands and fathers and killed them in the presence of their wives and daughters . . . kidnapped priests, monks, clergy, and laborers; put them in shackles and other instruments of torment called "monkeys" [*singez*], and then beaten them, by which some were mutilated, others driven mad.[74]

Indeed, throughout the entire war, the most methodical destruction, the cruelest atrocities, the most thorough robbery and extortion can be attributed to the work of garrisons, "free companies," "*écorcheurs*," and small bands or *routes* living permanently off the land. Soldiers on *chevauchée* generally had neither the time nor, really, the incentive to bother tracking down villagers hiding in the woods or to hold common peasants for ransom — and so did not need to resort to murders or tortures to inspire their victims to pay.[75] Even if the invaders were bent on bloodshed, the villagers could usually escape temporarily to the shelter of local fortresses or strong towns until the *coureurs* passed out of range. Things were very different, however, if a group of soldiers installed themselves in a castle, monastery, or town and used it as a base of operations to scour the land all around at their leisure. The well-known story of Hugues de Montgeron, a country prior in the diocese of Sens, vividly illustrates this situation:

In the year of our Lord 1358 the English came to Chantecocq and captured the castle on Halloween. The same evening they burned almost all of the town and then brought the whole countryside under their control, ordering the towns, both great and small, to ransom all their possessions — namely, bodies, goods, and movables — or else they would burn the houses. This they did in many places. Confounded and completely terrorized in this fashion, many of the people submitted to the English, paying them ransom money and agreeing to provide them with cash, flour, oats, and many other necessary supplies, if they would stop for a while the aforementioned torments because they had already killed many men in different places. Some they shut up in dark dungeons, threatening them daily with death, and continually making them suffer with whippings, wounds, hunger, and deprivation beyond belief. But others had nothing with which to pay ransom or were unwilling to submit to the power of the English. To escape from their hands these people made themselves huts in the woods and there ate their bread with fear, sorrow, and every misery. But the English learned of this and resolutely sought out these hiding places, searching numerous woods and putting many men to death there. . . . [I] put together a hut in the woods of les Queues and stayed there with many of my neighbors, seeing and hearing every day about the vicious and wicked work of our enemies: namely, houses burned and many dead left lying like animals

48

throughout the villages and hamlets. Seeing and hearing such things, I decided on December sixteenth to go to the city and stay there. But it happened that very night that these accursed English found their way to my hut so quietly that, in spite of the watchfulness of our sentinels, they almost captured me while I was asleep. But by God's grace and through the help of the blessed Virgin Mary I was awakened by the noise they made and escaped naked, taking nothing with me because of my haste except a habit with a hood. Crossing into the middle of the swamp I stayed there, trembling and shivering in the cold, which was then very great, while my hut was completely despoiled.[76]

That was just the beginning of the poor man's troubles. He took refuge with a relative in Sens, but the English followed him, sending him letters threatening to burn down his host's house unless Hugues made a deal with them. Eventually, he had to give in and purchased "protection" from them for four months. Unfortunately, the captain with whom he made his arrangement was captured by the French, and the other English would not honor it. Hugues was taken prisoner again but let free because he seemed to have nothing worth taking. His house was stripped of all movable goods; the soldiers drank his wine, stole his oats and his clothes, and ate all his pigeons. When harvest time drew near, he realized that he would have to pay protection money again or see his crops destroyed. What happened to him after that we do not know, for his account ends there.

There are any number of similar tales, and even worse ones.[77] One account from 1359, after describing how the English had destroyed towns and churches, dishonored women and maidens, and killed many of them and their children, adds: "when they captured the men, they hung them for two or three days, without food or drink, some by the arms, some by the genitals, others by the fingers of their hands or by the feet, and tortured and beat them to force them to talk, so that many died of it; and those who escaped their hands through ransom, [often] could not live, and if they did live, still they were driven mad or maimed."[78]

The sufferings of the population were worst in areas like Rouergue, the Cotentin, the Beauvaisis, or the Pas-de-Calais, where garrison warfare became a fact of daily life for long periods. A series of witnesses before a circa 1390 inquest complained of how the English had coursed through Quercy for at least fifty years, pillaging and killing. The results of this sort of constant warfare (aggravated, of course, by plague and general economic decline) are reflected in the state of the lands of the diocese of Cahors in 1387: of about 1,000 benefices, 250 were worthless because they were completely uninhabited, and another 400 could provide only half a living. The bishop's revenues, which at one point had reached 16,000 florins, were down to 3,000 by 1368, and to just 1,000 by 1388, according to his treasurer.[79] We have already seen the comments of Thomas Basin and Jean Juvenal des Ursins on the equally miserable state of the border areas in the north of France in the fifteenth century. But it was not border areas alone that suffered from the practitioners of *petite guerre*. In the late 1350s and the 1360s, in particular, the *routiers* and the "Companies" penetrated into almost every area of France. Sir Thomas Gray did not exaggerate—indeed, he understated—when he wrote that "they levied protection money from nearly all Normandy and many of the border areas around there, securing for themselves good fortresses in Poitou, Anjou, and Maine, and all the way into the Ile-de-France within six leagues of Paris."[80]

The following two maps—2.3 and 2.4—give some idea of how widespread these *routier* and free companies' garrisons were. The first shows the places in Quercy (in south-central France) that late-fourteenth-century papal records described as captured by the English, uninhabited, or worthless. The second shows the strongholds held by "English" companies in the Montfort-Dourdan district between 1358 and 1364, with shaded circles to indicate the areas within an easy hour's ride (7.5 kilometers) of places that were in enemy hands during at least three of those years.[81]

In the Nivernais, the "English" were said to occupy over one hundred fortresses. Eustache d'Auberchicourt, a "very able, very vigorous, very acquisitive knight," led a band of a thousand soldiers who held a dozen fortresses in Champagne and Brie and "held to ransom all the country between Troyes, Provins, Château-Thierry, and Châlons-sur-Marne" in 1359. Later, he moved on to pillage the environs of Reims. Other garrisons, mostly operating under the (at least nominal) authority of the king of England or of Navarre, dotted Périgord, Berry, the Bourbonnais, and Touraine.[82] Siméon Luce was able to identify over 450 strongholds, spread out over 36 departments of France, that were occupied by "Anglo-Navarrese" companies between 1356 and 1364 alone.[83] Sometimes these bands imposed themselves on the country-

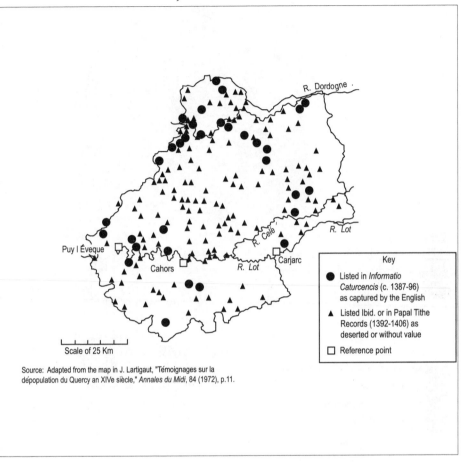

Map 2.3. The Devastation of Quercy at the End of the Fourteenth Century

side for extended periods. In Anjou, one band occupied the abbey of Louroux from 1355 to 1370, and another held Puy-Notre-Dame from 1359 to 1364.[84] Wherever they operated, the *routiers* and companies "inflicted great miseries on the countryside."[85]

Among these miseries was the virtual destruction of long-distance trade. "The English took many castles by force," complained Jean de Venette, " . . . wherefore the whole population and the very roads and highways had reason to mourn and grieve, for by reason of their seizures and depredations the highways were closed."[86] The same was true

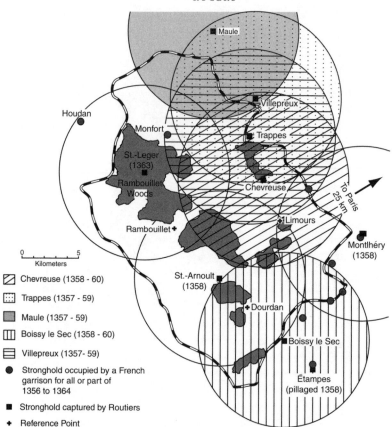

Map 2.4. Strongholds Occupied by Anglo-Navarrese Companies, 1356–1364

of many water routes. This "culpable interference in trade" added to the strains resulting from mass emigration from the unsafe country-side to the already overcrowded cities.[87] At the same time, the need to improve the defenses of towns all over the realm led not only to very onerous duties of watch and ward, as well as heavy construction and repair costs, but also to the destruction of a very large number of sub-urban monasteries, castles, and residential areas by the French towns-men themselves, either to clear the ground for new fortifications or to keep the enemy from using them as bases.[88] In 1360, to cite one of many examples, the citizens of Paris burned their own suburbs to keep them from falling into the hands of the English.[89] Away from the cities, the same logic led the French royal government to destroy entire settlements that were judged indefensible.[90]

To make matters worse for the common people, the nobility "bore hard upon them, extorting from them all their livelihood."[91] Sometimes this was to meet the cost of defense, to raise the ransom of a seigneur captured by the enemy, or to gather enough money to pay a band of *routiers* to give up a stronghold they had captured.[92] Other times, it was simply because in the chaos of war no one could check the nobles' greed. Bernard-Ezii, the sire d'Albret, admitted in his will of 1358 that some of his subjects, whom he had constrained to work on his construction projects, had been "harmed to excess" and should receive compensation.[93]

In such circumstances, it is little wonder that the social order threatened to collapse entirely. The commoners' revolt of 1358, the infamous "Jacquerie," did involve some truly horrible incidents.[94] It was, however, more than matched by the response of the nobles, who "burned the villages, killed the good people of the countryside without any pity or mercy whatsoever, robbed and pillaged all that they encountered—women, children, priests" until "there was no need for the enemy English to come to complete the destruction of the countryside.[95] For in truth the English, who had been the chief enemies of the realm before, could not have done what the nobles of France did."[96] This was only one of many instances where the grand war between England and France spawned or provided opportunities for the eruption of smaller conflicts, which together added substantially to the sum of misery suffered by the civilian population of France.

To all of this we can add the regions that were devastated by one or more of the great *chevauchées* as well as all the land that was during one portion of the war or another a disputed border territory and so subject to both the depredations of enemy garrisons and also to the "rapyn, oppressions and extorcions" of troops on its own side (such as the French troops who, as the regent John of Normandy admitted in the late 1350s, so pillaged the countryside, imprisoning and ransoming the peasants, that the inhabitants were too frightened to cultivate the land and so exposed themselves to death by famine).[97] All this considered, we can easily see that the descriptions of a ruined France that began this essay were no flights of fancy.

The degree of havoc wrought by the soldiers of this period will be surprising to many readers. Most people think of the Middle Ages as a time of devout Christianity and of chivalry—and indeed it was. Edward III, for example, from all outward signs considered himself a devout Christian, and certainly he was seen by his contemporaries as the very paragon of chivalry.[98] Yet it was he who was responsible for the most devastating *chevauchées* of the Middle Ages and he who released a plundering plague of *routiers* on sorrowing France. This raises the question of how chivalric, Christian monarchs, and the often devout knights who led their armies, justified inflicting such harsh methods of warfare on the innocent noncombatants of the enemy side.

In truth, however, medieval soldiers did not find any great difficulty on either score. Medieval religious thought recognized war as a valid, necessary, and indeed valuable way for sovereigns to settle international disputes, provided that the war was a just one. "We must understand that war comes from God," wrote one fourteenth-century authority, "and not merely that He permits war, but that He has ordained it . . . for the aim of war is to wrest peace, tranquillity, and reasonableness from him who refuses to acknowledge his wrongdoing."[99] The devastation of war was thus a form of punishment, a rod not spared, a means to the laudable end of bringing the wrongdoer to the right. If noncombatants supported their lord in his refusal to do justice, then they too were doing wrong and subject to the chastening scourge of war.[100] Furthermore, that condition did not have to be determined on an individual basis. If the king's council, which represented the community of the realm, decided upon the war, then the enemy soldiers could legitimately pillage his subjects and make war freely. The legitimacy of this position was enhanced by the fact that—despite Honoré Bonet's claim that "everyone knows that when it comes to deciding on war, or planning it, or undertaking it, poor men don't get involved; for they seek nothing but to live in peace"—the commons of both realms did indeed support the war efforts of their rulers with taxes and often even with personal military service, and usually quite willingly.[101] Thus, normally the medieval conception of *ius in bello*, at least in the case of a *bellum hostile* (a just war undertaken by a sovereign ruler), posed no legal impediment to attacks on civilians or their property.[102]

Furthermore, any residual moral qualms could usually be dissolved by blaming the enemy in one way or another.[103] And even if some soldiers did cross the line from allowable brutality to excessive barbarity, a share of their loot could often purchase absolution from the religious authorities, or a little more violence could extort it.[104]

Chivalry posed even less difficulty than religion, for the "laws of chivalry," as understood at the time, were meant primarily to regulate conduct of one *chevalier* toward another.[105] Peasants fell outside the charmed circle of fellowship in arms, despite the efforts of some churchmen to protect them under chivalry's aegis.[106] "A man may not torture a prisoner or extort money from him by way of ransom," wrote one medieval authority, "but it is different in the case of peasants, at least according to the custom of mercenaries."[107] Similarly, peasant women who were taken prisoner were often raped or forced to pay "ransom" in sexual services, a fate that ladies of the chivalric classes could usually escape, except during the sack of strong places taken by assault.[108] Thus, the sort of people we would now consider "civilians" were actually much *less* protected by the laws of chivalry than were the soldiers themselves. That is why, when they describe one of Edward III's *chevauchées*, the chroniclers — even the French chroniclers — often take the opportunity to criticize the French nobility for failing to protect their people rather than condemning Edward for causing such havoc. It also explains why brutal *routier* captains like Robert Knolles and Eustache d'Auberchicourt could receive the Garter, the ultimate accolade of chivalry.[109] They remained, according to the laws of chivalry, *sans reproche*.

And yet, to explain how a chivalrous, Christian king like Edward III could justify causing "innumerable evils" is not to explain *why* he did so.[110] After all, the legists and chroniclers may have accepted the legality of force against noncombatants, but they still regretted it.[111] Indeed, Edward III himself more than once admitted that devastation and bloodshed were things "which every good Christian should eschew, and especially princes and others who hold themselves for governors of men."[112] Furthermore, there are obvious practical reasons why the English monarchs might want to prevent the devastation of France. They claimed, after all, to be the legitimate rulers of that kingdom. As such, they had a clear duty to protect their subjects rather than preying on them and a clear interest in keeping intact what they hoped to acquire. Even on a purely military plane, the use of force against the population could have major disadvantages. H. J. Hewitt has argued that pillaging and destruction, which "took time, lowered morale, and might be contrary to the overriding interests of the campaign," could be (and were) "carried to lengths which exceeded military necessity, military advantage or even good sense."[113] William of Worcester, in the fifteenth century, argued that the pillaging conducted by the Lancastrian garrisons in Normandy virtually forced those who had been obedient subjects into "breking theire allegeaunce by manere of cohercion for suche rapyn, oppressions and extorcions."[114] Why then did such things occur? Did they result, as some contemporaries and many modern historians have thought, from the poor pay and worse discipline of the troops and the need for them to live off the land?[115]

The answer breaks down into five parts. Each must be considered separately, for each has a dynamic and a logic of its own: first, the *chevauchées*; second, the authorization of the *routiers* of the fourteenth century; third, the activities of the closely related "free companies"; fourth, the use and abuse of raids and "*appatis*" (contracts in which a group of soldiers agreed to refrain from devastating a village or an area in return for a payment in cash or supplies) by regular garrisons; and, fifth, siege warfare and strategies of precedent.

The great *chevauchées* of the fourteenth century, the most dramatic of the scourges that afflicted France, have often been described as nothing but "destructive but rather objectless" raids, characterized by an "absence of strategy, of policy, of any thought at all" and reflecting haphazard strategy or an incapacity to wage intelligent war.[116] More recent work, however, has generally discarded this view.[117] I myself have argued elsewhere that the devastation wrought by the *chevauchées* had a definite strategic rationale.[118] Edward III and his commanders intended to put the Valois monarchs in a lose-lose situation, where they would be faced with the grim choice of either launching an attack on the invading English army—an attack that would likely lead to battlefield defeat, as at Crécy or Poitiers—or else visibly and unequivocally failing in the foremost duty of kingship: to protect (or at least to avenge) the subjects of the realm. "All landed lords are duty-bound to guard their people," said the Comte de Foix; "it is for that that they hold their lordships."[119] Thus, the direct application of violence against civilians and their property was one of the most effective means for compelling a battle-shy opponent to accept the risks of a general engagement rather than relying on a highly effective strategy exhaustion.

There was another element to the strategic rationale behind the havoc caused by the English *chevauchées*: economic attrition.[120] Even if the Valois monarchy could not be brought to battle and decapitated nor toppled from its throne by political destabilization, then it could at least be hamstrung. Money was long since recognized as the "sinews of war," and the men guiding the English war effort in the fourteenth century were well aware of how much money their raids could cost to the French treasury.[121] Indeed, Sir John Wingfield, who served on the Black Prince's *grande chevauchée* of 1355, went to the trouble of having the records collected from the houses of the tax collectors in the towns that the English destroyed so he and the treasurer of England could keep track of how much damage they had done to the Valois fisc. His conclusion: "the countryside and good towns which were destroyed in this *chevauchée* found for the king of France more [money] each year in support of his war than did half his kingdom."[122] This economic aspect of the *chevauchée* helps explain why the troops took the trouble to destroy mills, fruit trees, livestock, and other means of production, even when there was no direct profit to be gained in doing so. Neither the desire for booty nor the need for the army to gather the supplies to live off the land can begin to explain the systematic destruction that these expeditions wrought. Indeed, by driving away the peasants the work of the *coureurs* could actually make it more difficult for the army to gather the supplies it needed, so the lack of supplies provided from base can hardly be used to explain the devastation they caused. The riches that the soldiers acquired through plunder on these expeditions were an important "bonus" but were not the primary motive.

The importance of devastation to each of the elements of the strategy at work here—provocation to battle, political destabilization, and economic attrition—should be obvious. Rather than a "futile and callous policy," ravaging was part of a successful and calculated (though certainly callous) use of force intended to achieve specific political goals.[123]

The *routiers* who, in the name of the king of England, plundered so much of the realm of France after the battle of Poitiers served a similar strategic purpose. They, as much as if not more than the English armies on *chevauchée*, were open evidence of the impotence of the Valois monarchy. They both took advantage of and magnified the political chaos that the war brought on. To contemporary observers it was a "marvel" that so many could suffer so much at the hands of so few.[124] Were it not for the large number of lords killed or captured at Poitiers — especially King John himself — the *routiers* could never have been so successful. But after that battle, "a hundred Frenchmen did not want or dare to meet twenty English in the field."[125] The *routiers* also contributed greatly to the economic attrition aspect of Edward's strategy: by the devastation they inflicted, by the wealth they extracted, and indirectly by forcing localities all over the realm to expend their resources on their own defense instead of contributing to the national war effort. For these reasons, Edward was fully willing to "authorize" them — to give them the position of soldiers fighting on behalf of a sovereign prince in a just war and so to extend to them important legal protections and at least a degree of moral legitimacy.[126] Nor was their connection to the English royal war effort merely nominal. Robert Knolles, for example, reportedly turned all the castles, towns, and fortresses he had taken in France over to his king in 1359.[127] Once Edward achieved his war aims with the peace of Brétigny in 1360, many of the *routiers* gave up their captured fortresses as required by the terms of the treaty, though often only after they had been paid a cash settlement to do so.[128]

Unlike the *coureurs* of an army on *chevauchée*, however, the *routiers* were generally not in the pay of the crown. Their wage was whatever they could seize from the enemy. Much like privateers equipped with letters of marque, the *routiers* provided a way for the monarch to sponsor military activity without paying for it. Thus, these bands had strong incentives to squeeze the peasantry and bourgeoisie of France dry. Since they had the time to extort at their leisure, the most effective way to do this was not by the haphazard plundering that characterized the *chevauchée* but rather through various ways of extracting what in a more modern context might be called "protection money."[129] Burning, torture, and murders, for them, were only particularly effective ways of encouraging larger and more rapid payments; they were not carried out to further a larger strategic goal. Since the greatest portion of the *routiers'* income came from ransoms and "truce" payments (*appatis*) they had no reason to cause the kind of destruction created by the *chevaucheurs* unless their victims proved hesitant to pay up. Indeed, destruction that reduced the ability of the peasants to pay their ransoms was actively counter to the *routiers'* interests.

The free companies, which operated in much the same way as the *routiers* but without the sanction of a sovereign to legitimize their activities, were even more dedicated to bleeding the maximum possible amount of wealth from the common people. If the *routiers* were privateers, the "free companions" were pirates. As Philippe Contamine has pointed out, contemporaries found this a significant distinction.[130] Since they by their very nature operated outside the laws of war, these "sons of Belial and men of iniquity . . . who assailed other men with no right and no reason other than their own passions, iniquity, malice, and hope of gain" showed even less restraint than the *routiers*.[131] The captain of one band whose motto declared him to be "everyone's enemy" was well justified; he and his men "killed men, women and children without mercy, and raped townswomen and maidens."[132] Since the companies did not require or receive the approval of a monarch, however, they must be considered a *result* of the Hundred Years' War rather than an element of its prosecution.[133]

Also closely related to the *routiers*, in practice if perhaps not in theory or intent, were the official garrisons paid and commanded as part of the regular royal forces primarily to guard frontier fortresses and secure control of the lands around them. When these garrisons were in peaceful areas, they were generally relatively well disciplined and imposed no particular burden on the people—indeed, they acted to their benefit in imposing civil order.[134] In border areas, however, they were constantly raiding into enemy territory, laying waste, taking plunder and—most profitable of all—seizing captives for ransom.[135] Whole crowds of "enemy" civilians were often rounded up like cattle and herded back to the garrisons' bases to be held for ransom.[136] As with the other types of war included in the larger conflict known as the Hundred Years' War, these activities had mixed motivations. A major part was, without doubt, greed. Garrison troops could make a huge amount of money on these raids, potentially far more than their regular pay, which was in any case often seriously in arrears. Of course, they also ran the risk of big losses, especially in ransom if they themselves were captured, but this gave them all the more motivation to collect enough money to be able to absorb such financial blows. The desire to harm the enemy and to "earn their pay" as soldiers certainly also came into play.[137] Sometimes the intent was to "comfort" one's own subjects by retaliating for enemy raids.

Because these garrisons were generally permanent (more so than even the bands of *routiers* or free companions who held so many strongholds in France) their raids, though individually limited in scope and destructiveness, had a horrible cumulative effect on the areas within their reach. It was such raids that left much of northern France "desolate and deserted" during the fifteenth century, the peasants having fled or living in huts that looked "more like the dens of wild beasts than the dwellings of people."[138] English Guienne, which had suffered a century of raiding by French garrisons by 1414 (in addition to the ravages of the Black Death), may have lost more than two-thirds of its population over that period.[139]

In many cases, the garrisons were expected to support the cost of their maintenance by, in effect, collecting taxes from all those around them, friend or enemy.[140] At its best, this system could simplify the government's duties. Instead of having the garrisons collect the money, send it to a central treasury, and then get it back as wages, the intermediate steps were eliminated, and the wages were collected by the soldiers directly in their locality. As Jean de Bueil explained, if the king couldn't provide payment of wages it was necessary for the soldiers to raise their own supplies and finances, as much from those of their own "obedience" as from the enemy population.[141] This was usually done through the means of *appatis* or *truages*—agreements reached on a town-by-town or parish-by-parish level, in which the local people agreed to supply cash or goods in kind in exchange for being spared by the soldiers.[142] Once such systems were established they usually required little if any violence against civilians to maintain, although the heaviness of the charge might entail substantial suffering. This was especially true for the hapless villages that found themselves forced to pay off both sides, which in the border areas was a very common situation. Sometimes a poor hamlet would find itself obliged to pay off several different garrisons, even eight or ten, on both sides. Thus, the *appatis* system, too, could contribute to the depopulation of areas within range of major garrisons, enemy or "friendly."[143]

As suggested earlier, however, the most intensely destructive episodes of the Hundred Years' War were the sacks of cities and towns, especially those taken by assault. Often such assaults were carried out in the course of a *chevauchée* or by a band of *écorcheurs, routiers,* or free companions seeking fat profits and a new base. In those cases, the logic behind them is best understood by placing them in the context of those types of operations, as explained in the last few paragraphs. Most extended sieges, however—which brought great suffering to the besieged whether or not they ended in an assault—were undertaken by royal armies fighting campaigns specifically oriented toward the capture of enemy strongholds. The duke of Lancaster's campaigns of 1345; Henry V's conquest of Normandy; the French reconquests of the 1370s, 1449–1450, and 1451; the Black Prince's recapture of Limoges in 1370; and the earl of Salisbury's operations in the 1420s all fall into this group. In these operations, the use of violence against the noncombatant bourgeoisie served what I call a "strategy of precedent." The only way to conquer a large number of fortified strong points in a short period of time (especially before siege cannon became capable of knocking down strong fortifications around the 1420s) was to convince the garrisons or the inhabitants that they were better off surrendering than fighting.[144] The more astute commanders of the day—and, for that matter, of other times when similar dynamics applied, as in the Reconquista or the Eighty Years' War—fully realized this fact and used it, in combination with the laws of siege warfare, to their advantage. When Henry V wanted to capture the castle of the town of Caen, where the garrison was holed up, "he sent worde to the lorde Montayny beyng capitain, that if he would yelde the castle by a daie, he should depart without dammage. And yf he would be foolishe and obstinate, all clemencye and favor should be from hym sequestred. When the capitain and his compaignions had well digested his message, beyng in dispaire of comfort, upon the condicions offred, rendred the Castle and yelded themselves."[145]

The basic principle of the laws of war at work here was that a stronghold taken by assault was not legally entitled to any mercy. Garrisons could legitimately be slaughtered, the property and even the lives of the inhabitants taken. The violent sack of a town that strongly resisted capture—especially if contrasted with the lenient treatment of another one that surrendered more readily—could lead to the prompt surrender of many others.[146] Even if a captured town was treated generously after it was taken, the agonies of hunger and bombardment it suffered during the siege could be enough to convince its neighbors to give up more easily. "When the renderynge of Roan [Rouen] was blowen throughe Normandy," for example, "it is in maner incredible to heare how manye tounes yelded not once desired [i.e., ordered to surrender], & how many fortresses gave up wythout contradiccion."[147]

The calculations on both sides that went into this sort of warfare were very complex and, considering the topic at hand, need not be fully addressed here. For our purposes, the key point is that when a royal army sacked a town the result could be bloody indeed. As the earl of Salisbury explained in his beautifully crafted letter to the town of le Mans, which he was about to besiege:

> we wish with all our heart to avoid the effusion of human blood and also to reduce and reunite the subjects of the king our said lord into his obedience, and rejoin them to his lordship by pleasant, friendly and gracious ways, without brutality or force . . . [but] you should know for certain that if you fail [to surrender], we will proceed to the encounter with you to execute the charge which the king and the regent have given to us in this area, so that the punishment which will be inflicted on you by the help of our Savior Jesus Christ will be a perpetual example and reminder to all others who will speak of it.[148]

Yet here, as with the *chevauchées*, the explanation for the sufferings of the "civilian" population had at least as much to do with strategy as with greed, bloodlust, and poor discipline combined. Noncombatants were made the victims of attack because attacking noncombatants *worked*, because it could facilitate the conquest of a fortified region, compel an enemy to do battle in the field, or hamstring him economically or politically. It is the effectiveness of methods of war like those employed by one of Edward III's partisans—"taking Frenchmen and putting them to ransom, living on the country and despoiling it, and leading the company under his command about the realm of France, and burning and setting afire places in it"—that transformed them from being just part of what a warrior "may" do in a *bellum hostile* to what he "*ought*" to do.[149]

The Hundred Years' War was no tourney, no game. A comparison for the chaos and suffering it caused within France can hardly be found.

What the great nineteenth-century historian of the war Henri Denifle referred to as "an endless and terribly monotonous suite of massacres, arsons, pillages, ransomings, destructions, losses of harvests and livestock, crimes, indeed of all calamities" characterized its 116-year-long course.[150]

Why was this war, fought in the midst of an age of honor, chivalry, and devout Christianity, so cruel? Part of the answer was simply the extraordinary scale and duration of the conflict, which grew beyond the ability of the fledgling royal states that waged it to control fully. A bigger part had to do with the laws of war of the day, which reflected a chivalric *mentalité* that placed relatively little weight on the sufferings of those separated from the men of war by class, profession, values, and outlook—in short, on the sufferings of "civilians." Perhaps the most important factor, though, was that neither side was willing to compromise its war aims easily, and so peace could only come with utter defeat—which, however, each side was strong enough to avoid. The preferred target of the English was the enemy army, but even when they hit it they found that battlefield victory alone did not give them their desired political results. When the French army refused to fight them, the English took their war directly to the people. The *chevauchées*, the towns sacked and burned, even the release of the *routiers* on the country: all these were intended to convince the French people and government that whatever the English wanted it was best to give them. The sufferings of defeat would be prolonged until they did so or until they learned to conquer in the field. Unfortunately for France, that took over a century. And, meanwhile, "if sometimes the simple and innocent suffer harm and lose their goods, there is nothing that can be done about that."[151]

Notes

1. The first and third quotations are from Jean Froissart, *Oeuvres*, ed. Kervyn de Lettenhove, 25 vols. (Brussels, 1870 etc.; Osnabrück, 1967 [reprint]), 2:342, 4:384, cf. 4:24; and Jean le Bel, *Chronique de Jean le Bel*, ed. J. Viard and E. Déprez, 2 vols. (Paris, 1904), 2:76. The second quotation is from Jean de Venette, *The Chronicle of Jean de Venette*, trans. J. Birdsall, ed. R. A. Newhall (New York, 1953), 66.

2. Jean Juvenal des Ursins, in *Écrites politiques de Jean Juvenal des Ursins*, ed. P. S. Lewis, 3 vols. (Paris, 1978), 1:149.

3. Thomas Basin, *Histoire de Charles VII*, ed. and trans. Charles Samaran, 2 vols. (Paris, 1933) 1:86. Petrarch: quoted in R. Boutruche, "The Devastation of Rural Areas during the Hundred Years' War and the Agricultural Recovery of France," in *The Recovery of France in the Fifteenth Century*, ed. P. S. Lewis (New York, 1972), 26. Cf. also Venette, *Chronicle of Jean de Venette*, 93.

4. Juvenal des Ursins, quoted in P. S. Lewis, "The Centre, the Periphery, and the Problem of Power Distribution in Later Medieval France," in *Essays in Later Medieval French History*, ed. P. S. Lewis (London, 1985), 166, referring specifically to his own diocese.

5. A. R. Bridbury, "Before the Black Death," *Economic History Review*, 2d ser., 30 (1977): 400. Cf. Harry A. Miskimin, *The Economy of Early Renaissance Europe, 1300–1460* (Englewood Cliffs NJ, 1969), 51. Bridbury continues: "Campaigns were few and brief. Armies were small, so small indeed that the biggest of them . . . did little more than provide an outing for the unemployed. Weapons were simple, so simple that the damage they were able to do was strictly confined to the neighbourhood in which they did it."

6. The quotation is from J. F. C. Fuller, *The Decisive Battles of the Western World*, ed. John Terraine (London, 1970), 29. Similarly, Philippe Contamine writes that chivalric warfare "easily changed into a sort of great tourney, half serious, half frivolous." *War in the Middle Ages* (London, 1984), 291. For Edward III's chivalric interests, see J. Vale, *Edward III and Chivalry* (Woodbridge, 1982).

7. Honoré Bonet [a.k.a. Bouvet], *L'Arbre des batailles*, ed. Ernest Nys (Brussels, 1883), 211; Jean de Bueil, *Le Jouvencel*, ed. Léon Lecestre, 2 vols. (Paris, 1887), 1:19; Mark W. Warner, "The Montagu Earls of Salisbury *circa* 1300–1428: A Study in Warfare, Politics and Political Culture" (Ph.D. diss., University College London, 1991), 172, quoting a contemporary description of the town of Sézanne several years after its sack by the English.

8. Cf. John A. Lynn, "How War Fed War: The Tax of Violence and Contributions during the *Grand Siècle*," *Journal of Modern History* 65 (1993), for an explanation of this valuable concept in an early modern context.

9. Froissart, *Oeuvres*, 25 vols., 6:235, 225. Basin, *Histoire de Charles VII*, 2 vols., 1:86, cf. 88. Cf. also Venette, *Chronicle of Jean de Venette*, 93.

10. *Rotuli parliamentorum*, ed. J. Strachey et al. (London, 1783–1832), 6 vols., 2:176; Denifle, *Désolation*, 2:77 n.

11. François de Monte-Belluna, "Le *Tragicum argumentum de miserabili statu regni Francie* de François de Monte-Belluna (1357)," ed. A. Vernet, in *Annuaire-bulletin de la Société de l'histoire de France* (1962–63), 139.

12. *Chevauchée* (literally a "ride") is a word used to describe a medieval war

expedition, especially one involving widespread destruction. For the Black Prince's letter, see Robert of Avesbury, *De gestis mirabilibus regis Edwardi tertii*, ed. E. M. Thompson (London, 1889), 434–37.

13. Denifle, *Désolation*, 2:186; for the identification of the sire d'Albret in 1357, see L. de Mas Latrie, *Trésor de chronologie* (Paris, 1889), col. 1533.

14. R. Boutruche, *La crise d'une société: seigneurs et paysans du Bordelais pendant la Guerre de Cent Ans* (Paris, 1947), 515, p.j. 22.

15. His pardon is cited in Newhall's notes to Venette, *Chronicle of Jean de Venette*, 281. See also the similar documents in Denifle, *Désolation*, 2:252; Claude Gauvard, *"De grâce espécial." Crime, état et société en France à la fin du Moyen Age* (Paris, 1991), 537, and Siméon Luce, *Histoire de Bertrand du Guesclin* (Paris, 1876), 582–83.

16. "Que à grant paine ils sèvent de quoy vivre." DD. Brouwers, "Indemnités pour dommages de guerre au pays de Namur, en 1432," *Annales de la société archéologique de Namur* (1932–33), 91.

17. Edward III's letter, in Avesbury, *De gestis mirabilibus regis Edwardi tertii*, 304–6.

18. *Chronique*, 2:80, confirmed on 2:85.

19. Wynkeley in Adam Murimuth, *Adae Murimuth. Continuatio chronicarum*, ed. E. M. Thompson (London, 1889), 215; Northburgh in Avesbury, *De gestis mirabilibus regis Edwardi tertii*, 358; see also *Chronica Johannis de Reading et anonymi Cantuariensis, 1346–1367*, ed. J. Tait (Manchester, 1914), 187. Cf. Henrici Knighton, *Chronicon*, ed. J. R. Lumby (London, 1895), 2:39.

20. Knighton, *Chronicon*, 2:10–11, 39, 66, 81, 85; Edward III in Avesbury, *De gestis mirabilibus regis Edwardi tertii*, 304–6; *Chronicon de Lanercost*, ed. J. Stevenson (Edinburgh, 1839), 318; le Bel, *Chronique*, 2:80, 85, 225; Wynkeley in Avesbury, *De gestis mirabilibus regis Edwardi tertii*, 358; Avesbury, *De gestis mirabilibus regis Edwardi tertii*, 455; Northburgh in Murimuth, *Adae Murimuth*, 215; *Récits d'un bourgeois de Valenciennes*, ed. Kervyn de Lettenhove (Louvain, 1877), 235; Froissart, *Oeuvres*, 5:379, 6:235; 8:282; letter in James Raine, *Historical Papers and Letters from the Northern Registers* (London, 1873), 386; 1339 Campaign Diary in Froissart, *Oeuvres*, 18:90; *Anonimalle*, 62 (fifteen leagues' breadth); cf. also *Anonimalle*, 45. 1339 (Cambrésis), 1346 (Crécy), 1346 (Neville's Cross), 1349 (Toulousain), 1355 (Ireland), 1355 (Scotland), 1355 (Languedoc), 1356 (Poitiers), 1356 (Normandy), 1356 (Scotland), 1359 (Reims), 1369 (Ponthieu), 1373 (Artois). Note that the meaning of these sources is often somewhat unclear due to varying usages of phrases like *in circuitu*, which some writers (e.g., Knighton) apparently use with the diameter distance, while others (e.g., Wynkeley) use it with the radius distance. One additional small piece of evidence to support a radius of devastation of

5 or more leagues is to be found in Denifle, *Désolation*, 2:90: while the Black Prince was at Narbonne in 1355, his pillagers were recorded as having reached at least to the walls of Béziers—which is about 14.3 modern miles (6 leagues) from Narbonne. Cf. Chandos Herald, *La Vie du Prince Noir*, ed. Diana B. Tyson (Tübingen, 1975), line 648.

Cf. also the 1435 strategy report of Sir John Fastolf, in *Letters and Papers Illustrative of the Wars of the English in France during the Reign of Henry the Sixth, King of England*, ed. J. Stevenson (London, 1861–64), 2 vols., 2:579, and for an example from 1461, see *Ingulf's Chronicle of the Abbey of Croyland, with the Continuations*, trans. H. T. Riley (London, 1854), 422.

21. See my *War Cruel and Sharp*, chap. 15. "*Coureurs*" (literally "runners") in this context refers to foragers, raiders, outriders, or pillagers. I have kept the original because no English word seemed quite satisfactory as a translation.

22. One league in France during most of the Middle Ages was equal to 3 Roman miles—4.411 kilometers or 2.68 modern miles. R. E. Zupko, *French Weights and Measures before the Revolution* (Bloomington IN, 1978), 95–96.

23. Jean le Bel, *Chronique*, 2:80.

24. And in 1356 the rate of advance was about the same. Alfred H. Burne, *The Crecy War* (London, 1990 [reprint of 1955 edition]), 258; H. J. Hewitt, *The Black Prince's Expedition of 1355–1357* (Manchester, 1958), 104, 107. For purposes of comparison, this is half again the speed that Turenne was able to make over three centuries later in "the most mobile of all the campaigns of Louis XIV." Martin van Creveld, *Supplying War* (Cambridge, 1977), 23.

25. See Jean le Bel, *Chronique*, 2:250; Knighton, *Chronicon*, 2:100, 111; Froissart, *Oeuvres*, 6:35, 229.

26. Juvenal des Ursins, *Histoire de Charles VI*, quoted in John Gillingham, "Richard I and the Science of War in the Middle Ages" in *War and Government in the Middle Ages*, ed. John Gillingham and J. C. Holt (Woodbridge, 1984), 85 n.

27. Many reports—e.g., Geoffrey le Baker, *Chronicon*, ed. E. M. Thompson (Oxford, 1889), 127–38; Gilles le Muisit, *Chronique et annales* (Paris, 1906), 130; letter of Wingfield in Avesbury, *De gestis mirabilibus regis Edwardi tertii*, 446–47—emphasize the destruction of mills, which represented a great capital investment. Cf. Michael Roberts, "The Military Revolution, 1560–1660," reprinted in *The Military Revolution Debate*, ed. Clifford J. Rogers (Boulder, 1995), 35 n. 86, for interesting testimony on the destructive power of fire, from the time of the Thirty Years' War.

28. Cf. J. Quicherat, "Récit des tribulations d'un religieux du diocèse de Sens pendant l'invasion Anglaise de 1358," *Bibliothèque de l'école des chartes*, 3d ser., 4 (1857); the illumination from the *Grandes Chroniques* reproduced in Richard Barber, *The Life and Campaigns of the Black Prince* (London, 1979), 48;

Denifle, *Désolation*, 2:16 (where the raiders even broke the bells of the abbey of St.-Armand), 284; and cf., for an earlier period, *Jordan Fantosme's Chronicle*, ed. and trans. R. C. Johnston (Oxford, 1981), 118.

29. E.g., see Denifle, *Désolation*, 2:13, 219–21.

30. Denifle, *Désolation*, 2:13. It is easy to see how the figures could mount so high when we consider that a raid on a single monastery could net 432 horses, 552 cattle, 800 pigs, and 8,000 sheep. Denifle, *Désolation*, 2:220. Cf. Denys Hay, "Booty in Border Warfare," *Transactions of the Dumfriesshire and Galloway Natural History and Antiquarian Society*, 3d ser., 31 (1954): 154.

31. PRO E359 (Lord Treasurer's Remembrancer, Enrolled Lay Subsidies)/ 14/13 (East Riding of Yorkshire, 1319); *Calendar of Close Rolls (1346–9)*, 448–49; J. F. Willard, "The Scotch Raids and the Fourteenth-Century Taxation of Northern England," *University of Colorado Studies* 5 (1908): 240.

32. C. T. Allmand, *Lancastrian Normandy, 1415–1450. The History of a Medieval Occupation* (Oxford, 1983), 170.

33. Robert Fossier, "Fortunes et infortunes paysannes au Cambrésis à la fin du XIIIe siècle," *Économies et sociétés au moyen âge, mélanges offerts à Édouard Perroy* (Paris, 1973), 87–103. Also discussed by Richard W. Kaeuper in his excellent *War, Justice and Public Order: England and France in the Later Middle Ages* (Oxford, 1988).

34. The higher figures virtually always resulted from the loss of livestock, though Mehaut d'Assonleville, for example, lost over 17 l.t. worth of cloth, armor, and other goods.

35. Fossier, "Fortunes et infortunes paysannes," 173.

36. Fossier, "Fortunes et infortunes paysannes," 174.

37. Venette, *Chronicle of Jean de Venette*, 66.

38. Excluding the large areas of the Cambrésis that lay outside the realm of France proper. L. Carolus-Barré, "Benoit XII et la mission charitable de Bertrand Carit dans les pays devastés du nord de la France. Cambrésis, Vermandois, Thiérache. 1340," *Mélanges d'archéologie et d'histoire* 62 (1950).

39. Carolus-Barré, "Mission charitable," 169–71.

40. Seventy-eight parishes in Laon, eleven in Reims, fifty-five in Noyon, and thirty in Cambrai (limited to areas within the realm of France). Carolus-Barré, "Mission charitable," 172.

41. The charitable disbursements were relatively constant (most often 15 or 20 sous tournois per household), and the variation was apparently more due to age, number of dependents, and social rank than to the amount of loss claimed. For example, in the parish of La Capelle-en-Thiérache, Colardus de Bray (along with his wife and seven children), claimed to have lost 200 pounds, while (two entries lower on the register) Colinus des Brochars and his sister,

orphan beggars, lost only 20 pounds, but both Colardus and Colinus received the same charitable payment of 20 sous.

42. Carolus-Barré, "Mission charitable," 189.

43. Carolus-Barré, "Mission charitable," 226. Considering the course of the campaign, it is difficult to imagine how the villagers of la Capelle could have failed to know of the English approach. Perhaps they expected the English army to be engaged by the nearby French royal host before arriving at their village.

44. Similarly, the dean of Issigeac, a small town near Bergerac, reported suffering 5,000 l.t. of damage because of a raid by Renaud de Pons and six hundred of his followers, who destroyed the town walls, the dean's mill, and fifty houses and carried off provisions and cattle, and the like. This was in 1301. Émile Labroue, Le livre de vie (Paris, 1891), 54–55.

45. This map is based on the one in Carolus-Barré, "Mission charitable." Edward III's route is drawn from information in Froissart, in Edward III's letter on the campaign, and in the contemporary "Ordonnance" in Kervyn de Lettenhove's appendices to Froissart's Oeuvres, 18:84–96.

46. Denifle, Désolation, 2:12; Froissart, Oeuvres, 3:21, 31–36. Also "Vaus" [Vaucelles?], "Pont-au-Nouvion" [Nouvion-le-Comte?], "Clari" [Clary?], and Vendeuil. Froissart also says that an English detachment burned Marle "horsmis le fortrèce," La Fère, and "tous les foursbours" of Ribemont, though Carolus-Barré describes these three as "towns not devastated." Froissart, Oeuvres, 3:21, 28, 35; Carolus-Barré, "Mission charitable," map.

47. One example of such an ecclesiastical community was the convent at Oregni. See Froissart, Oeuvres, 3:20. According to a petition of the deacon and chapter of St.-Géry, ten of the twelve hamlets from which they drew their revenues had been completely destroyed and another one was half destroyed. Denifle, Désolation, 2:10. On the other hand, Aubenton and a few of the smaller villages that received alms from the Carit mission were destroyed in a raid by the Count of Hainault in 1340, not during the 1339 campaign proper. Jean le Bel, Chronique, 1:171; Chronographia regum Francorum, ed. H. Moranvillé (Paris, 1891–97), 2:105–6; Jonathan Sumption, The Hundred Years War, vol. 1: Trial by Battle (London, 1990), 310–11. Also, some of the damage visible in the Carit report was done not by the English directly but by Frenchmen of the area. The French royal government had proclaimed that everyone should clear all valuables and supplies out of the path of the English army and take them into fortified places. Any goods left in the countryside "were abandoned to anyone who wanted to take them; because of which order, many were robbed and despoiled by their own neighbors." C. J. Rogers, "A Continuation of the Manuel

d'histoire de Philippe VI for the Years 1328–39," *English Historical Review* 114 (1999): 1265.

48. Carolus-Barré, "Mission charitable," 198–202.

49. Edward's letter in Avesbury, *De gestis mirabilibus regis Edwardi tertii*, 305. Similarly, the claim of the Lanercost chronicler that Edward laid waste an area sixty miles long and twenty-eight wide is remarkably accurate as a statement of the most widely separated points hit by his army, though the area put thoroughly to the torch was well smaller. *Chronicon de Lanercost*, 318.

50. Ordonnance in Froissart, *Oeuvres*, 18:93. It is interesting to note, however, that the *Chronicon de Parco Ludae* gives a similar figure—1,805 towns and villages, each with a parochial church—for the 1340 Tournai campaign, which was comparable in scope to the 1339 *chevauchée*. E. Déprez, *Les préliminaires de la guerre de cent ans. La papauté, la France et l'Angleterre (1328–1342)* (Paris, 1902), 332 n. 12.

51. Considering that damages reported were nearly six thousand l.t. at just one of the over two hundred villages mentioned in the Carit report (viz. La Capelle) and that that record leaves out a number of wealthy areas that were destroyed, such as la Fère, the suburbs of Marle, and the imperial Cambrésis.

52. Experience: Jean le Bel, *Chronique*, 1:159, 161; Froissart, *Oeuvres*, 3:20; cf. also le Bel on 1346 (*Chronique*, 2:77) and le Baker on 1355 (*Chronicon*, 130). Walls: Froissart, *Oeuvres*, 3:35, 21, 27. Quotation: le Bel, *Chronique*, 1:159.

53. For the last, Basin, *Histoire de Charles VII*, 86. More generally, see the excellent dissertation of R. P. R. Noël, "Town Defence in the French Midi during the Hundred Years War" (Ph.D. diss., University of Edinburgh, 1977).

54. Quoted in Brouwers, "Indemnités pour dommages," 89.

55. Brouwers, "Indemnités pour dommages," 91–92.

56. The damages ranged from the 21 crowns (18 l.t.) lost by Evrard Gane de Champlon to the 16,300 (14,083 l.t.) claimed by the provost, dean, and chapter of St. Begghe d'Andenne. Eleven abbeys, six chapters of canons, three priories, a convent, and three hospitals reported substantial damage, as did twelve parochial curés. The towns of Namur, Bouvingnes, and Wallecourt claimed 12,000 clinquars (13,680 florins), 6,000 crowns (8,640 florins), and 13,532 crowns (19,486 florins), respectively, which may represent an agglomeration of the losses of the petty bourgeois since the richer citizens of the towns made individual statements. For example, Colart de Wanherive, bourgeois de Namur, requested 450 clinquars (513 florins). Brouwers, "Indemnités pour dommages," 98–99. Most of the remaining claims came from local nobles, merchants, comital officials, and other individuals.

57. For example, Jean Hollignoulle claimed 1,200 crowns (1,368 florins) and

received 80 florins, while Jehan le Preudomme du Sart claimed only 250 crowns (360 florins) but received 100 florins.

58. Note that this matches well with the chronicler's claim of three hundred villages destroyed and the cost of the "destruction" of Cagnoncles—fifteen hundred livres. For currency conversion rates, see Brouwers, "Indemnités pour dommages," 94, 94 n. 1. The calculation of work years assumes 260 days of annual employment.

59. This is a rough guess, based on an overall assessment of the figures cited in Claude Gaier, "Analysis of the Military Forces in the Principality of Liège and the County of Looz from the Twelfth to the Fifteenth Century," *Studies in Medieval and Renaissance History* 2 (1965).

60. The city of London, for example, was given a higher tax assessment for the Fifteenths of 1332 and 1334 than were the entire counties (excluding the boroughs) of Middlesex and Lancaster, combined. PRO E359 (Lord Treasurer's Remembrancer, Enrolled Lay Subsidies)/14/18–20.

61. For example, see Froissart, *Oeuvres*, 5:114; A. Tuetey, *Les Écorcheurs sous Charles VII* (Montbéliard, 1874), 1:3.

62. The English also burned, according to the chronicles, St-Vaast-la-Hougue, Torigny, Cormolain, Gisors, Vernon, Poissy, St.-Germain-en-Laye, Rays, St. Cloud, the new royal palace of Montjoye, "the most pleasant of all the manors of the king of France," Fontaine-sur-Somme, Long-en-Ponthieu, Longpré-les-Corps-Saints, Oudeuil, Mareuil-Caubert, Saint-Josse, St.-Riquier, Beaurain, Étaples, Fauquembergues, Neufchâtel-Hardelot, the suburbs of Boulogne, and Wissant. They also plundered Oisemont and Montebourg and did much damage to Airaines, though it was not burned because it surrendered. Jean le Bel, *Chronique*; *Acta bellicosa*, in J. Moisant, *Le Prince Noir en Aquitaine* (Paris, 1894); G. Villani, *Cronica*; *Eulogium historiarum*, 206–12 passim; Gilles le Muisit, 2:263; Knighton, *Chronicon*, 2:39; *Récits d'un bourgeois de Valenciennes*, 235; Venette, *Chronicle of Jean de Venette*, 41; Holinshed, *Chronicle*, ed. J. Johnston (London, 1807), 635; Avesbury, *De gestis mirabilibus regis Edwardi tertii*, 358–59; quotation from *Chronica monasterii de Melsa*, ed. E. A. Bond (London, 1866–68), 3:57. The number of smaller towns, hamlets, and villages burned must have reached several hundred, if not into the thousands. Le Bel, whose chronicle specifically mentions nearly all of the towns just named, explained: "I am only naming to you the large towns, rich beyond measure, because I wouldn't know how to name the mid-sized ones, nor the common little villages, which were infinite," *Chronique*, 2:84–85. This list does not include the places damaged by Edward III's Flemish allies in the same campaign or those destroyed by the duke of Lancaster in the south. For more details on the Crécy campaign, see Rogers, *War Cruel and Sharp*, chaps. 10–11.

63. *Chronique*, 2:78. At Lisieux, "they found as much treasure or more." *Chronique*, 2:84. Froissart, *Oeuvres*, 4:408, adds that Caen was three times as large as St.-Lô.

64. Geoffrey le Baker, *Chronicon*, 133. In 1419, Rouen paid even more, three hundred thousand *écus*, to avoid destruction after being captured by Henry V. Allmand, *Lancastrian Normandy*, 13.

65. *Registres du trésor des chartes*, ed. Aline Vallée (Paris, 1984), vol. 3, no. 6660.

66. Denifle, *Désolation*, 2:235, cf. p. 262: The area around St.-Flour in Auvergne reportedly suffered over four hundred thousand florins' worth of damage between 1353 and 1363. The faubourgs of the town were pillaged and burned in 1360 and again in 1363; of the 206 taxable households listed there in 1344 only 6 remained in 1364.

67. As noted earlier, only one of the inhabitants of Cagnoncles was harmed, and the only casualties at La Capelle were two men killed, out of a population of around 450 people in each village.

68. Jean le Bel, *Chronique*, 2:82–3.

69. Letter of Northburgh in Avesbury, *De gestis mirabilibus regis Edwardi tertii*, 359.

70. The letter of Bartholomew Burghersh says five thousand killed or captured (Murimuth, *Adae Murimuth*, 203); the *Acta bellicosa*, 166, reports "over 2,500 corpses of the slain," aside from those killed in the pursuit in the fields. Giovanni Villani, *Cronica* in *Cronisti del Trecento*, ed. Roberto Palmarocchi (Milan, 1935), 390, sets the number of killed at five thousand; cf. *Eulogium historiarum*, 207.

71. According to a petition written several years later, given in Warner, "Montagu Earls," 172. Cf. the sack of Poitiers in 1346, described in Froissart, *Oeuvres*, 5:114; also Tuetey, *Les Écorcheurs*, 1:54

72. Juvenal des Ursins, *Écrites politiques*, 1:302.

73. Juvenal des Ursins, *Écrites politiques*, 1:308.

74. Juvenal des Ursins, *Écrites politiques*, 1:56–57, cf. 309–10. See also the complaint of the duke of Burgundy in Tuetey, *Les Écorcheurs*, 1:40, and Juvenal des Ursins, *Écrites politiques*, 1:22–3, 48.

75. The armies tended to acquire more booty than could be carried anyway. See le Bel, *Chronique*, 2:221–22, and Froissart, *Oeuvres*, 4:503–4.

76. The full account is published in J. Quicherat, "Récit des tribulations d'un religieux du diocèse de Sens pendant l'invasion Anglaise de 1358," *Bibliothèque de l'école des chartes*, 3d ser., 4 (1857); this translation is from Newhall's notes to Venette, *Chronicle of Jean de Venette*, 253, with some modifications.

77. For example, see Denifle, *Désolation*, 2:284, 213; Siméon Luce, ed., *Chronique des quatre premiers Valois (1327–1393)* (Paris, 1862), 71; Venette, *Chronicle of Jean de Venette*, 76–77; Juvenal des Ursins, *Écrites politiques*, 1:309–10; Jean Cabaret, *La Chronique du bon duc Loys de Bourbon*, ed. A. M. Chazaud (Paris, 1876), 19; Denifle, *Désolation*, 2:180–82; J. Lartigaut, "Témoignages sur la dépopulation du Quercy au XIVe siècle," *Annales du Midi*, n.s. 84 (1972): 10; Keen, *Laws of War*, 243; Fowler, *The Age of Plantagenet and Valois*, 169.

78. Published in A. Germain, "Projet de descente en Angleterre . . . ," *Publications de la Société archéologique de Montpellier* 26 (1858): 426.

79. Lartigaut, "Témoignages," 9; cf. Denifle, *Désolation*, 2:271 ff.

80. *Scalacronica*, 178. Cf. Jean le Bel, *Chronique*, 2:249 ff.; for Poitou, R. Mémain, "Les misères de la guerre en Bas-Poitou aux XIVe et XVe siècles" *Bull. de la Soc. des Antiquaires de l'Ouest*, 3d. ser., 12 (1941): 668. Understatement: cf. *Chronique Normande*, 146 n. 3, 145.

81. Quercy map based on Lartigaut, "Témoignages," 11; Montfort-Dourdan map based on information in Luce, *Histoire de Bertrand du Guesclin*, 501–4. 7.5 km/hr: calculated from le Bel, *Chronique*, 2:85.

82. Froissart, *Oeuvres*, 5:348 (quotation); Denifle, *Désolation*, 2:254, 240–42, 276, 255, 287.

83. Luce, *Histoire de Bertrand du Guesclin*, 1:459–509.

84. Denifle, *Désolation*, 2:291. Similarly, in the department of the Aube, Beaufort was held from 1356 to 1364, and Bouy, Trainel, and Veaurenier were held between 1359 and 1365.

85. *Scalacronica*, 187.

86. Venette, *Chronicle of Jean de Venette*, 84 (re: 1358), cf. 66 (re: 1356), 123, 85–86. A related chronicle, the *Chronique Normande*, has on p. 146: "And the merchants could not go securely through the countryside nor transport their merchandise without safe conducts or having paid for a 'truce,' except at the risk of their lives and their goods." One of the reasons given by King John for his submission to the treaty of Brétigny was that the war had destroyed commerce; at least, that seems to be the meaning of his phrase "en est . . . marchandise perie." A. Bardonnet "Procès-verbal de l'délivrance . . . des places françaises abandonnées par le traité de Brétigny," *Mémoires de la Soc. de Statistique, Sciences et Arts du Département des Deux-Sèvres*, 2d. ser, 6 (1866): 137.

For examples of the impact this problem had on individuals' lives, see Noël, "Town Defence in the French Midi during the Hundred Years War," 12, and *Lo Libre de vita* in Labroue, *Le Livre de vie*, 404–24. The latter is essentially a diary of all the acts of brigandage suffered by the inhabitants of Bergerac at the hands of neighboring garrisons (*routiers* and free companions of various sorts) between February 1379 and June 1382. Well over one hundred incidents are noted, mostly robberies and kidnappings.

87. Venette, *Chronicle of Jean de Venette*, 97, 99, 75–76, 83.

88. The seriousness of the burden of watch and ward should not be underestimated. In 1347, for example, the town of la Rochelle had to be given special concessions to prevent its depopulation, caused in part by the flight of many inhabitants seeking to escape "les grans gais et veilles toutes les nuyz" on the ramparts. *Trésor des chartes*, vol. 3, no. 6640. In Millau in the early fifteenth century, the system of watches apparently required each householder to stand guard for one night in every eight. Noël, "Town Defence," 112; cf. 126, 130.

Noël, "Town Defence," provides many examples of the financial burdens borne by French municipalities because of the war. See also Sumption, *Trial by Battle*, 367.

Regarding the suburban monasteries, castles, and residential areas, see *Chronique Normande*, variant, 146 n. 3: "And those who stayed in the cities, burgs, and towns also suffered much persecution in this time. All their suburbs were burned and destroyed by them or by their enemies in all the lands [between the Rhône and the Somme], and they [suffered] much to rebuild their walls and ditches . . . and to pay heavy taxes."

89. Venette, *Chronicle of Jean de Venette*, 98. The same was done at other times at Toulouse (Denifle, *Désolation*, 2:66), a city nearly as large as Paris, where over three thousand houses were reportedly destroyed (Froissart, *Oeuvres*, 5:344), and at Rouen (*The Brut or the Chronicle of England*, ed. F. W. Brie [Early English Text Society, original series], vols. 131, 136 [1906–8], 2:394–95). According to le Bel, even the bourgeois of Montpellier did so in 1355 (*Chronique*, 2:222). For other examples of places destroyed by townspeople for reasons of defense, see Brouwers, "Indemnités pour dommages," 101; le Bel, *Chronique*, 2: appendix 8; *Trésor des chartes*, vol. 3, no. 6226; Denifle, *Désolation*, 2:7, 64–65, 78, 81, 145, 221, 223, 227, 237, 241, 286, 289, 290, 291, 295, 297; Avesbury, *De gestis mirabilibus regis Edwardi tertii*, 210; and Venette, *Chronicle of Jean de Venette*, 84, 83, 86, 95.

90. Noël, "Town Defence," 19, 27–30.

91. Venette, *Chronicle of Jean de Venette*, 93, cf. 66: "The nobles despised and hated all others and took no thought for the mutual usefulness and profit of lord and men. They subjected and despoiled the peasants and the men of the villages. In no wise did they defend their country from its enemies. Rather did they trample it underfoot, robbing and pillaging the peasants' goods," and *Chronique Normande*, 146 n. 3: "And even the regent levied many wondrous taxes on the realm, and some lords took [the people's] wheat, oats, cattle, and

other food and gave them to the garrisons of their castles, and some allowed their men to be molested and their lands to be devastated."

92. For one good example of the costs this practice could impose, see Luce, *Histoire de Bertrand du Guesclin*, 584–90 (p.j. 51).

93. Boutruche, *Crise*, 515 (p.j. 22).

94. For example, see Denifle, *Désolation*, 2:213; *Chronique des quatre premiers Valois*, 71; Venette, *Chronicle of Jean de Venette*, 76–77.

95. Taken from a contemporary letter of Étienne Marcel, provost of merchants of Paris, who adds that they tortured clergy, profaned holy services, raped women in front of their husbands, burned or ransomed churches, and in brief acted with greater inhumanity and cruelty than any Saracen. As a result of the nobles' counterattack, wrote Marcel in another letter, "it is very doubtful whether this country, which used to be very fertile for wheat and wine, won't be entirely wasted and dead this year, or that there will be anyone to take care of the vines and pick the grapes, or anywhere to put the wine, since the casks in the villages are all burned, as are the villages themselves." Quoted in Froissart, *Oeuvres*, 6:468, 469.

96. Venette, *Chronicle of Jean de Venette*, 78. Venette, *Chronicle of Jean de Venette*, 76–77, and the *Chronique Normande*, 146 n. 3, suggest a close connection between the Jacquerie and the nobles' failure to defend the peasants from the *routiers*.

97. William of Worcester considered the depredations caused by English garrison troops to be one of the main reasons why the Normans "turned their hertis frome us." Quoted in Allmand, *Society at War*, 96; Walter Bentley expressed the same idea concerning the English presence in Brittany in the 1350s in the report printed in Froissart, *Oeuvres*, 18:339. Cf. Venette, *Chronicle of Jean de Venette*, 105, 113, for the parable of the sheepdog and the wolf, and Keen, *Laws of War*, 191, for the excesses of French troops in 1439: "femme violee, gens crucifiez, rotiz et pendus, homme roty."

On the peasants so frightened that they exposed themselves to death by famine, see Denifle, *Désolation*, 2:244, cf. 252 and Noël, "Town Defence," 151. For the fifteenth century, cf. Juvenal des Ursins, *Écrites politiques*, 1:308–9, 56–57.

98. W. M. Ormrod, "The Personal Religion of Edward III," *Speculum* 64 (1989); Jean le Bel, *Chroniques*, 1:118–19.

99. Bonet, *Tree of Battles*, 125. See also St. Augustine, quoted in Allmand, *Society at War*, 17.

100. Bonet, *Arbre des batailles*, 141 ("ayde et faveur"). John of Legnano similarly argues that a just war may be prosecuted against the residents of a hostile state "when the residents bear the burdens of the state," even in the case of "private persons, who are absolutely innocent, because of an offense of their

lord." Johannis de Lignano, *De Bello, de represalis, et de duello*, ed. and trans. T. E. Holland (Oxford, 1917), 316, 321; cf. Russell, *Just War*, 19, 275 (Vincent of Beauvais).

101. Bonet, *Arbre des batailles*, 141–42. Of course, they would have to support their ruler's wars, willingly or unwillingly, if they did not want to be punished as rebels.

102. Such a war was considered essentially a judicial duel writ large, an appeal to the court of God, who alone could judge between monarchs who shared no earthly lord. De Lignano, *De Bello, de represalis*, 308; Bonet, *Arbre des batailles*, 90–91; Edward III in Avesbury, *De gestis mirabilibus regis Edwardi tertii*, 379–80; cf. Rymer, *Foedera*, II:2:1127, 1131. See also Fastolf's similar view in Stevenson, *Letters and Papers*, 2:576; Henry V's cited in Christopher Allmand, *Henry V* (Berkeley, 1992), 110; Bonet's in *Arbre des batailles*, 83; and the Black Prince's in Chandos Herald, *La Vie du Prince Noir*, lines 848–52. In feudal or "*couverte*" war, by contrast, devastation was not permitted, though it was still often practiced. Keen, *Laws of War*, 104, 67 ff.

103. For example, Stevenson, *Letters and Papers*, 2:581; Edward III in Avesbury, *De gestis mirabilibus regis Edwardi tertii*, 379–81; Philip VI in Rymer, *Foedera*, II:2:1131.

104. *Memoriale presbiterorum*, written in 1344, observes that "many modern confessors . . . if some part of the plunder or something else is given to them, absolve *de facto* the plunderer." Quoted in W. A. Pantin, *The English Church in the Fourteenth Century* (Cambridge, 1955), 209, 274. Extortion: Seguin de Badefol, the "king of the Companies," for example, demanded that he receive papal absolution (as well as thirty thousand livres) before he would abandon the fortress of Anse. Labroue, *Le Livre de vie*, 80. Cf. Denifle, *Désolation*, 2:186, 284 and (on a grander scale) le Bel, *Chronique*, 2:324.

105. Keen, *Laws of War*, 19.

106. Efforts: Bonet, *Arbre des batailles*, 208–11; Keen, *Laws of War*, 189–90; Russell, *Just War*, 70. There is some reflection of this in the ordinances of war of Richard II and Henry V: *Black Book of the Admiralty*, 1:453 clause 3; 460 clause 3; 467 clauses 26, 28; 469 clause 33. In the case of laymen, however, as clauses 26 and 33 show, the point was merely to protect "civilians" who were *within the king's obedience*, not those loyal to the enemy.

107. Paris of Pozzo, quoted in Keen, *Laws of War*, 243. The torture of peasants to extract money was in fact common in the Hundred Years' War. See p. 55 earlier in this chapter, and Nicholas Wright, "Ransoms of Non-combatants during the Hundred Years War," *Journal of Medieval History* 17 (1991): 326–27, for examples; cf. Guillaume Trignant, "Commentaire du 'Jouvencel,'" in Jean de Beuil, *Le Jouvencel*, ed. Léon Lecestre (Paris, 1889), 269.

108. Peasant women: Wright, "Ransoms," 326–29. Noblewomen: Jean le Bel, *Chronique*, 2:83, 90–91.

109. Jean le Bel, *Chronique*, 2:234, 250–51, 273, 276, 285, 301; Froissart, *Oeuvres*, 6:112–13; Denifle, *Désolation*, 2:186, 228 ff.

110. From his letter to Clement VI in Avesbury, *De gestis mirabilibus regis Edwardi tertii*, 379–80.

111. Bonet, *Arbre des batailles*, 211, 141; Froissart, *Oeuvres*, 4:407, 5:114, 8:41.

112. Edward's letter in Rymer, *Foedera*, II:2:1131; cf. Avesbury, *De gestis mirabilibus regis Edwardi tertii*, 379–81, and *Calendar of Patent Rolls, 1345–8*, 516–17.

113. Hewitt, *Organization of War*, 93, 96.

114. Quoted Allmand, *Society at War*, 96.

115. C. T. Allmand, "The War and the Non-Combatant," in *The Hundred Years War*, ed. Kenneth Fowler (London, 1971), 167, 169–70, 177, 180. A. E. Prince, "The Army and Navy," in *The English Government at Work, 1327–1336* (New York, 1940), 365.

116. Oman, *History of the Art of War in the Middle Ages*, 1:160 (first quotation); J. M. Tourneur-Aumont, *La Bataille de Poitiers*, 404 (second quotation).

117. Notably H. J. Hewitt's *The Organization of War under Edward III, 1338–62*, and C. T. Allmand, *The Hundred Years War* (Cambridge, 1988).

118. Clifford J. Rogers, "Edward III and the Dialectics of Strategy, 1327–1360," *Transactions of the Royal Historical Society*, 6th ser., 4 (1994). The following two paragraphs are based on that essay.

119. Froissart, *Oeuvres*, 12:109.

120. Hewitt, in *Organization of War*, chap. 5, was the first to emphasize this aspect of the *chevauchée*, though Ferdinand Lot had made a passing observation on the subject earlier in *L'art militaire et les armées au moyen âge* (Paris, 1946), 352–53.

121. The idea of economic attrition as a component of military strategy was common in the late middle ages. E.g., see J. F. Verbruggen, *The Art of Warfare in Western Europe during the Middle Ages. From the Eighth Century to 1340* (Amsterdam, 1977), chap. 5, and M. Jusselin, "Comment la France se préparait à la Guerre de Cent Ans," *Bibliothèque de l'école des chartes* 73 (1912), doc. 6.

122. Avesbury, *De gestis mirabilibus regis Edwardi tertii*, 442. Cf. Rogers, "Edward III and the Dialectics of Strategy," 101. Cf. also Avesbury, *De gestis mirabilibus regis Edwardi tertii*, 457–58, for the secondary effects of the devastation on the French fisc.

123. Quotation from Philip Warner, *Sieges of the Middle Ages* (London, 1968), 172.

124. *Scalacronica*, 178; le Bel, *Chronique*, 2:249–50.

125. *Anonimalle*, 43.

126. This was important both because it could offer them justification for making war (without violating their chivalric or Christian duties) and also because it gave them protection under the laws of war. See Keen, *Laws of War*.

127. According to Knighton, *Chronicon*, 2:103. An ordinance of 1352 for Brittany allowed *routiers* who captured a stronghold from the French to keep the wealth contained therein for their own profit. However, it also required that they should then immediately turn the place over to a captain and garrison who would be assigned and paid to guard it and govern the locals (or at least the ones willing to enter into the king's obedience) in tranquillity. Froissart, *Oeuvres*, 18:340, 341. See also *Anonimalle*, 43.

128. Of the thirty-eight strong places known to have been held in 1360 by "Anglo-Navarrese" companies in the departments of Aisne, Allier, Ardennes, and Aube, for example, only eight are known to have been still so held in 1361. Precisely which of the thirty others were surrendered because of the Treaty of Brétigny cannot be determined, however. Luce, *Jeunesse de Bertrand*, 460–65. The *Récits d'un bourgeois de Valenciennes*, 312, mentions some exceptions but concludes that after 1360 "all the English and many of those of other nations departed from the realm of France by the command of the king of England."

129. For an excellent treatment of the subject of these payments (*appatis, truages, patises*, etc.), see Fowler, *Age of Plantagenet and Valois*, 165 ff. See also Labroue, *Le Livre de vie*, 27–31, 410–11, 413.

130. Philippe Contamine, "Les Compagnies d'Aventure en France pendant la Guerre de Cent Ans," *Mélanges de l'École Française de Rome* 87 (1975): 371–73, though Contamine himself finds this distinction "trop formelle."

131. The quotation is from Venette, *Chronicle of Jean de Venette*, 106; cf. 105.

132. Jean le Bel, *Chronique*, 322–23.

133. They did, perhaps, serve Edward III's strategic interests by increasing the pressure for peace felt by the French monarchy, but that was only a side-effect of their pursuit of their own ends.

134. Allmand, *Lancastrian Normandy*, 188.

135. Philippe Contamine, "Rançons et butins dans la Normandie anglaise (1424–1444)," in *La France aux XIVe et XVe siècles. Hommes, mentalités, guerre et paix* (London, 1981); Wright, "Ransoms."

136. Wright, "Ransoms," 327, 331 n. 17.

137. Froissart, *Chronicles*, 2:272, 3:158.

138. Jean de Bueil, *Le Jouvencel*, 1:19.

139. Margaret Wade Labarge, *Gascony: England's First Colony, 1204–1453* (London, 1980), 206.

140. These *appatis* were recognized by some contemporaries as a form of taxation. See the definition quoted by Philippe Contamine, "Rançons et butins

dans la Normandie anglaise (1424–1444)," 250. Cf. Keen, *Laws of War*, 138.

141. See Keen, *Laws of War*, 82–83, Alain Chartier, *Quadrilogue invectif*, ed. E. Droz (Paris, 1923); Basin, *Histoire de Charles VII*, 104–6. Cf. Labroue, *Le Livre de vie*, 418 (Johan de la Sala).

142. Fowler, "Truces," 204–5; Fowler, *Age of Plantagenet and Valois*, 166, for discussion. For substantial records of the operation of the system in Brittany, see PRO E101 (Accounts Various)/174/10–14.

143. Labroue, *Livre de vie*, 13, 29; Juvenal des Ursins, *Écrits politiques*, 1:57 (multiple payoffs). Juvenal des Ursins, *Écrits politiques*, 1:311 for depopulation: "the poor people, unable to pay [mutiple *patises*], have departed, so that the land is left entirely uninhabited, and of a hundred people only one remains."

144. Rogers, "Military Revolutions of the Hundred Years War," 66–73. As Clausewitz writes in *On War*: "If we want our adversary to comply with our will, we must place him in a situation which is more disadvantageous to him than the sacrifice which we demand from him." Carl von Clausewitz, *Vom Kriege* (Reinbek bei Hamburg, 1963), 14.

145. Edward Halle, *The Union of the Two Noble Families of Lancaster and York* (Menston UK, 1970 [facsimile of 1550 ed.]), Henry V, xxv.

146. For example, see Froissart, *Chronicles*, 1:256–69, 2:111 ff., 272 ff.; 3:142 ff.

147. Halle, *Union of the Two Noble Houses*, Henry V, xxxii dorso, cf. xlvii and *Brut*, 2:491.

148. For the full French text of the letter, see Warner, "Montagu Earls," appendix 2.

149. Emphasis added. See Keen, *Laws of War*, 98, bearing in mind the difference between *bellum hostile* and mere "just war," and see also Froissart, *Oeuvres*, 6:229, and *Chronique des règnes de Jean II et de Charles V*, ed. R. Delachenal (Paris, 1916), 2:146. There were dissenting opinions on this point, however: e.g., see Bonet, *Arbre des batailles*, 211.

150. Denifle, *Désolation*, 2:1; cf. Jean II's own description of the impact of the war, in "Procès-verbal de l'délivrance à Jean Chandos," 136.

151. Bonet, *Abre des batailles*, 142 (aultre chose ne s'en peut faire); cf. 125 and Chartier, *Quadrilogue invectif*, 24.

A Brutal Necessity?

The Devastation of the Palatinate, 1688–1689

John A. Lynn

Oh Mannheim! Oh Friedrichsburg! Vengeance! Vengeance! Vengeance! Speyer in cinders, Worms reduced to a heap of ruins, know only how to cry: Vengeance! Vengeance! Where are you ancient Nemesis, where are you god of vengeance! Alas, cities which flourished many years before Jesus Christ and now lie entirely ravaged, behold yourselves! Cry for your descendants! Cry for your children! Mix your tears with the Rhine that passes at your feet! Unite your voices together and cry: Vengeance! Vengeance! . . . It only remains for us to serve for all eternity as witnesses of French brutality and to cry, to all Europe, where we have been driven into exile: Vengeance! Vengeance!

From *Concusus creditorum*, 1689

This cry arose as a result of the cruel and systematic destruction known as the devastation of the Palatinate by troops in the service of Louis XIV of France from the fall of 1688 into the summer of 1689. Actually, it was not just the Palatinate that suffered, for the fire and fury of this destruction swept over Baden and Württemberg as well, although the worst struck along the Rhine from Worms to Speyer. At the time, it incited the disgust even of those who had endured the excesses of the Thirty Years' War a generation before, and for centuries thereafter the devastation of the Palatinate epitomized the horror that war visited upon civilians caught in its path. The fact that it so startled European sensibility demonstrates that the devastation of the Palatinate represented an extreme in the savage conduct of war, well beyond what was regarded as usual even in a harsh age.

Rather than memorialize the sad events of 1688–1689, this inquiry will concentrate on the political and military context so as to under-

stand the rationales behind such calculated destruction. That desolation was not simply the work of soldiers on the rampage, although
undisciplined excesses punctuated the tale of horror. The devastation
of the Palatinate was the conscious policy of French military figures at
the highest levels, men such as the marquis de Chamlay and Gilbert
Colbert, sieur de Saint Pouenges, advisors to and agents of the war
minister, the marquis de Louvois; that war minister himself; and the
supreme master of France, Louis XIV.[1]

The story of the devastation is one of aggression, miscalculation,
and excess. War between France and her German neighbors technically began with the proclamation of Louis's manifesto, his *Mémoire
des raisons*, on 24 September 1688. However, his enemies could not
even have heard of this declaration of grievances before French troops
invaded the Rhineland the next day. Louvois directed this attack in the
expectation that the war would last only three or four months, and the
whole purpose of the invasion was preemptive or "preventative."[2] It
made no sense to advertise its approach, so he successfully disguised
the preparations. The first target was Philippsburg, the last of the great
fortresses that guarded Rhine crossings east of Alsace. The French already held Huningue, Breisach, Freiburg, Strasbourg, and Fort Louis,
so the taking of Philippsburg would effectively seal the Rhine. For
public purposes, the Dauphin commanded the army that besieged the
fortress in October, while Marshal Duras held effective military command, and Vauban directed the siege.

After the surrender of Philippsburg on 30 October, the main French
army invested Mannheim, which did not hold out for long; the town
fell on 10 November and the citadel two days later. There, French success resulted not only from Vauban's skill but also from the fact that
the German garrison had not been paid for seventeen months.[3] With
Mannheim gone, the French crossed the river to besiege Frankenthal on 15 November, which capitulated in four days. In addition to
these fortresses, other towns surrendered without resistance, including Neustadt, Oppenheim, Worms, Bingen, Alzey, Kreuznach, Bach-
arach, Kaiserlautern, Heidelberg, Pforzheim, Heilbronn, and Speyer;
above all, the key fortress of Mainz accepted a French garrison. Louis
would also have liked to take Koblenz, but its lord, the Elector of Trier,
stubbornly refused to surrender it. In response, Louis ordered that
Boufflers bombard the city in order to burn its interior without the

necessity of conquering its walls. With terrible success, the bombard-ment gutted the city in November.[4] The burning of Koblenz foreshad-owed the destruction to come, but at the time it was only an isolated act of intimidation, not yet part of a consistent and thorough policy. It is not the initial conquest of Rhineland territory that threw a shadow across the radiance of the Sun King but the destruction of towns and villages that began in December and continued into the summer of the next year (see map 3.1).

Louis XIV had now mastered the Rhine south of Mainz to the Swiss border and had good reason to believe that the campaign was over. A measure of this is the fact that in mid-November Vauban received permission to take an extended leave to his estates. Louis demanded that the German princes knuckle under to the French ultimatum by 1 January 1689, but it was soon clear that they would not.[5] Instead of agreeing to surrender, the Imperial Diet declared war on 24 January. But, even before this, major German princes, including the electors of Brandenburg and Hannover, met in late October at Magdeburg to fashion an alliance against Louis XIV. Soon Louis faced the forces of Brandenburg, Hannover, Hesse-Cassel, Saxony, and Bavaria, in addi-tion to those of the Habsburg emperor, Leopold I, and on 26 Novem-ber the Dutch entered the war as well. Already in December, German cavalry opposed the French in the field. In addition, "Schnapphahns," a term normally meaning "highwaymen" but in this case partisans, emerged from the local peasantry to snipe at the French.

If the Germans princes were not willing to capitulate, then Louis re-solved to punish them for resistance and, perhaps, to intimidate them into submission.[6] However, most certainly he meant to make it as hard as possible for them to attack France by, as it were, clearing a firebreak to the north and east of the French fortress line that ran from Breisach to Strasbourg to Philippsburg to Landau.

The first discussions of destroying individual towns were connected with the nasty business of collecting contributions, or war taxes, from the Germans or with the attempt to deny the enemy the protection of town walls. In a notable letter of 27 October, Chamlay suggested to Louvois that the French demolish the fortifications of a list of towns situated between the Rhine—in its course from Philippsburg to Kob-lenz—and the French main fortress line from Landau to Saarlouis to Montroyal.[7] This was not, however, a matter of destroying everything

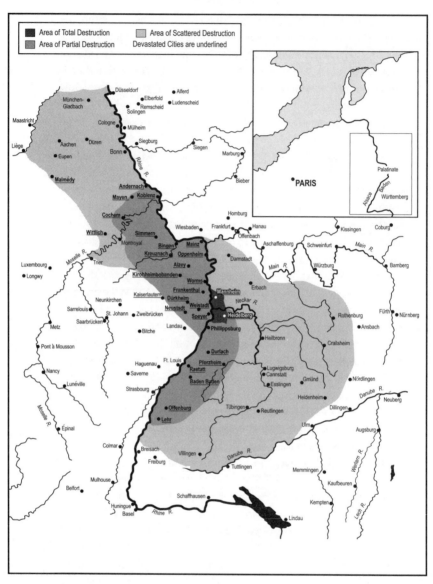

Legend:
- Area of Total Destruction
- Area of Partial Destruction
- Area of Scattered Destruction
- Devastated Cities are underlined

Map 3.1. Area of Destruction, 1688–1689

within entire towns but only of tearing down their defenses. In fact, as Chamlay stipulated, French troops could be put in the towns for winter quarters while or after the walls were rendered useless. Meanwhile, Louvois ordered General Montclair to drive east to the Neckar and "pillage and raze" Stuttgart, Esslingen, and Tübingen and to occupy Heilbronn, while tearing down its walls.[8] (The term *raze* is confusing here because in the first phase of destruction it meant only the demolition of fortifications.) At the same time, everything was to be done to extract the most money out of the frightened townspeople of Württemberg.

However, in the 27 October letter, Chamlay suggested more odious actions: "I would dare to propose to you something that perhaps will not be to your taste, that is the day after we take Mannheim, I would put the city to the sword and plow it under."[9] On 15 November, the news of Mannheim's surrender reached Versailles, and two days later Louvois echoed Chamlay's severe proposal in an order to the military intendant La Grange: "I see the king is rather disposed to entirely raze the city and citadel of Mannheim, and, in this case, to utterly destroy the houses, in such a manner that no stone stands on another."[10] Here the intention was not simply to squeeze what one could out of a conquered people. And here also, as is the case time and again, the documents put Chamlay in league with Louvois and, of course, their king to form a triumvirate that sealed the fate of the Palatinate.

As Louis and his servants realized that this would not be a brief and decisive parade of French glory, but rather a bitterly contested and probably long war, their methods turned savage. While French troops recoiled from the advancing Germans, Louvois wrote Montclair on 18 December: "His Majesty recommends to you to completely ruin [*faire bien ruiner*] all the places that you leave along the lower and upper Neckar so that the enemy, finding no forage or food whatever, will not try to approach there."[11] He was to fall back on Pforzheim, Heidelberg, and Mannheim.

Already by 20 December, Louvois had marked upon a fateful map all the cities, towns, villages, and châteaux intended for destruction. It is worth noting that the king agreed to the list of the doomed, only sparing certain religious buildings.[12] Thus, the devastation of the Palatinate, Baden, and parts of Württemberg resulted from decisions made in December. During late December and on into January, a string of letters demanded a faster pace of destruction. On Christmas Eve, Louvois wrote to castigate the military intendant La Grange: "I am surprised to learn . . . that you have not started the demolition on the pretense that there are 200 people [in Offenburg] . . . I beg you to know that I do not want to hear of such things and that I want to know that the demolitions are going on. . . . I am surprised not to have letters from M. de Montclair telling me that he has abandoned Heilbronn, Tübingen, Esslingen, and other places . . . after having put them in the condition that I ordered."[13]

The frenzy of destruction peaked from March through the first days of June. Under the direction of Tessé, a subordinate of Montclair, retreating French troops forced out the inhabitants and torched Heidelberg on 2 March.[14] On that day, Montclair reported that the destruction was complete. However, Louvois soon learned from another source that while the castle had been utterly destroyed, townsmen who possibly had been warned of French intentions and made advance preparations returned to put out the fires once the French had departed, so that instead of over four hundred houses destroyed, the fire only claimed about thirty to thirty-five. Louvois was furious.

Mannheim would not be so fortunate; it suffered the worst of this devil's work. On 13 January, truly an unlucky thirteenth for the people of Mannheim, Louvois condemned that city to destruction in an order to Montclair. "The king wills that the inhabitants of Mannheim be warned to withdraw to Alsace, and that all the buildings of the city be razed, without leaving any structure standing."[15] However, only in March did the French put Mannheim to the torch. On 4 March, Montclair told the magistrates that the French intended to tear down the dwellings in the town, and he had the gall to suggest that the townspeople demolish their own homes "to avoid disorder," but they refused.[16] Louvois wanted the inhabitants to evacuate the town and withdraw to Alsace.[17] The people of Mannheim were ordered to take their belongings and leave, but so little time was allowed—in some cases no more than four days—that they were permitted to put their belongings in churches for ten to twelve days until transport could be arranged.[18] As the citizens fled, they received help from at least some French officers.[19] The actual burning began on 8 March and proceeded on the following days.[20] Fire promised to do the job well, according to Montclair: "since the town is almost all built of wood, it will soon be consumed."[21]

Soldier work crews tore down walls and filled in ditches, and in addition peasants were rounded up and used as forced labor for this and other destructions.[22] Later, when the town had been evacuated and the destruction completed, Louvois ordered Montclair to kill any residents who tried to return to their homes.[23] In the words of Chamlay, Mannheim had been leveled, "like a field."[24]

The fate of Mannheim awaited other unfortunate towns. On 12 May, Duras wrote of the necessity to burn Speyer and Worms; Louvois approved, and on 21 May Chamlay set out a plan for the destruction of these two cities and Oppenheim.[25] The inhabitants were to be given six days to remove their furniture and other goods, and they would be encouraged to resettle in Alsace, Lorraine, and Burgundy, where they would be exempt from all taxes for ten years. Then on 31 May, fire consumed Oppenheim and Worms, although it is to be noted that the fortifications of both towns had already been razed, that is, breaches torn in the walls and ditches filled in, and only the residences stood to be fired.[26] Flames consumed Speyer the next day, 1 June, and Bingen on 4 June. Duras reported that amidst the smoking ruins of Worms not a single habitation remained standing.[27]

All in all, the French destroyed over a score of substantial towns, and to this toll must be added the numerous villages reduced to ashes, for as fires gutted the great towns they also charred the surrounding countryside. Tessé reported that while the French destroyed Mannheim they also burned all villages around it to a distance of four leagues, or twelve miles.[28] The French resolve to destroy everything in their paths spelled the end for barns as well as fine houses, as French war parties collected tribute and burned their way across the countryside. Montclair reported with some pride on one raid: "Lademburg was burned the day before yesterday by M. Mélac, and all the other villages from that town between the Neckar and the Bergstratt up to Landhoffen."[29]

While Louis and Louvois instructed soldiers to carry out their work in a disciplined manner, the line between destruction and pillage blurred. It proved nearly impossible to command a soldier to burn down a house but not to steal any of its contents or abuse its occupants. Certainly, to the average man in the ranks this must have seemed bizarre. In addition, much of the work was done by isolated patrols operating far from the eyes of senior commanders. The conduct of such raiders must have varied depending on the rapaciousness of the particular men involved, and undoubtedly some cared little for official directives or common decency. To make matters worse, soldiers were not always in control of themselves, but literally grew drunk with pillage. From Mannheim, Montclair complained, "As it would be impossible to limit drunkenness because all the cellars are filled with wine, I have ordered a halt to the work [of destruction] for four days so that the inhabitants can remove their effects without leaving anything in the cellars."[30]

It could be argued that for all their pious words about discipline, the French benefited from the misconduct of their soldiers, so that there was little real pressure to rein them in. General d'Harcourt testified to this in a way when he suggested vis-à-vis the city of Speyer, "I should be of the opinion to so strongly ill-treat the inhabitants that one might oblige them to absolutely desert the city, in such a way that it might remain as a desert, if one does not prefer to burn it."[31]

Soldiers committed the kind of excesses typical of the Thirty Years' War but which were thought to be barbaric anomalies by the late seventeenth century. Some of the same images used to condemn that earlier war were resurrected to condemn the conduct of French troops in the Palatinate. One artist copied Callot's great engraving, "The Pillage of a Large Farmhouse," from his "Misères et maleurs de la guerre" (1633), and simply changed the costumes to update the vision. A pamphlet detailed crimes committed against women near Heidelberg: "Some young girls, one of whom was only fourteen, were violated in the middle of the street in the presence of children and old folk. In the same way they used an old lady whose arms they held while others satisfied their evil passions. They even did this to a pregnant woman who had hid in a cellar, holding a child in her arms, and they satisfied their desires in turns before her husband's eyes."[32]

As is so often the case, brutality bred reprisal, and Germans murdered Frenchmen. A force of about two hundred German dragoons left its own bloody signature: "In the month of January of this year, the enemy, having surprised some sick soldiers in an outpost that had been abandoned, had the cruelty to cut their throats."[33] Obviously, such acts simply drove the French to commit further obscenities.

French troops mistreated the people in their path so brutally not primarily because they were of different national origins, for the consciousness of national identity then mattered less than it would in the nineteenth century. The most important difference between soldier and civilian was just that: one was a soldier and the other a civilian. As J. R. Hale has argued so well, in early modern Europe the man of arms looked down upon the villager, even though the soldier in all probability came from village stock himself.[34] Once the peasant took up the musket he was a peasant no longer; he adopted a different lifestyle with different values. Those who had spawned him became aliens and, all too often, the objects of his hate.

The campaign season brought a close to the devastation of the Palatinate, Baden, and Württemberg as German and Dutch forces advanced against the French and forced them back toward their fortress line. French sway in the Palatinate ended with the fall of Mainz. A combined allied army of about sixty thousand gathered around the city and finally opened siege trenches on the night of 22–23 July. On 8 September, the fortress asked for terms, and on 11 September the garrison marched out under the command of Huxelles.

The savage character of the devastation of the Palatinate stood out at the time, even though the seventeenth century was an era that witnessed the horrors of war on a grand scale and had become callous. Perhaps revulsion at the suffering inflicted by the Thirty Years' War engendered a hope that the brutality would end, or at least diminish, and thus the devastation of the Palatinate shocked all the more because it demonstrated that such horrors were not only a nightmare from the past but a terrible reality of the present.

A flood of pamphlets denounced French conduct, and with good cause. "Before, the French passed as an honest, humane, and civil nation, with a spirit opposed to barbarities; but today in the minds of their neighbors, a Frenchman and a cannibal are almost the same thing."[35] If they were as bad as cannibals, they were also no better than the Turk: "The French have made themselves feared by other nations, not so much by their virile courage and bravery as by their numbers and their tyrannical cruelty, in attacking without warning the Empire and especially the Palatinate and the Duchy of Württemberg where they encountered no resistance and have raged more cruelly than the Turk, one could say like living devils."[36]

The French actions in the Palatinate, Baden, and Württemberg helped to unite the Germans against the French. Although some German forces moved against Louis's army as early as November and

December 1688, the empire formally declared war on the French in January 1689. French barbarity, combined with the image of Louis's limitless ambition, helped to forge a European alliance against France, an alliance that included England, the United Provinces, Spain, Savoy, and the empire. In the long run, the devastation of the Palatinate fueled a bitter animosity within the German people against the French that festered for centuries within the national memory and, some would argue, contributed to the onset of the climactic wars of the twentieth century. As the passage that began this chapter cried, "It only remains for us to serve for all eternity as witnesses of French brutality and to cry, to all Europe, where we have been driven into exile: Vengeance! Vengeance!"[37]

The devastation of the Palatinate struck the people of the time as particularly heinous international crime, yet it was not the first time since the Thirty Years' War that war brought the horror of systematic destruction upon a civilian population. The Dutch War (1672–1678) saw the French lay waste to parts of the Dutch Netherlands in 1672–1674. Then in 1674 Turenne devastated the lands between the Main and the Neckar to impede any German advance against Alsace, and in 1677 the French wreaked havoc on the Meuse country, again to create a logistic obstacle against their enemies. Neither would the devastation of the Palatinate in 1688–1689 be the last such action during the wars of Louis XIV; the armies of Marlborough and Eugene of Savoy ravaged Bavaria in 1704. But it was not these other instances of brutal destruction but the devastation of the Palatinate that burned itself into the European conscience. And there is reason to believe that memories of the Palatinate were one of the influences that inspired Europeans to try to make the conduct of war more restrained and humane in the eighteenth century, although it would be impossible to establish an absolute link between the devastation of the Palatinate and the age of limited warfare that followed.

To understand French policy in the Palatinate, policy that ultimately cost Louis a great deal as well as victimizing the unfortunate civilians who stood in his way, that destruction must be considered in its political and military context. The factors to be put into the balance include Louis's war aims, his strategy of barriers, practices of extorting money and goods from occupied populations, shifts in the nature of French military command, and Louis's own propensity for brutality in international relations during the 1680s. The emphasis here will be less on the results of French conduct than on the expectations that justified that conduct. This intellectual labor is not an attempt to excuse French actions, although it will make them more explicable.

The monarch's rationales for war in 1688 have been fairly well understood from the beginning. As early as 1727, Quincy, in his classic history of Louis's wars, picked out three elements to the diplomatic background of the conflict: the tide of Habsburg victory against the Turks, the potential grab for the English throne by William III, and, as a precipitating factor, the dispute over designating a successor to the aging archbishop of Cologne.[38] Modern accounts have simply added more detail to this general picture.[39]

Strategically, Louis's concerns had become ultimately defensive, though immediately aggressive. As Clausewitz noted, "It had become almost a question of honor for Louis XIV to defend the frontiers of the kingdom from all insult, as insignificant as it might be."[40] A good case can be made that after the Dutch War, for all the Sun King's emphasis on glory, he was more interested in securing a defensible frontier than in conquest for its own sake. However, it would never have occurred to him to achieve that frontier by falling back to better position and thereby abandoning some of his territory to the enemy. On the contrary, if a more defensible line had to be sought, it must be gained by driving forward, by taking the offensive diplomatically or militarily. This is what the historian André Corvisier means when he refers to Louis's "aggressive defense."

The province most vulnerable to enemy attack was Alsace. During the Dutch War, allied forces had repeatedly campaigned in Alsace, and Louis could not tolerate such incursions. The Reunions of 1681–1684 can largely be explained by Louis's desire to shelter Alsace by seizing new lands and fortresses. And since his primary demand from the emperor by the late 1680s was a permanent agreement accepting the so-called Reunions, the desire to protect Alsace provided the ultimate rationale for both the onset of war in 1688 and, in a more immediate sense, for the devastation of the Palatinate. But in all things diplomatic, nothing is so simple.

Louis worried continually about the defense of France from the resurgent Austrian Habsburgs. Their war with the Turks had gone well for them, adding to Habsburg lands, population, and resources, and

Louis feared, apparently with good reason, that the Habsburgs would turn on him should they win a victorious peace from the Turks.[41] His manifesto of 24 September 1688 spoke of "the Emperor's long-established plans to attack France as soon as he could have peace with the Turks."[42] Perhaps a French attack across the Rhine would offset Habsburg victories in the east and encourage the Turks to continue their struggle and thus occupy the Habsburgs. In the words of Villars, "Nothing was more important for us than to present as powerful a diversion as that conducted by the Turk."[43] Before the war began, Louis XIV explained his design to his ambassador in Constantinople: "It is only too obvious that the Turks will profit from this conjuncture and that they will reestablish their affairs by the continuation of the war."[44] The ambassador was to persuade the Turks to continue in the war.

Louis hoped to gain permanent imperial recognition of his territorial acquisitions of 1679–1684, known as the Reunions. These gains included Strasbourg, Luxembourg, and other lesser fortresses and real estate. They not only expanded the borders of France; they secured those borders by forming a more rational fortress line praised even by Vauban, who in general was not enthusiastic about senseless conquest. In a way, Philippsburg was to be the last of the Reunions since it completed the defensive wall felt necessary by Louis. In 1688 he simply desired a quick and easy agreement to solidify his position; this, he thought, could be won in a four months' campaign, followed by a victorious peace in January. The devastation of the Palatinate was a monument to the failure of that policy.

Beyond French concern with the Habsburgs, English readers are apt to assume that the potential overthrow of James II weighed heavy on the mind of the Sun King, but this seems not to have been the case. Louis XIV never seemed to judge the English crisis correctly. In August, he feared an invasion of the island kingdom by William III, but then decided that, in the words of historian Geoffrey Symcox, "William did not pose an immediate threat."[45] Early in September Louis tried to bluff the Dutch into doing nothing by stating that any move against James II would be seen as an act of war against France; however, this simply made the States-General more willing to back William's claims. As it turned out, although Louis believed that William would do little or, at most, simply paralyze England with civil war, the French commitment to war along the Rhine freed William to devote his troops and attention to an English adventure that soon won him the crown. The fact that William secured the throne within a month of his sailing for England on 11 November made Louis's December decisions all the more worried.

As an additional guarantee for French borders, Louis wanted his candidate, Cardinal William Egon von Fürstenberg, elected to succeed the old and failing archbishop of Cologne upon his death. The archbishop held not only Cologne, but Liège, Münster, and Hildesheim, meaning that his territories could provide either a useful barrier, if they were friendly, or a dangerous threat, were they hostile. Louis worked hard to secure Fürstenberg's right of succession through election by the cathedral chapter, and it chose Fürstenberg, but Pope Innocent IX would not confirm the election, so the issue hung in the balance when the old archbishop died in June 1688. William III conspired against Fürstenberg's elevation to archbishop, and the ultimate decision deadlocked in the chapter and thus fell to the Pope, who continued to balk. Therefore, the controversy with the Pope grew hotter in August, and Louis even threatened an attack on the papal states. The crisis over the choice of a new archbishop of Cologne, more than anything else, precipitated war in the fall of 1688.[46]

Louis expressed certain lesser rationales as well, including disapproval of the way in which the Elector Palatine had treated Louis and, in particular, the wife of Philippe d'Orleans, the king's brother, but these were little more than smoke screens.[47] As stated earlier in this chapter, Louis's primary purposes could, in his judgment, be satisfied by a short war, and Louvois concurred that the war would last but four months. When it became clear that the war would pit a greater alliance against France than either the king or his minister had anticipated, they were caught off guard, and they turned to desperate measures to buy time to gear up for a major conflict.

Louis XIV based the defense of his lands upon a strategy of barriers. Natural obstacles were to be supplemented with fortress lines, and beyond these logistical barriers could be created to impede the enemy. Obviously, in the defense of his eastern frontier the Rhine provided the most important obstruction, but this would not suffice to bar an advance from Germany. In addition to rivers and mountains, great fortresses stood along the frontiers like so many sentinels. The most famous fortress line, the *pré carré*, guarded the frontier with the

Spanish Netherlands. In defense of Alsace, Louis and Louvois, assisted by Vauban, created a new system of defenses along the Rhine from the Swiss border north and then between the Rhine and the Saar and then across to Luxembourg. To complete this line, the French seized Strasbourg in 1681 and Luxembourg in 1684, then as the opening stroke of the War of the League of Augsburg, Louis dispatched his main army to take Philippsburg.

Just as Louis prized his own fortresses highly, he feared those of his enemies. Such strong points could be used defensively to resist French armies and offensively to serve as essential bases for attacks against French fortresses and territory. This explains his orders to French commanders to raze enemy fortifications in the Palatinate, Baden, and Württemberg. From the outset of the war, as he declared in his manifesto, he felt forced "to take up arms on the banks of the Rhine and to attack the fortifications which would give the Emperor [an] easy possibility to commence and sustain war against France."[48]

But beyond the barriers provided by nature or built by man, seventeenth-century warfare also relied upon what can be seen as logistic barriers. Logistic considerations determined victory or defeat, and, in fact, fortifications themselves played key logistical roles, from housing magazines to commanding supply routes to controlling resource areas.[49] While armies depended upon regular systems of supply, they could not maintain themselves in the field simply upon what their supply trains could haul up from the rear. Napoleon once said that the greatest natural barrier was a desert, precisely because it was devoid of what an army needed to subsist.[50] For that great captain, a logistical barrier posed a greater threat than a physical one. The argument that one must lay waste the enemy's land to deny him the ability to supply himself was already well established in the military literature of the sixteenth and seventeenth centuries.[51]

In a sense, the French devastated the Palatinate to create an artificial desert that would preclude the enemy from undertaking offensive operations. Chamlay expressed his desire to defend France not with field armies but with fortresses and a wasteland in letter of 9 November 1688:

If I were given the command of the army of His Majesty in Germany, I would respond . . . by keeping the enemies from undertaking any enterprise, without committing the king's army, and to reduce them either to not daring to lose sight of their own country, and by consequence to conduct only a disgraceful and fruitless campaign, or, should they want to leave their lands for some expedition, to expose themselves to ruin and desolation; for, finally, on what fortress could they prey, when, after having razed Palatinate and the Rhineland towns that one chose not to guard, one would provide strong garrisons and all sorts of munitions to Landau, Philippsburg, Huningue, Belfort, and Montroyal?[52]

Louvois echoed this logic of desolation in a letter to Montclair: "His Majesty recommends that you ruin the places you leave . . . so that, finding no forage or food whatever there, the enemies would not attempt to approach there."[53] In December, General d'Harcourt also counseled wide-scale destruction of towns occupied by the French, "ruining not only the walls, but also carrying away all the grains, wines, and cattle that one was not able to consume, and burning the forage that might remain, that would deprive the enemies of the means of acting in that region this winter, and even [in] the next campaign."[54] Other men on the spot believed that they might shelter behind scorched earth: "I always conclude to ruin that which is within the reach of the King's troops so that, the Germans ruining the rest of the surrounding countryside, they shall not be in a state to make any movement in the spring, nor even in a later season for lack of the food and rations that they draw only from the lands they occupy."[55]

For the same reasons at the same time, Louvois ordered that wheat not be sown on either bank of the Meuse to a distance of four leagues from the river, from Mézières to Verdun, for two years in order to make it difficult for an enemy to advance into France along that line.[56] This amounted to the creation of an artificial "wheat desert" over twenty miles wide, or about a two days' march.

Both the nineteenth-century historian and biographer of Louvois, Camille Rousset, and the twentieth-century historian and biographer of Louis XIV, John B. Wolf, compared the devastation of the Palatinate to the act of ripping down buildings and other obstacles from around a fortress to clear fields of fire, but this is a poor metaphor.[57] Clearing the lands in front of the French fortress line had nothing to do with striking the enemy but rather with starving him out or at least making his operations as difficult as possible.

To quarter troops, an enemy might make use not only of fortress walls and food but also of the very residential buildings of a town and, to store provisions, of large open structures. Therefore, buildings also had to be destroyed, generally by burning, so the enemy could find no comfort under their roofs. The war minister did not let his commanders forget. A letter of 17 December reminded Montclair of Louis's desire to have "Heilbronn, Tübingen, and Esslingen destroyed so that they could not serve as quarters for the enemy."[58] Apparently, one of the rationales that explain the bombardment of Koblenz was to deny it as winter quarters for German troops.[59] The emphasis on quarters was particularly apropos during the cold months, when troops needed shelter to survive. But more than beds were at stake. In late January, Louvois again chided Montclair, "It is annoying that you left Pforzheim in a condition that the enemies can establish a base there."[60] When Chamlay argued for the utter destruction of Oppenheim, Worms, and Speyer in May, he did so in part because the towns were "so filled with large buildings capable of containing large magazines."[61]

According to this line of argument, devastation was considered to be a necessary adjunct to French fortifications. Quincy defended the devastation or burning as a reaction to suddenly being overwhelmed and having to fight on too many fronts, since an outnumbered and overwrought French army needed to keep the enemy at arm's length as long as possible. In a sense, the combination of many barriers bought time for, and was itself a temporary substitute for, the expansion of the army, which reached such unprecedented proportions during the War of the League of Augsburg.[62]

An unpublished dissertation by Ronald Ferguson puts the devastation of the Palatinate in a very different context, that of contributions.[63] Contributions were war taxes imposed on an area, city, town, village, or even an estate by an occupying, passing, or threatening army. Essentially, contributions amounted to extortion, and the sanction against those who refused to pay this protection money was fire. In a practice known as "execution," war parties burned out those who did not comply.[64] Wallenstein pioneered the seventeenth-century styles of contributions and executions in the 1620s, but soon they became standard operating procedure for all armies, a procedure legitimated by international law.

There is no question that after 1659 the French army relied on contributions to pay a substantial portion of its bills. It is impossible to arrive at any exact figure, but a fair estimate would be that contributions accounted for 25 percent of the cost of war.[65] When the troops marched into the Palatinate in 1688 they immediately began to demand contributions and threaten executions; they would have regardless of French intentions concerning the ultimate fate of the Palatinate. But in addition, at this point the French regarded contributions as more than simply a way to pay for the war; they had become a device designed to impose peace on French terms. As Rousset pointed out: "The Germans were not rich; to surprise and seize their modest savings, to exhaust them through large contributions, to cut, in a word, the sinews of war, and by consequence to paralyze their first efforts, to hold them back to only a demi-campaign, to gain at one stroke both time and money, was it not all an advantage?"[66]

From the start, the intention was to make war feed war by quartering French troops on German lands, where they would be supported by demands made on the surrounding peoples. Duras believed he could quarter sixty thousand troops from Freiburg to Mannheim if he could raise the necessary contributions.[67] Boufflers also thought of winter quarters early in October: "All these places and all the Palatinate on this [west] side of the Rhine will afford means to His Majesty to winter a very numerous body of troops . . . and shall deprive the enemies of all means of undertaking anything on this side of the Rhine."[68] In addition, even battalions left to garrison French fortresses were to be funded by contributions.[69] While the besieging army still surrounded Philippsburg, Louvois instructed the intendant La Goupillière on 6 October, "You cannot work too soon at demanding contributions beyond the Rhine between the Main and the Neckar, and if one does not begin to bring money eight days after you have asked for it, you shall send [troops] to burn some houses in the farther regions, so as to spread terror."[70] Just a few days later Louvois ordered La Grange, another intendant, to demand contributions from "all the Estates, bailiwicks, and lordships beyond the Rhine."[71]

The French jockeyed to put themselves in locations best situated for the levying of contributions. According to Chamlay, "to establish a great contribution, it is absolutely necessary to make oneself master of Heilbronn."[72] Heidelberg, Pforzheim, Mannheim, and Mainz were also seen as important locations from which to collect payments. Chamlay prophetically argued: "Even if it should be true that the Imperials must come there, and you do not desire to wait for them, you would always have enough time to draw a great sum of money that I would estimate would be well over a million [livres]."[73]

Contributions were assessed on a number of levels, from villages to entire provinces. Oppenheim was to pay eighty thousand livres and fifty thousand rations of forage, and the French also demanded fifty thousand livres and fifty thousand rations of forage from Frankfurt.[74] By mid-October, the estates of Württemberg had worked out a deal and promised to send an initial payment of one hundred thousand livres.[75]

Already by the end of October the French mounted raids to burn out those who were tardy in their payments, and these "executions" escalated over the course of the French occupation. Duras issued orders to burn "towns or castles" since "I do not doubt that shall make the money come promptly."[76] This notion that burning was essential to get the money flowing seemed to be shared by all. La Goupillière even sent agents disguised as peasants to set fires "as far as Franconia," apparently with no other intention than simply to scare the population.[77] Chamilly reported that in his contribution raids in December, "I forgot nothing that could cause them fear."[78]

Contributions were, in fact, exhausting and ruining the country. As La Bretesche explained to Louvois: "When I had the honor to write you that the contributions of this area would not be considerable for this first year past, it was because I see the area is being absolutely ruined, and that all the people are abandoning it, forsaking all their horses, beasts, and crops, and [they do this] because of the threats of the Germans and [because of] the great contributions that one asks of them."[79] The destruction of the country made it harder and harder for the French to extort funds. Complaints multiplied about meager and slow contributions. In December, La Grange complained that the area would soon be devastated, which would make it impossible for the population to pay contributions.[80] In January, La Goupillière explained the slow pace of payments by the fact that "the poverty of the people is great," and in April he blamed their impoverishment upon the actions of French raiding parties: "because these troops have taken [amounts for themselves] that much exceed the contributions and because of the frequent executions that they have carried out in the villages."[81] The problem of collection was made all the more difficult, from the French point of view, by the presence of German cavalry that had arrived and by the actions of Schnapphahns: "all the peasants are armed and on their guard."[82]

To a degree, demanding large contributions was, in fact, intended to ruin the country. General d'Harcourt suggested in December: "I would also ruin the country beyond the Neckar as far as it shall be possible, not only by contributions in money, but also by drawing from it the greatest quantity of grains that one shall be able to bring down the Neckar, burning all the forage that one could not consume, and razing all the castles that one might have the time to ruin."[83] Obviously, for d'Harcourt and others, demanding excessive contributions was simply an organized form of pillage equivalent to burning fodder and ripping down castles.

Ronald Ferguson argues that the destruction of many towns had more to do with the logic of contributions than with leaving a logistical barrier in front of the French army as it withdrew; therefore, to him the devastation of the Palatinate followed as a consequence of contributions policy. He interprets Chamlay's letters of 27 October and 9 November as primarily concerned with contributions. Mannheim could be sacrificed because "for you that place is good for nothing, it will not produce any contribution money."[84] More importantly, the same towns that were valuable to the French for gathering contributions could have been used by the allies as well, so as the French withdrew they had to destroy them. Towns like Heilbronn that were key collection points would not have been razed if the enemy had not approached in force. However, since Ferguson's entire research focuses only on contributions, he seems committed to claiming contributions as a rationale exclusive of all others, but this is a fundamental error. Supporting an army in the field required drawing on local resources, and part of creating a logistic barrier demanded eliminating the possibility of the enemy drawing contributions from a region. For that reason, there is no conflict, rather there is an almost necessary link between the process of creating a logistic barrier and of denying contributions to the enemy.

Ferguson's work must be put in the balance, for he makes valid points on his way to what is too extreme a conclusion. What is clear is that, first, much of the burning of German towns came not from a

policy of total destruction but as encouragement or punishment associated with contributions and, second, the fate of certain towns rested
on their value in the process of collecting contributions.

While it would be hard to prove, it is reasonable to suggest that
French conduct in the Palatinate may have also flowed from Versailles's
lack of confidence in its generals. The great captains of Louis's younger
days were all gone. A cannonball struck down Turenne in 1675, while
at the close of that year Condé retired, and Créquy, "one of the greatest
captains of the century," died in 1687.[85] Marshal Luxembourg's star
still lay low on the horizon. To be sure, Louis would soon recognize
the talents of Luxembourg, but that great captain had yet to prove
himself. He had, in fact, languished in disgrace after the Dutch War,
both because of his conduct in that war and because he was put on
trial during the infamous affair of the poisons that rocked the French
court in the early 1680s.[86]

When, in his letter of 9 November, Chamlay expressed the hope that
a barrier of devastated territory and secure French fortresses would
defend France without having to risk an army on the battlefield, he
linked this strategy to a belief that great generals would no longer be
needed:

> The difference that exists between the present situation of the king's
> affairs and that of [the Dutch War], is that in those previous times,
> the fate of His Majesty and of his kingdom was in the hands of a
> man who, either by being killed or by making a bad decision, could
> condemn it in a moment, or at least compromise it in some way by
> the loss of a battle [after] which it had been difficult to reestablish.
> Whereas, presently, because of the great conquests that have been
> made, and because of the advantageous situation of the fortresses
> that have been fortified, the King finds himself able to grant com-
> mand of his armies to whomever it pleases him, without having any-
> thing to fear from the mediocre capacity of those to whom he con-
> fides it.[87]

Considering the context in which these odd remarks were made leads
one to wonder if Chamlay praised the French fortress line and encouraged devastation because he lacked faith in French military leadership.
After all, Chamlay was serving with the main army under the command of the Dauphin and Marshal Duras. The Dauphin was a cipher,

and Duras was a man of limited will and suspect talent. If this was the best field commander that Louis had, perhaps it was best not to base a campaign plan upon the capacities of his generals. And if as a consequence the French were to adopt a defensive plan that would eventually see them hunkering down in their fortresses, the devastation of the surrounding territory made a great deal of sense. That devastation also announced that the French had no intention of carrying out an offensive of their own since it would have been equally hampered by the impossibility of drawing supplies from the barren ruins of the Palatinate.

It might be charged that Chamlay's comments of 9 November amounted to little more than whistling in the dark, but if he was trying to make the best of a bad situation it just reinforces the notion that he and his masters could not count on their generals in the field. This also fed into Louis's propensity to direct warfare from Versailles, to conduct, in conjunction with his war minister, *guerre de cabinet.* That style of high command speaks both to Louis's and Louvois's desires for personal control and also to their limited respect for the men who led their armies. In fact, the tone of Louvois's letters to the front suggests not confidence but frustration with the likes of Duras, Montclair, and Tessé. About the only general who enjoyed the king's complete backing was Vauban, and he, of course, fed right into the obsession with positional warfare.

If one tries to follow the decision-making process only in the recorded documents of the period, then the driving forces behind the devastation of the Palatinate appear to be Louvois and Chamlay. However, a knowledge of the workings of the French court and government makes it clear that these administrators acted in the name of the king and that without the sanction of Louis XIV they would have been powerless. The knowledgeable and wise historian Andrew Lossky concludes: "In the first half of his reign Louis seems to have kept or chosen his ministers because their main ideas were consonant with his own; in the second half, because they reflected some aspect of his personality."[88] During the 1680s Louvois seems to have fallen into both categories but ultimately more the second; the minister embodied something basic in the king himself. Thus, the responsibility for French actions in the Palatinate ultimately rests with Louis.

But to what extent can Louis be charged with malice aforethought?

Lossky regards Louis's decision to devastate the Palatinate as an "irrational outburst, with little or no premeditation."[89] Perhaps; however, the argument in this essay is that elements of the brutal destruction were discussed at the very start of the campaign and that the basic decisions seem to have been made as early as December 1688, even though the fires that consumed Mannheim, Worms, Oppenheim, Speyer, and Bingen were not lit until March, May, and June 1689. So while Louis did not envision the campaign's apocalyptic end when he ordered French troops across the border, he and his agents framed a policy of destruction over several months and could have called it off at any time. Also, to dismiss the devastation as irrational and impulsive misses the point that the individual actions undertaken were not in themselves unprecedented or senseless. Rather, the extent of systematic destruction over such a large area constituted an extreme application of standard military practices.[90] The result shocked by its lack of moderation, but it did not come out of the blue.

Moreover, while it may not have been premeditated in the strict sense of the word, Louis's brutality in the Palatinate was entirely consistent with a long chain of brutal actions that stretched back to 1680. Louis and Louvois repeatedly appealed to brutality as a way of reaching their foreign policy goals even in the midst of what was supposed to be peacetime.

The logic of Louis's "aggressive defense" of beleaguered Alsace required that he close off the Rhine to the east and secure fortresses from Landau to Luxembourg on the northern flank. Through a process of "Reunion" from 1680 to 1684, Louis staked claims to adjacent territories in French courts, secured favorable verdicts, and then enforced those judgments with armed might. In this manner, he gained Saarbrücken, Zweibrücken, and Montroyal. It also provided him with a pretext for attacking Luxembourg, which he began to blockade in 1681 and finally took by siege in 1684. During the same period, Louis's troops marched into Strasbourg to take this vital bridgehead along the Rhine.

The Reunions led to a brief war with Spain, 1683–1684, that saw French armies act with unusual harshness in the enforcement of contributions. When the Spanish demanded payments from French-controlled villages, Louvois ordered an escalating toll of reprisals for enemy executions. In this demonic arithmetic, the French condemned ten or twenty enemy villages or houses to be burned for every one village or house under Louis's protection that the Spanish executed, but at the very worst the multiplier jumped to one hundred.[91] Such reprisals were apparently intended to affect public opinion and force the inhabitants to pressure Spanish officials. Louis must have been encouraged by the minor war with Spain since in terms of achieving his goals this was his most successful war.[92]

In another case of violence used in lieu of diplomacy, when Louis thought that Genoa was too friendly to Spain during the 1683–1684 war he ordered his fleet to bombard the city. In May 1684, the French lobbed exploding shells into the city, destroying two-thirds of it, and then Louis assembled forces at Casale to threaten an overland invasion. The humiliated doge of Genoa had to journey to Versailles in 1685 and present his abject apology to Louis for wrongs Genoa never committed. Only in this way did Genoa escape further punishment.

Louis also attempted to bring religious unity to France by violent means. After trying to bully French Protestants, or Huguenots, into converting by quartering ill-behaved cavalry upon them (the *dragonades*), Louis banned their faith altogether when he revoked the Edict of Nantes in 1685. He hounded Huguenots in France and wherever they sought refuge. One of the darkest blots on his record is the way in which he forced the duke of Savoy to attack his own Protestant community, the Vaudois, because Louis saw them as a source of refuge for Huguenots. Louis made the duke accept French troops to aid in this attack, which amounted to genocide, and in April 1686 French and Piedmontese swept forward, killing those who dared to resist them and collecting some six thousand prisoners, men, women, and children. At the end of the campaign Marshal Catinat, in command of the French, wrote, "This county is completely desolated; there are no more people or beasts at all."[93] After the survivors were herded into concentration camps and began to perish, Louis commented, "I see that illness delivers the Duke of Savoy from the trouble caused by the need to guard the rebels from the valleys of Luzerne, and I do not doubt at all that he easily consoles himself for the loss of such subjects who make room for better and more faithful ones."[94]

Since harsh policies seemed to work, is it any wonder that Louis continued to employ them? The string of cruel actions that Louis undertook during the 1680s probably both gave him confidence in the efficacy of brutality and desensitized him to the human misery brought by his policies. In the case of the devastation of the Palatinate, Chamlay may have voiced the policy first and Louvois may have enforced it, but behind both stood the overpowering presence of Louis XIV. The Sun King might just as well have actually penned Louvois's advice to Chamlay: "Forget any idea that you have anything to gain from the Germans by friendship or moderation."[95]

To claim that the devastation of the Palatinate was an "irrational outburst, with little or no premeditation" does not adequately take into account that it was entirely consistent with Louis's actions in the 1680s. Consistency may not be the same thing as premeditation, but it demonstrates a damnable habit. The attack on the Rhineland was certainly an appeal to violence, so it all comes down to how much more violent and inexcusable was the total, as opposed to the only partial, destruction that any attack had to entail. Louis and Louvois had demonstrated their tendency to go too far repeatedly in the past, so why would it not be expected that they would give way to excess again? Perhaps it was not malice aforethought, but it was not too difficult to foresee what Louis would do.

This essay has argued that the devastation of the Palatinate followed from an exaggerated application of contemporary military practices, called into use because of political miscalculations by Louis and his advisors. Faced by unexpected resistance and the emergence of a hostile alliance, they were willing to resort to extremes to hold the front and buy time for French military mobilization. But this does not excuse the decisions that Louis made because it cannot be denied that he was willing to cause great harm to German civilians in the name of his own bankrupt policy. Louis XIV thought a great deal about his *gloire*, about his immortal reputation. Were Louis in the docket to defend his actions before the bar of history, there is no doubt that he would claim that what he ordered done, though unfortunate, was a brutal necessity imposed upon him by circumstance. But history has delivered a verdict against him, and it is best expressed in the words of contemporaries: "There is no amount of time that can abolish, nor torrential rain that can wash away, nor fire that can efface, nor gilt and paint that can make beautiful the memory that King Louis left there, in causing to flow the blood and tears of thousands of oppressed and innocent people."[96]

Notes

1. Chamlay and Ste. Pouenges were both important advisors and were both at the front in 1688–1689. Chamlay left a voluminous correspondence, and according to his biographer, Ron Martin, seemingly wrote down whatever crossed his mind, traits that make him a much-used source. Ste. Pouenges may have rivaled Chamlay in influence; however, since he did not leave the paper trail that Chamlay did, historians have emphasized the role of Chamlay in these matters over that of Ste. Pouenges. This chapter does the same.

2. See the discussion in John B. Wolf, *Louis XIV* (New York, 1968), 443–56. "One of his letters after another, as well as the proclamations in which he fairly shouted that he was the aggrieved party in the dispute, were all based on the assumption that there would be peace by January 1689" (443). Thus, Louvois and Louis expected a three to four months' conflict. "This war was to be a *Blitz*" (446).

3. Camille Rousset, *Histoire de Louvois*, 4 vols. (Paris, 1862–64), 4:144.

4. Vauban opposed the bombardment: "What will be the good of it? . . . Would it not be better to husband our bombs than to waste them in useless expeditions which produce nothing?" Service Historique de l'Armée de Terre, Archives de Guerre (hereafter cited as AG), A^{1}832, 2 November 1688, Vauban to Louvois, in Rousset, *Louvois*, 4:142. Louvois seemed to enjoy the prospect, as he praised Boufflers: "The king has seen with pleasure that after having thoroughly burned [*bien brûlé*] Koblenz and done all the harm possible to the palace of the Elector, you returned to Mainz." AG, A^{1}812, 14 November 1688, Louvois to Boufflers, in Rousset, *Louvois*, 4:143.

5. Wolf, *Louis XIV*, 450–51.

6. Kurt von Raumer, *Die Zerstörung der Pfalz von 1689* (Munich, 1930), 81, argues that one of the four primary rationales for the devastation of the Palatinate was the "Theory of Intimidation," but that while intimidation is implicit in the discussion, after the Germans stiffen their resistance the correspondence explicitly deals with defense along the frontier, not with scaring the Germans into a diplomatic capitulation to French demands.

7. AG, A^{1}826, 27 October 1688, Chamlay to Louvois, in Rousset, *Louvois*, 4:160.

8. AG, A^{1}871, 19, 20, 29 November and 6 December 1688, Louvois to Montclair, in Rousset, *Louvois*, 4:164.

9. "J'oserai vous avancer une chose qui ne sera peut-être pas de votre goût, qui est que dès le lendemain de la prise de Mannheim, je mettrois les couteaux dedans et ferois passer la charrue dessus." AG, A^{1}826, 27 October 1688, Chamlay to Louvois, in Rousset, *Louvois*, 4:163.

10. AG, A^{1}871, 17 December 1688, Louvois to la Grange, in Rousset, *Louvois*, 4:164.

11. AG, A^{1}871, 18 December 1688, Louvois to Montclair, in Rousset, *Louvois*, 4:165.

12. AG, A^{1}871, #175ff, cited in Wolf, *Louis XIV*, 452.

13. AG, A^{1}871, #177, Louvois to La Grange, in Wolf, *Louis XIV*, 453.

14. The interchange of correspondence on Heidelberg follows an interesting course. That from the officials in the field to Louvois is contained in volume AG, A^{1}875. On 2 March, Montclair claimed that destruction by fire was near total, and on 4 March Tessé reported that 432 houses had been burned. On 6 March, Montclair again claimed that "400 to 500" houses had been burned. However, on 17 March, the intendant La Grange informed Louvois that the estimates from Montclair and Tessé had overstated the destruction and that only thirty to thirty-five houses had actually been lost because the people had come back into the town to fight the fires. However, he also suggests that "they had apparently been warned of what was to happen since the majority had water stored even in their attics." The letter of 2 March from Montclair, AG, A^{1}875, states that Tessé did his duty, "not withstanding the large offers which were made to him to bring some moderation" in the destruction. The "offers" that Tessé turned down may have bought critical information from someone else.

15. Letter in Rousset, *Louvois*, 4:166.

16. AG, A^{1}875, 4 March 1689, La Grange to Louvois.

17. Rousset, *Louvois*, 4:166.

18. On these details, see AG, A^{1}875, 6 March 1689, La Grange to Louvois.

19. Raumer, *Die Zerstörung der Pfalz*, 144.

20. Raumer, *Die Zerstörung der Pfalz*, 145.

21. AG, A^{1}875, 6 March 1689, Montclair to Louvois, from Mannheim.

22. A number of documents in AG, A^{1}875, discuss the use of soldiers in demolition. For example, in a letter of 9 March 1689, Tessé reported to Louvois that for the hard work of demolishing the citadel, "There was not a battalion that did not furnish 400 men for the work." For examples of peasant labor, see AG, A^{1}829, 6 December 1689, La Grange to Louvois, from Speyer, quoted in Ronald Thomas Ferguson, "Blood and Fire: Contribution Policy of the French Armies in Germany (1668–1715)" (Ph.D. diss., University of Minnesota, 1970), 113; AG, A^{1}875, 6 March 1689, Huxelles to Louvois.

23. AG, A^{1}872, 16 May 1689, Louvois to Montclair, in Rousset, *Louvois*, 4:168–69.

24. AG, A^{1}876, 21 May 1689, Chamlay to Louvois, in Rousset, *Louvois*, 4:178.

25. AG, A^{1}876, 12 May 1689, Duras to Louvois, in Rousset, *Louvois*, 4:177–78. On Louvois's response, see Rousset, *Louvois*, 4:178. AG, A^{1}876, 21 May 1689,

Chamlay to Louvois, in Rousset, *Louvois*, 4:178–79. Corvisier credits Chamlay with broaching the proposal on 21 May, but this would seem to be in error. André Corvisier, *Louvois* (Paris, 1983), 463.

26. AG, A^{1}875, 31 March 1689, La Goupillière to Louvois, states that it was five or six days since Oppenheim was entirely razed, and Worms was then razed as well. However, since there was not enough earth to fill all the ditches, the French made "dams" so one could cross at several places. In a letter of 17 April 1689, Duras stated that Oppenheim was "well razed" but that the work had not been quite so well accomplished at Worms, where other labor was to proceed. AG, A^{1}875, 17 April 1689, Duras to Louvois.

27. AG, A^{1}882, 31 May 1689, Duras to Louvois, from Odernheim, in Ferguson, "Blood and Fire," 116.

28. AG, A^{1}875, 9 March 1689, Tessé to Louvois, from Mannheim.

29. AG, A^{1}875, 6 March 1689, Montclair to Louvois, from Mannheim. Unattached to any particular regiment, Mélac became a specialist at leading destructive raids. On Mélac, see Ferguson, "Blood and Fire," 102–4.

30. AG, A^{1}875, 6 March 1689, Montclair to Louvois, from Mannheim. Another account from a contemporary pamphlet, *Balance française*, says of the French: "The noble wine of the Neckar was left to flow in the cellars onto the ground. . . . As badly as these brutes had treated the precious drink, they have not failed to avail themselves of it greedily, and more than one drank 10 measures, which would be difficult to do for a German who professed to be a heavy drinker." *Balance française*, 75, in Gillot, *Le règne de Louis XIV et l'opinion publique en Allemagne*, 186. Wine seemed to be an object of comment and worry. When La Goupillière searched the Elector's palace at Mainz, he detailed the 366 casks of wine, along with the 250 in the chancellor's cellar and the 700 that belonged to the nephew of the Elector. La Goupillière put guards on the wine. Ferguson, "Blood and Fire," 106–7.

31. AG, A^{1}829, 28 December 1688, d'Harcourt to Louvois, from Speyer, in Ferguson, "Blood and Fire," 113–14 n.

32. *Balance française*, 165, in Gillot, *Le règne de Louis XIV et l'opinion publique en Allemagne*, 186.

33. Charles S. Quincy, *Histoire militaire de Louis le Grand roi de France*, 7 vols. (Paris, 1726), 2:168.

34. J. R. Hale, *War and Society in Renaissance Europe* (Baltimore, 1985). He speaks of a "mental frontier between the man of war and the man of peace" (129).

35. *Soupirs de France*, 13e mémoire, in Rousset, *Louvois*, 4:183.

36. *Balance française*, 75, in Gillot, *Le règne de Louis XIV et l'opinion publique en Allemagne*, 185.

37. *Concusus creditorum* (1689) in Gillot, *La règne de Louis XIV et l'opinion publique en Allemagne*, 188.

38. Quincy, *Histoire militaire*, 2:119–21. Villars noted that the two major considerations were, first, the fact that the Turks might soon make peace, and, second, the likely disorder that would result from William's attempt to take the English throne, thus neutralizing England or leading it back to James II. Villars, *Mémoires du maréchal de Villars*, ed. Charles de Vogüé, 6 vols. (Paris, 1884), 1:100–101.

39. The most recent treatments of French rationales for the War of the League of Augsburg are Geoffrey Symcox, "Louis XIV and the Outbreak of the Nine Years War," in *Louis XIV and Europe*, ed. Ragnhild Hatton (Columbus, 1976), 179–212, and Paul Sonnino, "The Origins of Louis XIV's Wars," in *The Origins of War in Early Modern Europe*, ed. Jeremy Black (Edinburgh, 1987), 112–31. See as well John A. Lynn, "A Quest for Glory: The Formation of French Strategy under Louis XIV, 1661–1715," in *The Making of Strategy: Rulers, States and War*, ed. Williamson Murray, MacGregor Knox, and Alvin Bernstein (Cambridge, 1994), 178–204. Raumer in his *Die Zerstörung der Pfalz*, argues hard and long that the French had harbored a desire to take over the Palatinate practically from time immemorial and that the French also sought a natural frontier along the Rhine as a matter of principle. Both these arguments are weak, particularly the first, and the "natural frontiers" concept has taken some hard knocks in modern scholarship, particularly by Gaston Zeller.

40. Carl von Clausewitz in Jean Bérenger, *Turenne* (Paris, 1987), 514.

41. On the validity of Louis's fears, see Ragnhild Hatton, "Louis XIV and his Fellow Monarchs," in *Louis XIV and Europe*, 33.

42. B.N., Recueil Cangé, vol. 33, folios 174–78, *Mémoire des raisons*, in Wolf, *Louis XIV*, 650 n. 19.

43. Villars, *Mémoires*, 1:101.

44. Louis to his ambassador Girardin, 10 September 1688, in Charles Gérin, "Le pape Innocent IX et l'élection de Cologne en 1688," *Revue des questions historiques* 33 (1883): 122.

45. Symcox, "Louis XIV and the Outbreak of the Nine Years War," 202.

46. "It was thus the failure of Louis' plans to retain his hold on Cologne which led him into the initial decision to use armed forces." Symcox, "Louis XIV and the Outbreak of the Nine Years War," 197.

47. In his *Mémoire des raisons*, Louis complained of "injustices and violent usurpations of the Elector Palatine." B.N., Recueil Cangé, vol. 33, fols. 174–81, *Mémoire des raisons*, in Wolf, *Louis XIV*, 650 n. 19.

48. B.N., Recueil Cangé, 33:174–81, *Mémoire des raisons*, in Wolf, *Louis XIV*, 650 n. 19.

49. See the discussion of early modern logistics in *Feeding Mars: Logistics in Western Warfare from the Middle Ages to the Present*, ed. John A. Lynn (Boulder, 1993). In particular, see John A. Lynn's contribution, "Food, Funds, and Fortresses: Resource Mobilization and Positional Warfare in the Campaigns of Louis XIV," 137–60.

50. "The frontiers of nations are either large rivers, or chains of mountains, or deserts. Of all these obstacles to the march of an army, deserts are the most difficult to surmount, mountains come next, and large rivers hold only the third rank." *Napoleons' Maxims* in *Roots of Strategy*, ed. T. R. Phillips (Harrisburg PA, 1940), 407.

51. The much-read Roman classic *De Re Militari* by Vegetius stated: "the main and principal point in war is to secure plenty of provisions for oneself, and to destroy the enemy by famine." Ascanio Centorio in his *Discorsi di Guerra* (Venice, 1567) advocated destroying the countryside and starving the enemy. See Frank Tallett, *War and Society in Early-Modern Europe* (London, 1992), 66.

52. AG, A^1827, 9 November 1688, Chamlay to Louvois, in Rousset, *Louvois*, 4:161–62.

53. AG, A^1871, 18 December 1688, Louvois to Montclair, in Rousset, *Louvois*, 4:161–62.

54. AG, A^1829, 28 December 1688, d'Harcourt to Louvois, in Ferguson, "Blood and Fire," 110–11. When the troops were ready to go on campaign, he would completely raze Heilbronn, Heidelberg, and Mannheim.

55. AG, A^1829, 14 December 1688, La Bretesche to Louvois, in Ferguson, "Blood and Fire," 97.

56. AG, A^1853, 29 July 1689, Louvois to the intendants of Champagne, Lorraine, and the Moselle, in Rousset, *Louvois*, 4:226.

57. Rousset, *Louvois*, 4:158. Wolf, *Louis XIV*, 451 repeats this strange metaphor without citing Rousset. Raumer, in *Die Zerstörung der Pfalz*, 82, refers to a *Glacis-Theorie*, but his is explicitly concerned with supply.

58. AG, A^1871, 17 December 1688, Louvois to Montclair, in Wolf, *Louis XIV*, 453.

59. Ferguson, "Blood and Fire," 77.

60. AG, A^1871, 27 January 1689, Louvois to Montclair, in Wolf, *Louis XIV*, 453. This is Wolf's translation, and his "Pfortzen" must, in fact, be Pforzheim.

61. AG, A^1876, 21 May 1689, Chamlay to Louvois, in Rousset, *Louvois*, 4:179.

62. On the expansion of the army, see John A. Lynn, "Recalculating French Army Growth during the *Grand Siècle*, 1610–1715," *French Historical Studies* 18 (fall 1994).

63. Ferguson, "Blood and Fire." I must acknowledge my debt to Ferguson in this section; I have used both his arguments and his references.

64. On seventeenth-century contributions in general, see Fritz Redlich, "Contributions in the Thirty Years' War," *Economic History Review*, 12 (1959–60): 247–54, and Fritz Redlich, *De praeda militari: Looting and Booty 1500–1815*, supplement 39, *Vierteljahrschrift für Sozial- und Wirtschaftsgeschichte* (Wiesbaden, 1956).

65. On the French army and contributions, see John A. Lynn, "How War Fed War: The Tax of Violence and Contributions during the *grand siècle*," *Journal of Modern History* 65, no. 2 (June 1993): 286–310.

66. Rousset, *Louvois*, 4:158. John B. Wolf picks up on the same argument: "These detachments had as their primary mission the imposition of contributions upon the German people from Bonn to Hesse, thereby making them pay for a good part of the campaign, and forcing their lands to furnish food and fodder for the French armies. Louvois assured the king that this policy would encourage the German princes to be accommodating, and at the same time it would deprive the empire of the resources necessary for any serious resistance to the French invasion." Wolf, *Louis XIV*, 447.

67. AG, A^{1}826, #52, 23 October 1688, Duras to Louvois, in Ferguson, "Blood and Fire," 63.

68. AG, A^{1}825, #14, 2 October 1688, Boufflers to Louvois, in Ferguson, "Blood and Fire," 69.

69. This involved thirty battalions at Montroyal, Landau, and Belfort. Ferguson, "Blood and Fire," 63.

70. AG, A^{1}824, #125, 6 October 1688, Louvois to La Goupillière, in Ferguson, "Blood and Fire," 67.

71. AG, A^{1}825, #73, 10 October 1688, Louvois to La Grange, in Ferguson, "Blood and Fire," 70.

72. AG, A^{1}825, #23, 4 October 1688, Chamlay to Louvois, in Ferguson, "Blood and Fire," 69. It is very illustrative that this note was written from the besieging army's camp at Philippsburg. Chamlay clearly believed that even with the demands of the siege, he must plan for contributions.

73. AG, A^{1}825, #23, 4 October 1688, Chamlay to Louvois, in Ferguson, "Blood and Fire," 70.

74. AG, A^{1}826, #60, 23 October 1688, La Goupillière to Louvois, in Ferguson, "Blood and Fire," 74–75.

75. AG, A^{1}826, #30, 31, 19 October 1688, La Grange to Louvois, in Ferguson, "Blood and Fire," 72.

76. AG, A^{1}826, #79, 26 October 1688, Duras to Louvois, in Ferguson, "Blood and Fire," 79–80.

77. AG, $A^1$826, #77, 25 October 1688, La Goupillière to Louvois, in Ferguson, "Blood and Fire," 92.

78. AG, $A^1$829, 14 December 1688, Chamilly to Louvois, in Ferguson, "Blood and Fire," 94.

79. AG, $A^1$874, 14 December 1688, La Bretesche to Louvois, in Ferguson, "Blood and Fire," 100.

80. AG, $A^1$829, 6 December 1688, La Grange to Louvois, in Ferguson, "Blood and Fire," 101. For other complaints, see AG, $A^1$874, 4 January 1689, La Goupillière to Louvois, in Ferguson, "Blood and Fire," 101; AG, $A^1$875, 25 March 1689, La Goupillière to Louvois, from Mainz.

81. AG, $A^1$874, 18 February 1689, La Goupillière to Louvois, from Mainz, in Ferguson, "Blood and Fire," 105; AG, $A^1$875, 20 April 1689, La Goupillière to Louvois, from Mainz.

82. AG, $A^1$875, 9 March 1689, Huxelles to Louvois, from Mainz.

83. AG, $A^1$829, 28 December, d'Harcourt to Louvois, from Speyer, in Ferguson, "Blood and Fire," 110–11.

84. AG, $A^1$826, #93, 27 October 1688, Chamlay to Louvois, in Ferguson, "Blood and Fire," 83.

85. Quincy, *Histoire militaire*, 2:119.

86. This scandal involved the use of poisons by upper-class women to eliminate inconvenient family members and lovers. At the center, were several "witches" who dispensed the lethal goods. Luxembourg was not accused of using poisons, but he was charged with employing witchcraft. His incarceration and trial went on for months, and he was acquitted.

87. AG, $A^1$827, 9 November 1688, Chamlay to Louvois, in Rousset, *Louvois*, 4:162.

88. Andrew Lossky, "Some Problems of Tracing the Intellectual Development of Louis XIV, 1661–1715," in *Louis XIV and the Craft of Kingship*, ed. John Rule (Columbus OH, 1969), 321–22.

89. Lossky, "Some Problems of Tracing," 333.

90. Judging by Quincy, *Histoire militaire*, the French seemed relatively unconcerned with the moral aspect of the devastation of the Palatinate. Quincy devotes only two paragraphs to the subject in volume 2 (p. 167), while devoting thirty pages (175–204) to the siege of Mainz, which to Quincy clearly was an item of greater importance.

91. On 11 July 1683, Louvois ordered that since parties from Luxembourg had pillaged two villages, French troops were to pillage twenty in Limbourg. *Letters of Louvois*, ed. Jacques Hardré, University of North Carolina Studies in the Romance Languages and Literatures, no. 10 (Chapel Hill, 1949), 297. On 15 December 1683, Louvois ordered ten times the damage to be done to

the Spanish that they had inflicted on French, Hardré, *Letters of Louvois*, 327. On 24 October 1683, Louis ordered Humières to do twenty times as much to the Spanish as they did to the French. Louis XIV, *Oeuvres de Louis XIV*, ed. Philippe Grimoard and Philippe Grouvelle, 6 vols. (Paris, 1806), 4:26. Later, Louis ordered burning fifty houses or villages for every one the enemy burned, *Oeuvres* 4:270; AG, A¹722, #13–16, 24 October 1683, Louis ordered Humières to burn fifty houses or villages for every one the enemy burned on Louis' domains; on 26 October 1683, Louvois ordered Boufflers to do thirty times as much damage as the enemy did (Hardré, *Letters of Louvois*, 290–91); and on 2 January 1684, Louvois ordered Humières to burn one hundred times as much as the Spanish burned in executions (Hardré, *Letters of Louvois*, 336).

92. This is Wolf's conclusion. Wolf, *Louis XIV*, 420.

93. AG, A¹ 776, 9 May 1686, Catinat to Louvois, in Rousset, *Louvois*, 4:24.

94. Louis to the marquis d'Arcy, 8 November 1686, in Rousset, *Louvois*, 4:28.

95. "Otez-vous de l'esprit que vous ayez rien à ménager avec les Allemands, ni par amitié, ni par modération." Louvois in Corvisier, *Louvois*, 461.

96. *Balance française*, 178, in Gillot, *La règne de Louis XIV et l'opinion publique en Allemagne*, 190.

4

Liberation or Occupation?

Theory and Practice in the French Revolutionaries'
Treatment of Civilians outside France

T. C. W. Blanning

Relations between the French Revolution and the civilian population of Europe began in a mood of carefree optimism but soon turned into tragedy. The optimism was part and parcel of the revolutionaries' fundamental outlook, as expressed in the Declaration of the Rights of Man and the Citizen proclaimed by the National Assembly on 26 August 1789—not "the rights of *French* Man and the *French* Citizen," but the rights of all men and all citizens everywhere. This abstract, rational universalism underpinned the revolution's radically new political culture, which Lynn Hunt has defined as "the values, expressions, and implicit rules that expressed and shaped collective intentions and actions" and has lauded as "the chief accomplishment of the French Revolution."[1] Of the great revolutionary triad—liberty, equality, and fraternity—the last named advertised explicitly the brotherhood of mankind. It was in this spirit that a number of foreign luminaries such as Bentham, Schiller, Pestalozzi, Kosciuszko, and Washington were made honorary French citizens.

The implications for foreign civilians in their encounters with French armies seemed obvious. Any conflict between the new France and the *people* of another country was simply unthinkable. As the National Assembly stated on 22 May 1790 in its first programmatic statement on foreign relations: "the French nation renounces the undertaking of any war with a view to making conquests, and affirms that it will never use its power against the liberty of any other people."[2] Of course, that did not rule out war altogether, but it did mean that the revolutionaries were making a clear distinction between their attitude toward the rulers of Europe and their subjects (see map 4.1). So when the hawks in the new Legislative Assembly, which met for the first time on 1 October 1791, began to press for war with Austria, they were insistent that their quarrel was only with the Habsburg emperor and his evil advisers. Indeed, one of their most potent arguments was based on the premise that the oppressed peoples of Europe were only waiting for the arrival of a French army to rise in revolt against their old regimes and to fraternize with their liberators. The leader of the war party, Jacques-Pierre Brissot, made the point most eloquently in his celebrated speech of 29 December 1791:

> The French Revolution has turned diplomacy upside down. Although the common people of the various nations are not yet free, they do pull some weight in the political balance because now kings have to take their opinions into account. The British people are all in favor of the French Revolution, and the British government will have to pay attention to what they think. In almost all the provinces of the Habsburg Monarchy there is seething unrest that announces imminent insurrection. In Belgium the bitter hatred of the Austrians can end in only one way—with the total victory of liberty, and the best way to accelerate this process would be a war. War with France would lead inevitably to a collapse of discipline in the Austrian army. If the Emperor Leopold does begin a war against us, then we shall appeal to the fraternal feelings of his subjects.[3]

During the initial stages of the war, which began on 20 April 1792, the question of how to treat foreign civilians remained academic, for the first French attempt to invade Belgium (the Austrian Netherlands) was a fiasco. It was not until the autumn, after the Austro-Prussian invasion had been checked at the battle of Valmy on 20 September and the revolutionary armies went on the offensive that the problem became acute. It appeared to have been resolved by the celebrated "Edict of Fraternity" passed by the National Convention on 19 November, which declared in the name of the French nation that "it will grant fraternity and assistance to all peoples who wish to recover their liberty, and instructs the Executive Power to give the necessary orders to the generals to grant assistance to these peoples and to defend those citizens who have been—or may be—persecuted for their attachment to the cause of liberty. The National Convention further decrees that the Executive Power shall order the generals to have this decree printed

Map 4.1. Europe, 1796

and distributed in all the various languages and in the various countries of which they have taken possession."[4] Far from making war on
foreign civilians, the revolutionaries intended to liberate them. It was
with the memorable slogan *Guerre aux châteaux, paix aux chaumières!*
that the revolutionary armies poured over the frontiers.

It was at this point that a contradiction inherent in the Revolution's
political culture became apparent. As François Furet has shown, it was
undermined by two related problems: first, there was a highly unsta-
ble marriage between liberal individualism and the unitarian concept
of national sovereignty, and, second, the revolutionary definition of
the nation was more restrictive than it seemed because it excluded the
privileged.[5] Only if everyone everywhere freely took the same decisions would these theoretical fault lines remain hidden.

It was not to be. On 15 December 1792, less than one month after the Fraternity Edict, the National Convention issued another decree, this time concerning how the newly liberated territories were to be governed. It starkly revealed the contradictions that were to plague the Revolution's relations with the civilian population of Europe. The first few articles were impeccably liberationist, ordering the abolition of "feudalism" in all its various forms; the introduction of "peace, succor, fraternity, liberty and equality"; and the organization of elections to establish a new regime. However, it was also decreed that no one would be allowed to vote who had not taken an oath to embrace revolutionary ideology and that "The French nation declares that it will treat as an enemy any people that refuses to accept liberty and equality and seeks to keep, recall, or compromise with their old princes and privileged orders." Perhaps more ominous still was the news that "The Executive Power will send commissars to liaise with the generals on the best means of clothing and feeding the French armies, and of raising the money necessary to pay for its upkeep." As Georges Lefebvre wrote, this decree "instituted the dictatorship of revolutionary minorities under the protection of French bayonets, and undertook to secure the fortunes of other peoples, without consulting them, at their expense."[6]

It was with a mixture of anger and surprise that the revolutionaries made the discovery that most of the Belgians and Germans they had sought to liberate did not wish to be forced to be free. When elections were held in accordance with the 15 December decree, it was only through intimidation that even a small number of voters could be induced to take the necessary oath and vote. At Aachen, so an eyewitness recorded, the electors meeting in the Capuchin church refused six times to obey the summons to vote. Losing patience, General Dampierre then led 350 soldiers into the church to lend his seventh summons additional authority. It did not have the desired effect. An intrepid young man jumped up and shouted (in French) "You can aim your cannons at us, and you can mow us down, but you cannot force us to exchange our true liberty for a chimera." The assembly then elected unanimously and derisively as their new mayor an elderly beggar sitting outside the church. More troops were brought in to purge the assembly until just twenty to thirty collaborators were left.[7] It was ironic that the first use of force employed by the French armies against civilians was to make them vote the right way.

Disillusionment led swiftly to a change of policy. With the war going badly in the spring of 1793 and France once again threatened by invasion, the National Convention formally abrogated the Fraternity Edict after less than five months. Following Danton's appeal that "above all else we need to look to the preservation of our own body politic and to lay the foundations of *French* greatness," it was decided on 13 April 1793 that never again would the French nation seek to interfere in the domestic affairs of another state. From now on it was to be revolution in one country.[8]

What was more, the French people had demonstrated that of all the peoples of Europe only they were mature enough to appreciate the benefits of liberty, equality, and fraternity. As Robespierre told the National Convention in May 1794: "The French people seem to have outstripped the rest of the human race by two thousand years," adding that one was tempted to conclude that they now constituted an entirely new species.[9] This conviction was shared by the military men in the occupied regions. General Dampierre found the perfect metaphor for the recalcitrant citizens of Aachen: "You are just too backward to be able to appreciate the true concept of divine liberty. You will have to be treated like an invalid who has to be forced by his friends to undergo a painful but necessary operation."[10] When this sense of superiority collided with the particularist loyalties of occupied Europe, the result was deep contempt. Reporting from Naples in 1798, a French commissar told Bonaparte: "I have to tell you, General, that the idea of a revolution made in Italy by Italians horrifies me. There would just be no end to the chaos created by passion and ignorance. . . . In Italy, there is nothing but hatred for France. Lombardy regards us with abhorrence, Genoa likes us no better, Rome loathes us; the common people are decadent and degenerate."[11] Bonaparte's own abrasive verdict on the Italians was "effeminate and corrupt, as cowardly as they are hypocritical."[12]

The turn away from universalism was accelerated by the fall of Brissot and his colleagues in June 1793. Robespierre and his colleagues then adopted a much more hardheaded approach to the exploitation of occupied territories. Ironically, it had been Robespierre who had produced two perceptive insights on the likely conduct of the rest of Europe when he vainly tried to halt the war party during the winter of 1791–1792, namely: "Liberty cannot be exported on the points of bayonets" and "No one loves armed missionaries."[13] Now that he was in charge, however, he was ready to pursue the war *à outrance*. On 15 September 1793, the National Convention decreed that "the generals commanding the forces of the Republic on land and sea, renouncing from henceforth every philanthropic idea previously adopted by the French people with the intention of making foreign nations appreciate the value and benefits of liberty, will behave toward the enemies of France in just the same way that the powers of the coalition have behaved toward them; and they [the French generals] will exercise with regard to the countries and individuals conquered by their armies the customary rights of war."[14]

Within the space of less than eighteen months, in other words, the French revolutionaries had ceased to regard foreign civilians as oppressed slaves waiting to be liberated and now saw them rather as resources to be exploited. When seeking to explain this process, it is important to bear in mind that the revolutionaries believed they were fighting a war quite different from anything in the past. The rhetoric of the hawks that eventually attracted almost unanimous support for the war (only 7 deputies out of 745 voted against) laid great emphasis on the impending conflict as a Manichaean struggle between absolute good and absolute evil, a final showdown between old and new. It was with cries of "total victory or death" that the Brissotin deputies brought their audience to its feet.[15]

Once the war was underway, this passionate conviction meant that unless a quick victory could be achieved, the war would be very difficult to stop. Especially after they had executed Louis XVI (21 January 1793), the revolutionaries had burned their boats. So important was their cause that *anything* could be done to ensure its victory. The crucial moment was 23 August 1793 when the National Convention mobilized every last man, woman, child, animal, and inanimate object in France for the war effort. This is usually referred to as "the *levée en masse*," but it should really be called "the declaration of total war." It also represented the liberation of the state from those former constraints of law, custom, and religion that had restrained its ambition. The implication for foreign civilians is obvious: if the regime could call on its own people for every last ounce of effort, then how much more could they demand from the subjects of its enemies?

This pressure from the revolutionary decision makers was intensified by a fundamental imbalance between revolutionary ambitions and revolutionary resources. On the last occasion that France had established hegemony in Europe, under Louis XIV, she had been clearly the most populous, the most prosperous, and the best administered state in Europe. One hundred years later she was none of those things. As her population had increased by only 30 percent in the course of the century, her "demographic primacy was over," as Pierre Goubert neatly put it.[16] By the spring of 1793, the Revolution was at war with most of the rest of Europe—the Habsburg monarchy, Prussia, Great Britain, the United Provinces, the Holy Roman Empire, Spain, the Kingdom of the Two Sicilies, and Sardinia-Piedmont—and so was outnumbered many times over. Moreover, the Revolution had inherited bankruptcy from the old regime and was facing the monumental task of reconstructing the country's administration from scratch.

Just to survive in the face of these odds was an extraordinary achievement, then to conquer most of western and southern Europe was truly phenomenal. But there was a terrible price in overexertion to be paid—and it was mainly charged to the account of foreign civilians. As William McNeill has written: "After their first victories, the armies then moved onto foreign soil. From that time onward, the costs of their support devolved largely upon populations outside French borders; economic recovery within France and return to a market system for supplying urban centers with food became possible once again."[17] The *levée en masse* of 1793 created an army of at least three-quarters of a million and possibly more.[18] This great horde, the largest in the history of the Europe until that point, could not have been sustained from the domestic resources of France—*even if* a stable government had been able to tap the country's resources to the full. There was only one way out, and it was identified by the Committee of Public Safety on the very day that the National Convention abandoned its previous "philanthropic" attitude (15 September 1793): "One of the first principles of the conduct of war is to nourish war by war."

This account of the development of French policy between 1789 and the autumn of 1793 demonstrates the limitations of approaching the subject through revolutionary theory and government policy. It would have made little sense to Belgian or German civilians, who had felt exploited from the start. The very first French troops to cross the eastern frontier did so on 9 September 1792, when they occupied briefly the small town of Merzig on the Moselle in the electorate of Trier—and looted it.[19] In the words of John Lynn's bleak epigram: "Pillage, like death, arrives hand in hand with war," and never more so than during the 1790s.[20] Plundering by French soldiers became the most obtrusive, ubiquitous, constant—and hated—feature of revolutionary warfare. There is no room for doubt on this score, as there is a mountain of evidence from every possible different quarter: from those on the receiving end, from the looters themselves, from their commanding officers, and from the political commissars accompanying the French armies. The archives of the war ministry at Vincennes are stuffed with day-to-day accounts of the latter's depredations as they swept across Europe.[21]

To convey some impression of the scale and intensity of the suffering this inflicted, the following provides one example of each of the categories mentioned:

Our people have been attacked and robbed on the streets, and our women have even had their scarves torn from their necks. Cellar doors have been smashed and the barrels stove in; what the soldiers could not drink, they allowed to gush away on the ground. They have forced their way into homes and stolen money. The hovels of the poor have been spared no more than the homes of the well-off. (The town council of Zweibrücken to the commissar attached to the army of the Moselle, November 1793)[22]

The 14th company lacked any discipline, and all the soldiers were thieves. Every night we went off looting potatoes; I was sorry I got mixed up in this pillaging, which was all the more inexcusable because we never lacked supplies. (French soldier of the Army of the Rhine, June 1794)[23]

What upsets me most in all this is the behavior of the soldiers. They are laying the country waste, they are looting, they are stealing—everywhere there is devastation. (Lieutenant Villiers of the Sambre-et-Meuse army, September 1795)[24]

Everything that we hear of Custine's army, camped between Mainz and Landau, fills us with horror. It is nothing but thieving, dereliction of duty, and corruption on every side. (Commissars Simon and Grégoire, reporting from Strasbourg, January 1793)[25]

More important for our purposes, however, are the explanations of what contemporaries clearly perceived to be the special character of revolutionary looting. They are not difficult to summarize: the French armies were much larger than anything seen in the past, they were worse provisioned from their own resources (indeed, they were usually not provisioned at all), they had no money, and they lacked discipline. The combination was best summed up by the artilleryman Bricard in his diary: "as we received no victuals, we were obliged to live from pillaging."[26] In fact, the French soldiers looted for profit just as vigorously as they did for survival, selling or even just spoiling what they did not need for themselves. It is not difficult to imagine why a fighting man, living in daily fear of a violent death, should allow normal ethical standards to lapse. This was well put by another French soldier, reflecting in his memoirs on a crime he now felt guilty about: "If I were to judge our action today, I should find it reprehensible; but at the time it seemed entirely legitimate. We found ourselves in enemy territory, and it seemed to us that everything belonged to us by right of conquest, a right hallowed by time, however abominable and monstrous it may be."[27]

There was little danger that the exercise of that "right" would be interrupted by the authorities. Certainly, there were many officers who were ashamed and indignant about the conduct of their men, not least because of the military problems it created. Of the rich selection of despairing pleas for better behavior, the following *cri de coeur* from General Kléber, commanding the right wing of the Sambre et Meuse in the autumn of 1796, must suffice:

> It is with amazement matched only by sorrow that I learn of the presence among my troops of people who seem to want to make the French name accursed by their despicable and ferocious behavior. There can be no doubt that it is just these men whose criminal excesses on the right bank of the Rhine have made the local population there so bitterly opposed to us and have given them no choice but to take up arms against us and to oppose force with force, as they have been stripped of everything save the hope of exacting revenge

before they die for the rape of their wives and daughters, the burning of their homes, the theft of their livestock, and so on.[28]

There was little Kléber or any of his colleagues could do. Gone were the days when the rank and file were supposed to fear their officers more than the enemy and could expect brutal and summary punishment for indiscipline. It was partly for his allegedly excessive and "aristocratic" attention to good order that General Custine was sent to the guillotine in 1793. The new attitude was well summed up by Robespierre: "Indiscipline! This word, parroted in such an odious fashion by aristocratic and Machiavellian forces, is nothing more than a constant accusation leveled against the civic virtues of the citizen-soldiers who began the Revolution."[29] The soldier of the Revolution was also a citizen, entitled under the new disciplinary code to a judicial hearing, representation by counsel, trial by a jury consisting partly of men of the same rank as himself, and the right of appeal. Of course, that could not work in wartime. John Lynn's verdict on the Armée du Nord can be extended to include all the other armed forces: "The evolution of discipline and military justice never succeeded in eliminating the disorder or misconduct of French forces." After a unit in Belgium in the spring of 1793 had shown more enthusiasm for looting than official military operations, Carnot bluntly told the Committee of Public Safety: "If every soldier who steals as much as a pin is not shot on the spot, you will never accomplish anything."[30]

It was the appreciation that indiscipline had harmful military effects as much as concern for the civilians that prompted government and officers to try to maintain order. Every now and again a really determined general such as Custine in 1792 or Jourdan in 1794 set an example by having a few culprits shot, but they were always fighting a losing battle.[31] Part of the problem, to which the despairing authorities often referred, was that the officers themselves relied on what their men could steal to keep body and soul together. Higher up the military hierarchy, the generals celebrated the general relaxation of civilian control that followed the coup d'état of 9 Thermidor (27 July 1794) and the end of Robespierre's reign of terrorist virtue by helping themselves to the spoils of war. In the autumn of 1796, Commissar Haussmann reported to Paris that "the pen falls from my hand" as he tried to describe the looting that was going on in Germany by all ranks: it was now more difficult to find the innocent than the guilty, and no prosecutions were possible because all the prisons of the republic would not be large enough to hold the offenders.[32]

The military commanders of the old regime had also liked to live well on campaign. On the eve of the Revolution, Louis Sébastien Mercier jeered that, in the event of war, French officers feared danger less than deprivation of their luxuries. Alleging that in the Seven Years' War the generals had even insisted on Seine water being sent to the front for their coffee, he coined the sour epigram that a French officer would rather lay down his life than give up his *équipage*.[33] But whereas these sybarites had been able to have the good things of life sent from home, their revolutionary successors had to make do with what they found locally. On arrival in a foreign town, the first thing a general did was to issue a long shopping list to the local authorities. In September 1796, the town council of Koblenz complained that General Poncet had demanded a one-off delivery of nine hundred bottles of wine and a *daily* delivery of twenty-four flagons of white wine and twelve of red, six bottles of champagne and four of Malaga, twelve lemons, "several bottles" of Arak, two sugar loaves, four pounds of coffee, twenty pounds of beef, ten pounds of venison, six dozen eggs, fifty pounds of mutton, appropriate quantities of butter, fresh fruit, and so on and so forth.[34] No wonder that the citizens of Bonn complained that one French general and his staff cost three times more than their former prince (the Elector of Cologne) and his court.[35]

A frequently voiced objection to freelance looting, whether committed by generals or common soldiers, was the need to keep all foreign resources intact for official exploitation. The Revolution had been born in bankruptcy and never became solvent. Not even the nationalization of the lands of the crown, church, and émigrés — the *biens nationaux* — was equal to the bottomless pit of expenditure that the war quickly became. Far from solving the regime's financial problems, as the hawks had promised, the war made them critical.[36] The increasingly reckless printing of paper money — the *assignats* — reached a wonderfully fitting climax on 19 October 1795 when the floor of the printing house collapsed under their weight.[37] In short, there was never any prospect of the government being able to supply the armies at the front with the basic necessities of life. They were on their own, encouraged to live off the land they had conquered, to "nourish war with war."[38] As Alan Forrest has put it in his excellent recent study of the revolutionary armies: "By 1793, there was no way that French agriculture could feed the men fighting in the revolutionary armies, even had the government wished it to do so, and in September, the Committee of Public Safety ordered its commanders to procure the food stocks they needed, as well as supplies of clothing, arms, equipment, and transport, from the peoples of the occupied territories. As far as was possible, the war would in future be fought and paid for by the defeated nations, and it would be their responsibility to maintain and supply those of the armies deployed outside France."[39]

In other words, hard on the heels of pillaging soldiers came requisitioning commissars. Indeed, they often arrived together. Concerned above all to feed their armies, the generals ordered vigorous requisitions. A good example was provided by Hoche in January 1794 when he told his divisional commanders: "You are in a rich country; that is all you need to be told: requisition, don't wait for the needs of the poor sansculotte to show themselves, anticipate them—he will love you for it as a result. And if he feels that way toward you, you are sure to be victorious. . . . Have as much seized as possible. Begin with food, then cloth, leather, and linen. The grain is to be taken to Landau, the other items to headquarters, so that it can be sent on to the interior."[40]

Perhaps the best definition of requisitions was supplied by Charles-Alexis Alexandre, a commissar with the Sambre-et-Meuse army in 1794: "What is meant by this word 'requisitions'? It is the right exercised by the strong over the weak, by the victor over the vanquished, to make the latter provide the products of the conquered territory and the private luxuries of its people to satisfy the needs, whims, and pleasures of the former." He went on to argue that during the early stages of an invasion it was natural and inevitable that the armies would have to live off the land, but when requisitions became a permanent system of exploitation it was "an affliction that covered the land and laid it waste."[41]

The favored technique was to assemble the notables of the community, present them with a list of requirements to be supplied within a short space of time, and either take a number of hostages to encourage compliance or impose billeting. It was always official policy that the poor should be spared and the rich fleeced (especially the clergy and aristocrats among them), but it proved very difficult to implement. As so often, the best of intentions were constantly frustrated by the immediate needs of the army. Unfortunately, most of the rich foreigners did not wait to be fleeced but fled from the front to the interior, together with all their portable valuables. In their absence, the burden fell on the middling sort and the poor—just the classes that might have been expected to respond most favorably to revolutionary ideology. As an Augustinian friar of Cologne recorded in his diary in January 1796: "although this enemy of our country declared peace to the cottages and war to the châteaux, he oppresses the poor with special severity. Their houses are filled with his soldiers, who also have to be kept in victuals."[42]

A large army on the move, with no recourse to supplies from home, needed to raise locally an extraordinary variety of articles. The following list, compiled from requisitions made in the northern Rhineland in 1794, will give some impression of the voracity of the French military machine: bandages, beans, beds, bed linen, beetroot, bells, blankets, boats, boots, buttons, cabbage, cinnamon, cloaks, cloth (of every conceivable kind), cocoa, coffee, cooking pots, copper, currants, dye, fire appliances, gaiters, ginger, hats, hay, hemp, honey, hops, household utensils, indigo, ink, iron, juniper, lead, leather, mattresses, meat, medicine, nails, oats, office furniture, paper, peas, pens, pepper, pickaxes, potash, rice, rye, sailcloth, salt, shirts, shoes, shovels, soap, stockings, straw, tin, vinegar, weapons, wheelbarrows, wine, wool and yachts.[43]

Most in demand, of course, were draught animals and livestock—and the forage necessary to feed them. Especially for the poorer peasants, the loss of a cow could mean the difference between subsistence and starvation. So when, for example, the French took every fifth cow from the Münstereifel region in October 1794, they condemned many of its inhabitants to penury.[44] Of course, they were well aware of the damage they were causing but protested that they could do no other. As Commissar Gillet ruefully conceded in August 1795, it was very harmful to requisition horses at harvest time—but the war could not be fought without artillery and ammunition.[45] Unable to supply more than a fraction from domestic resources, the French appetite for draught animals was insatiable. In June 1796, Commissar Haussmann announced an order from Paris to requisition *every* horse on the occupied left bank of the Rhine that was suitable for use in the cavalry, for transport, or for artillery.[46] Since many of the animals requisitioned were not used for military purposes at all but promptly sold for cash by corrupt commissars or soldiers and since many of the remainder died of neglect, passive resistance to requisitions was dogged. Yet in the face of the dreaded punitive billeting (*Exekution*), all the peasants on the receiving end could do was to remove their livestock to the forests, a solution that could work only in the very short term.[47]

It was not enough to be penniless to avoid the pressure of requisitions, for labor was also conscripted to build fortifications, to widen and strengthen roads, to transport supplies, and to perform a thousand and one menial tasks, from making boots (with requisitioned leather) to herding requisitioned sheep (with the assistance of requisitioned sheepdogs). Typical of the complaints that flooded in was the doleful account of the conditions between the Meuse and the Rhine written by a local official at Kempen in November 1796.[48] The need to provide forced labor for work on batteries, fortifications, and the new roads, he maintained, was proving the most onerous of all the many burdens of war. For the past four months, the district had been obliged to provide each day one hundred laborers and thirty carts. Incessant backbreaking toil in all weathers had broken the health of many. To make matters worse, the French supervisors were deliberately spinning out the work to prolong the benefits they enjoyed from racketeering, intercepting the meat rations intended for the workers, selling exemptions, and the like. Only recently, a young man "of good family" had been killed by a saber blow from a French soldier while working on the road from Neuss to Brühl.

The effect the immediate demands for forced labor had on relations between the French armies and the foreign civilians in their path can easily be imagined. The Protestant pastor at Steinen near Lörrach recorded in his diary in July 1796 that when the French had arrived earlier that summer relations with the local people were initially quite good. The trouble began when forced labor was exacted: "Every day 1,800 workers have to present themselves for work on the fortifications. This mass of people is ordered around, tyrannized, sworn at, flogged, and generally maltreated in the most disgraceful manner by a handful of French soldiers, many of whom are just boys. But everyone has to keep quiet and bow his neck humbly and obediently to the iron yoke of the long-awaited liberty. Moreover, it is all arranged for the extortion of money—anyone who turns up late or works badly is fined."[49] There was no redress. In the following month, at Lörrach itself, the local official, Hugo by name, was unwise enough to lodge a protest against General Tuncq's demand for two thousand laborers equipped with five hundred picks and fifteen hundred shovels to march off to work on the fortifications at Huningue in Alsace. As Hugo pointed out, to remove what amounted to one-fifteenth of the district's total population at harvest time spelled economic ruin. On receipt of this remonstrance, General Tuncq went round with a force of dragoons, rousted Hugo from his bed in the middle of the night, personally thrashed him to the accompaniment of shouts of "*bougre, coquin*," and packed him off to prison at Huningue.[50]

Anyone with a roof over his or her head was also liable to billeting. As was noted earlier, the original intention to make war only on the châteaux and to spare the cottages had foundered on the mobility of wealth. However fast they may have been in comparison with the lethargic Austrians or Prussians, the French could not help but give advance warning of their arrival. So the rich and privileged had plenty of time to gather up their portable possessions and flee to safety. It was the ordinary people who could not afford to leave, and it was on them that the main burden of housing their uninvited guests fell. At Bonn in October 1794, the arrival of the French army meant that *every* household in the city was affected by billeting.[51] In March of the following year, the town was so full that it was estimated that every house was entertaining at least four soldiers.[52] The numbers involved could be considerable. Georg Ludwig Firmond, a merchant at Saarbrücken, recorded in his diary that in May 1794 he was playing host to five officers, a female camp follower, a servant, and sixteen private soldiers.[53] Living as he did on one of the main invasion routes into Germany, billeting became a regular affliction for the wretched Firmond. His entries for the year 1797 show that French soldiers were billeted on him constantly throughout the year.[54] Billeting was also a problem inside France, of course, as the villagers of Villeneuve-sur-Vannes in the Haut-Sâone memorably pointed out when they complained that between 1 January and 1 September 1794 they had been obliged to house troops on no fewer than seventy-two occasions.[55]

It was not only soldiers who had to be housed and fed. One of the last orders issued by General Hoche before his sudden death in the summer of 1797 was to complain about "a second army" of rapacious civilians who had flowed into the occupied regions to have themselves housed, fed, and often paid as well by the communities they battened on. Often outnumbering the soldiers, they claimed to be "administrators" or "agents," but in reality most of them had no official status. He ordered the institution of official passes, but it may be doubted whether this made much impact.[56] Certainly, the same sort of complaints were still being made several years later.[57] Whether those billeted were civilians or military personnel, the temptation to indulge their appetites at the expense of their hosts proved irresistible for many, if not most. One example of the innumerable complaints must suffice. A citizen of Frankfurt am Main recorded in his diary on 2 August 1796: "Today at twelve noon two squadrons of cavalry were billeted in the inns in the Friedberg alley, at the cost of the city. They behaved so badly that the publicans and all their staff either ran away or hid themselves. The bill for what the soldiers consumed and the damage they caused amounted to 1,500 gulden."[58]

In short, only someone who was destitute, homeless, and physically incapacitated could expect to escape scot-free from the demands of the French military. Yet even these unfortunates suffered indirectly, for the invaders destroyed traditional sources of charitable relief without finding an alternative. When they expropriated the churches, closed monasteries, expelled religious orders, and confiscated the stocks of *monts de piété*, they also hit the poorest hardest.[59] The result was a rapid increase in destitution. In 1795, it was estimated that between 20,000 and 30,000 out of the 60,000 inhabitants of Brussels were destitute, 16,000 out of 55,000 at Ghent, 5,543 out of 25,000 at Malines, and so on. During the terrible winter of that year, the dread word *mortalité* was again in circulation. At Verviers, for example, 3,000 out of a total population of around 9,000 succumbed to malnutrition and hypothermia.[60] Conditions were the same in Germany. On Christmas Day 1797, a supporter of the French, Mathias Metternich, published a devastating critique of the French occupation in his newspaper, in the course of which he claimed that it was no exaggeration to state that more than half of the inhabitants had been reduced to despair. In the following month, he reported the case of Friedrich Schober, who had cut the throats of his wife, daughter, and infant son before killing himself and leaving the following suicide note: "I did not commit these murders out of wickedness but because of my love for my wife and children, and to prevent them being reduced to begging: for it is hard, it is very hard, that I should have lost all of my possessions because of the war and can no longer provide my family with a home or a roof over their heads.—Pray for my wife and children, and for me too: it is a terrible thing to have sacrifice one's own son."[61]

This review of relations between French armies and foreign civilians in the 1790s makes it clear that the violence resulted primarily from the paramount need of the army to survive. Where the local population was able and willing to deliver money, food, and any other articles their conquerors demanded, some sort of coexistence could be achieved. The acts of vandalism, drunkenness, rape, assault, and theft perpetrated by individual soldiers were frequent but fortuitous—it was never official policy to terrorize the population gratuitously. Refusal or inability to pay a levy or to supply requisitioned goods was punished by arrests, hostage taking, or punitive billeting, but coercion was always used selectively. The real trouble started when local civilians retaliated against their despoliation by organizing themselves into guerrilla bands.

It was then that the heavy hand of the French came down with all its irresistible force. It was rare that a community failed to learn the lesson that open confrontation with disciplined firepower could end in only one way. In May 1796, for example, a great horde of peasants, variously estimated at five to six thousand and thirty to forty thousand, massed around Pavia, took control of the city, and drove out the French and their collaborators. Retribution was not long coming. When General Bonaparte's army ran into the insurgent forces at Binasco, not only were those who could not run away fast enough slaughtered but the town was burned to the ground for good measure. As a reward, Bonaparte handed over to the victors the main prize of Pavia and its inhabitants for an orgy of rape and looting.[62]

From one end of Europe to the other, direct action by civilians was punished swiftly and brutally. For example, in the Saar region in July 1794 the village of Edesheim was burned down after shots had been fired at French soldiers passing through. In the same month, the small town of Kusel was fired "to serve as an example in this evil region, where the local people have taken up arms against us," as Commissar Hentz put it. In October 1795, a group of peasants at Westhofen near Cologne attacked a barge that had been blown ashore, killing or wounding its French occupants; General Grenier promptly had the village burned to the ground. Throughout the retreat from Franconia during the summer of 1796, the Sambre-et-Meuse army torched villages whenever fired on by guerrillas.[63] Such episodes could be multiplied, if not ad infinitum, then certainly ad nauseam.

A more ambivalent form of resistance to the French was banditry. Always endemic in the heavily wooded regions of the Low Countries and the Rhineland, it flourished during times of war and never more so than during the 1790s. One of the most prominent of the "German Jacobins," A. G. F. Rebmann, offered the following cogent explanation of its intensification:

> Every protracted war, every conquest, and every revolution affecting whole countries have occasioned not only the large-scale dramatic upheavals that change the very composition of great states but also have brought changes that may be less striking but have just as dire consequences for individual sections of the population. In times such as these, all social order is dissolved and force alone rules; every hope of earning a living from peaceful trade and from one's honest labor is destroyed; lawfully gained resources are expropriated; fortune smiles on the intrepid and daring outlaw, and many men are forced to become first beggars and then, out of despair, criminals.[64]

Long-term population pressure and pauperization certainly accounted for some of the increase in violent crime during the period, but the connection with the French invasion is unmistakable. This can be shown in several ways. First, the bandits sought to intimidate the communities they raided by pretending to be French soldiers, shouting out in what they hoped would pass for French and singing the "Marseillaise." Second, they used French depredations to justify their resort to crime, as did Johann Müller, for example, when he told his interrogators that it had been the gang rape of his wife by a group of soldiers that had turned him into an outlaw. Third, and most important, they traded on the unpopularity of the invaders to win the support of the local communities. As the department of the Sarre pointed out in 1799 when bemoaning their failure to control banditry, "whatever measures are taken to purge these regions, they will all be in vain so long as the bandits continue to find refuge among—and indeed support from—the rural population, whom they take great care to cultivate by claiming to rob only Jews."[65]

None was more adroit at manipulating wartime conditions than the legendary bandit "Schinderhannes," the sobriquet of Johannes Bückler, the German Robin Hood. From 1797 until his eventual capture in 1802, he and his gang roamed the central Rhineland with impunity, supporting themselves with highway robbery, horse stealing, cattle rustling, and burglary. If he had not enjoyed at least the tacit support of the local people, his career would have been over in a matter of months, as the French themselves complained. As it was, he managed to project the not entirely unjustified image of a "social bandit" who spared the peasants and preyed only on Jews and French. As one commentator observed: "it is a characteristic of the region in which the bandits are based that these two nations [the Jews and the French] are hated. So crimes against them are motivated not just by a wish to rob them but also by a variety of fanaticism that is partly political and partly religious."[66] By the time he was captured and guillotined, "Schinderhannes" had become a legend in his own lifetime throughout Central Europe.

So had his slightly older contemporary, Michele Pezza or "Fra Diavolo," who has achieved even greater posthumous fame thanks to a Dumas novel (Dumas père was in command of the French task force that eventually tracked him down), an Auber opera, and a Laurel and Hardy film. He already had two murders to his credit when he escaped from penal service in the Neapolitan army in 1797 and took to the hills. His counterrevolutionary credentials were established by the murder of his father by Polish soldiers serving in the French army that sacked his home town of Itri in 1799. Fra Diavolo took revenge by forming a coalition of bandit gangs to harass the French occupying force to the north of Naples, thus accelerating the collapse of the short-lived "Neapolitan Republic."[67] Although by far the most famous, he was only one of scores of Italian bandits who formed the sharp end of civilian resistance to the French. In the papal states too, banditry intensified with the breakdown of law and order in the wake of the French armies.[68]

If banditry supplies ambiguous evidence of the fate of civilians in the path of revolutionary war, since it thrived both before and after the French invasions, unalloyed counterrevolutionary risings do not. So tenacious is the belief in the essential benevolence of the French Revolution that it is not often appreciated just how widespread and deep was the active resistance it provoked. Even in those regions that were directly "reunited" to France, Lafayette's optimistic forecast, made in July 1789, that the Revolution would "go around the world" was disproved. In the new Belgian departments annexed in 1795, for example, discontent fueled by a potent brew of economic deprivation and religious persecution made life difficult for the French authorities throughout this period. Their dismissal of the Belgians as "imbecilic and fanatical idiots" or simply as "enemies" was heartily reciprocated by the objects of their contempt.[69] Growing hostility eventually erupted in the "Peasants War" of 1798, triggered by the imposition of conscription.[70] Combined with the "Klöppelkrieg" in neighboring Luxembourg, the insurgents kept a large French army at full stretch during the autumn and early winter.

South of the Alps, the triumphant progress of General Bonaparte and the Army of Italy was punctuated by violent resistance to their exactions. Particularly revealing was the episode at Lugo, in the papal province of Ferrara at the end of June 1796. With a population of some sixteen thousand, Lugo was prosperous, fiscally privileged, conservative, and fiercely loyal to the Pope. So when the familiar commissars arrived to organize a levy and to impose requisitions, a clash could not be long delayed. Not for the first or last time in Italy, it was sparked off by the confiscation of a religious symbol, in this case the statue of Saint Ilaro, the town's patron saint. After they had taken it back by force and paraded it through the streets, the insurgents issued an appeal to the other communities of the Romagna, calling on them to rise against the French "in defense of their protectors the Saints, their sovereign, their state, and their fatherland." Despite the best efforts of the bishop of Imola, Cardinal Chiaramonti (the future Pope Pius VII), to prevent the inevitable retribution, on 6 July there was a bloody encounter that forced the French to retreat, leaving two hundred dead and many more wounded, including the commander, General Pourailly. As at Binasco two months earlier, a terrible revenge was exacted. General Augereau now brought up a major force, forced his way past obstinate resistance into the city, and proceeded to lay it waste, allowing his soldiers to do with it as they liked for twenty-four hours. It was enough. When they eventually withdrew to the north to meet a new Austrian advance, all that was left of Lugo was a smoking ruin.[71]

The French revolutionary armies were most at risk from civilian attack when they were retreating. It was then that their needs were greatest, that they misbehaved most spectacularly—and that civilians became foolish or brave enough to ignore previous retribution. So in 1796 in Germany and in 1799 in Italy there were many bloody confrontations. There is a particularly good account by artilleryman Bricard of the retreat of the Sambre-et-Meuse in 1796 that brings out well the harrowing cycle of deprivation, violence, and counterviolence. When news of the French advance across the Rhine reached them, all the inhabitants of the right bank took to their heels, seeking refuge for themselves, their livestock, and their property in the forests. Finding only deserted villages, the soldiers retaliated by burning what they could not loot. So when, later in the year, the defeated army began to retreat back across Germany to the Rhine the peasants were waiting to exact a terrible revenge on stragglers and the wounded, which only led to more villages being put to the torch and the sword. Bricard was an eyewitness to one pathetic incident when a dozen peasants appeared at the head of his convoy, thinking that it was an Austrian force and boasting to the commander of the large number of *carmagnoles* they had just massacred. When asked who had actually done the killing, they all rushed forward to claim the credit—and were duly shot out of hand.[72]

For military historians, the news that the armies of the French Revolution looted, raped, murdered, requisitioned, levied, conscripted forced labor, and caused general mayhem will not be surprising. The armies of the old regime did all those things as well. What was special about the French was the size of their armies, their lack of resources, and their lack of discipline. Above all, perhaps, it was the discrepancy between promise and reality that caused the most offense. They came as self-proclaimed liberators, but they behaved like conquerors. This was not because their national character was fatally flawed (as many Germans liked to believe), nor was it because their ideology was essentially evil (as counterrevolutionaries liked to believe). Their failure to liberate rather than exploit, to spare the *chaumières* while sacking the *châteaux*, derived from the nature of revolutionary warfare. No one grasped this better than Clausewitz, who deserves the last word: "When the French Revolution suddenly brought a national army back on the stage of war, the governments' means were no longer adequate. . . . The French revolutionary leaders cared little for depots and less for devising a complicated mechanism that would keep all sections of the transport system running like clockwork. They sent their soldiers into the field and drove their generals into battle—feeding, reinforcing, and stimulating their armies by having them procure, steal, and loot everything they needed."[73]

Notes

1. Lynn Hunt, *Politics, Culture and Class in the French Revolution* (London, 1986), 3, 15.

2. *Archives Parlementaires de 1787 à 1860: Recueil Complet des Débats Législatifs et Politiques des Chambres Françaises* (Paris, 1883), 15:662.

3. *Archives Parlementaires,* 36:602.

4. *Archives Parlementaires,* 53:472–74.

5. François Furet, *Revolutionary France, 1770–1880* (Oxford, 1992), 87, 103.

6. Georges Lefebvre, *The French Revolution from Its Origins to 1793* (London, 1962), 277.

7. Joseph Hansen, *Quellen zur Geschichte des Rheinlandes im Zeitalter der französischen Revolution,* 4 vols. (Bonn, 1931–38), 2:703.

8. *Archives Parlementaires,* 62:3.

9. T. J. Reed, *The Classical Centre: Goethe and Weimar 1775–1832* (London, 1980), 183.

10. Hansen, *Quellen,* 2:703.

11. Franco Venturi, "L'Italia fuor d'Italia," in *Storia d'Italia,* vol. 3, *Dal primo Settecento all'unità* (Turin, 1973), 1158–59.

12. Giacomo Lumbroso, *I moti popolari contro i Francesi alla fine del secolo XVIII (1796–1800)* (Florence, 1932), 80.

13. Jacques Godechot, *La Grande Nation. L'expansion Révolutionnaire de la France dans le Monde 1789–1799,* 2 vols. (Paris, 1956), 1:85; Marc Bouloiseau, Georges Lefebvre, and Albert Soboul, eds., *Oeuvres de Maximilien Robespierre,* vol. 8, *Discours* (Paris, n.d.), 81.

14. *Archives Parlementaires,* 74:231.

15. I have discussed this in my *The Origins of the French Revolutionary Wars* (London, 1986), 105–13.

16. Pierre Goubert, "La force du nombre," in *Histoire Économique et Sociale de la France*, ed. Fernand Braudel and Ernest Labrousse, vol. 2, *Des Derniers Temps de l'Acircumflexge Seigneurial aux Préludes de l'Acircumflexge Industriel (1660–1789)* (Paris, 1970), 20.

17. William H. McNeill, *The Pursuit of Power: Technology, Armed Force and Society since A.D. 1000* (Oxford, 1983), 193.

18. Jean Delmas, ed., *De 1715 à 1871*, in *Histoire Militaire de la France*, ed. André Corvisier (Paris, 1992), 2:228.

19. Hansen, *Quellen*, 2:363.

20. John A. Lynn, *The Bayonets of the Republic. Motivation and Tactics in the Army of Revolutionary France, 1791–94* (Urbana IL, 1984), 113.

21. A sample can be found in chapter 3 of my *The French Revolution in Germany. Occupation and Resistance in the Rhineland 1792–1802* (Oxford, 1983).

22. Ludwig Molitor, ed., *Urkundenbuch zur Geschichte der ehemals Pfalz-bayerischen Residenzstadt Zweibrücken* (Zweibrücken, 1888), 222.

23. Pion des Loches, *Mes Campagnes (1792–1815). Notes et Correspondance du Colonel de l'Artillerie* (Paris, 1889), 24.

24. Hansen, *Quellen*, 3:615 n. 5.

25. Archives Nationales, Paris, F1^e 40.

26. Bricard, *Journal du Canonnier Bricard (1792–1802)*, 2d ed. (Paris, 1894), 191.

27. Baron Boulart, *Mémoires Militaires sur les Guerres de la République et de l'Empire* (Paris, 1892), 10–11.

28. Hansen, *Quellen*, 3:837.

29. Quoted in Georges Michon, "La Justice Militaire sous la Révolution," *Annales révolutionnaires*, 19 (1922): 24.

30. Lynn, *The Bayonets of the Republic*, 113, 115.

31. Jacques Godechot, *Les Commissaires aux Armées sous le Directoire*, 2 vols. (Paris, 1937), 1:67–68.

32. Godechot, *Les Commissaires*, 362. There are many more examples in this volume.

33. Louis Sébastien Mercier, *Tableau de Paris*, new ed., 12 vols. (Amsterdam, 1783–88), 8:184–85.

34. Godechot, *Les Commissaires*, 1:601.

35. Blanning, *French Revolution in Germany*, 121.

36. See p. 117 in this chapter.

37. William Doyle, *The Oxford History of the French Revolution* (Oxford, 1989), 322.

38. Blanning, *The French Revolution in Germany*, 76.

39. Alan Forrest, *Soldiers of the French Revolution* (Durham NC, 1990), 131.

40. Ernest Cuneo d'Ornano, ed., *Hoche, sa Vie, sa Correspondance*, 2 vols. (Paris, 1892), 2:49.

41. Jacques Godechot, ed., *Fragments des Mémoires de Charles-Alexis Alexandre sur un Mission aux Armées du Nord et de Sambre-et-Meuse* (Paris, 1937), 145.

42. Hermann Cardauns, ed., *Köln in der Franzosenzeit: Aus der Chronik des Anno Schnorrenberg, 1789–1802* (Bonn, 1923), 112.

43. Blanning, *French Revolution in Germany*, 109.

44. Jakob Katzfey, *Geschichte der Stadt Münstereifel und der nachbahrlichen Ortschaften* (Cologne, 1854), 1:395.

45. Alphonse Aulard, *Recueil des Actes du Comité de Salut Public, avec la Correspondance Officielle des Représentants en Mission et le Registre du Conseil Exécutif Provisoire* (Paris, 1933–55), 60: 244.

46. Archives du Ministère de la Guerre (Service Historique de l'Armée, Château de Vincennes), B/51.

47. For references to peasants decamping to the forests with their animals, see, e.g., General Gouvion Saint Cyr's complaint to Moreau of 18 June 1796, Archives du Ministère de la Guerre, B/51; Hermann Cardauns, ed., *Die Franzosen in Coblenz 1794 bis 1797. Aufzeichnungen des Coblenzer Professors Minola* (Koblenz, n.d.), 70; F. W. Lohmann, *Geschichte der Stadt Viersen von den ältesten Zeiten bis zur Gegenwart* (Viersen, 1913), 703; L. de Lanzac de Laborie, *La Domination Française en Belgique. Directoire-Consulat-Empire, 1795–1814* (Paris, 1895), 259.

48. Hauptstaatsarchiv Düsseldorf [DI], Lande zwischen Maas und Rhein, 2593, Kempen 30 Fructidor 4 (16 September 1796).

49. Adolf Schmidthenner, *Das Tagebuch meines Urgroßvaters* (Freiburg in Breisgau, 1908), 118.

50. Archives du Ministère de la Guerre, B2/53.

51. Werner Hesse, *Geschichte der Stadt Bonn während der französischen Herrschaft (1792–1815)* (Bonn, 1879), 44.

52. Peter Friedrichs, *Verfassung und Verwaltung der Stadt Bonn zur Zeit der französischen Herrschaft (1794–1814)* (Bonn, 1911), 142.

53. "Firmondsche Chronik," *Mitteilungen des Historischen Vereins für die Saargegend*, 7 (1900): 56.

54. "Firmondsche Chronik," 91–106.

55. Jean-Paul Bertaud, *La Révolution Armée. Les Soldat-Citoyens et la Révolution Française* (Paris, 1979), 134.

56. Stadtarchiv Bonn FR 9/11 proclamation dated 25 Prairial V [13 June 1797].

57. See, for example, the complaints made in Aschaffenburg in 1800—

Vienna, Haus-, Hof- und Staatsarchiv, Mainzer Erzkanzler Archiv, Militaria, fasc. 132, of. 171.

58. Lorenz Finger, ed., "Vaterstädtisches und Vaterländisches. Auszüge aus S.G. Fingers Tagebüchern von 1795 bis 1818," *Archiv für Frankfurts Geschichte und Kunst*, n.s., 6 (1877): 196.

59. For examples from either end of Europe, see Carlo Zaghi, *La Rivoluzione Francese e l'Italia. Studi e Ricerche* (Naples, 1966), 133, 146; Giovanni Assereto, *La Repubblica Ligure: Lotte Politiche e Problemi Finanziari (1797–1799)* (Turin, 1975), 120; and Simon Schama, *Patriots and Liberators. Revolution in the Netherlands, 1780–1813* (London, 1977), 289.

60. Paul Verhaegen, *La Belgique sous la domination française, 1792–1814*, vol. 1, *La conquête, 1792–1795* (Brussels, 1922), 529.

61. *Politische Unterhaltungen am linken Rheinufer*, 1 Pluviôse VI 20 January 1798].

62. Lumbroso, *I Moti Popolari*, 15–25.

63. Aulard, *Recueil*, XV, 208, 432, 492; Hansen, *Quellen*, 3:678; Heinrich Scheel, *Süddeutsche Jakobiner. Klassenkämpfe und Republikanische Bestrebungen im Deutschen Süden Ende des 18. Jahrhunderts* (Berlin, 1962), 275.

64. Quoted in Blanning, *The French Revolution in Germany*, 287–88. This chapter contains an extended examination of banditry in the Rhineland during the 1790s.

65. Blanning, *The French Revolution in Germany*, 291.

66. Anton Klebe, *Reise auf dem Rhein durch die Deutschen Staaten, von Frankfurt bis zur Grenze der Batavischen Republik, und durch die Französischen Departemente des Donnersbergs, des Rheins und der Mosel und der Roër im Sommer und Herbst 1800*, 2 vols. (Frankfurt am Main, 1802), 2:37–38.

67. Gaetano Cingari, *Brigantaggio, Proprietari e Contadini nel Sud (1799–1900)* (Reggio Calabria, 1976), 39–56.

68. Giorgio Candeloro, *Storia dell'Italia Moderna*, vol. 1, *Le Origini del Risorgimento* (Milan, 1956), 343.

69. Verhaegen, *La Belgique sous la Domination Française*, 2:353.

70. The best short account is still that given by Henri Pirenne, *Histoire de Belgique*, 7 vols. (Brussels, 1926), 6:110–16.

71. There is a good account of the Lugo episode in Zaghi, *La Rivoluzione Francese e l'Italia*, 148–68, although Zaghi is unreasonably severe in his condemnation of the folly of the counterrevolutionaries.

72. Bricard, *Journal*, 200–227.

73. Carl von Clausewitz, *On War*, ed. and trans. Michael Howard and Peter Paret (Princeton, 1976), 332.

5

"Rebels" and "Redskins"

U.S. Military Conduct toward White
Southerners and Native Americans
in Comparative Perspective

Mark Grimsley

We begin with two mornings, three years apart. The first is a mild winter day in coastal South Carolina, on the flat tidal plain of the Savannah River. Blue-coated soldiers have entered the little village of Barnwell. Officially their orders are to pass through the town and seize or destroy only certain classes of public property. In brutal fact they believe their commanding officer desires the wreckage of everything in their path as they invade the state that first seceded and thereby unleashed the carnage that has consumed their lives and comrades for four years. The troops set fire to the town: public buildings, residences, everything. Then they leave, telling each other with grim satisfaction that the town ought properly to be rechristened "Burnwell." The civilians in their wake are aghast, in shock.[1]

The second is a chill autumn dawn in the former Indian Territory, now Oklahoma. Blue-coated soldiers have surrounded a nameless village on the Washita River. Officially, their orders are to surround and capture a party of Indian raiders believed to have attacked several white settlements in the region *and also* to wreck everything in their path. They open fire: unlike Barnwell, this little makeshift village is defended. But the inhabitants are taken by surprise, and within minutes the settlement is overrun. While a covering force screens against a possible counterattack from other Indians in the vicinity, the soldiers peel off into work details, systematically leveling the Indian lodges, shooting the nine hundred ponies in the village, and giving most of the Indians' possessions to the flames. Afterward there are no Indians left behind in the village to bewail the attack, for all have been made prisoners and escorted into captivity. And over a hundred of them, mostly old men, women, and children, are dead.[2]

It is commonly agreed that nineteenth-century America had two experiences with "total war": the first against the Southern Confederacy, the second against the Western Plains Indians (see map 5.1).[3] A number of historians have discerned similarities in the military methods employed, particularly the emphasis on the destruction of supplies and attacks on noncombatants. Such commonalities imply that however potent racial views may have been in white America's overall stance toward Native America, the role of race in the final military contest with Native America was not central. This point is suggested even by Francis Jennings, a distinguished historian highly critical of white America's conduct toward Native Americans. Writing of Maj. Gen. William T. Sherman, he remarks: "Any photograph of Sherman's Civil War devastation of Atlanta will reveal his style of war. Why should anyone expect him to be more merciful to alien Indians than to people of his own kind?"[4]

Yet in fact Sherman—and his counterparts within the Union army— *did* behave with considerably more mercy toward Southern whites than white America showed in its final wars with Native America. What happened at Barnwell, South Carolina, in February 1865 lay at the extreme end of the spectrum of Union conduct toward Southern civilians. What happened along the Washita River in November 1868, on the other hand, was fairly typical of the U.S. Army's conduct toward Native Americans. The difference reflects the salience of race and culture in the latter struggles.

Russell F. Weigley spoke some years ago of an "American way of war." It has long seemed to some historians that America has had two ways of war—one for enemies who are similar to white Americans in culture and ethnicity, one for enemies who are not.[5] Yet if this is correct (and some would say it is screamingly obvious), one still has to confront the dominant view in the literature, which suggests that the last wars against the Plains Indians were principally an extension and amplification of the methods used against white Southern civilians. There is a certain comfort in this view, for many military historians admire the soldiers whom they study and with considerable justice cherish a respect for the devotion to duty that soldiers exhibit, the hardihood and

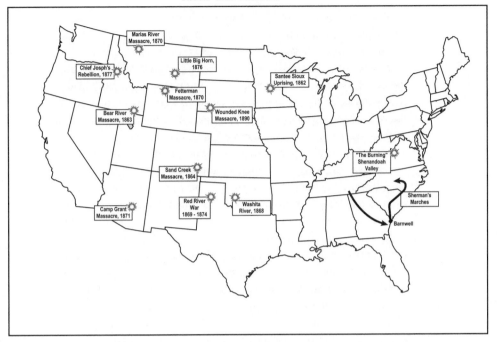

Map 5.1. The United States, 1861–1890

self-reliance they display, the sacrifice their vocation demands. There is also a certain plausibility: after all, the officers who presided over the destruction of Indian autonomy in the late nineteenth century were often the same men who had helped destroy the Confederacy in 1861–1865.[6]

Yet the contrasts between the wars against the Confederacy and Native America are compelling. They begin with the basic legal principles by which the two struggles were conducted. The laws and customs of European warfare contain two main strands of thought, one applicable to wars between nation-states, the other to internal rebellions. Although the Federal government explicitly denied the Confederacy's legal existence, it granted full belligerent rights to Southern armies and waged the Civil War largely as a contest between two nations. By extension, Union armies generally treated Southern civilians as if they were citizens of a foreign nation — subject to military rule and the seizure of their crops, to be sure, yet not to imprisonment or summary execution provided they refrained from guerrilla activity. This point is so obvious that it is easy to overlook. But as William T. Sherman liked to emphasize, the Federal government's decision amounted to a substantial act of forbearance, for by rights it could have applied the insurrectionary principle sweepingly, executed virulent secessionists, confiscated property wholesale, and even "banish[ed the inhabitants] and appropriate[d] their lands to a more loyal and useful population."[7]

Military policy toward Native Americans, on the other hand, routinely followed the insurrectionary principle, which in effect not only denied legitimacy to Native American combatants, but placed them in the same legal category as bandits or highwaymen. It did so despite the fact that Native Americans were not citizens of the United States but belonged instead to separate nonstate societies that until 1871 were officially regarded as "domestic dependent nations."[8] American units on the Western frontier did not automatically kill every Indian they encountered, but the widespread sense that Indians were illegitimate combatants—insurgents, simple bandits, or (in General Philip H. Sheridan's expressive phrase) "fiends"—made killing much easier to contemplate, condone, or excuse.[9]

It is sometimes suggested that the more relevant parallel is with Union policy toward Confederate guerrillas, who did fall under the insurrectionary principle and were therefore entitled, as one Union general put it, to "the rights due to pirates and robbers": in other words, no rights at all.[10] And undeniably, Union punishment of guerrilla activity was severe. The guerrillas themselves were often killed when caught, and reprisals against local civilians could take the form of arrests, hostage taking, expulsions, or the destruction of homes. But historians who equate Union treatment of Confederate guerrillas and Indian warriors overlook a crucial distinction. By according the Confederacy belligerent rights, the Union gave white Southerners a legitimate avenue of resistance through service in the Confederate army. Moreover, the Union bound itself to extend the customary protections of war even to partisan soldiers taken in arms, provided they displayed their weapons openly and wore distinctive identifying emblems. A guerrilla might choose to fight the Union while ignoring these injunctions, but a Native American had no choice: he was regarded as an insurgent no matter how he fought, even if he displayed arms openly and eschewed the moral camouflage of the peaceable civilian. Moreover, those who supported him were also regarded as insurgents, whether they carried arms or not.

During their clashes with the Western Indians, U.S. forces quickly discovered that it was almost impossible to destroy a Native American war party in open combat since Indians normally avoided battle except under favorable conditions, and their small numbers and high mobility made them hard to locate amid the vastness of the Far West. Accordingly, one of the army's favorite tactics was to swoop down upon a hostile party while it was ensconced in a village, ideally at dawn. This tactic practically guaranteed casualties among Native American women, children, and the elderly. Two well-known examples of this tactic are the Battle of the Washita, already discussed, and the Marias River Massacre on 23 January 1870, in which Maj. Edward M. Baker and two squadrons of the U.S. Second Cavalry killed 173 Piegan Indians, including 53 women and children, many of them ill with smallpox—and, incidentally, belatedly discovered they had attacked the wrong settlement.[11]

Sheridan defended the tactic of village attacks against criticism by eastern humanitarians, averring that it was no different than what had been practiced during the Civil War: "During the war did any one hesitate to attack a village or town occupied by the enemy because women and children were within its limits? Did we cease to throw shells into Vicksburg or Atlanta because women and children were there?"[12] But this was disingenuous. The bombardments of Vicksburg and Atlanta were rather desultory and produced few civilian casualties.[13] The affected townspeople knew for days if not weeks of the enemy's approach and could have departed (as many did). By contrast, the success of the Western village attacks depended upon the Native Americans' *not* knowing of their enemy's approach. And whereas the presence of noncombatants at Vicksburg and Atlanta was incidental to operations against the Confederate armies defending them, the presence of noncombatants in a Native American village was of central importance. As Richard Slotkin points out, "the greatest opportunities for white victory would occur when the presence of women and children immobilized the warriors and forced them to defend their ground."[14] Finally, while the Union army could readily discriminate between military and civilian targets at Vicksburg and Atlanta, during a village attack combatants and noncombatants were hopelessly intermingled. The result, predictably, was a level of noncombatant casualties far higher than anything seen during Civil War military operations, including sieges.[15] In short, Sheridan was not drawing an appropriate comparison. Rather, he was cloaking a morally dubious act in the mantle of one more easily defensible.

The principle of "double effect" helps to underscore the difference between the bombardment of besieged Southern cities and direct attacks on Native American villages. It is well explicated by political scientist and social critic Michael Walzer. "Double effect," he writes, "is a way of reconciling the absolute prohibition against attacking noncombatants with the legitimate conduct of military activity," which may unavoidably expose noncombatants to harm. Its key condition, he continues, is that "[t]he intention of the actor is good, that is, he aims narrowly at the acceptable effect [e.g., the death or incapacitation of combatants]; the evil effect [death or injury to noncombatants] is not one of his ends, nor is it a means to his ends, and, aware of the evil involved, he seeks to minimize it, accepting costs to himself."

One may complain that during the Atlanta bombardment, Sherman failed to minimize the risk of causing harm to civilians. But causing harm to them was neither his objective nor a means to his objective. By contrast, while injury to Native American women and children was plausibly not the objective of Custer at the Washita or Baker at the Marias, the presence of women and children was an important means to ensure the vulnerability of the otherwise elusive Native American warriors. According to the principle of double effect, this is morally unacceptable. "A soldier must take careful aim *at* his target and *away from* nonmilitary targets," Walzer explains. "He can shoot only if he has a reasonably clear shot; he can attack only if a direct attack is possible. He can risk incidental deaths, but he cannot kill civilians simply because he finds them between himself and his enemies." Ethically, then, the U.S. Army could have resorted to attacks on Native American villages only if it were prepared to take significant steps to avoid noncombatant casualties — for example, by using forces sufficient to surround the village, offering the Native Americans an opportunity to surrender, and permitting noncombatants a chance to leave the battle area.[16]

Yet although this conclusion cannot be gainsaid, it is perhaps only fair to point out that the army found itself chronically shorthanded during most of its campaigns and that even surprise attacks were fraught with considerable risk. At the Battle of the Big Hole (Montana) on 9 August 1877, a column under Col. John Gibbon surprised a Nez Perce encampment but failed to prevent the escape of most of the warriors, who scrambled to cover and shot down fully a third of Gibbon's men. But as usual, many of the Nez Perce killed in the opening attack were women and children. Estimates of Indian losses are notoriously hard to establish reliably, but the evidence suggests that as many as two-thirds of the eighty to ninety dead were noncombatants.[17]

The telling contrast between conduct toward white Southerners and Native Americans was also evident with regard to the destruction of property. Even historians fully aware that the Union military operations resulted in few civilian deaths dwell heavily on the devastation of Southern croplands, the burning of Southern towns, the looting of Southern homesteads. If these acts stopped short of the actual killing of noncombatants, surely they opened a Pandora's box that soon led to such killings? "The battlefields of the Civil War," declares a recent assessment, "were classrooms in which American officers learned the tactics they would apply with devastating effect against Native Americans."[18] But it is far from certain that they did. Indeed, despite a surface plausibility, such a formulation hinders more than it assists understanding.

Federal policy toward Southern civilians passed through three main stages, all of them strikingly different from the tactics employed in the Far West.[19] Initially, Union forces pursued a policy of conciliation, which deliberately sought to exempt Southern civilians from the burdens of war. The entry of Northern armies into the Confederacy was generally accompanied by promises to preserve the civilians' constitutional rights, particularly their right to property, including slaves. This policy was predicated on the assumption that a relatively small faction in Southern life—the so-called slaveholding aristocracy—had duped ordinary Southerners into secession by playing on their fears. By defusing these fears through a conciliatory policy, Northern commanders expected to woo Southern civilians back to their former allegiance.

Conciliation remained the dominant Union policy until the failure of McClellan's Richmond offensive in the early summer of 1862, when support for it abruptly evaporated. It vanished partly because frustrated Northerners grew impatient with this scornfully dubbed "kid glove" policy and partly because the Lincoln administration came to believe that, while considerable Union sentiment might exist in the South, it showed little sign of bursting forth. In mid-August 1862, the War Department issued a general order, drafted primarily by Lincoln himself, ordering military commanders throughout much of the South to "seize and use any property, real or personal, which may be necessary" for military purposes.[20] The administration's embrace of emancipation was, in part, a way to signal its impatience with conciliation. As Lincoln explained to a member of his cabinet, "We [want] the army to strike more vigorous blows. The Administration must set an example, and strike at the heart of the rebellion."[21]

It would be wrong, however, to mistake rejection of conciliation for the inauguration of the "hard war" policy that dominated the Union war effort in 1864–1865. Taken at face value, both Lincoln's order and the Emancipation Proclamation seem endorsements of warfare upon the Confederacy's economic base. But the primary significance of the order was not so much the promulgation of a new policy as a signal that the existing strategy—the destruction of Southern armed forces—must be pursued more vigorously. That, of course, widened the parameters of acceptable measures against Southern civilians, but it took time for commanders to exploit them.

What followed conciliation, then, was less the hard war measures of 1864–1865 than what might be called the pragmatic policy. Like conciliation, the pragmatic policy was essentially a conservative program that emphasized the need to win victory by battlefield success, not by subjecting Southern civilians to the burdens of war. Although it permitted greater severity toward those who engaged in or abetted guerrilla warfare and offered larger scope for Union foraging operations, it did not yet view the Southern population and economic infrastructure as major targets. The pragmatic policy differed from conciliation primarily in that it lacked a coherent strategic purpose. It was designed simply to keep civilians out of the way while Union armies continued to seek victory on the battlefield.

With that qualification established, however, it remains correct to view the period after the Emancipation Proclamation as one in which Northern policymakers increasingly came to grips with the fact that the war's nature had dramatically changed. The pragmatic policy was essentially a transitional period as Northern commanders evolved a strategy toward civilians that conformed with the increasingly hard-nosed political view of the conflict. Nevertheless, it predominated in most theaters of the conflict for many months — roughly from July 1862 to February 1864. Only then did it give way to widespread employment of the final hard-war policy.

How did this policy come about? In spite of its apparent novelty, Sherman, Grant, and Sheridan did not regard it as a departure from traditional warfare. Instead, they viewed it as an effort to claim the full extent of the destruction permissible within the existing rules of war, particularly the recognition of the logistical imperative that armies must find ways to supply themselves and, by extension, to deny supplies to the enemy. It was this imperative, more than any other factor, that gave rise to the hard war measures of the Civil War.

Americans in 1861 scarcely expected the conflict to reach the dimensions or destructiveness it eventually assumed. Most thought that a handful of battles would settle the outcome, a belief that stemmed partly from an underestimate of the enemy's determination and partly from the Napoleonic heritage, which suggested that victory might be won in a single, decisive armed collision. Nevertheless, despite the emphasis placed on audacious maneuver and shattering combat, the mobility of Napoleonic armies ultimately depended on their ability to derive sustenance from the countryside over which they passed. The resultant foraging operations were frequently disorderly and not readily distinguishable (in the eyes of hapless civilians) from simple pillaging. Hence, the burden Napoleonic warfare placed on the civilians in their path was far from light.

This gritty reality remained very much the underside of the Napoleonic system, overlooked amid the seductive prospect of the Austerlitz-style battle of annihilation. It rapidly surfaced, however, when American commanders attempted to replicate Napoleon's accomplishments. Despite the availability of rail and river transportation, Union and Confederate generals found that these avenues usually could not supply their army's complete needs. More critically, however, Civil War armies — particularly Union armies — found themselves obliged to operate in areas where suitable rail and water communications were unavailable. When that occurred they had to find other means of subsistence. Wagon trains alone proved completely inadequate; foraging from the country became essential.

By mid-1862, large-scale foraging operations had begun. These occurred mainly in the West, where Union supply lines broke down much more frequently than in Virginia. The vast distances in the trans-Appalachian theater created longer "pipelines," which Union quartermasters had difficulty keeping full, so that spot shortages were not uncommon. And as western armies drew more of their food and forage locally, they came to appreciate the importance of foodstuffs as a military resource to a degree that eastern commanders never did. Within a year, western commanders were not only seizing supplies from the countryside but also destroying surplus supplies so as to deny them to the enemy.

Extensive foraging, Union commanders recognized, inevitably meant hardship for civilians. They attempted to minimize it by forbidding abuses and by issuing instructions that Southern families should be left enough supplies for their own use. Even so, the civilian inhabitants suffered a great deal. Partly in an attempt to justify the hardship thus inflicted, Union commanders began to see foraging as a form of punishment. Eventually, they deliberately sharpened its bite in order to produce political and psychological effects.

What was this policy like in operation? The familiar image is one of widespread devastation. Then and later, Southerners condemned these destructive raids as little better than atrocities, portraying them as wanton, cruel, and above all *indiscriminate*. At least two writers, for example, have drawn direct connections between Sherman's march and the 1968 My Lai Massacre.[22] Yet the dominant theme of the Union *chevauchées* was less an *erosion* of values than an ongoing *tension* between competing sets of values. Union soldiers clearly came to understand the need to destroy Southern war resources. They also embraced the conviction that some Southern civilians deserved punishment for their role in starting or sustaining the war. But the same sense of justice that created this desire for retribution also insisted that punishment should fall upon the guilty. The result was indeed severity, but it was a directed severity aimed — and, for the most part, aimed effectively — at certain portions of the Confederate population and economic infrastructure.

This can be seen in many Federal orders concerning conduct toward Southern civilians. With the collapse of conciliation, Union commanders typically divided these civilians into three classes: loyal Unionists, who merited protection and who should be paid for goods requisitioned; neutral or passive citizens, who might also be protected but who remained subject to forced loans and military requisitions, with receipts given but payment to be made after the war upon proof of loyalty; and active secessionists. For the last category severe measures were authorized: "they may be treated as prisoners of war," ran a typical pronouncement, "and be subjected to the rigors of confinement or to expulsion as combatant enemies. . . . We have suffered very severely from this class, and it is time that the laws of war should be more rigorously enforced against them. A broad line of distinction must be drawn between friends and enemies, between the loyal and the disloyal."[23]

This trinary scheme appears repeatedly and persistently in Federal correspondence. It also seems, by and large, to have been understood and accepted by rank-and-file soldiers. The desire for a just retribution appears often in soldier letters and diaries. William T. Patterson, a sergeant in Sheridan's army, reflected the anguish that attended his commander's decision to burn private homes in retaliation for the murder of a Union staff officer. His reluctance to see the population around him de-housed stemmed less from softheartedness than from a desire to see justice done. "If it was at Berryville, Charlestown or Winchester [towns in the secessionist lower Shenandoah Valley] I would say burn in retaliation of Chambersburg [Pennsylvania, one-third of which had been torched by a Confederate force under Col. John McCausland], but this place is the most loyal or at least most innocent of any I have seen the Valley."[24] Such considerations mattered to Federal soldiers. Even in 1864, after years of warfare, most of them still retained a basic morality. Although not averse to destruction, they wanted to see the hard hand of war descend on those who deserved it and usually only in rough proportion to the extent of their sins.

This element of morality is critical to understanding the combination of severity and restraint that marked Union conduct during the war's final year. It clearly did not prevent destruction on a scale that desolated much of the South, but it channeled it in some directions and away from others. Public and quasi-public property like railroads, warehouses, and factories received the rough ministrations of Federal troops more often than private property. Plantations—the lairs of the slaveholding aristocracy—were targeted far more often than small farms.[25] Policy dictated that the Southern population be divided according to the loyal, neutral, and actively disloyal, with different standards of conduct for each. The policy worked because the rank and file recognized and understood such distinctions. Not only was the Northern soldier a member of one of the most politically aware societies on earth, he was also strongly tied to his community—representatives of which marched and fought beside him—and to the values of the society that bred him.[26]

The experience of South Carolina in February 1865 underscores this point. Until then, the unauthorized destruction that attended Sherman's march through Georgia was mainly, in the phrase of corps commander Maj. Gen. Alpheus S. Williams, the work of "the few (ever found in large bodies of men) who were disorderly and vicious."[27] From the moment that Federal troops crossed the Savannah River, however, incidents of pillaging and arson accelerated dramatically. The perpetrators were no longer the marginal soldiers alone but included many of the best, most motivated troops. What happened to South Carolina forcefully underscored the substantially directed nature of the severity that had preceded it. It showed what a Federal army could do when it *wanted* to wreak indiscriminate havoc.

The reason for this massive increase in violence—noticed and widely remarked upon by contemporary observers—was simple. South Carolina was almost universally believed to be filled, from one end to the other, with the most virulent, dedicated disunionists. Yet as soon as Sherman's forces crossed into North Carolina their destructive orgy stopped. The Tarheel State received much the same treatment as Georgia—possibly even a bit milder, since North Carolina was not part of the Deep South, was known to harbor significant Unionist sentiment, and had been one of the last states to secede. Certainly, a number of Federal commanders issued directives encouraging gentler behavior.[28] The abrupt cessation of the maelstrom that engulfed South Carolina formed one of the strongest proofs of the sense of discriminating righteousness that animated the Federal rank and file.

Except in South Carolina, Federal troops largely destroyed only what they were told to destroy. Their foraging activities, although liberal, usually concentrated on crops and livestock belonging to secessionist planters. The whirlwind of pillaging and arson that struck the Palmetto State was unique in scale; it showed what Union soldiers could really do if they wished. If the desolation inflicted on the South possesses significance, it is also significant that it was not far worse. The America of 1864–1865 witnessed a new *chevauchée* — as systematic and extensive as anything Europe had seen, but also more enlightened because it was conducted not by brutes but by men from good families, with strong moral values that stayed their hands as often as they impelled a sense of retribution. Certainly, the North's war upon Southern resources was hard, but it was also channeled, and by choosing to wage the war as a contest between two nations the Union government threw its moral and legal authority squarely behind the preservation of distinctions between combatants and noncombatants. Field commanders reinforced the distinction through a stream of orders that forbade pillaging and wanton destruction. Critics who cite the orders as evidence of continued depredations miss the crucial point: in war, nothing undercuts the claims of personal conscience faster than the demands of public authority.[29] By insisting on proper conduct toward Southern civilians, Union generals encouraged rather than undermined their soldiers' consciences.

Finally, the policy held up in no small measure because it made moral and political sense to the citizen-soldier in the ranks: men who accepted the need for a destructive war but wished its effects to be visited as much as possible on those who deserved it, and then in rough accord with the extent of their sins. This wish occasionally persisted even in the face of guerrilla activity, something that provoked Union soldiers more than anything else. A Federal brigade commander, for example, interceded with Sheridan to save a Virginia community from being burned in retaliation for the bushwhacking of a Union officer. His men wholeheartedly approved, and when informed that Sheridan had rescinded the order, "there was louder cheering than there ever was when we made a bayonet charge."[30] Told to burn houses near the sites of guerrilla activity in West Virginia, a Union colonel demurred nevertheless. "To men who have taken the oath [of allegiance], unless charges could be made and sustained, I do not feel authorized to apply [the] order. . . . I would rather spare two secesh than burn up one Union man's property."[31] But for the moral force of such distinctions, the Federal policy of directed severity would not have been possible.

149

Although it is common to locate the germ of the hard war policy within the fertile mind of William T. Sherman, the real source was the logistical imperative by which Civil War armies sometimes found it necessary to take supplies from the countryside and, by extension, to deny them to the enemy. A number of Union commanders resorted to foraging and area denial well before Sherman did; such methods were obvious solutions to obvious military problems. It requires little imagination to realize that if the Civil War had never taken place, the military problems of a war against the Plains Indians would have suggested their own solutions in much the same way. Faced with an opponent too mobile and too elusive to destroy in conventional battle, army officers resorted to attacks on villages, which were comparatively easy to locate; to the destruction of supplies that fed the warriors; and to the killing of the ponies on which Indian mobility rested. One does not need Sherman's marches to explain what inspired these measures. One does not even need the ample historical precedent of the colonial "feedfights," operations in which English colonists, unable to defeat their Indian adversaries in open combat, systematically ravaged the crops on which the Indians' livelihood depended.[32]

The destruction of Native American property followed a considerably different pattern from that of the Civil War. Although Southern barns and outbuildings might be destroyed, it was relatively uncommon for Union troops to burn private dwellings. But U.S. troops in the West routinely burned entire Native American villages. The emphasis in both official orders and actual practice was to leave white Southern civilians enough provisions to get by. In the West, the norm was to destroy provisions so thoroughly as to force the Native Americans to choose between life on a reservation and outright starvation. The pattern during the Civil War was to distinguish between Union, secessionist, and neutral or passive civilians. In the West, distinctions between the peace and war factions of a tribe were seldom made. Union foraging parties often gave white Southerners receipts for supplies taken, and after the war a Southern Claims Commission gave compensation to those who could demonstrate their loyalty. No such niceties applied in the contest against Native America.

Both struggles, of course, saw depredations by the rank and file. Southern tales of purloined silverware and rifled wardrobes have a strong factual basis. But the stories of widespread murder and rape by

Union soldiers in the South do not. Few white Southern women suffered rape or sexual abuse.[33] In the West, however, the rape of Native American women was common and frequently remarked. The Sand Creek Massacre is a particularly well-known case, but there were many others. A California newspaper reported in 1862 the gang rape of several Indian women by a military patrol.[34] At Bear River (Idaho Territory), where an estimated 250 Northwestern Shoshoni Indians were slaughtered in January 1863, women were raped even as they lay dying from wounds. There were also reports of forced concubinage on the part of Custer's cavalry after the Battle of the Washita.[35] "Under these circumstances," writes Sherry L. Smith, "officers apparently saw the Indian women as the spoils of war, as sexual conveniences."[36]

One historian offers two explanations for the widespread rape of Native American women: first, "It is women, after all, who are the repository of racial purity," so that rape was a vicious symbolic expression of the whites' desire to eradicate the Native Americans as a distinct people; and, second, "the rape of women has been a traditional part of a conquering army's celebration."[37] Both points seem reasonable, but the second raises questions about the rarity of such conduct among Union soldiers. If rape is a traditional act of conquering soldiers, why does the reality of Union conduct toward Southern white women so little resemble the myth?

There is a pervasive belief that participation in war is inherently brutalizing. "Humans regress under prolonged stress or discomfort," notes one social psychologist; "they become more primitive."[38] A U.S. officer in Vietnam remarked that his troops were decent enough young men. But subjected to sufficient fear, exhaustion, stress, and "a little mob pressure," he continued, "those nice kids . . . would rape like champions. Kill, rape, and steal is the name of the game."[39] But although much may be said in support of such a view, it is too simple. It overlooks, for example, the role that conscious indoctrination and informal military culture play in encouraging the depersonalization of the individual.[40] The persistence of restraint among Union soldiers during the Civil War suggests that brutalization is not a foregone conclusion. Men raised to regard rape as wrong continued to regard it as wrong even after three years of combat, illness, and hardship. If rape was more widespread in the West, something was at work besides the inherent brutality of war.

In short, it is misleading to see the Indian Wars as merely an extension and amplification of the tactics employed during the Civil War. The treatment of noncombatants during the two contests was qualitatively different. The legal principles by which they were conducted underscored the distinction between combatant and noncombatant during the Civil War but undercut it during the Indian wars. The tactics employed resulted in few civilian deaths during the Civil War but hundreds during the fighting in the West. The destruction of property was far more sweeping and complete in the latter struggles as well. Finally, incidents of rape were rare among the Union armies in the South, far more common in the West.

Where does this recognition get us? One hopes it does not simply return us to the old, unproductive squabble about whether the U.S. Army fought honorably or pursued a "deliberate, if bungled, program of genocide."[41] The historiography of the Civil War passed through stages in which the North's "hard war" policy was viewed through the lens of morality and subsequently through the lens of total war. The lens of morality tended to yield a lot of finger-pointing, and the lens of total war tended to emphasize destructiveness and political "realism" while overlooking evidence of restraint. This author found that exploring the significance of both severity and restraint afforded the most satisfying explanation of Union conduct toward Southern civilians. The same method might be useful with regard to the Indian wars. When one examines Anglo-American conduct toward Native Americans, the differing patterns of severity and restraint yield clues to the underlying dynamics.

It is fairly apparent that much of the qualitative difference between the Civil War and Indian Wars can be laid at the door of racial antagonism. White soldiers treated Southern whites with forbearance because in language, culture, and ethnicity they seemed basically similar. They treated Indians more harshly because the Indians seemed different, alien.[42] But this commonplace idea lacks nuance. It cannot account for the bloody white-on-white irregular warfare that wracked much of the borderlands during the Civil War. The Lawrence massacre in August 1863 was only the most spectacular example of this kind of warfare, which faithfully mirrored the white-on-red contests out west in all respects but one: one sees comparatively few instances of rape and sexual assault.[43]

Similarly, sheer racism cannot account for the differences in white attitudes toward Native Americans. The U.S. Army fought the Indians using tactics that often showed a reckless disregard for the lives of noncombatants, and regular troops both experienced and inflicted atrocities.[44] Yet by and large the army reflected an eastern assessment of Native Americans that saw them as inferior, savage, and fated for assimilation or extinction—but that could also muster some pity for a dying culture and could acknowledge that the Indians had often been treated unjustly. Volunteer troops from states east of the Mississippi who occasionally fought in the West exhibited a similar ambivalence. For example, a Utah observer noted (with some surprise) that the colonel of the Sixth Ohio Cavalry was "decidedly against killing Indians indiscriminately, and will not take any general measures, save on the defensive, until he can ascertain satisfactorily by whom the depredations have been committed, and then not resort to killing until he is satisfied that peaceable measures have failed."[45]

The prevalent attitude of western whites was far more virulent. Many embraced an ideology of outright extermination. "Indian hunting"—collective violence against Native Americans by groups of white civilians—was common in the West and epidemic in California, where Anglo Americans slew some 4,500 Indians between 1848 and 1880, a figure roughly equivalent to the total killed in battles against the U.S. Army. One might also point to the Camp Grant massacre in April 1871, in which a mixed group of Papago Indians, Hispanics, and Anglo Americans from Tucson (Arizona Territory) fell upon an unoffending encampment of Pinal and Aravaipa Apaches, killed between 86 and 150 people, raped the surviving women, mutilated the corpses, and sold 29 children into de facto slavery.[46] A number of California Native Americans were captured and sold into slavery as well.[47]

Some years ago, Barbara Fields suggested that race is "profoundly and in its very essence ideological" and that during the nineteenth century it became "the ideological medium through which Americans confronted questions of sovereignty and power."[48] By this logic, the human predisposition to create "in-groups" and "out-groups" is manipulated and exploited in order to deny the possibility of community between one group and another and, in so doing, to deny the sense of mutual moral responsibility on which society normally rests.[49] Other scholars, building upon this fundamental insight, have forcefully argued that racial categories are not transhistorical but instead are powerful social constructions. The key distinction thus turns out to be not so much racial difference per se as the willingness or unwillingness to acknowledge potential political community. This is hardly an automatic consequence of a common ethnicity or culture. During the American Revolution, for example, the antagonism between Whigs and Loyalists could be nearly as vicious as anything the Indian Wars could produce. The same was true of the internecine strife in the Southern upcountry during the Civil War, and it is possible that the lethal postwar labor strife can be seen in a similar light. White Southerners got off more easily the more they seemed likely to resume their status as U.S. citizens, and because the goal was to restore the South to the Union, some measure of forbearance was extended to virtually all white Southerners.

The degree of forbearance accorded Native Americans was greatly less, in large measure because few whites were willing to contemplate the extension of community to Native Americans except on terms that whites absolutely controlled. But because "whiteness" was as much socially constructed as other racial categories, it seems clear that white racial ideology, while retaining certain fundamental features, could vary according to place and circumstances.[50] This had implications for the terms on which whites could contemplate coexistence with Native Americans. For eastern humanitarians, the terms amounted to assimilation within the dominant white culture. The defensiveness of army officers when confronted by charges of atrocities, coupled with the humanitarian impulses of a few officers like George Crook and Oliver O. Howard, suggests that the army was not deaf to the idea that Native Americans might eventually be included on some subordinate basis. But it was also responsive to white America's demand that the West must be made safe for its own voracious development and that Indians who stood in the way—however courageous or shamefully wronged—must be made to submit.[51]

It is usually thought that Southern whites, too, were made to submit; this is a cherished bit of Civil War mythology. The North's hard war against Southern property is seen as a principal instrument toward this end. But the goal of Union policy was really to detach Southern whites from their allegiance to the Confederacy. This accomplished, the relative mildness of Reconstruction and the speed with which self-rule returned to the white South are, on the whole, remarkable.

Too much can be made of the U.S. Army's humanitarianism in the conduct of this difficult mission. The denial of community between whites and Indians except on white terms made it easy to define Indian resistance as illegitimate and to employ tactics that would have seemed barbaric, extreme, and unthinkable if employed against Southern whites. But it is fortunate that the U.S. government chose to make the regular army its principal instrument in the post–Civil War Indian conflicts rather than to continue the large-scale use of western volunteer troops, for among westerners the denial of community with Native Americans was all but complete. If the Union citizen-soldier's continued sense of connection to his home society was a key factor in preserving restraint during the Civil War, that same sense of connection helped make the western citizen-soldier into an implacable Indian destroyer. It is worth recalling that the Third Colorado Volunteers, who perpetrated the Sand Creek massacre, were enlisted for only a hundred days, had a social composition similar to other Civil War regiments, slaughtered the Black Kettle encampment in their first and only engagement, and returned to Denver festooned with scalps and women's genitalia, to receive a heroes' welcome.[52]

Notes

1. John G. Barrett, *Sherman's March through the Carolinas* (Chapel Hill NC, 1956), 52, 58; Joseph T. Glatthaar, *The March to the Sea and Beyond: Sherman's Troops in the Savannah and Carolinas Campaigns* (New York, 1985), 142–43.

2. Jeffry Wert, *Custer: The Controversial Life of George Armstrong Custer* (New York, 1996), 275–77. See Stan Hoig, *The Battle of the Washita: The Sheridan-Custer Indian Campaign of 1867–69* (Garden City NY, 1976), esp. appendix C, 200–201.

3. "Total war" is employed here in its familiar usage, as a conflict in which the boundaries between combatants and noncombatants are blurred or broken down.

4. Francis Jennings, *The Founders of America: How Indians Discovered the Land, Pioneered in It, and Created Great Classical Civilizations, How They Were Plunged into a New Dark Age by Invasion and Conquest, and How They Are Reviving* (New York, 1993), 376.

5. This point is suggested in Don Higginbotham, "The Early American Way of War: Reconnaissance and Appraisal," *William and Mary Quarterly*, 3d ser., 49 (1991): 234.

6. For examples of this interpretation, see Russell F. Weigley, *The American Way of War: A History of United States Military Strategy and Policy* (New York, 1973), 153–63; Robert M. Utley, *Frontier Regulars: The United States Army and the Indian, 1866–1890* (New York, 1973), 149–50 (as well as other works by Utley); Jerry M. Cooper, "The Army's Search for a Mission, 1865–1890," in *Against All Enemies: Interpretations of American Military History from Colonial Times to the Present*, ed. Kenneth J. Hagan and William R. Roberts (Westport CT, 1986), 178–82; and Lance Janda, "Shutting the Gates of Mercy: The American Origins of Total War, 1860–1880," *Journal of Military History* 59, no. 1 (January 1995): 7–26. It is also suggested in a number of other works, including Charles Royster, *The Destructive War: William Tecumseh Sherman, Stonewall Jackson, and the Americans* (New York, 1991), 393–99; and Paul Andrew Hutton, *Phil Sheridan and His Army* (Lincoln NE, 1985). Richard Slotkin reverses the usual interpretation, saying that "Sherman's march had its roots in colonial- and Revolutionary-era Indian campaigns" (*The Fatal Environment: The Myth of the Frontier in the Age of Industrialization, 1800–1890* [paperback ed., New York, 1994], 304.) John F. Marszalek does much the same, suggesting that Sherman's experiences in the Second Seminole War influenced his later treatment of Southern civilians. See his *Sherman: A Soldier's Passion for Order* (New York, 1993), 195–96. The principal dissent from the dominant view is Robert A. Wooster, *The Military and United States Indian Policy, 1865–1903* (New Haven CT, 1988), 136–42, 214. Wooster's objection emphasizes that the Civil War and the wars against the Plains Indians were very different contests and that the U.S. Army recognized them as such. He includes a paragraph on racism as a key difference, with emphasis on the fact that white Southern civilians were seldom killed by Union forces, whereas Native American women, children, and the elderly were not infrequently slain in western warfare.

7. Sherman to Roswell M. Sawyer, 31 January 1864, *War of the Rebellion: A Compilation of the Official Records of the Union and Confederate Armies*, 128 vols. (Washington DC, 1880–1901), Series I, vol. 32, pt. 2, 279. Cited hereafter as OR. Unless indicated, all citations are to Series I.

8. An obscure rider to an Indian appropriations bill outlawed further treaty-making with Native American tribes, and U.S. policy shifted during the late 1860s and 1870s toward regarding Indians as "wards of the nation" rather than members of semisovereign tribes. But the precise legal status of Indians remained in flux for some time. The appropriations rider is reprinted in Francis Paul Prucha, ed., *Documents in United States Indian Policy*, 2d ed. (Lincoln

NE, 1990), 136. The most thorough discussion of U.S. Indian policy during the last half of the nineteenth century is Francis Paul Prucha, *American Indian Policy in Crisis: Christian Reformers and the Indian, 1865–1900* (Norman OK, 1976).

9. The so-called Quaker or Grant Peace Policy of 1869 strongly buttressed this way of regarding Indians because it established reservations for most Native Americans and regarded as hostile any Native Americans who strayed from them. See Francis Paul Prucha, *The Great Father: The United States Government and the American Indians* (abr. ed.; Lincoln NE, 1986), 152–80 passim. The Sheridan quotation is in Hutton, *Phil Sheridan and His Army*, 185.

10. See John M. Gates, "Indians and Insurrectos: The U.S. Army's Experience with Insurgency," *Parameters* 12 (March 1983): 59–68. General Order No. 92 (Army of the Mississippi), 12 July 1862, OR 17, pt. 2:97. The formulation is that of Maj. Gen. William S. Rosecrans, but the principle represented official Union policy. See General Order No. 100 (U.S. War Department), 24 April 1863, section 4. More familiarly known as Lieber's Code, the order is conveniently reprinted in Richard Shelly Hartigan, *Lieber's Code and the Law of War* (Chicago, 1983).

11. Robert M. Utley, *Frontier Regulars: The United States Army and the Indian, 1866–1891* (New York, 1973), 198.

12. Sheridan to Sherman, 18 March 1870, Box 91, Philip H. Sheridan Papers, Library of Congress; quoted in Hutton, *Phil Sheridan and His Army*, 185.

13. While not precisely known, civilian deaths caused by the Union bombardment of Atlanta are estimated at about twenty over a three-week period. See Albert Castel, *Decision in the West: The Atlanta Campaign of 1864* (Lawrence KS, 1992), 488. The figures for Vicksburg were even less: between five and ten people over the course of a forty-seven-day siege. See Peter F. Walker, *Vicksburg: A People at War, 1860–1865* (Chapel Hill NC, 1960), 203 n.

14. Slotkin, *Fatal Environment*, 400.

15. Field engagements produced even fewer civilian losses. During the three-day battle of Gettysburg, for example, only one civilian lost her life: Jennie Wade. The fact that she is a minor celebrity of the battle—her house in the town has been preserved—eloquently testifies to the rarity of such deaths. The same might be said of Judith Henry, killed by a shell at the First Battle of Manassas. Even during Sherman's destructive marches through Georgia and South Carolina, almost no civilian deaths are recorded.

16. Michael Walzer, *Just and Unjust Wars: A Moral Argument with Historical Illustrations*, 2d ed. (New York, 1992), 151–59, 174. Quoted material is from pages 153, 155, and 174, respectively.

17. Merrill D. Beal, *"I Will Fight No More Forever"*: *Chief Joseph and the Nez Perce War* (Seattle, 1963), 112–43, esp. 128–29.

18. Janda, "Shutting the Gates of Mercy," 26.

19. This and succeeding paragraphs recapitulate the argument made in Mark Grimsley, *The Hard Hand of War: Union Military Policy toward Southern Civilians, 1861–1865* (Cambridge, 1995).

20. Lincoln to Stanton, 22 July 1862, in *The Collected Works of Abraham Lincoln: Supplement, 1832–1865*, ed. Roy P. Basler (Westport CT, 1974), 141. Lincoln's directive was published as General Orders No. 109, 16 August 1862, OR, Series III, 2:397.

21. Gideon Welles, "The History of Emancipation," *Galaxy* 14 (December 1872): 842–43.

22. See John Bennett Walters, *Merchant of Terror: General Sherman and Total War* (Indianapolis, 1973), xiii; and James Reston, *Sherman's March and Vietnam* (New York, 1984).

23. Henry W. Halleck to William S. Rosecrans, 5 March 1863, OR 23, pt. 2:107–8.

24. Entry for 4 October 1864, MS. Diary of William T. Patterson, 116th Ohio, Ohio Historical Society, Columbus.

25. Throughout the war, accounts of foraging by Union troops refer overwhelmingly to large plantations, secessionists, wealthy planters, rich mansions, and the like. See, e.g., entry for 3 February 1865, Jesse S. Bean Diary, Southern Historical Collection, University of North Carolina at Chapel Hill, entries for 26 and 28 November 1862; 18, 24, and 25 January 1863; 12 July 1863; 13 March 1865, diary of George P. Metz, Metz Papers, Special Collections, William R. Perkins Library, Duke University, Durham, North Carolina; Charles B. Tompkins to his wife, 6 May 1863, Charles Brown Tompkins Papers, Special Collections, William R. Perkins Library, Duke University, Durham, North Carolina. It was also usual for Northern soldiers to overlook the homes of the poorer whites. In several instances, Union soldiers, Robin Hood-like, distributed spoils taken from planters to the "poorer Class of inhabitance [*sic*]." See Robert Bruce Hoadley to his cousin, 26 May 1863, Hoadley Papers, Special Collections, William R. Perkins Library, Duke University, Durham, North Carolina.

26. For more on this point, see Michael Barton, *Goodmen: The Character of Civil War Soldiers* (State College PA, 1981); Earl J. Hess, *The Union Soldier in Battle: Enduring the Ordeal of Combat* (Lawrence KS, 1997); and James M. McPherson, *For Cause and Comrades: Why Men Fought in the Civil War* (New York, 1997).

27. A. S. Williams's report, 9 January 1865, OR 44: 212.

28. General Orders No. 8 (Henry Slocum's Twentieth Corps), 7 March 1865, OR 47, pt. 2:719; Sherman to Maj. Gen. Judson Kilpatrick, 7 March 1865, OR 47, pt. 2:721; Special Orders No. 63 (Francis P. Blair's Twenty-seventh Corps), 10 March 1865, OR 47, pt. 2:760–61.

29. The literature on this point is substantial, but see esp. Herbert C. Kelman and V. Lee Hamilton, *Crimes of Obedience: Toward a Social Psychology of Authority and Responsibility* (New Haven CT, 1989).

30. S. Tschappat to John Wayland, 16 March 1912, in John Wayland, *A History of Rockingham County, Virginia* (Staunton VA, 1943), 149–50.

31. Col. A. D. Jaynes to Maj. John Witcher, 21 June 1864, OR 37, pt. 1:659.

32. On the "feedfights," see Alden T. Vaughan, "'Expulsion of the Salvages': English Policy and the Virginia Massacre of 1622," *William and Mary Quarterly*, 3d ser., 35, no. 1 (January 1978): 57–84.

33. Glatthaar, *March to the Sea and Beyond*, 72–74; George C. Rable, *Civil Wars: Women and the Crisis of Southern Nationalism* (Urbana IL, 1990), 160–61; Lee Kennett, *Marching through Georgia: The Story of Soldiers and Civilians during Sherman's Campaign* (New York, 1995), 306–7; Grimsley, *Hard Hand of War*, 81, 199, 220; Stephen V. Ash, *When the Yankees Came: Conflict and Chaos in the Occupied South, 1861–1865* (Chapel Hill NC, 1995), 200–201; and Drew Gilpin Faust, *Mothers of Invention: Women of the Slaveholding South in the American Civil War* (Chapel Hill NC, 1996), 200. Significantly, African-American women seem to have been sexually abused with much greater frequency. On this point, as well the question of rapes upon white women, see the excellent discussion in Reid Mitchell, *The Vacant Chair: The Northern Soldier Leaves Home* (New York, 1993), 102–10.

34. *Red Bluff (CA) Beacon*, 9 October 1862, excerpted in *The Destruction of California Indians*, ed. Robert F. Heizer (1974; Bison Books ed., Lincoln NE, 1993), 283.

35. Brigham D. Madsen, *The Shoshoni Frontier and the Bear River Massacre* (Salt Lake City UT, 1985), 193.

36. Sherry L. Smith, *The View from Officer's Row: Army Perceptions of Western Indians* (Tucson AZ, 1990), 82. Documentary evidence on this point is suggestive but sketchy. See, e.g., Frederick W. Benteen to Theodore W. Goldin, 17 February 1896, in *The Benteen-Goldin Letters on Custer and His Last Battle*, ed. John M. Carroll (1974; Lincoln NE, 1991), 271: "[Custer issued] an informal invitation . . . for officers desiring to avail themselves of the services of a captured squaw, to come to the squaw round-up corral and select one! . . . Custer took first choice, and lived with her during the winter and spring of 1868 and '69." See also Paul Andrew Hutton, *Phil Sheridan and His Army*, 74, 389.

37. Sarah Deutsch, "Landscape of Enclaves: Race Relations in the West,

1865–1990," in *Under an Open Sky: Rethinking America's Western Past*, ed. William Cronon, George Miles, and Jay Gitlin (1992; New York, 1993), 117.

38. Ervin Staub, *The Roots of Evil: The Origins of Genocide and Other Group Violence* (Cambridge, 1989), 45. Here Staub is paraphrasing the opinion of another writer, M. Scott Peck, but the next sentence makes it clear that he endorses Peck's view.

39. Quoted in Richard Holmes, *Acts of War: The Behavior of Men in Battle* (New York, 1985), 392.

40. On this point, see Dave Grossman, *On Killing: The Psychological Cost of Learning to Kill in War and Society* (Boston, 1995).

41. Diana Vári, "A Monstrous Wrong without Guilt," *Reviews in American History* 3, no. 1 (March 1975): 81. In this essay, which reviewed Robert M. Utley's *Frontier Regulars*, Vári encapsulated the terms of the debate caustically but vividly: "On one side stands a loosely related group of historians who advocate the innocent motives if sometimes malign acts of the government, army, and even philanthropists. They describe the other side as smarmy dreamers who believe that the army was always sadistic and the plains Indians were sweet kids who were just plain misunderstood. Strange, but I never thought of Quanah Parker and the boys that way" (Vári, "A Monstrous Wrong without Guilt," 81–82).

42. There is an extensive literature on white perceptions of Native Americans. See, e.g., Robert F. Birkhofer, *The White Man's Indian: Images of the American Indian from Columbus to the Present* (New York, 1978); Ronald Takaki, *Iron Cages: Race and Culture in 19th-Century America* (New York, 1979), esp. chaps. 5 and 8; Reginald Horsman, *Race and Manifest Destiny: The Origins of American Racial Anglo-Saxonism* (Cambridge MA, 1981), 189–207; and Richard Drinnon, *Facing West: The Metaphysics of Indian-Hating and Empire-Building* (Minneapolis, 1980).

43. For the Lawrence Massacre, see Thomas Goodrich, *Bloody Dawn: The Story of the Lawrence Massacre* (Kent OH, 1991). On the question of rape and sexual assault, see Michael Fellman, *Inside War: The Guerrilla Conflict in Missouri during the American Civil War* (New York, 1989), 199–214.

44. A brief but perceptive summary of atrocities during the Plains warfare (both Indian and white) is in Thomas W. Dunlay, *Wolves for the Blue Soldiers: Indian Scouts and Auxiliaries with the United States Army, 1860–1890* (Lincoln NE, 1982), 201–5. See also Don Rickey, *Forty Miles a Day on Beans and Hay: The Enlisted Soldier Fighting the Indian Wars* (Norman OK, 1963), 231–34.

45. Quoted in E. B. Long, *The Saints and the Union: Utah Territory during the Civil War* (Urbana IL, 1981), 87.

46. Richard White, *"It's Your Misfortune and None of My Own": A History*

of the American West (Norman OK, 1991), 337–40; Don Schellie, *Vast Domain of Blood: The Story of the Camp Grant Massacre* (Los Angeles, 1968).

47. Albert L. Hurtado, *Indian Survival on the California Frontier* (New Haven CT, 1988), 145, 211. California law permitted the indenture of loitering and minor Indians, and in a number of instances Indians were enslaved extralegally. As late as 1862, a Union officer reported that Indians were being enslaved in his district. Thomas E. Ketcham to John Hanna Jr., 3 April 1862, OR 50, pt. 1:982.

48. Barbara J. Fields, "Ideology and Race in American History," in *Region, Race, and Reconstruction: Essays in Honor of C. Vann Woodward*, ed. J. Morgan Kousser and James M. McPherson (New York, 1982), 144, 168.

49. On the inherent human tendency to construct in-groups and out-groups, even on the basis of trivial differences, see Staub, *The Roots of Evil*, 58.

50. The literature on what Theodore W. Allen has termed "the invention of the white race" is substantial and growing rapidly. See Allen's *The Invention of the White Race*, 2 vols. (London, 1994, 1997); David Roediger, *The Wages of Whiteness: Race and the Making of the American Working Class* (London, 1991); David Roediger, *Towards the Abolition of Whiteness: Essays on Race, Politics, and Working Class History* (London, 1994); and Noel Ignatiev, *How the Irish Became White* (New York, 1995). Three older works with implications for the construction of whiteness are Takaki, *Iron Cages*; Alexander Saxton, *The Indispensable Enemy: Labor and the Anti-Chinese Movement in California* (Berkeley, 1971); and Winthrop D. Jordan, *White over Black: American Attitudes toward the Negro, 1550–1812* (Chapel Hill NC, 1968). Most of these works implicitly deal with whiteness as it was constructed and understood east of the Mississippi. A good study that addresses white racial identity in the Far West is Tomás Almaguer, *Racial Fault Lines: The Historical Origins of White Supremacy in California* (Berkeley, 1994).

51. This tension in the views of many U.S. officers is sensitively explored in Thomas C. Leonard, *Above the Battle: War-making from Appomattox to Versailles* (Oxford, 1978), 43–58.

52. Lonnie J. White, "From Bloodless to Bloody: The Third Colorado Cavalry and the Sand Creek Massacre," *Journal of the West* 6, no. 3 (October 1967): 535–81; Raymond G. Carey, "The 'Bloodless Third' Regiment, Colorado Volunteer Cavalry," *Colorado Magazine* 38, no. 3 (October 1961): 275–300. See also Stan Hoig, *The Sand Creek Massacre* (Norman OK, 1961); and David Svaldi, *Sand Creek and the Rhetoric of Extermination: A Case Study in Indian-White Relations* (Lanham MD, 1989).

The Immorality of Expediency

The German Military from Ludendorff to Hitler

Holger H. Herwig

"Unprincipled as a German civil servant, godless as a Protestant cleric, and dishonorable as a Prussian officer."[1] This aphorism, coined by the Prussian conservative Ewald von Kleist-Schmenzin as the Third Reich neared its *Götterdämmerung* in 1945, aptly summarizes the immorality of Germany's ruling elite under Adolf Hitler. Kleist, the scion of a noble clan that had left fifty-eight sons on Frederick the Great's battlefields, was hanged on Hitler's orders at Plötzensee on 9 April 1945. This chapter addresses that part of his comment dealing with the "dishonor" of the Prussian officer corps.

The Prussian officer corps had been forged administratively by Frederick William I and fused with the crown by the blood that it spilled so liberally in Frederick the Great's three Silesian wars. Its code of ethics stemmed from the Pietist fundamentalism espoused by Samuel von Pufendorf and Christian Thomasius at Halle University and encapsulated in Immanuel Kant's categorical imperative. Christian, conservative, honest, decent, and scrupulous—these words readily describe the corps that fought the three wars of German unification against Denmark, Austria, and France in the middle of the nineteenth century.

But thereafter, perhaps because of the very success of these wars, the Prussian officer corps developed a different ethos. When the historical section of the General Staff wrote the history especially of the Franco-Prussian War, it chose the heroes of its pantheon carefully. Civilians in the form of the militia (*Landwehr*) were quickly relegated to the footnotes of that history. Otto von Bismarck's skillful diplomacy, which had allowed Prussia to tackle each adversary one on one, was blithely ignored. So was the Iron Chancellor's sagacious policy of constantly

163

reassessing the war as it escalated beyond the initial clash of forces. The General Staff's writers instead attributed victory solely to the regular army—its discipline, drill, and weaponry—and in particular to its staff officers whose elite members Bismarck soon sarcastically derided as "demigods." At the War Academy (Allgemeine Kriegsschule), tactics (four hours), mathematics (four hours), military history, weapons, fortifications, and staff work (each three hours) were drummed into the heads of the army's best and brightest. Economics, foreign affairs, and politics were negated as not being worthy of study. At no time did imperial Germany develop institutions analogous to the British Imperial Defence College or the French Centre des Hautes Études Militaires.[2] Military action was seen not as simply another "means of politics" but as an end in itself, a cure-all for whatever ailed Germany. Civilian critics such as Hans Delbrück were not tolerated and their works denigrated by the military professionals.

The Schlieffen plan, drafted in the winter of 1905–1906, became the embodiment of this new mentality of "blinkered professionalism" (*Fachidiotie*). Germany's very survival was staked on a two-front gamble, a roll of the dice in northern France, winner take all. Operational effectiveness substituted for statecraft. The will to win replaced logistics. It is still shocking to read in Schlieffen's notes that the German army in 1906 was fully eight army corps shy of the required forces for the right wing of the "wheel" through Belgium and that it did not possess the five or six army corps needed to invest fortress Paris! In fact, no plans existed even on paper in 1905–1906 to create these critical forces.[3] Mere facticity?

Instead, intricate mobilization and deployment plans took the place of statecraft. Wishful thinking replaced strategy. Critics of the Schlieffen plan were either hounded out of office or publicly disgraced. Politicians and statesmen dared not challenge the voluminous railroad timetables that had replaced alliances in the planning of war. Put differently, civilians were kept out of the military knowledge loop. Chancellor Theobald von Bethmann Hollweg, in turn, proudly recalled after the Great War that he had never considered it to have been his "business" to take part in the "military for and against" discussions of the Schlieffen plan. Indeed, he admitted that he had not even known of its existence before 21 December 1912, when the General Staff had apprised him of the basic contours of Schlieffen's blueprint for victory.[4]

At about the same time, Kaiser William II had blurted it out at a state banquet in front of the king of Belgium.

The German officer corps, like German society as a whole, was seduced by the heady wine of social Darwinism and crude racism. The official records of soldiers and statesmen alike before 1914 are liberally sprinkled with prognostications regarding the "inevitable showdown" between the "Teutons" on the one hand and the "Gauls" and "Slavs" on the other. Even the elder Helmuth von Moltke painted a graphic picture of a "Germanic center in Europe" besieged by both a "Slavic East" and a "Romance West."[5] Ancient Germanic texts such as the Nibelungen saga were revived to shore up a highly romanticized alliance with the crumbling Austro-Hungarian Empire. Eight decades before Samuel P. Huntington "discovered" the concept, wars were already depicted as being fought not just between nations but ever more between "civilizations."[6] International relations were reduced to the "either-or" of world power or demise, centered on the theory of the survival of the fittest. Whether Germany's future lay in the East (as the army believed) or on the high seas (as the navy countered), there was almost universal consent that this path lay across the strewn corpses of "lesser" states.

To be sure, the German military-diplomatic elite was not alone in this line of thinking. Popular culture was, if anything, ahead of high culture in thinking along such "modern" lines. Countless civilian pressure groups lobbied government and public alike to accept war as both moral and inevitable. Not only the Pan-Germans and the various veterans associations with their nearly three million members in 1913 but also the Protestant and Catholic clergy publicly touted war as a panacea. In the words of a prominent Protestant theologian, Professor Alfred Uckeley, "God is the god of the Germans. Our situation is akin to that of Israel. We are God's chosen among the peoples of the earth. It stands to reason that our prayers for victory are heard."[7]

Academia joined the chorus. In 1912, Hans Delbrück demanded that the German fleet do more than protect trade; its real role was to accord Germany that "portion of world domination" due it on the basis of its role as a "cultural nation."[8] Not surprisingly, as the historian Wolfgang J. Mommsen has shown, there had developed in Germany by 1914 the "topos of inevitable war."[9] Leading public figures as diverse as Chancellor von Bethmann Hollweg, the writer Oswald Spengler, the Social Democrat August Bebel, and the Conservative Ernst von Heydebrand und der Lasa, joined Generals Friedrich von Bern-hardi, Axel von Freytag-Loringhoven, and August Keim in viewing war not only as inevitable but also as morally regenerating. Many Germans yearned for an end to what they referred to as the "foul peace" that Bismarck had imposed on Europe. Tired of hearing of the great deeds of their grandfathers and fathers in taverns and beer halls, they thirsted for deeds of their own. The younger Helmuth von Moltke merely reflected the public sentiment when he declared at the alleged "crown council" on 8 December 1912 that "he considered war to be inevitable and: the sooner, the better."[10] In many ways, the outbreak of war in July–August 1914 was in every respect the logical outcome of a decades-old self-fulfilling prophecy.

World War I both deepened existing ideological trends and added new dimensions. The war began with Germany's cavalier dismissal of Belgian neutrality, a "scrap of paper" that needed to be sacrificed to the dictates of railroad timetables; it ended with German plans to annex and "resettle" European Russia—megalomania triumphant. In between lay a host of policies and plans that, taken together, constituted a bridge from the Second to the Third Reich.

First, and most obviously, the German "wheel" through Belgium fell most severely and directly upon its civilian inhabitants. Immediately, irresponsible German newspapers—particularly the *Kölnische Volkszeitung*—fanned the flames of passion by circulating atrocity tales by Belgian *francs-tireurs* and saboteurs through headlines such as "The Beast in Belgium" and "Horrors in Liège." The Allies, in turn, quickly mounted an equally scurrilous propaganda campaign concerning alleged German atrocities (child molestation, murder, rape, even cannibalism) in Belgium. But there is no question concerning the reality of civilian suffering. The historian Henri Pirenne calculated that as many as 5,500 Belgian civilians were deliberately killed by the German army in 1914.[11] The number of those summarily executed by the Germans is estimated at 1,200 in the province of Liège, 2,000 in Namur province, 839 in Brabant province, and 350 in Hainaut province. As well, numerous towns such as Aerschot in Brabant were torched. Most tragically, the Germans set fire to the center of the historic city of Louvain (Leuven), razing the cathedral of St. Pierre and the city's ancient library. As well, about sixteen thousand houses were destroyed throughout Belgium, and an estimated half a million civilians fled the

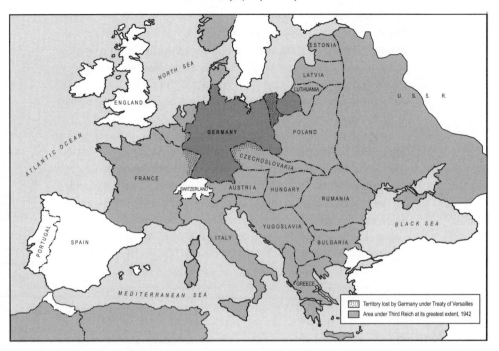

Map 6.1. Europe, 1919–1938

country, many to neighboring Holland. German authorities imposed a monthly payment of forty to sixty million francs on the Brussels government for the maintenance of their forces in Belgium and from mid-1915 to late 1916 deported about 500 Belgian workers per week to German munitions plants. Women and teenagers were used as forced labor on fortifications and roads.

When Germany sought to enhance its war effort through passage of the so-called Hindenburg Program, Belgian civilians once more became the targets of exploitation. By summer 1916, the Central Powers had "recruited" twelve thousand Belgian workers for German munitions plants as well as for Hungarian weaving mills and Bohemian glassblowing industries. In October 1916, General Erich Ludendorff, the army's First Quartermaster-General, demanded that twenty thousand Belgian workers be deported to Germany per week! Although that intake slowed to two thousand civilians per week by December, the deportations, amounting to about sixty thousand laborers, continued well into February 1917.[12] The workers were transported to the Reich in cattle cars and arrived half-starved and (in winter) half-frozen. Another sixty thousand Belgians worked behind the German front in France. About 170 factories were destroyed, while 160 more remained on the German governor-general's list for destruction by war's end. These actions presaged the more brutal exploitation of Europe's labor force after 1939.

Second, the German use of chlorine gas at Ypres in March 1915 is interesting for the mental gymnastics that cleared the way for its use. The Reich, as a signatory to the Hague Peace Conference of 1899, was pledged not to use "poison or poisoned weapons"; "arms, projectiles, or material calculated to cause unnecessary suffering"; or "projectiles" designed for the "diffusion of asphyxiating or deleterious gases."[13] The General Staff in 1915 deployed legal sophistry to bring its use of gas against Allied armies composed primarily of conscripted civilians within the Hague Conventions. The prohibition of "poison or poisoned weapons," the Second Army Supreme Command argued, applied only to the deliberate poisoning of food and water and the use of projectiles steeped in poison. And since the matter of "asphyxiating or deleterious gases" was dealt with in another provision of the Hague Convention, German leaders argued, the first clause of the final document did not pertain to "gas" warfare per se. Additionally, General Erich von Falkenhayn, then chief of the General Staff, suggested that since the German gas shells contained both a gas-producing compound and an explosive charge to produce fragmentation, they could be said to serve a dual purpose, that is, not "gas warfare" alone. And finally, German staffers suggested that the release of gas from cylinders obviously did not involve the use of "projectiles."[14] Obviously, no one could control where the gas went, or whether it blanketed soldiers or civilians. Falkenhayn's use of the disingenuous code name "Disinfection" for the Ypres action certainly presaged the Third Reich's predilection for similar euphemisms.

Third, the German unrestricted submarine campaign in the Great War gave further evidence of "redefining war." Under established "prize" rules, U-boats had to warn intended victims of their fate and to secure their civilian crews. Under the more radical "unrestricted" form of warfare, U-boats were free to dispatch merchant ships and ocean liners without warning and with impunity. Unrestricted U-boat warfare was argued always on the basis of tonnage count, never on that of morality or politics. The torpedoing of liners such as the *Lusitania* and *Arabic* in 1915 and of the *Sussex* in 1916 with significant loss of civilian passengers—to name but some of the most prominent cases—was seen but as unpleasant annoyances. That this game of "playing *va banque* with moderate chances . . . against half the world," as Lt. Comdr. Ernst von Weizsäcker termed the U-boat campaign, was not in the national interest was admitted by only a handful of naval officers and political leaders.[15]

Most German military, naval, and political leaders easily fell victim to the allure of statistics. The human cost was peripheral to tonnage count. Adm. Henning von Holtzendorff, chief of the Admiralty Staff, hired an army of civilian bankers, economists, insurance brokers, and university professors to assure the nation that victory lay in simple mathematics. Britain, Holtzendorff argued, had about eleven million tons of shipping at its disposal, including neutral vessels trading to Allied ports. If about half of the neutral three million tons of shipping could be scared off the seas by unrestricted U-boat warfare and if the Kaiser's "pirate ships" could destroy an average of six hundred thousand tons per month for a period of six months, then Great Britain would lose 39 percent of its tonnage, a "final and irreplaceable loss."[16]

The vast majority of German policymakers were so dazzled by these voluminous statistical compilations of world shipping tonnage, rye and wheat production, and monthly potential merchant ship sinkings, that it readily accepted bringing the United States into the war on the side of the Allies since it would be immaterial to the outcome of the conflict. Admiral von Holtzendorff assured Field Marshal Paul von Hindenburg, chief of the General Staff, that the underwater campaign was sure to bring the United States into the war—"a serious matter," to be sure—but that this would have to be taken into the bargain because the Reich could not turn its back on the weapon "that will bring us victory at the right moment."[17] Hindenburg readily concurred. "We fully expect war with America and have made all preparations for it. The situation cannot get any worse."[18] General Ludendorff bluntly stated that the decision for unrestricted submarine warfare was purely military and that it did not involve the politicians. Privately, Ludendorff informed the industrialist Hugo Stinnes: "The United States does not bother me . . . in the least; I look upon a declaration of war by the

United States with indifference."[19] Ludendorff was even more direct to Hindenburg: "I do not give a damn about America."[20] Grand Admiral Alfred von Tirpitz, the architect of the High Sea Fleet, caustically dismissed American sea power as well: "The Yankee fleet is of no consequence to us."[21] Such cavalier treatment of a potentially explosive political-strategic issue by imperial planners helped assure Germany's defeat in the Great War.

Moreover, it should be noted that civilians stood front and center in German calculations. Admiral von Holtzendorff spoke in his famous December 1916 U-boat memorandum about a "grip of fear" that would bring the war home to Britain's population. The island's notoriously "refractory" workers would strike as food supplies were cut off by the U-boats and thus cripple the war effort. "Disorder" would be the order of the day among the civilian population. "The psychological effect upon Englishmen" of drastically reduced foodstuffs, Holtzendorff crowed, "is of no less importance than the direct result upon imports."[22] Put differently, caloric intake among British women and children became a measure of survival or defeat—"wastage" in the cold terminology of the day, in much the same sense as soldiers killed, maimed, or wounded.

Fourth, one can detect a major redefining of German military theory and practice in late 1916 with the appointment of the Third Army Supreme Command of Hindenburg and Ludendorff. It would not be too far off the mark to suggest that the tenure of the duumvirate constituted the demarcation line between the sober, rational planning of the elder Moltke and Bismarck and the genocidal expansionism of Adolf Hitler and the Third Reich. Military brilliance, charisma, fanaticism, reckless leadership, efficiency, the craft of operations, and the pursuit of military excellence—these terms have all been used by historians to describe the age of Ludendorff in German military planning. Above all, Ludendorff regarded himself as an "engineer" of war. Ordnance on target replaced the "science" or the "art" of war in his vocabulary.

Most pertinent to the theme of "civilians in the path of war" was Hindenburg and Ludendorff's decision to withdraw from the so-called Ancre knee between Arras and Soissons in February–March 1917. Citing the Russian "scorched-earth" policy in Poland in summer 1915 as a precedent, Ludendorff dictated that "Operation Alberich" (named after the malicious king of the dwarves in the Nibelungen saga) was to lay waste all territory abandoned—basically, a strip of land twelve to fifteen kilometers in depth in front of the new 150-kilometer-long "Siegfried" line as well as another five-kilometer-deep strip behind it. The Allies, in his words, were to "find a totally barren land."[23]

First, more than nine hundred trains comprising 37,100 wagons hauled away all usable war materials and raw supplies as well as 126,000 French civilians. The largest single contingent removed consisted of 40,000 inhabitants of the city of St. Quentin; about 14,000 residents chose to stay behind. German military authorities brought the French civilians to railheads with whatever they could carry with them in wagons and then selected those "capable of work" from those "incapable of work."[24] Most of the former were "resettled" in Belgium and in the new German rear echelon; many of those unable to work were removed to Germany. Next, every village was reduced to rubble. Trees were felled; streets mined; bridges blown up; creeks dammed up; rail lines unscrewed; combustible materials burned; and telephone wires rolled up.[25] It was a staggering feat of "engineering" and one that most clearly affected civilians who happened to be in the wrong place at the wrong time. The only sour note was sounded when the general government in occupied Belgium experienced difficulties "recruiting" forced labor to construct the new Siegfried positions.[26]

But there existed also an ideological, political, and racial side to Ludendorff. Together with his aide, Col. Max Bauer, Ludendorff launched what the historian Martin Kitchen has termed a transitional phase of early or proto-fascism.[27] The Third Army Supreme Command's radical positions on the issue of German war aims, in the opinion of the historian Andreas Hillgruber, foreshadowed much of what was to come under the Third Reich.[28] Hindenburg and Ludendorff proposed nothing less than to dismember Russia and to return it to its Petrine dimensions. "Border states" such as the Ukraine, Georgia, the Crimea, and Transcaucasia were to be created on the shores of the Black Sea. The Russian Black Sea Fleet was to be seized by Germany as "war booty."[29] And while General Max Hoffmann already saw the Crimea as "our Mediterranean" coast—a not altogether surprising desire after three winters of warfare in Poland and Russia—Rear Adm. Walter von Keyserlingk, head of the Operations Division of the Admiralty Staff, crowed that Russia was "ready to be colonized for the second time in its thousand-year history. . . . The ideal colonizers are the Central Powers."[30]

The Baltic states, according to General Paul von Bartenwerffer, chief of the Political Division of the General Staff, were to be placed under German sovereigns as future reservoirs of raw materials and settlement lands for army veterans. Hindenburg not only desired the Baltic states for "the maneuvering of my left wing in the next war" but also as colonial land, from which the indigenous inhabitants were to be removed and the region repopulated with "physically and mentally healthy human beings." Ludendorff, who regarded the local population as being "a mixed race" without "a culture of its own," coveted Courland and Lithuania primarily as resettlement regions for retired German soldiers and counseled removal of the indigenous population.[31] William II envisaged a return to the glory days of Prussia's greatest king. "*Balticum* is a whole, in personal union under Prussia's king, who has conquered it! Just as under Frederick the Great!"[32] Little wonder that one million German soldiers occupied Russia at the time of the critical "Michael" offensive in France in the spring of 1918.

Ludendorff also saw the Great War as a *Kulturkrieg*, a clash of cultures. Racial or *völkisch* overtones dominated his thoughts, especially with regard to the East. As he later put it, "war is the highest expression of the racial will of life."[33] More than that, war was a truly national effort. It obliterated the neat dividing line between political and military considerations. The warrior became the statesman. He could demand total mobilization in the name of the nation, put forth total goals as its objective, and conduct total war in its behalf. Civilians were but pawns in the larger game of resettlement and colonization.

Military planners in the Weimar Republic sought to extract "lessons" from the Great War, but these centered by and large on the nuts and bolts of operations, tactics, and technology. Defeat was studied in terms of the number of shells on target, heavy guns per divisional front, machine guns per battalion, and gas laid down per square meter of front. Few, if any, military planners asked whether the use of force was still relevant for Germany in the 1920s.

The study of future wars—that is, primarily politics and strategy— was largely left to "popular" writers. In 1920, the ubiquitous General

Friedrich von Bernhardi sought to discredit the "civilian critic" Hans Delbrück by showing that the offensive, if properly conducted, remained the alpha and the omega of modern "aggressive warfare."[34] Two years later, Kurt Hesse, a civilian, by contrast stressed the "psychological component" of warfare—that is, issues such as motivation and the will to win—and called for the emergence of a modern-day charismatic *Führer* as the cure-all for Germany's military ills.[35] Yet another civilian writer, Max Schwarte, saw salvation in still greater concentration on technology: a symbiosis of soldier and worker, officer and statesman; and a new emphasis on mechanization and motorization.[36]

General Hans von Seeckt, the father of the Reichswehr, displayed a narrow military professionalism with regard to the war of the future. The chief of the Army Command reiterated not only the central role of cavalry in combat but also the traditional Prussian view that the direction of the war should remain in the hands of a small, highly professional military elite. In his view, organized violence had to be institutionalized and monopolized. Above all, it had to be removed from civilian interference or control, be it from the Right or the Left. Questions such as the role of industry, the place of logistics, and the influence of public opinion in war lay beyond Seeckt's horizon.[37]

But there existed within the Reichswehr a minority faction that looked back to the wars of liberation against Napoleon—the myth of the civilian soldier—as an ideal worthy of revitalization. In 1924–1925 Joachim von Stülpnagel, a division chief in the thinly disguised general staff (Troop Office), added national hatred to the arsenal of German warfare. Stülpnagel sought to erase the dividing line between civilians and soldiers and to turn blood and treasure alike into "tools of war." Specifically, he envisaged a peoples' war (*Volkskrieg*) whereby German army regulars and militia irregulars would conduct guerrilla-style warfare against even overwhelming enemy armies, drawing them deeply into Germany in order to splinter them, and then to decimate and demoralize them with terrorist and scorched-earth policies. Poison gas, flooding, assassinations, and kidnappings would highlight the new "citizen" style of warfare. Stülpnagel was quite willing to dismiss the fact that Germany's seven divisions possessed ammunition for only one hour of fighting. Instead, he lectured fellow officers (including the future war minister Werner von Blomberg) that wars against France and Poland could be conducted by *Simplicissimus* peasants defending fortified potato cellars and *Götz von Berlichingens* fighting from hidden forest paths![38] Better a "heroic result" than cowardly inactivity.

What all these writers had in common once more was what the historian David Schoenbaum has called "the redeeming grace of heroic generalship"—the triumph of "tactical virtuosity" and the "magic of new technologies" as substitutes for Bismarckian *Realpolitik*.[39] None addressed the reality of German industrial production, treaty constraints, or alliance relations. None evaluated the role of civilians, either as combatants or as victims of a future war. That task remained for Defense Minister Wilhelm Groener. In 1928–1930, after having tested Stülpnagel's guerrilla tactics in two war games with devastating results (annihilation in a two-front war), Groener penned a realistic assessment of Germany's military options taking these factors into account.[40] It was a sobering document. A military solution to Germany's security problems, Groener concluded, was not in the cards. He rejected out of hand suicidal operations as anathema to military professionalism.[41] Economic recovery, followed by alliance revisions, alone promised future revisions of the Versailles *Diktat*. Wars, in Groener's view, had to remain short and their conduct tightly under the control of the nation's professional political and military elite. His realistic calculus never had a chance in the turbulent climate of the late Weimar Republic, and Groener was quickly hounded out of office. The majority of Germans favored more arms and more soldiers, which alone could assure future wars. Germany's military by 1930 was bent on restoring the past in order to fight the wars of the future.[42]

Ideology also dictated German naval strategy as the Weimar Republic began to yield to the Third Reich. Commander (later Admiral) Wolfgang Wegener, in what was truly the one strategic thought ever developed by the navy, posited Anglophobia as the central driving force in naval planning. In place of Tirpitz's "risk theory," which concentrated on a naval Armageddon in the south-central North Sea, Wegener developed an "Atlantic strategy" whereby Germany would seize Norway, the French Channel coast, and the Faeroe Islands (he actually preferred the Shetlands) as the vital prerequisites for a "Second Punic War" against "perfidious Albion."[43] Yet again, army and navy failed to coordinate their strategies. And neither embedded its wishful planning in the broader parameters of German industrial strength or diplomatic possibilities.

Still, Wegener's emphasis on geography as a factor in strategic planning brought to center stage another "ideology" that linked the Weimar Republic to the Third Reich: geopolitics. Geopolitics was most closely associated with General Karl Haushofer, who greatly admired Wegener's work and who in 1924 tried to explain Carl von Clausewitz's *On War* to the Landsberg prison inmates Adolf Hitler and Rudolf Hess.[44] It emphasized control of the Eurasian "heartland" from Vilna to Vladivostok. The language of geopolitics—"justified war," "emasculation of racial enemies," "the natural law of *Lebensraum*," "servants of the Anglo-Saxons," and "the *Volk* in chains"—certainly became part and parcel of Nazi rhetoric.[45]

But it did not remain rhetoric. Intoxicated by the pure opium of Wegener and Haushofer, the Kriegsmarine in January 1942, for example, proposed to divide the world with the fellow "Aryan" ally in Tokyo along a line running north to south at 70 degrees longitude—that is, from the Kara Sea to Omsk, Tashkent, Bombay, Karachi, and the Indian Ocean.[46] Thereby, Germany would control half the globe from India to Greenland; Japan the other half from India to Hawaii—once more, megalomania triumphant. General Franz Halder, chief of the General Staff and no stranger to such musings, later laconically noted of German admirals: "These people dream in continents."[47]

The Third Reich reaped the whirlwind of the Wilhelmian and Weimar "politics of despair": social Darwinism, racism, military professionalism, megalomania, and geopolitics. Hindenburg and Ludendorff's concepts of eastern colonization, for example, became the centerpiece of Hitlerian expansionism. Falkenhayn's penchant for disingenuous code names became part of the official language of the Third Reich (*Aktion, Endlösung, Kanada, Kugel, Sonderbehandlung,* etc.). And Falkenhayn's callous disregard of the Hague Conference agreements on gas warfare in 1915 was but the precursor of Hitler's casual setting aside of international conventions on warfare especially in spring 1941. Wegener and Haushofer's geopolitical calculus became the cornerstones of Nazi rhetoric and policy. In all they did, the Nazis took up earlier developments and radicalized them into their well-known brutality.

Three days after coming to power, Hitler convened his military chiefs and laid out before them the main tenets of his "program": authoritarian rule at home, rapid rearmament, radical revision of the Versailles Treaty, and the conquest and "ruthless Germanization" of lands in the East. The party would secure the inner front—read, civilians—so that the army could concentrate on a policy of aggression. Hitler found no opposition that 3 February 1933. General Walther von Reichenau summed up the feelings of many officers: "We are National Socialists without party cards . . . the best and most serious."[48]

Four years later, on 5 November 1937, Hitler repeated his expansionist aspirations to Germany's military and diplomatic leaders. The Führer asked his military adjutant, Col. Friedrich Hossbach, to take careful notes since Hitler regarded his comments as a sort of political testament. For our purposes, it suffices to note that Hitler proposed that Austria and Czechoslovakia be seized by Germany as the necessary prerequisite for the main *Drang nach Osten*: a war to the bitter end against Soviet Russia by 1943–1945. None of the generals (Werner von Blomberg, Werner von Fritsch) or admirals (Erich Raeder) present at the meeting objected to the planned destruction of Austria and Czechoslovakia or to the extension of the war into the East. They limited their "critique" to suggestions that Hitler might not be correct in arguing that Britain and France would stay out of a general European war.[49]

To be sure, there were to be fundamental differences of opinion especially between Hitler and General Ludwig Beck, the chief of the General Staff from 1934 to 1938, as to the *pace* of rearmament, but very few on the *principle* of rearmament leading to war. In 1937, the German army estimated that it could be ready for war only by 1943 and that its defensive deterrent against France (the Westwall) would not be completed until 1953! Hitler would have none of this. General Alfred Jodl tersely noted in his diary in May 1938: "Sharp controversy between Hitler and army leaders. Hitler says: we must go ahead this year, the army says, we cannot."[50]

Equally significant, the German officer corps maintained its narrow military professionalism from the Weimar Republic into the early Nazi period. While historians such as Gordon Craig, Harold Gordon, and Francis Carsten, among others, have highlighted the army's political role under the republic, recent scholarship has stressed the officer corps' retreat into professionalism. Tactics (six hours) and military history (four hours)—a euphemism for more tactics—once more dominated the curriculum of the *Kriegsakademie* in Berlin. Logistics and intelligence were ignored. Nor had Seeckt been interested in developing strategic or economic experts.[51] And politics had been omitted entirely.

In fact, under what the historian Klaus-Jürgen Müller has called the "twin-pillars concept" of army and state, German officers readily abandoned politics to Nazi party *Bonzen* in order to concentrate on military effectiveness. In league with Hitler, these officers demanded radical revisions of the Versailles Treaty of 1919 and effectively pursued hegemony in Europe for the new Greater Germany. While Gens. Wilhelm Keitel and Alfred Jodl joined General von Reichenau as enthusiastic supporters of the charismatic Führer—whom Kurt Hesse had called for in the early 1920s—senior army officers such as Gens. Franz Halder, Walter von Brauchitsch, and Erich von Manstein, to name but three, retreated in the best tradition of the Weimar Republic's Reichswehr into their cherished world of military professionalism. They shared the regime's hegemonic expansionism and saw in Hitler's *Ostpolitik* the continuation of Hindenburg and Ludendorff's eastern and military policy from 1916–1918. All too many officers appreciated the attack on the Soviet Union in June 1941 as nothing less than an ideological life and death struggle against the instigator of the German revolution of 1918 and as revenge for the "rape of East Prussia" by Tsarist armies in World War I.[52]

In the end, German army officers were forced by Hitler to abandon their historic claim to control strategy. While the old professional school continued to view war as an exercise in elite politics, the Nazis offered instead an apocalyptic vision of war, a limitless escalation of violence. Hitler's pseudoscientific laws of race and ideological assertions of will were designed to overcome friction in war. Perhaps not all officers shared Hitler's Napoleonic policy of total war for unlimited goals, but they worshipped him as a man of action and success. Most were quite willing to retreat into the comfortable world of operational planning. Few possessed the intellectual strength or integrity to challenge Hitler. Few, if any, appreciated that their wars of conquest had civilians as secondary as well as tertiary targets. In short, they became content to act as a functional elite in the service of their Führer.

Few realized that in the process they would lose even this functional military role to the SS (Schutzstaffel) by 1944. Above all, they became ready executors of Hitler's insane policy of biological extermination and genocide.

It is necessary briefly to define the basic contours of Hitler's "program" to fully comprehend the shared mentality of Hitler and his generals and the nature of the campaign waged in the East beginning in 1941 against both Red Army combatants and Russian civilians. From day one of his political career, Hitler stressed the twin doctrines of race and space. The Führer nurtured a virulent, vulgarized version of social Darwinism. The rise and fall of civilizations, he argued, was directly related to their success or failure in maintaining racial purity. Human beings, like plants and insects, either survived or perished. This was a fundamental law of nature, one that had nothing to do with morality and everything to do with the will to fight (*Kampf*). In the case of Russia, Hitler from the start envisaged a cataclysmic war between two irreconcilable ideologies.

Space, to Hitler, translated not only into the radical annexationism of Hindenburg and Ludendorff, but also into the heartland notions of Haushofer: control of the Eurasian land mass stretching from Germany to the Urals. Under the slogan of "blood and soil" (*Blut und Boden*), Hitler sought nothing less than the conquest of Soviet Russia and the eradication of what he called the "Jewish-Bolshevik bacilli" that ruled the land. Conquest of Lebensraum went hand in hand with biological extermination. The traditional distinction between combatant and civilian was set aside from the start. Hitler sought nothing less than to establish a new order by destroying the enemy in the East. Once more, as with Wilhelmian writers, it was all or nothing: *Weltmacht oder Niedergang*, world power or demise.[53] If there was a "rational" calculus behind the Führer's vision of the new order, it ran roughly as follows: the "logic of escalatory war" combined with the "terrorist logic of national regeneration" would allow a purified German society to establish its hegemony over Europe.[54]

Hitler openly trumpeted these views in *Mein Kampf*, in his unpublished "Second Book" of 1928, and in the countless speeches that he delivered in the 1920s and 1930s. Few, if any, leaders have ever proclaimed their "program" so openly and so frequently. Only charlatans and mythmakers would deny its existence.

The steps toward the barbarization of war in the East are well known and will be analyzed in the next chapter by Truman Anderson. On 10 February 1939—that is, well before the attack on the Soviet Union— Hitler instructed field commanders that the coming struggle would be "purely a war of *Weltanschauungen,* that is, totally a people's war, a racial war." He asked the Wehrmacht's leadership elite to pledge un- conditional loyalty to him as their ideological Führer.[55] No objections were recorded. Hitler repeatedly referred to the coming war as a "racial war" and readily used terms such as "liquidation" to describe his ulti- mate objective with regard to enemy civilians. On the last day of July 1940, having defeated France, Hitler again returned to this theme in announcing to the military his "irrevocable decision" to destroy the Soviet Union. General Halder noted the gist of the Führer's speech in his diary: "Decision: Russia must be finished off in the course of this confrontation. Spring 1941. The sooner we destroy Russia, the better. Operation makes sense only if we seriously cripple the state in one blow."[56] Yet again, Hitler left no doubt that the operation was to destroy both the Soviet regime and the "Jewish-Bolshevik conspiracy" that it entailed. The army registered no protests against this policy.

But did Hitler really mean this? Or were these merely the idle mus- ings of a deranged mind? After 1945 German admirals and generals used sympathetic or biased listeners to put across their *Through the Looking Glass* interpretation of the war in the East. They assured will- ing listeners that they had conducted a "clean" and "decent" campaign as honorable Christian soldiers, defending Western civilization against Asian barbarism, and that in the process they had spared civilians as best they could. They dismissed tales of Wehrmacht atrocities as ac- cidents or isolated occurrences of every war—or laid them at the feet of the SS. This fairy tale historiography made its way into altogether too many Anglo-Saxon works on the Wehrmacht, especially those by political scientists, few of whom have ever darkened the inside of the Federal Military Archive at Freiburg.

Thanks in large measure to the efforts of the (then West) German historians at the Militärgeschichtliches Forschungsamt, we can now reconstruct the genesis and design of Operation Barbarossa (22 June 1941) on the basis of the well-documented historical record. Hitler, in his famous Directive No. 21 of 3 March 1941, instructed General Jodl, head of operations of the Oberkommando der Wehrmacht, that the war with the Soviet Union would be waged as an ideological struggle designed to end with the "eradication" of the "Jewish-Bolshevik intelligentsia."[57]

How did the army respond? On 26 March 1941 the Wehrmacht and the SS signed a draft agreement parceling out areas of responsibility for the coming war of annihilation. One day later, Chief of Army Command Brauchitsch instructed his staff to view the coming German-Soviet struggle as a racial war ("the struggle of race against race") and to use all possible harshness to conduct it.[58] On 30 March, General Halder accepted Hitler's command that the war would be an ideological and racial one, that the Wehrmacht needed to shed antiquated notions of "soldierly comradeship," and that the troops were to conduct a campaign of "extermination" against Bolshevik leaders and intellectuals.[59] Soldiers and civilians alike were to be treated as hostile.

Hitler translated what some might dismiss as ideological musings into binding orders shortly before the invasion of the Soviet Union. The "Decree Concerning the Exercise of Military Jurisdiction" of 13 May and the "Guidelines for the Treatment of Political Commissars" of 6 June 1941 set the tone for the coming war. Troops were ordered to shoot suspected guerrillas "while fighting or escaping"; officers were admonished to submerge "feelings of justice" to "military necessity." Final battle orders to the Wehrmacht called for "ruthless and rigorous measures" not only against Bolsheviks and guerrillas but also against Jews and Russian civilians.[60]

Individual unit commanders understood these instructions. While General Heinz Guderian later claimed that his Panzer Group Two never even received Hitler's so-called commissar order of 6 June 1941, in fact the head of Guderian's own Forty-seventh Panzer Corps openly referred to "the Führer's calls for ruthless action against Bolshevism" in his battle reports and stated that Communist officials and their sympathizers should be "taken aside and shot," but only by an officer.[61] General von Reichenau, commander of Sixth Army in 1941, instructed his forces that the "essential goal of the campaign" was to destroy Bolshevik power and to "eradicate" Asian influence on Western civilization. In the process, Reichenau decreed, the army would also eliminate "Jewish subhumanity."[62] General von Manstein, head of Eleventh Army, demanded nothing less than the "eradication" of the "Jewish-Bolshevik system" in the Soviet Union and ordered his soldiers to show no mercy as the new "carrier of a racial conception."[63] General Hermann Hoth, chief of Seventeenth Army, exhorted his "racially superior" German soldiers "to save European culture from Asian barbarism," from "an Asiatic mode of thinking and primitive instincts."[64] As late as January 1943, General Wolfram von Richthofen, commander of Fourth Airfleet, reread the chapters of Hitler's *Mein Kampf* "concerning Russia and Eastern policies" and found them "really very interesting" and providing "answers for almost all questions" in the present war.[65] And Field Marshal Fedor von Bock, commander-in-chief of Army Group Center, allowed that every soldier had the right to gun down "from in front or from behind" any Russian suspected of guerrilla activities.[66]

Countless similar citations could be repeated from divisional commanders as well, each showing yet again that such orders did not languish in army group archives. But perhaps a final word on the nature of the campaign in the East should go to General Erich Hoepner, head of Panzer Group Four: "The war against Russia . . . is the old battle of the Germanic against the Slavic peoples, of the defense of European culture against Muscovite-Asiatic inundation, and the repulse of Jewish Bolshevism. This battle must . . . therefore be conducted with unprecedented severity . . . [and] must be guided . . . by an iron resolution to exterminate the enemy remorselessly and totally."[67] It is clear from these selections that the "clash of civilizations" in the East recognized no line of demarcation between combatant and civilian.

The criminality of the campaign in the East can also be traced through two specific orders issued by Hitler. On 4 October 1939, the Führer had put out a directive granting all troops "amnesty" for any "acts of barbarism"—be they against soldiers or civilians—that they committed in Poland. Hitler reissued that directive on 13 May 1941— and expanded it also to include Soviet prisoners of war. With that, Hitler effectively set aside the Geneva Convention on the treatment of POWs as well as the Hague Convention of 1907 on the rights of civilians in war.[68] Little wonder that the historian Christian Streit entitled his book on the Russian campaign in general and the Wehrmacht's treatment of Soviet prisoners of war in particular *Keine Kameraden* (No comrades).[69]

The brutalization of warfare in the East can readily be gleaned from a very few statistics. The Wehrmacht captured slightly more than 5.7

million Red Army soldiers in the course of Operation Barbarossa; about 3.3 million (or 57 percent) died while in captivity.[70] Additionally, Adolf Eichmann of the SS placed the number of Jewish civilians "liquidated" in the East at 6 million. But the killing was not one-sided. The Wehrmacht suffered 1.3 million battlefield casualties (or 40 percent of the 3.2 million soldiers with which it had invaded the USSR in June 1941) just in the first year of the Russian campaign.[71]

Recent examinations of German military "justice" also show the brutalization of discipline within the Wehrmacht. During the Great War, imperial Germany had executed 48 citizen-soldiers for various transgressions against military discipline; Britain and France, by comparison, dispatched 346 and 650, respectively. But under the Third Reich, as the German historian Manfred Messerschmidt has shown, German military courts placed somewhere between 300,000 and 400,000 citizen-soldiers on trial for ideological or political crimes. Messerschmidt calculates that roughly 50,000 soldiers were sentenced to death and that at least 6,000 were executed. Omer Bartov, an American historian, places the latter figure at about 13,000 to 15,000. Again by comparison, the United States executed one citizen-soldier for "desertion with intent to hazard or avoid duty" and none for "political" actions. Great Britain executed one citizen-soldier (out of a total of forty sentenced to death) for treason.[72]

In a total perversion of morality and legality, the German navy in Norway insisted (successfully) after 26 May 1945 that the British confirm and carry out all sentences involving more than two years' incarceration (and thus capital offenses) passed by German military courts against sailors convicted of ideological and political crimes — primarily lèse-majesté, that is, insulting the "honor" of the Führer. Leaving out the fact that such sentences were carried out in the name of an *Unrechts-regime* that had murdered millions of civilians and soldiers throughout Europe, one can only wonder whether the irony ever dawned on British leaders that they were performing this duty as late as spring 1946 — that is, well after the "first soldier of the German Reich," Hitler, had "deserted" (*Fahnenflucht*) on 30 April by way of suicide.[73]

What the historian Michael Geyer called the German "escalatory ladder to apocalyptic war" on the Eastern Front in 1941 reached its climax with Propaganda Minister Joseph Goebbels's infamous Sportspalast speech on 18 February 1943.[74] Whipping his listeners up into "a frenzied atmosphere of emotion," Goebbels asked them no less than ten times whether they were prepared to accept "total war" in all its desperate implications. Like the French patriots who voted nearly unanimously for "total war" in the National Convention on 23 August 1793, the Germans present in the Sportspalast in 1943 also responded enthusiastically in favor of total war. And Goebbels fully understood the criminality of the Third Reich. "We have burned our bridges," he wrote in November 1943 in the paper *Das Reich.* "We will go into history books either as the greatest statesmen or as the greatest criminals."[75] Few would disagree with that assessment.

Still, were the various and sundry army orders for the conduct of the war in the East ever followed? Or did they merely languish on the dusty shelves of army corps headquarters? Some historians have warned that we should not equate rhetorical orders with battlefield actions. We will be able better to answer this critical query when the voluminous Wehrmacht records housed in the former Soviet Union have all been returned to Germany and assessed by professional historians. For the time being, we are left with the historian Jürgen Förster's example of the 707th Infantry Division, which in Belorussia in a single month in 1941 shot 10,431 out of a total of 10,940 "captives."[76]

Perhaps the final word on the nature of the biological war of extermination that Germany conducted in the East beginning in 1941 should belong to the architect of that campaign, Reichsführer SS Heinrich Himmler. Speaking before SS-Gruppenführer in Posen on 4 October 1943, Himmler addressed what he called a "difficult chapter" in German history, one that his listeners understood but also one that Himmler assured his listeners could never be publicly revealed. "I mean now the evacuation of Jews, the rotting out of the Jewish people." That policy was being conducted as "a moral duty toward our people." Himmler acknowledged the physical difficulties faced by his ideological warriors as a result of the constant "piles of corpses" before them. "To have gone through that, and still . . . to have remained decent people, that is what has toughened us. It is a glorious page of our history, which has never been written and never will be."[77] For Himmler well knew the magnitude of his crimes against civilians.

To conclude: if some of the foregoing remarks seem overly harsh it is because they are intended to be so. After all, what makes modern

German history so distinct is not its quaint literary heritage, its charming rural setting, or its diverse regional peculiarities; rather, it is its aggressive, militaristic policies in the launching and conduct of two world wars. German social historians conveniently tend to ignore this point.

With regard to the topic of ideology and war, it should be obvious from the preceding that the Germans never quite got it "right" after Bismarck. Generals and statesmen alike developed and then clung desperately to the notion that military action was the one and only "cure-all" for whatever ailed the nation, or for whatever they thought it needed to do to feel secure. In the all-consuming drive to redefine war from 1871 to 1939, morality was jettisoned for the sake of expediency. International neutrality agreements were swept aside, gas was deployed in contravention of international agreements, and merchant ships were ruthlessly torpedoed whenever the goddess efficiency demanded such actions. Civilians were viewed as but inert impediments in the path of war—and removed or "resettled" as policy dictated.

But the Russian campaign raised even this redefinition of war to new and different heights. Thucydides argued in the Athenian case that what is necessary is also what is just. German generals in the East after 1941 may have felt that their actions were somehow wrong, yet they argued even more vociferously that they were also just. Perhaps they were simply closing ranks and defending one another as part of a group psychology. Yet we need to recognize that what was "normative" to Hitler and his military paladins was (and remains) immoral and illegal to us today. The German conduct of the Russian campaign had little to do any more with traditional concepts of self-interest, normative reality, or even expediency. It had nothing to do with established norms of behavior toward "civilians in the path of war." In its crassest forms, as manifested by many SS units, it became *Kampf* for the sake of *Kampf*. To some, it mattered little whether they killed or were killed.[78]

The Russian campaign from the start was one of plunder and exploitation, ruthless starvation and massive destruction. Edward III in France during the Hundred Years' War or Louis XIV in the Palatinate in 1688–1689 could have appreciated its character. Yet it was more: in the end, Barbarossa, perhaps the greatest *chevauchée* in history, ended in senseless and meaningless violence and destruction as ends in themselves. Michael Geyer has argued that what he terms the "expanding torrent of destruction" became the "main operational and tactical rationale" for war. Barbarossa's only operational goal for Hitler and his generals "was to inflict damage and destruction, to destroy the enemy state and to batter enemy societies and their armed forces into submission."[79] In the end, they also destroyed the very notion of professional warfare. Hitler, Goebbels, and Himmler certainly understood the immense gamble that they had undertaken in Russia; all three clearly appreciated that they would jointly celebrate victory—or hang. If one can even use the word *morality* in connection with the brutalization of warfare after 1941 it would have to be as the morality of predators—social Darwinism in its ultimate extreme form.

David Schoenbaum has suggested that the German generals'"original sin" was that of an "arrogant *Fachidiotie*, the blinkered professionalism of specialists indifferent to the context and consequence of their profession."[80] I would suggest that their "sin" was really not "original"; rather, it was incremental. Arrogance compounded by crude racism and social Darwinism led to war in 1914; megalomania compounded by geopolitics and genocide defined the war after 1939.

The price of the Russian campaign was paid by Germany's officers, political leaders, and above all by its people. Between November 1945 and October 1946, the Allies tried twenty-four major NSDAP members and organizations as well as German generals and admirals with crimes against peace and humanity and with planning aggressive war. The International Military Tribunal at Nürnberg handed out twelve death sentences. Those hanged included Generals Jodl and Keitel; Admirals Raeder and Dönitz received prison sentences.[81] One can well argue that the trials did not nearly reach deep enough into the Third Reich's criminal elite. But the German people to this day carry with them the burden of what the historian Charles Maier has called their "unmasterable past." Their every action—for example, moving the capital back to Berlin or reinterring Frederick II's remains at Potsdam—is judged against the Nazi past, the sins of the fathers visited on the sons to the third or fourth degree. Perhaps Schoenbaum was on the mark in assessing Bismarck's successors as sheer opportunists, Faustian romantics seduced by the glittering allure of an expediency that led them into the depths of immorality—and into decimating a good part of Europe's civilian populations.

Notes

1. Cited in Bodo Scheurig, *Ewald von Kleist-Schmenzin — Ein Konservativer gegen Hitler* (Oldenburg, 1968), 145.

2. Holger H. Herwig, "The Dynamics of Necessity: German Military Policy during the First World War," in *Military Effectiveness*, ed. Allan R. Millett and Williamson Murray, vol. 1, *The First World War* (Boston, 1988), 83.

3. Jehuda L. Wallach, *The Dogma of the Battle of Annihilation: The Theories of Clausewitz and Schlieffen and Their Impact on the German Conduct of Two World Wars* (Westport, 1986), 58.

4. Theobald von Bethmann Hollweg, *Betrachtungen zum Weltkriege* (Berlin, 1919) 2 vols., 1:167; see also, Herwig, "Dynamics of Necessity," 86–89.

5. See Helmuth von Moltke, *Ausgewählte Werke* (Berlin, 1925) 4 vols., 3:13.

6. Samuel P. Huntington, *The Clash of Civilizations?: The Debate* (New York, 1997).

7. Martin Greschat, "Krieg und Kriegsbereitschaft im deutschen Protestantismus," in *Bereit zum Krieg. Kriegsmentalität im wilhelminischen Deutschland 1890–1914*, ed. Jost Dülffer and Karl Holl (Göttingen, 1986), 49.

8. Hans Delbrück, "Deutsche Ängstlichkeit," *Preussische Jahrbücher* 149 (1912): 365.

9. Wolfgang J. Mommsen, "The Topos of Inevitable War in Germany in the Decade before 1914," in *Germany in the Age of Total War*, ed. Volker R. Berghahn and Martin Kitchen (Totowa NJ, 1981), 23–45.

10. Cited in *Der Kaiser . . . Aufzeichnungen des Chefs des Marinekabinetts Admiral Georg Alexander v. Müller über die Ära Wilhelms II.*, ed. Walter Görlitz (Berlin, 1965), 125.

11. See Henri Pirenne, *La Belgique et la guerre mondiale* (Paris, 1928), 64–65; and John Horne and Alan Kramer, "German 'Atrocities' and Franco-German Opinion, 1914: The Evidence of German Soldiers' Diaries," *Journal of Modern History* 66 (1994): 1–33.

12. See Holger H. Herwig, *The First World War: Germany and Austria-Hungary 1914–1918* (London, 1997), 260–61.

13. *The Reports of the Hague Conference of 1899 and 1907*, ed. James B. Scott (Oxford, 1917), 126 ff., 170 ff.

14. See Ulrich Trumpener, "The Road to Ypres: The Beginnings of Gas Warfare in World War I," *Journal of Modern History* 47 (1975): 468; and Reichsarchiv, *Der Weltkrieg 1914 bis 1918*, vol. 8, *Die Operationen des Jahres 1915* (Berlin, 1932), 35–48.

15. Lieutenant Commander Ernst von Weizsäcker, cited in Holger H. Herwig, *The German Naval Officer Corps: A Social and Political History 1890–1918* (Oxford, 1973), 188.

16. Holger H. Herwig and David F. Trask, "The Failure of Imperial Germany's Undersea Offensive against World Shipping, February 1917–October 1918," *The Historian* 33 (1971): 612–13.

17. Holtzendorff to Hindenburg, 22 December 1916. Politisches Archiv, Auswärtiges Amt, Bonn, Der Weltkrieg No. 18 *geheim*, Krieg, 1914.

18. Cited in Holger H. Herwig, "Miscalculated Risks: The German Declarations of War against the United States, 1917 and 1941," *Naval War College Review* (fall 1986): 89.

19. Ludendorff to Stinnes, 15 September 1916, Bundesarchiv-Militärarchiv (hereafter BA-MA), Freiburg, Nachlass Vanselow, F 7162.

20. Cited in Karl-Heinz Janssen, *Die graue Exzellenz. Zwischen Staatsräson und Vasallentreue. Aus den Papieren des kaiserlichen Gesandten Karl Georg von Treutler* (Frankfurt, 1971), 210.

21. Cited in Herwig, "Miscalculated Risks," 89.

22. Holtzendorff's memorandum in *Stenographische Berichte über die öffentlichen Verhandlungen des 15. Untersuchungsausschusses der Verfassungsgebenden Nationalversammlung nebst Beilagen* (Berlin, 1920), 2:227. Also, Holger H. Herwig, "Total Rhetoric, Limited War: Germany's U-Boat Campaign, 1917–1918," in *Great War, Total War: Combat and Mobilization on the Western Front, 1914–1918*, ed. Roger Chickering and Stig Förster (Cambridge, 2000), 189–206.

23. Germany, Reichsarchiv, *Der Weltkrieg 1914 bis 1918*, vol. 12, *Die Kriegführung im Frühjahr 1917* (Berlin, 1939), 121–22, 124.

24. *Der Weltkrieg 1914 bis 1918*, 125, 132.

25. A graphic account is provided by Ernst Jünger, *Im Stahlgewitter. Ein Kriegsbuch* (Berlin, 1926), 139.

26. *Der Weltkrieg 1914 bis 1918*, 12:123.

27. See Martin Kitchen, "Militarism and the Development of Fascist Ideology: The Political Ideas of Colonel Max Bauer, 1916–1918," *Central European History* 8 (1975): 199–220.

28. Andreas Hillgruber, *Deutschlands Rolle in der Vorgeschichte der beiden Weltkriege* (Göttingen, 1967), 58–67; and *Die gescheiterte Großmacht. Eine Skizze des Deutschen Reiches 1871–1945* (Düsseldorf, 1981), 53–58.

29. Naval diary entry of 27 February 1918, BA-MA F 4055, Kommando der Hochseestreitkräfte: KTB. See also Holger H. Herwig, "Admirals *versus* Generals: The War Aims of the Imperial German Navy 1914–1918," *Central European History* 5 (1972): 225–26.

30. BA-MA, Nachlass Keyserlingk, N 161, vol. 1:8.

31. See Holger H. Herwig, "Tunes of Glory at the Twilight Stage: The Bad Homburg Crown Council and the Evolution of German Statecraft, 1917/18,"

German Studies Review 6 (1983): 481, 483; Erich Ludendorff, *My War Memories 1914–1918* (London, n.d.), 1:178–79; Vejas Gabriel Liulevicious, *War Land on the Eastern Front: Culture, National Identity and German Occupation in World War I* (Cambridge, 2000).

32. See Winfried Baumgart, *Deutsche Ostpolitik 1918: Von Brest-Litovsk bis zum Ende des Ersten Weltkrieges* (Vienna, 1966), 68; and Holger H. Herwig, "German Policy in the Eastern Baltic Sea in 1918: Expansion or Anti-Bolshevik Crusade?," *Slavic Review* 32 (1973): 339–45.

33. Erich Ludendorff, *Der totale Krieg* (Munich, 1935), 10.

34. Friedrich von Bernhardi, *Vom Kriege der Zukunft. Nach den Erfahrungen des Weltkrieges* (Berlin, 1920).

35. Kurt Hesse, *Der Feldherr Psychologos. Ein Suchen nach dem Führer der deutschen Zukunft* (Berlin, 1922).

36. Max Schwarte, *Der Krieg der Zukunft* (Leipzig, 1931). See Wilhelm Deist, "Die Reichswehr und der Krieg der Zukunft," *Militärgeschichtliche Mitteilungen* 45 (1989): 81–92.

37. See Hans Meier-Welcker, *Seeckt* (Frankfurt a. M., 1967), 636; and *Handbuch zur deutschen Militärgeschichte 1648–1939* (Munich, 1979), vol. 5, 529 ff.

38. BA-MA, N 5/10 "Gedanken über den Krieg der Zukunft," 14–38.

39. David Schoenbaum, "The Art of the Impossible: German Military Policy between the Wars," in *Ideas into Politics: Aspects of European History 1880–1950* (London, 1984), 100.

40. See Wilhelm Deist, "Die Aufrüstung der Wehrmacht," in *Das Deutsche Reich und der Zweite Weltkrieg*, vol. 1, *Ursachen und Voraussetzungen der deutschen Kriegspolitik* (Stuttgart, 1979), 382 ff.

41. Michael Geyer, *Aufrüstung oder Sicherheit. Die Reichswehr in der Krise der Machtpolitik 1924–1936* (Wiesbaden, 1980), 191–95, 208–9. See also Gaines Post Jr., *The Civil-Military Fabric of Weimar Foreign Policy* (Princeton, 1973), 203–38.

42. See Edward W. Bennett, *German Rearmament and the West, 1932–1933* (Princeton, 1979), 235–41, 338–55.

43. See Wolfgang Wegener, *The Naval Strategy of the World War*, trans. and ed. Holger H. Herwig, Classics of Sea Power (Annapolis MD, 1989).

44. On Clausewitz, see the analysis by Williamson Murray, "Clausewitz: Some Thoughts on What the Germans Got Right," *German Military Effectiveness* (Baltimore MD, 1992), 193–216.

45. See Hans-Adolf Jacobsen, "'Kampf um Lebensraum.' Karl Haushofers 'Geopolitik' und der Nationalsozialismus," *Aus Politik und Zeitgeschichte: Beilage zur Wochenzeitung Das Parlament* 34–35 (August 1979): 17–29; and in greater detail, *Karl Haushofer. Leben und Werk* (Boppard, 1979), 2 vols.

46. See Vice Admiral Kurt Fricke's memorandum of 17 December 1941. BA-MA, PG 32220–21 Case 272. I. SKL Teil C 15.

47. Diary entry of 12 June 1942. Franz Halder, *Kriegstagebuch. Tägliche Aufzeichnungen des Chefs des Generalstabes des Heeres 1939–1942* (Stuttgart, 1964), 3:333. See also Holger H. Herwig, *Politics of Frustration: The United States in German Naval Planning, 1889–1941* (Boston, 1976), 238–39.

48. Cited in Klaus-Jürgen Müller, *The Army, Politics and Society in Germany, 1933–45* (New York, 1987), 34.

49. See Gerhard L. Weinberg, *The Foreign Policy of Hitler's Germany: Starting World War II 1937–1939* (Chicago, 1980), 35–40.

50. Manfred Messerschmidt, "German Military Effectiveness between 1919 and 1939," in *Military Effectiveness*, ed. Allan R. Millett and Williamson Murray, vol. 2, *The Interwar Period* (Boston, 1988), 236.

51. Messerschmidt, "Military Effectiveness," 244. See also David N. Spires, *Image and Reality: The Making of the German Officer, 1921–1933* (Westport, 1984); and James S. Corum, *The Roots of Blitzkrieg: Hans von Seeckt and German Military Reform* (Lawrence KS, 1992).

52. The German official history of the Great War claimed that the Russians had taken 10,000 "hostages" in East Prussia, destroyed 17,000 buildings, and stolen or slaughtered 135,000 horses, 250,000 cows, and 200,000 hogs. Reichsarchiv, *Der Weltkrieg 1914 bis 1918*, vol. 2, *Die Befreiung Ostpreussens* (Berlin, 1925), 325–30.

53. See the summations in Holger H. Herwig, *Hammer or Anvil? Modern Germany 1648-Present* (Lexington, 1994), 273, 312.

54. Michael Geyer, "German Strategy in the Age of Machine Warfare, 1914–1945," in *Makers of Modern Strategy from Machiavelli to the Nuclear Age*, ed. Peter Paret (Princeton, 1986), 574.

55. *Heeresadjutant bei Hitler 1938–1943. Aufzeichnungen des Majors Engel*, ed. Hildegard von Kotze (Stuttgart, 1974), 45.

56. Halder, *Kriegstagebuch*, 2:49. Entry for 31 July 1940.

57. See *Das Deutsche Reich und der Zweite Weltkrieg*, vol. 4, *Der Angriff auf die Sowjetunion* (Stuttgart, 1983), 414.

58. *Das Deutsche Reich und der Zweite Weltkrieg*, 4:416–17.

59. Halder, *Kriegstagebuch*, 2:336–37.

60. See Jürgen Förster, "New Wine in Old Skins? The Wehrmacht and the War of 'Weltanschauungen', 1941," in *The German Military in the Age of Total War*, ed. Wilhelm Deist (Leamington Spa UK, 1985), 310–13.

61. Cited in Omer Bartov, *Hitler's Army: Soldiers, Nazis, and War in the Third Reich* (New York, 1991), 86.

62. Bartov, *Hitler's Army*, 129–30. Order of 10 October 1941.

63. Bartov, *Hitler's Army*, 130. Order of 20 November 1941.

64. Bartov, *Hitler's Army*, 131. Order of 25 November 1941.

65. Bartov, *Hitler's Army*, 25, 132.

66. *Das Deutsche Reich und der Zweite Weltkrieg*, 4:435.

67. Cited in Förster, "Old Wine in New Skins?," 310.

68. *Das Deutsche Reich und der Zweite Weltkrieg*, 4:431, 433.

69. Christian Streit, *Keine Kameraden. Die Wehrmacht und die sowjetischen Kriegsgefangenen 1941–1945* (Stuttgart, 1978).

70. Bartov, *Hitler's Army*, 83.

71. Bartov, *Hitler's Army*, 44.

72. Bartov, *Hitler's Army*, 95–96; and Manfred Messerschmidt and Fritz Wüllner, *Die Wehrmachtjustiz im Dienste des Nationalsozialismus. Zerstörung einer Legende* (Baden-Baden, 1987), 29–30, 50, 87.

73. Messerschmidt and Wüllner, *Die Wehrmachtjustiz*, 260–67.

74. Geyer, "German Strategy in the Age of Machine Warfare," 593.

75. Cited in Hans-Ulrich Thamer, *Verführung und Gewalt. Deutschland 1933–1945* (Berlin, 1986), 679–80.

76. Förster, "Old Wine in New Skins?," 318.

77. Cited in Thamer, *Verführung und Gewalt*, 703.

78. This is abundantly clear from the expert studies by Charles W. Sydnor Jr., *Soldiers of Destruction: The SS Death's Head Division, 1933–1945* (Princeton, 1977); and James J. Weingartner, *Hitler's Guard: The Story of the Leibstandarte SS Adolf Hitler 1933–1945* (Carbondale IL, 1974).

79. Geyer, "German Strategy in the Age of Machine Warfare," 593.

80. Schoenbaum, "The Art of the Impossible," 103.

81. See Bradley F. Smith, *Reaching Judgement at Nuremberg: The Untold Story of How the Nazi War Criminals Were Judged* (London, 1977).

Yeline

A Case Study in the Partisan War, 1942

Truman O. Anderson

Yeline is a tiny Ukrainian village located near the border with Belarus in the Shchors district of the Chernihiv region. It is a casualty of Ukraine's two most recent disasters: the Chernobyl nuclear accident and the lurching transition to a market economy. Only a few births are recorded each year, and the village has become a community of the elderly. The young understand that their best opportunities lie elsewhere, and those who can leave Yeline tend to do so. The people who remain subsist on inadequate state pensions and the contaminated produce of their gardens and woodlands. Though Yeline seems destined to become a ghost town, it has risen from the ashes once before.

In early 1942, Yeline became the base of the most important Soviet partisan group then operating in German-occupied Ukraine. Partisan attacks on local garrisons and police detachments soon drew security troops to the area, and at the end of March a mixed force of German and Hungarian soldiers burned Yeline and several neighboring villages to the ground after a two-day battle. Many of the inhabitants were arrested and later put to death, and the remainder became homeless refugees under the most deplorable of conditions. This chapter will examine the background, conduct, and aftermath of this battle as a detailed case study of the partisan war, with emphasis on the actions of the German chain of command.[1] It also aims to explore the interaction of the occupiers, the insurgents, and the civil population and to illustrate the circumstances of the partisan war. Before turning to this story, however, it is necessary to establish its context within the broader history of military violence to civilians, the history of the German military during the Third Reich, and the history of the German-Soviet war.

As Mark Grimsley and Clifford Rogers state in the introduction to this collection, reprisals against civilians have been a feature of war from antiquity to the present day. The rise of industrial economy and the spread of nationalist mentalities in the nineteenth and twentieth centuries greatly exacerbated the problem, and international humanitarian law has lagged well behind in its efforts to constrain the various forms of punitive violence to civilians. Indeed, it was not until the Geneva Convention of 1949 that international law actually prohibited reprisals against civilians and their property.

The law of war was formally codified for the first time at the end of the nineteenth century. The Hague Conventions of 1899 and 1907 had given occupying armies broad powers to suppress "irregular" resistance and had imposed a correspondingly strict definition of "lawful" resistance upon potential insurgencies, a definition that effectively proscribed covert warfare. People who took up arms outside of these were liable "to be treated summarily as highway robbers or pirates."[2] This state of affairs reflected the convenience of the most powerful signatory states, all of whom projected themselves in the role of the occupier and wished to discourage guerrilla resistance. International jurists genuinely feared that granting too much license to guerrillas was likely to blur the lines that separated combatants from noncombatants. There was, in other words, a humanitarian argument against guerrilla insurrection, one that seemingly justified harsh repressive measures in order to prevent chaos. Thus, as the world prepared for renewed conflict in 1939, international law still reflected the view that the civil population of an occupied territory should go about its business peacefully or suffer the consequences. The German, French, British, and American armed forces each authorized the use of reprisals against noncombatants under certain circumstances and allowed the execution of guerrillas who did not qualify as lawful combatants.[3]

The events of World War II brought an end to this consensus in favor of the rights of occupying armies. The Geneva Convention of 1949 imposed an absolute prohibition on reprisals for several reasons. First, the moral imperative of resistance to Nazi occupation had cast the problem in a different light. Second, German reprisals had been so extreme and so numerous that the humanitarian logic of such measures seemed ridiculously misguided in retrospect.

This propensity for repressive violence to noncombatants is an important feature of the literature on the Wehrmacht and the brutalization of warfare. Revisionist studies that began to appear in the late 1960s and early 1970s laid to rest the early Cold War view that the Wehrmacht had fought a clean, professional war free of the bestial taint of Nazism. It has become clear that the Wehrmacht, at an institutional level, was a willing partner in the Third Reich's outrages against humanity.

Opinions vary as to how deeply the Wehrmacht's affinity for National Socialism's racial dogmas and cult of *Härte* ("brutal severity") is rooted in the German past. Holger Herwig, in his contribution to this volume, has suggested the era of the wars of unification as the point of the German military's descent into increasingly purposeless violence. The Franco-Prussian War and World War I indicate that the German army was already prone to react harshly to irregular resistance long before Adolf Hitler made *Härte* and blind obedience the twin summits of military virtue. Historians also disagree over the importance of ideological radicalization versus other factors that contributed to the escalation of German violence to civilians during World War II, including conditions at the front, the supply system, reciprocal Soviet brutality, and the frustrations of antipartisan warfare. The influence of Nazism on the mindset of rank-and-file soldiers is also a contested issue, though the indoctrination that young Germans received in the Nazi-controlled school system and the Hitler Youth is significant. Despite these variations in interpretation, the myth of the "clean Wehrmacht" of the early postwar years is dead and buried.

German forces tended to modulate the severity of their violence in accordance with the ethnicity of the subject population. Racial hierarchy was enshrined in antipartisan doctrine and reprisals in eastern Europe and the Balkans became more frequent and more severe than in the West. In Belarus alone no fewer than 628 villages were destroyed by German troops, and perhaps as many as 350,000 people lost their lives as a direct consequence of antipartisan operations.[4] The influence of Nazi ideology is also apparent in that, in all theaters occupied by the Reich, reprisal violence was frequently directed toward Jews in preference to other victims. The most striking example of this phenomenon was in Serbia, where Jews held in concentration camps around Belgrade were executed en masse in retaliation for partisan attacks on

German units operating in the countryside.[5] Furthermore, the terms *reprisal* and *punitive measure* (*Repressalie* and *Sühnemaßnahme* in German) were also borrowed to cover the deliberate extermination of Soviet Jews by SS and security forces working independently or in conjunction with army units.[6]

It is important not to lose sight of variations in occupation policy and practice, even on the Eastern Front. Some officers within the Ostheer recognized the counterproductive effects of sweeping reprisals and argued for a more moderate course of action from a very early point in the campaign.[7] Events in Ukraine had their own special trajectory, thanks largely to the influence of Alfred Rosenberg and Ukraine specialists of his Reichsministerium für die besetzten Ostgebiete (Reich Ministry for the Occupied Eastern Territories). In discussions with the leadership of Army Group South prior to the invasion, Rosenberg conveyed the idea that Ukrainians were a racially valuable people who would merit the status of dependent allies in the war with Stalin's regime. Capt. (Professor) Hans Koch, Rosenberg's liaison to the staff of Army Group South, was a particularly ardent champion of German-Ukrainian cooperation, and his opinions had a lasting influence on several key figures, including Lt. Gen. Karl von Roques, the commanding general of the rear area of Army Group South (Heeresgebiet Süd).

Early in the campaign, von Roques had instructed his forces to view Ukraine as the "*Lebensraum* of a friendly people" and had granted ethnic Ukrainians a number of privileges withheld from Russians, Poles, and Jews. Most important, Roques joined other eastern front generals in directing that Ukrainians should be spared from reprisal violence.[8] As partisan activity increased in Ukraine from October onward, however, the Heeresgebiet abandoned this policy and began to punish Ukrainian communities as well. But both von Roques and his successor, Erich Friderici, remained committed to a pro-Ukrainian concept of occupation policy.[9] Hitler's appointment of the vicious Gauleiter Erich Koch as the governor of Reichskommissariat Ukraine scuttled Rosenberg's vision of Ukraine as a German satellite. But in those parts of Ukraine that remained outside Erich Koch's jurisdiction, the German army continued to argue for what they supposed to be "decent" or "reasonable" treatment of the ethnic Ukrainian majority until the Wehrmacht was driven back into the Reichskommissariat in late 1943. It is important to note that these pro-Ukrainian sympathies within the officer corps were not altruistic. The fighting at Yeline took place at a time when the German army authorities were struggling to reconcile their professed policy of reasonable treatment for Ukrainians with their fervent desire to eradicate the Soviet partisan movement and all those who supported it.

The involvement of Hungarian forces is another factor that complicates the Yeline story. Soldiers of the Honved are generally depicted as reluctant partners who behaved in a more civilized fashion than their German allies. There is ample evidence in the records of Heeresgebiet Süd, however, to demonstrate that some Hungarian commanders were as likely to advocate reprisals as their Wehrmacht counterparts when faced with a serious partisan threat.

The early stages of the partisan war in the USSR were chaotic and improvised. Stalin's contributions to his country's disastrous defeats in the early weeks of Barbarossa included his refusal to countenance the development of a partisan organization in the years before the outbreak of war. As a result, the Soviet Union had no underground structure in place when the Wehrmacht struck on 22 June 1941. Not until 18 July did the government provide any formal instructions for the formation of a resistance movement, and even then confusion, inefficiency, and rivalry between the Communist Party, the army, and the NKVD remained the norm. Stalin did not create a central staff for the partisan movement until May 1942, and it had little impact on the struggle until well into the war's second year. In the interim, local, district, and regional Communist officials led the insurrection as best they could in loose cooperation with the army and NKVD.

Hitler and his senior generals were united in their expectation of a short, successful campaign against the USSR. They were certain that the decisive battles against the Red Army would take place west of the Dvina and Dnipro rivers within a period of six to eight weeks. A thin web of German garrisons, augmented by a small number of specialized security divisions, was thought sufficient to protect the army's communications while hostilities were in progress. Once the fighting was finished, control of the occupied portions of the USSR would pass to civilian governors (*Reichskommissare*) appointed by Hitler. The army therefore did not expect to play a significant role in the administration of conquered lands for very long. Though "fanatical" irregular resistance was expected, the army felt confident that this problem could await permanent resolution. Repressive measures long favored by the German military (but deliberately intensified for Barbarossa) would help keep the partisans in check and compensate for the relative weakness of Wehrmacht ground forces in the rear areas.

Hence, neither the Soviets nor the Germans were really prepared to fight a partisan war. The German advance swept over the western regions of the USSR so quickly that Communist officials were unable to organize effective opposition. Spontaneous popular resistance was virtually unheard of. The situation began to change when a quick victory eluded the German forces. As the war dragged on into the fall of 1941, partisan resistance stiffened, mainly due to the added time available to underground organizers before the arrival of the Wehrmacht.

In Ukraine, the German forces deployed in Heeresgebiet Süd fought a series of battles with partisans at Nykopil and Novomoskovs'k in the swampy Dnipro bend area from October to December and smaller engagements against less formidable groups around Myrhorod in the Poltava region. Both contests involved the killing of noncombatants, including the selective execution of persons denounced by their neighbors as "partisans" or "communists" as well as full-scale reprisals with both Jewish and Ukrainian victims.[10] The reprisals against Ukrainian villages showed that von Roques's policy of favorable treatment of Ukrainians was already being undermined by the Wehrmacht's draconian approach to antipartisan warfare. By the end of December, however, most of the partisan groups encountered during the autumn had been destroyed or scattered, and Heeresgebiet Süd, now commanded by Friderici, officially reaffirmed its policy of "reasonable" treatment of the ethnic Ukrainian majority.[11]

In January 1942, the northern boundary of the Heeresgebiet came to rest in the Chernihiv region. Here, in the forests between the river Desna and Ukraine's borders with Belarus and Russia, second-rate Hungarian units attached to the Heeresgebiet confronted a well-entrenched partisan organization under the capable and ruthless leadership of A. F. Fedorov, the chairman of the Chernihiv regional committee (*obkom*) and Khrushchev's personal choice to lead the underground struggle.[12]

Fedorov's group combined the *obkom* and its regional partisan detachment with smaller units that had been organized in each of the region's constituent districts (*raiony*). Its membership was typical of partisan units at this stage of the war. The nucleus was formed of party officials chosen by Fedorov himself. The majority of the partisans were party members and nonparty volunteers recruited locally before the German occupation of the region had begun. Fedorov had also allowed isolated soldiers from the Red Army to join, and peasants and villagers continued to trickle into the detachment over time. The group therefore fluctuated in size from a few hundred partisans and camp followers to more than one thousand. It possessed adequate stores of food and equipment, had a network of fortified camps in the forests, and was able to arrange resupply by airdrops from Moscow from time to time. Most important among its advantages was its proximity to the operational boundary between German Army Groups South and Center and to the immense Briansk forest to the northeast. The former made coordination of antipartisan operations difficult for the Germans, while the latter offered a refuge from pursuit.

Fedorov's group also enjoyed the cooperation of local villagers, many of whom rarely saw a German or Hungarian soldier and therefore found the partisans' authority much more credible than the invaders'. Many of the partisans visited the villages at night to see members of their families or to obtain supplies and information. In some instances, the entire detachment was billeted in a given village rather than in the forests. Most communities had an underground cell of one kind or another. Often this was organized by members of the Communist Party youth, the *komsomol*, or by villagers who had relatives serving with the partisans. Fedorov's headquarters had a printing press and circulated thousands of leaflets throughout the area, often with the help of these underground cells. Yeline, which had provided Fedorov with many of his sledges, became his main base of operations in February 1942.

Fedorov's partisans attracted the attention of the Heeresgebiet command through a series of small but bloody encounters with elements of the Hungarian 105th Light Division in January and February 1942. Most of the combat-ready units that were assigned to the Heeresgebiet had been sent forward to shore up the German line in the face of the Soviet winter counteroffensive. Only the local garrisons (*Kommandanturen*) and a few battalions of overage soldiers remained behind. The task of protecting the northern sector of the Heeresgebiet (designated Feldkommandantur 194 — abbreviated FK194) therefore fell to this Hungarian division, itself deprived of two reinforced battalions. Commanded by Brig. Gen. Imre Kolossváry, it was strung out eastward from Chernihiv in a series of small enclaves at Horodnia, Nizhyn, Bakhmach, Novhorod-Sivers'kii, and Iampil'. These isolated positions were essentially unreachable by road during the winter. Moreover, the Hungarian troops were unequipped for fighting in extreme weather. Fifty percent were reservists who, in Kolossváry's opinion, should never have been sent to the Eastern Front in the first place, given their age and physical condition. Mail and supplies were infrequent, and wounded men had to be evacuated cross-country to Chernihiv before receiving medical attention. Serious frostbite was commonplace (267 cases by the beginning of April), and while in the field the men were quartered in the villages and lived in the most primitive of conditions: "In resting places even officers were billeted in unheated Ukrainian houses or in houses heated with dung from the outside, used simultaneously as stalls (for animals) and a dwelling for people. Leaving aside the time spent in combat, one cannot rest, care for and clean one's body in such conditions and in such an environment—one can only become infected with lice (*verlausen*)."[13]

All of these shortcomings made Hungarian patrols a very attractive target for Fedorov's partisans. Their preferred victims, however, were members of the Ukrainian police detachments raised by the Germans from the most disaffected or opportunistic elements of the population, particularly from those whose families had suffered most from "dekulakization," collectivization, and the purges. These men, usually equipped only with small arms, were the everyday face of German authority in much of occupied Ukraine. Since the partisans acted not only as a military force but also as the long arm of the Stalinist government, they sought to make examples out of the policemen and German-appointed village chiefs (*starosty*). Fedorov's leaflets made it clear that active resistance to the Germans was the sacred duty of every Soviet citizen. Attacks against the police therefore served not only as a warning to would-be collaborators, but also a violent reminder to everyone else that a middle course between the Germans and the partisans did not exist. Between 15 and 18 January partisans attacked the village of Orlivka in the Novhorod-Sivers'kii district. There they killed twenty-six policemen and seventeen of their kinsmen, burned thirty-four houses, and made off with nineteen "recruits." Lieutenant Colonel

Würfel, the German commander of FK194, pleaded with the Heeresgebiet staff to take some action lest cooperation with German authorities cease altogether.[14] There was to be no response for some time, however, for in February the Heeresgebiet was forced to hand over even more of its manpower along with sixteen hundred sledges—the only reliable means of transportation apart from the railroads—to the Eleventh Army.

The Hungarians were therefore left more or less on their own. On 5 February, a mixed Hungarian and Ukrainian patrol from the Third Battalion, Thirty-second Infantry Regiment (105th Brigade) suffered two men killed and two wounded in a partisan ambush near Ivanivka.[15] On 17 February, another Hungarian patrol from the 105th Brigade was ambushed near Yeline. In the initial encounter, the Hungarians suffered twenty-two men killed and nine wounded as the partisans rained fire upon them from all directions (including the treetops). The brigade later reported that reinforcements had arrived and, in the ensuing action, the Hungarians claimed to have killed 139 "partisans" and burned the village of Luky-Hutor. It is highly likely that many of these 139 dead were not actual partisans but simply residents of Luky-Hutor killed for their presumed support of the guerrillas.[16]

This constant bloodletting continued in the following month. A group from the Forty-sixth (Hungarian) Infantry Regiment, probing eastward from Konotop toward Hlukhiv (Sumy region), sustained eighty-six combat casualties and an "undetermined" number of frostbite cases during the first week of March.[17] A few days later, Fedorov's partisans attacked Huta-Studenets'ka (Koriukivka district) and killed the district chief of police. Among his papers they discovered orders that revealed the presence of a mixed Hungarian-Ukrainian detachment at nearby Ivanivka, under the command of Lieutenant Kemery.[18] In the hours before dawn on 11 March three of Fedorov's companies attacked and overwhelmed Kemery's small force, driving it from the village, killing twenty-two Hungarian soldiers and wounding thirteen more. While occupying Ivanivka, the partisans executed thirty policemen and burned six homes in reprisal for collaboration. According to a report written by Lieutenant Colonel Würfel, they also cut off the hands of several of the policemen's children and persuaded ten more men to join them in the forest. German air support (rare in the partisan war) and Hungarian reinforcements from nearby Turia and Snovs'ke forced the partisans back into the woods the following afternoon.[19]

These attacks made it clear to the Heeresgebiet command that these "Snovsk" or "Yeline" partisans would have to be dealt with. Neither the Germans nor the Hungarians could protect collaborators from partisan reprisals. At the very least, this failure would make it very difficult to recruit policemen in the vicinity. The guerrillas also posed a threat to German control of the area's collective farms and to the rail line between Gomel and Bakhmach, which could be put out of service for weeks if the Desna bridge at Makoshina were demolished. On 3 March, the interested commanders met at Kiev to coordinate a counterattack. These included Brigadier General Kolossváry, his administrative superior Lieutenant General Olgyay (commander of the corps known as the Royal Hungarian Occupation Group), Lieutenant Colonel Würfel of FK194 and Lieutenant Colonel Kiefer, commander of FK197. The Heeresgebiet commander, von Roques (recently returned from medical leave), made a reinforced German guard battalion (Wachbataillon 703) available for the operation, along with three Secret Field Police groups (Geheimefeldpolizei or GFP) under the personal command of GFP Director Stephainski, the senior GFP officer in the Heeresgebiet. These units would join elements of the Second Battalion, Fifty-fifth (Hungarian) Infantry Regiment in an attempt to encircle the main body of Fedorov's partisans in their camp near Yeline.

The Heeresgebiet had a fairly good picture of the size and structure of Fedorov's group.[20] At this early stage of the partisan war, German intelligence was still profiting from popular discontent with Communist rule and could count on a number of desertions from the guerrilla ranks. Interrogation of partisans captured during the fighting at Ivanivka revealed that Fedorov's principal base, located southeast of Yeline, consisted of a network of dugout bunkers and storehouses large enough to accommodate roughly six hundred men. Camouflaged barns housed horses and cattle, and the Soviets were known to be well equipped with light and heavy automatic weapons, mortars, skis, sleds, and radios. The Germans also believed that there were partisans and their followers (mainly family members) quartered in the surrounding villages of Yeline, Bezuhlivka, Mostki, and Mlynok.[21]

Overall command of the operation fell to Lieutenant Colonel Würfel. His plan of attack called for a "hammer and anvil" approach over two consecutive days. On the first day, the Hungarian force would attack from the north and occupy Yeline, then on the second the bulk of the German troops (Wachbataillon 703) would eliminate the main body of the partisans in their camp. Würfel anticipated that Fedorov would attempt to withdraw to the northeast and planned dispositions to prevent this. The western and southwestern approaches to the guerrillas' enclave were left open.

While Wachbataillon 703 moved to the Ivanivka area by rail, Stephainski's GFP groups 708, 721, and 730 intensified their intelligence gathering. From reconnaissance patrols, informants, and prisoners a very detailed knowledge of the partisan camp's layout was developed, including the location of many of the bunkers, security outposts, and the paths leading into and out of the position. They also recruited guides to assist German troops during their advance through the woods. During these preparations, a GFP team encountered a small partisan patrol near Radomka, about thirty kilometers due east of the Yeline encampment. All five men in the patrol were killed in the ensuing firefight. A working Soviet army radio, complete with codebooks, thus fell into German hands. Also recovered was a sketch of various routes leading from the Yeline area toward Kholmy. Stephainski assumed that this patrol had been sent to scout the path of Fedorov's withdrawal.[22]

Armed with this intelligence, Lieutenant Colonel Würfel set 22 March as the day of the attack. He established his headquarters at Ivanivka while the attacking forces made their final dispositions. These were as follows (see map 7.1).

The Hungarian battalion (Second Battalion, Fifty-fifth Infantry Regiment) assigned the task of sealing off the northern edge of the forest, assembled first at Snovs'ke, and from there moved northward on horse-drawn sledges along the west side of the forest up the left bank of the river Snov to Pishchanka. On the first day of the attack, it would advance as a battalion from Pishchanka and deploy small blocking positions as it proceeded through Bezuhlivka to Yeline. On the second day, it would send detachments eastward to Mostki and southward to Mlynok and establish contact with the German units advancing from the south. In addition to eighty-two Ukrainian policemen from Horodnia, it was joined by GFP Group 708 plus the heavy

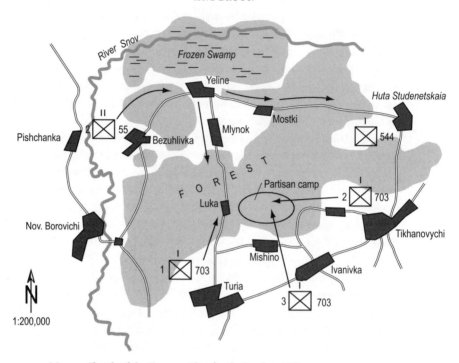

Map 7.1. Sketch of the German Plan for the Battle at Yeline on
22 March 1942

machine gun and antitank platoons of Wachbataillon 703. German air
support would also be available to the battalion during the attack.

Wachbataillon 703 arrived in the area on 17 March and deployed
in the villages along the southern edge of the forest. It was divided
into three company-sized elements, each reinforced with a squad of
GFP, a heavy machine gun team, and up to thirty-five Ukrainian policemen. Each company would advance simultaneously on the second
day of the operation. The First Company would attack north from
Turia toward Luka and destroy the partisan position in that village.
The Third (the largest group) would advance from Ivanivka and attack
the camp from the south, while the Second Company attacked it from
the east (from Tikhanovychi). Farther to the north, a company from
Landesschützenbataillon 544 was to take up a blocking position along
the eastern edge of the forest and prevent the escape of the guerrillas,

establishing contact with the Hungarians on its right, and the Second Company of the Wachbataillon on its left.[23]

Despite terribly cold weather and a recent snowfall, all of the attacking elements reached their assembly areas and deployed according to plan. At nine o'clock in the morning on 22 March, the attack began with the advance of the Hungarians toward Yeline. Bezuhlivka was reached without incident by mid-morning. Leaving behind a detachment of thirty Ukrainian policemen for security, they continued onward. Another group of policemen, however, sent out to protect the battalion's right flank, blundered into disaster. Ordered to take up a blocking position astride a trail that ran parallel to the battalion's line of march, the leader of this group instead brought his men onto the trail and began heading for Yeline. The partisans ambushed the group from the rear with devastating effect. By the time a Hungarian officer arrived, seventeen men had been killed and fifteen were missing.[24] According to Fedorov's account of the episode the missing men surrendered to one of his lieutenants and revealed to the Soviets that the Germans would attack the camp the following morning.

The Hungarians made their way to Yeline without further incident and began their assault at mid-afternoon. According to the account written by Lieutenant Colonel Csendes, the commanding officer of the Second Battalion, partisans fired upon the leading Hungarian companies as soon as they emerged from the tree line. The attack faltered under this fire until three German aircraft bombed the town. The remaining partisans withdrew, leaving Yeline to its fate.[25]

Two platoons set off to pursue some people whom the Hungarians had seen running in the direction of Mostki. Csendes sent another to search and burn Mlynok, which lay roughly four kilometers to the south. According to Csendes, both Yeline and Mlynok were completely deserted. Even the furniture had been removed from the homes. All of this indicated that the residents had known in advance that the village would be attacked and, fearing a reprisal, had moved out to the forest, taking as many of their belongings and livestock as possible. Not everyone had left, however, for the Hungarian soldiers counted eighty-six corpses scattered throughout Yeline. The detachments sent to the outlying villages returned after nightfall, having killed a further fourteen "partisans" encountered on the road to Mostki.

The attacking companies of Wachbataillon 703 trudged off at two o'clock in the morning on 23 March. The night march proved grueling as the men of the battalion struggled through fresh snow that was often hip deep. Things went well enough for the First and Second Companies on the flanks, which captured a series of Soviet outposts. By one o'clock in the afternoon, the First Company had occupied Luka. But in the center the Third Company's attack came to an abrupt halt when it reached the partisans' main defensive perimeter around the camp. Thanks to the desertion of the Ukrainian policemen the day before, the partisans knew when and where the German blow would fall. Fedorov's men waited until the Germans got within twenty-five or thirty meters of their positions and then opened fire. The advance soon lost all impetus. Most of the Third Company's light machine guns seized up from the cold, and as the battalion commander attempted to reorganize his forces and direct supporting mortar fire, he found his radio communications disrupted by Soviet interference. Partisan sharpshooters firing from the trees made efforts to reorganize very hazardous. An armorer, brought forward from Ivanivka, put most of the machine guns back in working order while the Second Company came up to support the Third, but it wasn't until nearly one o'clock in the afternoon that the Germans were able to set the attack back in motion. Eventually, as dusk approached and the pressure of the assault mounted, the partisans withdrew from the camp. Instead of pursuing the fleeing guerrillas, the German troops set about the task of destroying the partisans' abandoned bunkers and storehouses. The battalion then set off for quarters in Turia, Ivanivka, and Tikhanovychi, which were reached without further incident.[26]

In the north, the Hungarians had resumed their operations at four o'clock that morning. The main body of the battalion went east to Mostki, leaving an outpost just south of Mlynok to guard the road. A small patrol of partisans, interrupted while mining the road between Yeline and Mostki, fired on the battalion, killing one man and wounding another. The partisans fled, leaving behind six mines and a wounded comrade, whom Csendes ordered shot following a hasty interrogation. The troops arrived in Mostki before dawn and found it deserted. Csendes sent the German heavy machine gun platoon attached to his command farther east toward a tiny outlying village called Hutor Muryka. After searching Muryka, this platoon, led by a Captain Ulmke, moved on to reconnoiter the tree line beyond the village. Partisans concealed in the edge of the forest allowed Ulmke's group to come within fifty meters and then opened fire from three sides. Ulmke and two of his men were killed before Csendes could extricate them from the ambush. During the afternoon, Lieutenant Colonel Würfel authorized the battalion to withdraw to Bezuglovka. Csendes ordered Muryka burned to the ground. On the way back, the battalion also set fire to the houses along the southern edge of Yeline in order to screen their retreat.[27]

The initial results of the operation were mixed. Wachbataillon 703 estimated that at least one hundred partisans had been killed in the battle for the camp and many more wounded. How they established this figure is not clear, however. The battalion commander's report on the action states it was the result of "careful estimation" and also notes that the partisans dragged their wounded and dead into the forest, leaving behind many blood trails. This statement creates the impression that none of the dead were actually seen by the battalion within the perimeter of the camp, for bodies found after battle were ordinarily described as "counted dead" in German reports.

The Hungarians claimed 101 partisans killed, including the 86 dead found strewn throughout Yeline.[28] It is not possible to establish how many of these dead were members of Fedorov's detachment and how many were civilians. That the Hungarians lost only one man in the operation hints that there were few genuine partisans in Yeline itself, as does the Hungarians' failure to report so much as a single rifle or cartridge captured.

Lieutenant Colonel Würfel ordered another search of the area on 26–27 March. Wachbataillon 703 returned to the partisan camp on the twenty-sixth and found two boys (aged ten or twelve) who were able to tell the Germans something of the partisans' movements (he did not specify what information the boys gave or what became of them). Other than this, the Germans' search produced nothing.[29] The Hungarians, however, found that the villagers had returned to Yeline. According to Csendes, one or two partisans fired on the battalion as it entered the village at 0500. A house-to-house search turned up 230 people (all of whom he called "partisans"). Thirty who resisted arrest were shot immediately. The remainder were handed over to the GFP. The battalion then burned Yeline systematically, destroying everything. In addition to the captured "partisans," the battalion brought in twenty-two horses, thirty-eight cattle, and one Soviet parachute, but still no weapons. What was left of Mlynok was also put to the torch.

Over the course of the next two days, the Hungarians collected another 36 prisoners along with seventy-eight cattle and three barrels of oil. The prisoners were transported to Snovs'ke and the cattle surrendered to the local German agricultural leader. Between 29 March and 4 April, the GFP made further searches of the neighboring villages. Including the 236 prisoners brought in by the Hungarians, they arrested a total of 536 persons. Three hundred and six were sent to a civil internment camp at Gomel (located in *Heeresgebiet Mitte*). The remainder were released. This marked the close of the operation.[30]

The German officers who participated in the Yeline operation considered it a great success. Interestingly, the Hungarian reaction was a bit different. Lieutenant Colonel Csendes was skeptical about what had been achieved. Accepting the German estimate of the partisans' casualties, he nevertheless reckoned that at least three hundred guerrillas had successfully withdrawn.[31] Regardless of their differing points of view, all the participants agreed that whatever remained of Fedorov's group had made good its assumed escape to the northeast toward Briansk.

Fedorov's account of the battle provides a plausible explanation for this perception. He maintained that the bulk of his detachment withdrew in good order to the *southwest* on the night of 23 March, bringing its weapons, its wounded, and much of its baggage train. Fedorov stated plainly that the German attack had forced them from their initial perimeter into fallback positions before the withdrawal. During the withdrawal, however, he sent a smaller group to the northeast for the express purpose of deceiving the Germans. There is no direct evidence that German intelligence took this bait, but the Heeresgebiet continued to believe that Fedorov's detachment had fled toward Briansk for some time.[32]

Fedorov also conceded that his command suffered significant casualties, albeit far fewer than the Germans and Hungarians claimed. Altogether, he reckoned his own losses at twenty-two men dead and fifty-three wounded. These figures seem plausible for two reasons. First, they are roughly proportional to the casualties that the Germans sustained during their assault (twenty-seven dead and twenty-seven wounded). That the Germans, attacking a well-prepared position, did not lose more men is a bit surprising, though their superiority in mortars may account for this. Second, as noted earlier, the German estimate of the partisans' losses seems unreliable.

Fedorov's numbers, however, raise several important questions about what happened in Yeline, for they obviously do not allow for the "body count" offered by Lieutenant Colonel Csendes. It is unlikely that Csendes invented the story of being fired upon from the village, for no such pretext would have been necessary to justify his subsequent actions. At the same time, the Hungarians' lack of casualties and failure to capture anything but livestock indicates that the partisan presence in the village amounted to nothing more than an outpost on the twenty-second. Most of the dead found by the Hungarians after the German air strike were therefore civilians.

Yeline comprised 516 homes in March 1942, and even allowing for the loss of men to service in the army or in the ranks of the partisans, the balance of the population was missing when the Hungarians arrived. From Soviet sources it is clear that they were hiding in the nearby woods. They did not expect a follow-up visit, however, and were once again in their homes when Csendes's battalion came back on 26 March.

By this stage in the German-Soviet war, many units of the German army had become accustomed to shooting some of the civilians encountered during antipartisan operations as "partisans" or "helpers." As noted earlier, within Heeresgebiet Süd this tendency had been moderated to some degree by the command's policy toward the ethnic Ukrainian element of the civil population. The Heeresgebiet staff, however, viewed Yeline and the surrounding villages as "partisan" controlled, and pro-Ukrainian bias would not stop Heeresgebiet officers from ordering brutal reprisals when it seemed warranted by the pro-Soviet behavior of a given community.[33]

In a statement given to representatives of the NKVD on 19 August 1944, Aleksei M. Peven', a Yeline resident who witnessed the destruction of the village by Csendes's troops, claimed that seventy-three persons were shot at the outset of the raid for resisting the Hungarians' orders to assemble in the village school. These victims allegedly included elderly people, women, and children. Those who had complied watched as their homes went up in flames. They were then taken to nearby Shchors, where they remained for a week, subsisting on a diet of one hundred grams of bread (roughly one or two slices) and some broth each day. Sixty elderly persons, including Peven' (who was fifty-eight years old) were segregated from the rest of the prisoners and taken by rail to what he called a "prisoner of war camp" at Gomel. They remained there for three months under somewhat better conditions, receiving five hundred grams of bread and two servings of broth per day. They were released and instructed never to return to Yeline on pain of death. Peven' claimed that the remaining three hundred persons who had been arrested were shot by the Germans at a location near Gomel. Once again, the victims included a number of women and children.[34]

There is no reference whatsoever to the fate of the Yeline detainees in Heeresgebiet records. In an interview conducted in August 1997, Yevdokia M. Kadeniak, an elderly Yeline resident who was present during the fighting in March 1942, also claimed that most of those sent to Gomel had been shot.[35] If this is correct, then the pacification of the Yeline area was ultimately achieved not only by driving off the partisans and destroying the village but by executing many of the inhabitants as well.

In many ways, revelation of these killings raises more questions than it answers. Given the ruthlessness of German methods on other parts of the Eastern Front, why were these victims not killed outright? What criteria were used in determining who was arrested and who was released during the initial gathering of prisoners? Why did the Germans then further segregate the group sent to Gomel, and why did they kill some of the prisoners taken there and release the others? Analysis of the Heeresgebiet's previous antipartisan operations suggests a probable explanation: the persons executed may have been identified by the GFP as relatives of partisans serving with Fedorov. The 444th Security Division had used this tactic during the Heeresgebiet's operations at Novomoskovs'k in the previous autumn, as had the Sixty-second Infantry Division (then temporarily detailed to antipartisan duty with the Heeresgebiet) in the Myrhorod area. This information was often obtained simply from denunciations by pro-German villagers, which in 1941 had not been difficult to obtain. Perhaps this was again the case once Fedorov had departed. The Ukrainian policemen who took part in the Yeline operation, most of whom seem to have been recruited from the district, could also have provided the denunciations.

It is important not to lose sight of the terrible suffering of those persons who escaped arrest and execution. In the weeks that followed they lived as refugees and underwent tremendous hardships. This was especially true of women with small children. They could expect little help or sympathy from other people in such desperate circumstances. Kadeniak, a war widow and the mother of three, found that no one would help her after Yeline had been burned: "I went to the meadow. There people were making a fire but didn't let me join them, [they] said that my children would cry." After five days she and another woman set off for a village called Pliutsy in Russia, where she found refuge with relatives of her dead husband.[36]

In the months that followed the destruction of Yeline, partisan activity in the northern reaches of the Heeresgebiet slackened, chiefly due to the spring flooding that made sustained operations impossible for both the partisans and their German and Hungarian pursuers. By June, however, Heeresgebiet forces found themselves facing two well-organized partisan groups in the Sumy region, under the leadership of Sidor Kovpak and A. N. Saburov. As had been the case with Yeline, it was the Hungarians who were taking most of the casualties, and the disparate burdens of the two allies placed serious strain on their relationship. The Hungarian generals accused the Germans of saddling them with the most difficult areas and, incredibly, of coddling the Ukrainians, while the Germans claimed that the Hungarians' wanton destruction of villages was wasting valuable resources and driving the rural inhabitants into the arms of the partisans.[37] There was a strong element of hypocrisy in the Germans' complaints, for many of the officers involved did not hesitate to order extreme reprisals. Würfel himself authorized the execution of 116 persons at Nizhyn in early July in reprisal for the killing of a GFP sergeant.[38] Yet Friderici, who replaced von Roques permanently in June, continued to demand moderation.

Conflict over the treatment of the population was partially defused by compromise in September and October when a small number of villages on the northern edge of the Heeresgebiet were evacuated and destroyed. Tension between the Heeresgebiet's pro-Ukrainian position and the pressures of mounting partisan warfare, however, were never fully resolved before being overtaken by events in 1943.[39] As Friderici's jurisdiction shrank in the face of the Soviet advance, the SS role in antipartisan operations within Heeresgebiet boundaries increased. This development had dire consequences for the population. One example clearly illustrates this point. In May and June of 1943, Heeresgebiet forces played a supporting role in a joint operation with SS and police units called WEICHSEL the objective of which was to destroy partisan units operating in the so-called wet triangle between the Desna and the Dnipro. Walter Schimana, brigadier general of police and of the SS, commanded the main German battle group involved in the fighting. At the close of the operation, his staff proudly reported the destruction of 103 villages. Four thousand and eighteen "bandits" were allegedly killed in action by his troops and 18,860 persons evacuated and made available for forced labor. Schimana's task force lost only twenty-eight men killed in action and fifty-six wounded.[40] Though units operating in the rear area of Army Group Center (Heeresgebiet Mitte) had proved willing to wipe out village after village in areas merely traversed by the partisans, the Heeresgebiet operations directed by Friderici or von Roques had never reached this standard of destructiveness.

What do events at Yeline tell us about the character of the partisan war on the Eastern Front? A few observations seem warranted. The Heeresgebiet's reaction to Fedorov's activity in the northern sector of the Chernihiv region is probably best described as an attenuated example of the radicalized warfare typical of the Wehrmacht's antipartisan operations in the occupied USSR. Even when allowing for the German military's long-term proclivity for harsh reprisals, the importance of the army's relaxation of military law for operation Barbarossa is clear. It is also worth noting that the brutal destruction of Yeline was counterproductive from the Germans' point of view. Such measures undermined the command's professed policy of more favorable treatment of Ukrainians, and, coupled with Germany's plunder of the economy and forced deportation of Ukrainian laborers to the Reich, they gave momentum to the progressive alienation of rural Ukraine from German authority during 1942. Also, after Fedorov's departure, this area was visited time and again by partisan groups ranging southward and westward out of the Briansk forest. Since the Germans were unable to protect the local people from the guerrillas, the inhabitants had no option but to provide the partisans the support they demanded.

It is important to recognize that the use of repressive violence in this operation was more temperate than was typical of antipartisan operations taking place elsewhere on the Eastern Front. This is clear in several particulars. First, the joint German and Hungarian operation occurred because of a genuine partisan threat to control of the vicinity. This fact alone sets the operation apart from contemporary "antipartisan" operations in Belarus, where the most trivial of pretexts was often invoked to justify the destruction of villages. Second, the operation engaged the partisans themselves. At Yeline, the objective had actually been to encircle and destroy an armed enemy force, and both the Germans and the Hungarians suffered losses in the fighting. Third, the devastation and executions that took place at Yeline were confined to the area where the partisans had actually been based. Fedorov himself noted the importance of Yeline to his detachment in his memoir, and there seems little reason to doubt that his men were being supported by the villagers.

The records of Heeresgebiet Süd suggest that the most likely cause of this partial attenuation of repressive violence was the commanding general's belief that German occupation policy ought to involve an element of preferential treatment for ethnic Ukrainians. Despite Alfred Rosenberg's political weakness among the Nazi leadership, his elaborate racist dogmas, which allowed for some distinctions between Soviet ethnic groups, seem to have had a material influence on the commanders and staff of Heeresgebiet Süd. Nevertheless, the people of Ukraine suffered horribly under German rule in both political and military jurisdiction, and the favoritism displayed toward Ukrainians by military authorities was itself part of a racist mindset. Such variations in policy and mentality should not be ignored, even if they existed chiefly at the level of frustrated intent.

The Yeline story also sheds some light on the relationship between rural Ukrainian communities and the Soviet partisan movement at this early stage in the German-Soviet war. Two observations are tenable based on the German documents used in this study. First, it is clear that the Heeresgebiet had been able to raise a significant number of policemen in the north of FK194 prior to Fedorov's raids. The police casualties reported at Orlivka and Ivanivka in January and February make this clear enough, as does the significant indigenous police presence in the German and Hungarian operation at Yeline. There was, in other words, some collaborationist element to be found in this area. Second, terror was an important feature of Fedorov's influence in the area. His attacks on the scattered units of the Hungarian 105th Light

Division were coupled with raids against village police detachments. In these raids, the violence was not confined to the killing of policemen but involved reprisal executions of members of police families and the destruction of numbers of their homes. The mutilation of policemen's children described by Lieutenant Colonel Würfel is particularly disturbing.

The story of what happened at Yeline provides an illustration of the predicament of the civil population in the German-Soviet partisan war. A Soviet victory offered a better future for the Ukrainian peasantry than did Germany's "New Order," for it was Adolf Hitler, rather than the Ukrainophile officials of the Ostministerium, who would have determined the fate of Ukraine had Germany won the war in the east. Yet few Ukrainians could have understood the situation so clearly in this comparatively early stage of the war, and it is not surprising that individual responses to German occupation ranged from active, zealous collaboration to bitter resistance in the Soviet underground. Many people sought merely to accommodate whichever force confronted them at the time. Tragically, neither the Soviet nor the German regimes would tolerate such a middle course, and the result was tremendous suffering for all those caught in the path of war.

Notes

1. Such a study is possible only because of an unusual wealth of documentary sources. Detailed descriptions of the fighting at Yeline have survived within the records of Heeresgebiet Süd, the rear area of Army Group South. These documents, housed in the German Federal Military Archive (Bundesarchiv-Militärarchiv) in Freiburg, include reports written by the participating Hungarian and German battalion commanders and one produced by a senior German counterintelligence officer who also took part in the battle. Several radio messages transmitted during the action have survived, along with routine situation reports made by higher-level German and Hungarian commands that refer to events at Yeline. The author has obtained a series of situation reports made by the Hungarian chain of command from the Hungarian Military Archive (Hadtörtnélmi Levéltar) in Budapest, and some Soviet documentation is also available. The most valuable item is a survivor's eyewitness account given to the NKVD in August 1944. Also useful are the published account provided by the commander of the Soviet partisan detachment and

the reminiscences of one surviving witness whom the author interviewed in August of 1997. By carefully comparing these very diverse sources, it has been possible to reconstruct the history of the fighting at Yeline in some detail.

2. The "Lieber Code" (U.S. Army General Order no. 100), section I, article 82. Reproduced in its entirety in Leon Friedman, ed., *The Law of Warfare. A Documentary History*, vol. 1 (New York, 1972), 158–86. Lieber's ideas formed the basis for the Brussels Declaration of 1874, which in turn formed the foundation of the 1899 and 1907 Hague Conventions.

3. British Manual of Military Law, 1929, Amendments (no. 12), chap. 114, "The Laws of Land Warfare"; U.S. Basic Field Manual FM27–10, *Rules of Land Warfare* (Washington DC, 1940); Zentrale Stelle für Landesjustizverwaltungen in Ludwigsburg, *Geisel und Partisanentötungen im Zweiten Weltkrieg: Hinweise zur rechtlichen Beurteilung* (Ludwigsburg, 1968), 17.

4. Paul Kohl, *Der Krieg der deutschen Wehrmacht und der Polizei 1941–1944. Sowjetische Überlebende berichten* (Frankfurt a.M., 1995), 13; Christian Gerlach, "Deutsche Wirtschaftsinteressen, Besatzungspolitik und der Mord an den Juden in Weißrußland 1941–1943," in Ulrich Herbert, ed., *Nationalsozialistische Vernichtungspolitik 1939–1945. Neue Forschungen und Kontroversen* (Frankfurt a.M., 1998), 263.

5. Walter Manoschek, *Serbien ist Judenfrei* (Munich, 1993); Richard Fattig, "Reprisal: The German Army and the Execution of Hostages during the Second World War" (Ph.D. diss., University of California at San Diego, 1980); Christopher Browning, "Wehrmacht Reprisal Policy and the Mass-murder of Jews in Serbia," *Militärgeschichtliche Mitteilungen*, 33 (1983), no. 1: 31–47.

6. Helmut Krausnick and H. H. Wilhelm, *Die Truppe des Weltanschauungskrieges. Die Einsatzgruppen der Sicherheitspolizei und des Sicherheitsdienstes 1938–1942* (Stuttgart, 1981), 186–87, 234–35; Bernd Boll and Hans Safrian, "Auf dem Weg nach Stalingrad," in *Vernichtungskrieg: Verbrechen der Wehrmacht 1941 bis 1944*, ed. Hannes Heer and Klaus Naumann (Hamburg, 1995), 279–80; Erhard Wiehn, ed., *Die Schoah von Babij Jar. Das Massaker deutscher Sonderkommandos an der jüdischen Bevölkerung von Kiew 1941 fünfzig Jahre danach zum Gedenken* (Konstanz, 1991).

7. OKH/GenStbdH/H Wes Abt. (Abw.), Az. Abw. III Nr. 2111/41 12.7.41, BA-MA RH 27–7/156; 62. Infanterie-Division Abt. Ia/Ic Nr. 1784/41 geh. betr. Befriedung, Sühnemaßnahmen, 11.11.41, BA-MA RH26–62/41.

8. Bfh. rückw. H. Geb. 103 Abt. Ic 968/41 geh. 11.7.41, Besondere Anordnungen für die Behandlung der ukrainischen Frage, USNA (U.S. National Archives Microfilm Series) T-501/5; (Abschrift) Rückw. Heeresgebiet Süd Abt. VII Nr. 103/41, 16.8.41 Anordnung Abt. VII Nr. 7, BA-MA Alliierte Prozeße Nr. 9 NOKW-1691; Sich. Div. 454 Abt. Ia, Anlage zum Divisionsbefehl Nr. 59 8.9.41, Merkblatt

über Sofortaufgaben der Ortskommandanturen, BA-MA 26–454/6a-b.

9. Dienstreise zu OKH 25.11.41, USNA T-501/6; Bfh. rückw. H.Geb. Süd, Abt. VII/123/41 geh. 14.12.41, Anordnung Abt. VII. Nr. 31, USNA T-501/6.

10. For documents pertaining to the struggle in Dnipro Bend area, see: Rückw. H.Geb.Süd KTB (Ia), entries of 18.11.41, 12.12.41–16.12.41, 19.12.41 USNA T501/4; Tätigkeitsbericht der Abteilung Ic zum Kriegstagebuch der Sicherungs-Division 213 (no date), BA-MA RH26–213/6; Sich. Div. 444 Abt. Ia 21.1.42, Bericht über die Bekämpfung der Banditengruppen im Waldgebiet Nowomoskowsk-Pawlograd, BA-MA RH22/19; Rückw. H.Geb. Süd Tagesmeldung an Heeresgruppe Süd, 4.1.42, BA-MA RH22/19; Anruf Sich. Div. 444 6.1.42, Vorläufiger Abschlußbericht über Banditenbekämpfung im Waldgebiet Nowomoskowsk, BA-MA RH22/19; Sich. Div. 444 Abt. Ia 22.1.42, Erfahrungsbericht beim Banditenunternehmen Nowo Moskowsk-Pawlograd, BA-MA RH22/19; Befh. H.Geb. Süd Abt. Ia 3571/42 geh. 10.1.42, Abschrift, 10 Tägige Meldung to Gen. St. d.H./Gen. Qu., Abt. K.Verw., BA-MA RH22/19.

For Soviet accounts of this fighting, see Stenogramma zapici vospominanii Panchenko, Trofima Ivanovicha, TsDAHO 166/3/245. See also: Dokladnaia Zapiska o partizanskom dvizhenii, o sostoianii podpol'nykh part-organizatsii i o polozhenii del v levoberezhnykh raionakh Dnepropetrovshchiny so vremeni ikh okkupatsii fashistskimi voiskami, TsDAHO 1/22/7. This is a retrospective report from 12 March 1943 written by A. Fedorov.

The operations of Heeresgebiet forces in the Myrhorod area are also extensively documented in both German and Soviet records. For the more important German documents, see Rückw. H.Geb. Süd KTB (Ia) entries from 3.11.41–31.12.41,USNA T-501/4; 62. Infanterie-Division KTB (Ia) entries 28.10.41–31.12.41, BA-MA RH26–62/39; Tätigkeitsberichte (Abt. Ia 62. Inf. Div.) für die Zeit vom 26.11.41–14.11.41, BA-MA RH26–62/41; (Fernschreiben) Tagesmeldung 9.11.41 62. Inf. Div. Ia/Ic an Befh. rückw. H.Geb. Süd Ia/Ic, USNA T-501/6; (Fernschreiben) 9.11.41 Befh. H.Geb. Süd an 62. Inf. Div., USNA T-501/6; (Fernschreiben) 10.11.41 62. Inf. Div. Ia an Befh. H.Geb. Süd Ia/Ic, USNA T-501/6; (Fernschreiben) 12.11.41 62. Inf. Div. Ia/Ic an Befh. H.Geb. Süd Ia/Ic, USNA T-501/6; Fernspruch 13.11.41 20.00 Uhr Betr. Strafaktion Oberst Sins (sic), BA-MA RH26–62/56; (Fernspruch) (Abschrift) von I.R. 190 an 62. I.D., Meldung betr. Baranowka, BA-MA RH26–62/41; Ortskommandantur Mirgorod Gendarmeriegruppe 8.11.41 BA-MA RH26–62/41; Tätigkeitsbericht (62. Inf. Div.) für die Zeit 26.11.41–14.11.41, entry of 10.11.41,BA-MA RH26–62/41; (Abschrift), II. Infanterie-Regiment 164 Abt. Ia betr. Säuberungsaktion 12.11.41, BA-MA RH22/173; Infanterie Regiment 190 Abt. Ia 17.11.41 betr. Meldung über den Verlauf der Unternehmungen gegen Banden bis einschl. 17.11.41, BA-MA RH26–62/56; Inf. Rgt. 164 Tagesmeldung 24.11.41 and 25.11.41, BA-MA RH26–62/56; 62. Inf. Div. Ia/Ic Fernschreiben

(Tagesmeldung) to Bfh. rückw. H.Geb. Süd Ia/Ic 24.11.41, BA-MA RH26–62/60; "Nibelungen" (Inf. Rgt. 164) Nachtrag zur Tagesmeldung 27.11.41, BA-MA 26–62/56.

Soviet records of the fighting between partisans and the Sixty-second Infantry Division center on the activities of the "Victory" detachment, which had been organized by officials of the Myrhorod regional communist party. See Prilozhenie k protokolu n37 Otchet ob antifashistskom podpol'e i partisanskoi dvizhenii na territorii Poltavskoi oblasti v period Velikoi Otechestvennoi Boiny 1941–1943 g., DAPO 15/1/2016; Sekretar' Poltavskogo Obkomu KP/b/U no Propagande i Agitatsii, Mirgorodskii RKKP/b/U vysylaem listovki vypushchennye partizanami v period nemetskoi okkupatsii Mirgorodskogo raiona, 24.7.46, DAPO 105/1/265., 1944; Poltavskii oblastnoi sovet deputatov trudiashchikhsia g. Poltava, otchet o deiatel'nosti podpol'nykh organizatsii KPbU i o partizanskoi oblasti v period vremennoi nemetsko-fashistkoi okkupatsii, sent. 1941–sent. 1943 gg., DAPO 4085/4/5; Kharakteristika Baranovskogo S-soveta s. 1941 r. po 1944 r, DAPO (Derzhavnyi arkhiv Poltavs'koi oblasti) 1876/8/108; Shishaskii raion kompartii Ukrainy, khronologicheskaia zapiska raionnoi komissii . . . DAPO 105/1/358; Shishaki Raikom Kompartii Ukrainy, Pokazanie ob'iasnitel'nie zapiski i drugie dokumenty . . . DAPO 105/1/357.

11. Bfh. rückw. H.Geb. Süd, Abt. VII/123/41 geh. 14.12.41, Anordnung Abt. VII. Nr. 31, USNA T-501/6.

12. Fedorov's memoir is a key source of information for historians examining the history of the Soviet partisan movement in Ukraine. The first edition, published in 1948, is propagandistic in nature and offers a Stalinist view of issues like the relationship between the partisans and the inhabitants. When used in conjunction with German sources, however, the book remains quite useful. Fedorov, *Podpol'nyi Obkom Deistvuet*.

13. 621./105 le. Div. Ia 7.4.42 zusammenfassende Meldung / bis zum 31.3.42, BA-MA RH22/34. Note that Kolossváry's chief of staff signed this document in the general's absence.

14. Feldkommandantur (V) 194 420211 an Befehlshaber d. rückw. H.-Geb. Süd, Abtlg. Ia-nachrichtl. Befehlshaber d. rückw. H.-Geb. Mitte, Ia Betr.: Lagebericht für die Zeit vom 14.1. bis 10.2. 1942, BA-MA RH22/203.

15. Nr. 210/Inf. Brig. 105 Abt. Ib. vom 3.3.42, Meldung über die Unternehmung von Iwanowka, BA-MA RH22/24.

16. (Fernspruch) Nr. 1094/Bes. Gr. Abt. Ia Feldpost Nr. 13 17.2.42 1315 Uhr Olgyay Generalmajor und Befh. der Bes. Gruppe, BA-MA RH22/22; Nr. 210/Inf. Brig. 105 Abt. Ib. vom 3.3.42, Meldung über die Unternehmung von Iwanowka, BA-MA RH22/24.

17. (Fernschreiben) Nr. 1167/Bes. Gruppe Abt. Roem Eins A an Befh. rückw.

H.Geb. Süd 2,3,42m BA-MA RH22/24.

18. Fedorov, *Obkom Deistvuet*, 202–3; Nr. 210/Inf. Brig. 105 Abt. Ib. vom 3.3.42, Meldung über die Unternehmung von Iwanowka, BA-MA RH22/24.

19. FK (V) 194 Sammelheft über Erfahrungen in der Partisanen-Bekämpfung gem. Anordnung Befh. rückw. H.Geb. Süd Ic vom 7.1.1942, entry of 12.3.42, BA-MA RH22/173; Nr. 210/Inf. Brig. 105 Abt. Ib. vom 3.3.42, Meldung über die Unternehmung von Iwanowka, BA-MA RH22/24; K.megsz. csop. psag. 1221/I.a. 42.III.12. 4073/7/M. l.vkf.-1942, Hadörténelmi Levéltár Budapest (HL) 1.89. VKF: 1. osztály: Számnélküli iratok: Fasc. 265–66.

20. 341./55./II Batl. 4.4.42. Anlage Nr. 2 zu 621./105.le.Div. Ia. 7.4.42., Abschliessende Meldung über die vom 21.3. bis 2.4.1942. gegen das Partisanenlager im Walde von Jelino durchgeführte Unternehmung, BA-MA RH 22/34.

21. Der ltd. Feldpolizeidirektor beim Befh. H. Geb. Süd, 30.4. 1942, Bericht über die Partisanenkämpfe im Raume nordostwärts Snowsk, BA-MR RH22/27.

22. Der ltd. Feldpolizeidirektor beim Befh. H. Geb. Süd, 30.4. 1942, Bericht über die Partisanenkämpfe im Raume nordostwärts Snowsk, BA-MR RH22/27.

23. Wach-Bataillon 703 Abt. Ia 3.24.1942, Herrn Befehlshaber rückw. Heeresgebiet Süd über Feldkommandantur 194, Gefechtsbericht, BA-MA RH22/24.

24. 341./55./II Batl. 4.4.42. Anlage Nr. 2 zu 621./105.le.Div. Ia. 7.4.42., Abschliessende Meldung über die vom 21.3. bis 2.4.1942. gegen das Partisanenlager im Walde von Jelino durchgeführte Unternehmung, BA-MA RH 22/34.

25. 341./55./II Batl. 4.4.42. Anlage Nr. 2 zu 621./105.le.Div. Ia. 7.4.42., Abschliessende Meldung über die vom 21.3. bis 2.4.1942. gegen das Partisanenlager im Walde von Jelino durchgeführte Unternehmung, BA-MA RH 22/34; K.megsz. csop. pság. 1275./I.a. 42.III.24 4072./18/M.l. vkf., HL 1.89.VKF: 1. osztály: Számnélküli iratok: Fasc. 265–66.

26. Wach-Bataillon 703 Abt. Ia 3.24.1942, Herrn Befehlshaber rückw. Heeresgebiet Süd über Feldkommandantur 194, Gefechtsbericht, BA-MA RH22/24; Der ltd. Feldpolizeidirektor beim Befh. H. Geb. Süd, 30.4. 1942, Bericht über die Partisanenkämpfe im Raume nordostwärts Snowsk, BA-MR RH22/27.

27. 341./55./II Batl. 4.4.42. Anlage Nr. 2 zu 621./105.le.Div. Ia. 7.4.42., Abschliessende Meldung über die vom 21.3. bis 2.4.1942. gegen das Partisanenlager im Walde von Jelino durchgeführte Unternehmung, BA-MA RH 22/34.

28. The final figures provided by Lieutenant Colonel Csendes do not tally with those given in the course of his narrative. My figures here are based upon the narrative rather than the summary given at the end of the report. 341./55./II Batl. 4.4.42. Anlage Nr. 2 zu 621./105.le.Div. Ia. 7.4.42., Abschliessende Meldung über die vom 21.3. bis 2.4.1942. gegen das Partisanenlager im Walde von Jelino durchgeführte Unternehmung, BA-MA RH 22/34.

29. Wach-Bataillon 703 Abt. Ia 3.24.1942, Herrn Befehlshaber rückw. Heer-

esgebiet Süd über Feldkommandantur 194, Gefechtsbericht, BA-MA RH22/24; Der ltd. Feldpolizeidirektor beim Befh. H. Geb. Süd, 30.4. 1942, Bericht über die Partisanenkämpfe im Raume nordostwärts Snowsk, BA-MR RH22/27.

30. Der ltd. Feldpolizeidirektor beim Befh. H. Geb. Süd, 30.4. 1942, Bericht über die Partisanenkämpfe im Raume nordostwärts Snowsk, BA-MR RH22/27; 341./55./II Batl. 4.4.42. Anlage Nr. 2 zu 621./105.le.Div. Ia. 7.4.42., Abschliessende Meldung über die vom 21.3. bis 2.4.1942. gegen das Partisanenlager im Walde von Jelino durchgeführte Unternehmung, BA-MA RH 22/34.

31. Der ltd. Feldpolizeidirektor beim Befh. H. Geb. Süd, 30.4. 1942, Bericht über die Partisanenkämpfe im Raume nordostwärts Snowsk, BA-MR RH22/27; 341./55./II Batl. 4.4.42. Anlage Nr. 2 zu 621./105.le.Div. Ia. 7.4.42., Abschliessende Meldung über die vom 21.3. bis 2.4.1942. gegen das Partisanenlager im Walde von Jelino durchgeführte Unternehmung, BA-MA RH 22/34; Wach-Bataillon 703 Abt. Ia 3.24.1942, Herrn Befehlshaber rückw. Heeresgebiet Süd über Feldkommandantur 194, Gefechtsbericht, BA-MA RH22/24.

32. Fedorov, *Obkom Deistvuet*, 216–19.

33. See note 18.

34. Protokol Doprosa Svidetelia (kopiia), 1944 goda, avgusta 19 dnia, c. Elino . . . Peven' Aleksei Minovich, TsDAHO 166/3/242.

35. Interview with Yevdokia Malafeyevna Kadeniak, Yeline, 9 August 1997.

36. Interview with Yevdokia Malafeyevna Kadeniak, Yeline, 9 August 1997.

37. The following documents figure in the German and Hungarian debate over reprisal violence in the spring and summer of 1942: 621./105. le. Div. Ia. 7.4.42, 5. zusammenfassende Meldung / bis zum 31.3.42, BA-MA RH22/34; Bfh. rückw. H. Geb. Süd Abt. Ia 5522/42g. 420301 an OKH Gen. St. d. H./Gen. Qu., Abt. Kriegsverwaltung, BA-MA RH22/24; Anlage 3./zu Nr. 2270/Bes. Gr. Ost Ia vom 4.7.42, Nr. 2195/Bes. Gr. Ost Ia vom. 25.6.42 (Auszugsweise Übersetzung), BA-MA RH22/46; (Fernschreiben) Armeegruppe von Weichs an Befh. H.Geb. Süd 420703, BA-MA RH22/47; Der Kommandierende General der Sicherungstruppen und Befehlshaber im Heeresgebiet Süd Abt. Ia Nr. 8791/42 an OKH/Gen Qu / K. Verw. betr.: Monatsbericht . . . 15.7.1942, BA-MA RH22/299; Anlage 3./zu Nr. 2270/Bes. Gr. Ost Ia vom 4.7.42, Nr. 2195/Bes. Gr. Ost Ia vom. 25.6.42 (Auszugsweise Übersetzung), BA-MA RH22/46; Befh. H. Geb. Süd Abt. VII/III/Ic Nr. 8449/42g., 2.7.42, BA-MA RH22/173; FK (V) 194 Br. B. Nr. 1297/42 18.7.42 Betr.: Lagebericht für die Zeit vom 18. Juni-17 Juli 1942, BA-MA RH22/47; Nr. 2543/Bes. Gr. Kmdo. Ost, Ia vom 7.8.42. Betr.: Vorschlaege zu den Richtlinien für die Partisanenbekaempfung, BA-MA RH22/56.

38. (Fernschreiben) Tagesmeldung FK (V) 194 an Befh. H.Geb Süd Ia 9.7.42, BA-MA RH22/51; Der kommandierende General der Sicherungstruppen und Befh. im Heeresgebiet B Abt. Ia-Nr. 9340/42 g., 15.8.42 Betr.: Monatsbericht 1.

"Contrary to Our National Ideals"

American Strategic Bombing of Civilians in World War II

Conrad C. Crane

This collection has highlighted a number of instances where military operations against civilians were used to influence their governments. On the eve of World War I at least one military theorist believed that it was inevitable that future wars would be decided primarily by the mood of the civil population, and not by statesmen or generals. Polish banker Ivan Bloch predicted that the next conflagration would be devastating, total, and protracted, and the resilience and perseverance of civil society would decide the victor.[1] The Great War was indeed characterized by four years of bloody ground stalemate that eventually produced revolutions to bring down the empires of Russia and the Central Powers. Probably the most effective Allied operation of the conflict was the British sea blockade, which denied resources to the German home front as well as the war machine and contributed significantly to their collapse. Ironically, the hardships of the naval blockade produced almost eight hundred thousand civilian deaths, the same toll as the Allied bombing of German cities in World War II that has received so much moral condemnation.[2]

Proponents of the fledgling air weapon that had just made its debut took many lessons from the Great War concerning the ability of the airplane to avoid indecisive land combat and strike directly at vulnerable civilian will. Air Chief Marshal Hugh Trenchard, chief of the British Air Staff and the father of the independent Royal Air Force, estimated that the psychological "yield" of his air attacks on Rhenish towns was twenty times greater than the damage from actual physical destruction. When sizing up aerial options against the civil population of Britain's most likely enemy in 1923, France, Trenchard claimed that "the French in a bombing duel would probably squeal before we

219

did." Echoing Bloch to some degree, the British chief of Air Staff argued, "The nation that would stand being bombed longest would win in the end."[3] Giulio Douhet, impressed by reports of German attacks on London and a firsthand observer of the reaction of his fellow Italians to Austrian bombing raids, went even further. He predicted that air fleets dropping a mixture of high explosive, incendiary, and gas bombs on enemy cities would end wars in only a few days. People would panic at the mere sight of airplanes and demand an end to the conflict, "driven by the instinct of self-preservation." Such wars could not last long "since the decisive blows will be directed at civilians, that element of countries at war least able to sustain them."[4]

Air warfare had much in common with earlier forms of combat. Like the tank, or even the bayonet, the airplane could have quite a psychological effect just from the fury of its application. Similar to intense artillery bombardments, air raids would subject the people in the target area to significant shock and stress. Blast effects could stun and disorient, and the fear of imminent death and destruction could bring terror. As an American memorandum noted in 1943, however, air warfare differed "in the range of its potential destruction. The air gives uncurbed bestial instincts a wider field of expression, leaving only humanity and common sense to dictate limitations."[5] While avoiding the direct targeting of noncombatants, Army Air Corps planners in the 1930s looked at ways to disrupt the economic and social network of a whole country, destroying an enemy nation's war-making capacity while producing civilian exhaustion or resignation to the omnipotence of airpower.[6] Actual examples of city bombing during that same decade showed that less desirable effects were also possible. Civilians might just become apathetic and resigned to their fate, or they might even be made more determined in their resistance.

By the late 1930s, American airpower publicist Alexander de Seversky was portraying an air campaign against enemy cities as a sort of aerial blockade reminiscent of the seapower theories of Alfred Thayer Mahan. But the average citizen did not perceive any resemblance between the bombing of Shanghai or Madrid and the Royal Navy's blockade of Germany. As the preliminary conflicts that would develop into World War II crackled around the world, American public opinion clamored against the immoral aerial bombardment of civilians. Newspaper editorials proclaimed that the laws of war were becoming "scraps of paper," pictures of casualties from Japanese bombing in-spired support for China, and even bubblegum cards displayed the gore of the "horrors of war" from air attacks on Spanish cities.[7] United States Army Air Forces (AAF) leaders were especially sensitive to pub-lic opinion, since the airmen believed they needed all the support they could get to achieve the independent status they desired. Between the wars, army aviators had exploited American dreams that the air-plane could revolutionize daily life and transform the world for good, and at the core of precision-bombing doctrine was the belief that the American public would not stand for the indiscriminate aerial bom-bardment of civilians.[8] Air Corps Tactical School texts stressed that direct attacks on the civil populace had to be "rejected as an air objec-tive due to humanitarian considerations."[9] Terror bombing in China, Ethiopia, and Spain appeared to be ineffective and often counterpro-ductive. West Point lesson plans emphasized that, contrary to the the-ories of airpower advocates like Douhet, the bombing of cities seemed to strengthen civilian resolve. Military strategists noted that such raids often just led to reprisals on the attacker's cities.[10] Efficiency as well as humanity militated against bombing cities and supported precision doctrine. Most AAF leaders and airmen believed in it wholeheartedly, as it seemed to be the quickest and cleanest way to end the war.

Actual wartime public opinion was not as intolerant of civilian casu-alties as the AAF perceived, however. Pearl Harbor transformed Amer-ican public opinion about terror attacks on civilians. A poll on 10 December 1941, revealed that 67 percent of the population favored un-qualified and indiscriminate bombing of Japanese cities, while only 10 percent gave an outright "no." Subsequent surveys produced simi-lar results. A majority of Americans favored urban bombing even if it brought Axis retaliation against U.S. cities. This implied a deep com-mitment or resignation to total warfare and reflected the intense anxi-ety about a war that appeared to be going so disastrously. For religious reasons, most Americans expressed resistance to bombing Rome, but by early 1944 three-quarters of those polled approved bombing his-toric religious buildings and shrines if military leaders believed such attacks were necessary.[11]

The majority of public opinion on killing enemy civilians ranged between avid support for vengeful urban attacks and resigned accep-tance of a regrettably unavoidable practice. The average American may not have been aware of the extent of the destruction bombing wreaked on cities; posters depicted Allied bombers attacking factories instead of people, and periodicals described b-17s dropping explosives down industrial smokestacks. Even if they had known the exact results of bombing, it would not have made much difference. Most American families had experienced the deaths of loved ones, friends, or neighbors. If bombing enemy civilians would speed victory and save American lives it had to be done.

Many Americans were comforted, however, by the belief that the AAF avoided indiscriminate killing of civilians whenever possible. In turn, AAF leaders perceived a public opinion in line with the position of publications like the *New Republic*, which stated that it did not approve of terror bombing but added that, to the best of its knowledge, most bombardment was directed at military objectives.[12] A subtle, important interaction existed between public perceptions of American strategic bombing and the attitudes of the leaders carrying it out. Air force planners interpreted public opinion as favoring precision attacks on industrial and military targets without indiscriminate civilian casualties. This is one of the key influences that shaped AAF bombing doctrine and practice. Military reports and news releases designed to demonstrate the accuracy and effectiveness of pinpoint bombardment in turn shaped public opinion. This is another example of a trend that can be traced back to the American Civil War, as "management of, or compliance with, public opinion" has become "an essential element in the conduct of war."[13] In World War II, American leaders did everything they could to dispel any impressions of American terror bombing.

This often caused men in high places to present different public and private positions on the bombing of enemy civilians. The commander-in-chief, Franklin D. Roosevelt, is a good example. When the Germans invaded Poland on 1 September 1939, he immediately issued a plea to all belligerents to cease "the ruthless bombing from the air of civilians in unfortified centers of population" that "has sickened the hearts of every civilized man and woman, and has profoundly shocked the conscience of humanity." He asked for a public affirmation that all parties would avoid such acts, "upon the understanding that these same rules of warfare will be scrupulously observed by all of their opponents."[14] This plea was largely a political ploy. A week earlier, ambassador to France William Bulitt had proposed that such an appeal should be made at the start of hostilities. The assumption was that England, Poland, and France would agree, while Germany would not, thus showing the moral superiority of the Allies and swaying world opinion against Germany. After consultation with Cordell Hull, Roosevelt agreed to send the message. The Allies did indeed respond favorably, but so did Germany. And the Germans were able to claim by 11 September that the Poles were violating the rules of warfare by resisting in open cities and shelling their own people, thus justifying retaliation from the air.[15]

FDR's true feelings are probably better demonstrated by a statement he made to Henry Morgenthau on 4 August 1941 on how to defeat Hitler. The president declared, "Well, the way to lick Hitler is the way I have been telling the English, but they won't listen to me. . . . I have suggested again and again that if they sent a hundred planes over Germany for military objectives that ten of them should bomb some of these smaller towns that haven't been bombed before. There must be some kind of factory in every town. That is the only way to break the German morale."[16] While factories would be the technical targets, FDR's actual objective was to smash civilian will, not the economy. An AAF operation similar in concept named Clarion was planned in Europe in 1945 and generated much controversy over whether it aimed to terrorize noncombatants. According to Michael Sherry, Roosevelt revealed as early as 1938 that he believed the morale of the German people could be cracked by the terror of aerial bombardment.[17] It appears, however, that the president intended to rely on bombing to produce a shock effect and impression of invincibility rather than kill civilians directly to break their will.

At least in private, FDR showed a willingness early in the war to attack civilian morale from the air. So did the AAF's commanding general, General Henry "Hap" Arnold, who had what one aide called "an open mind" on terror bombing.[18] In 1941, Arnold wrote in a book he co-authored with then Col. Ira C. Eaker that "bombing attacks on civil populace are uneconomical and unwise" because "bombers in far larger numbers than are available today will be required for wiping out people in sufficient numbers to break the will of a whole nation."[19] Arnold kept his options for future civilian bombardment open, and his memoirs and diaries reveal even more flexibility on the subject. He was impressed by the damage and civilian listlessness caused in London during the Blitz by a relatively small number of *Luftwaffe* bombers, and he envisioned great results from larger fleets of American planes.[20]

In public Arnold called terror bombing "abhorrent to our humanity, our sense of decency," and a policy he did not believe in.[21] In private he told his air staff that "this is a brutal war and . . . the way to stop the killing of civilians is to cause so much damage and destruction and death that the civilians will demand that their government cease fighting." He added, however, "This doesn't mean that we are making civilians or civilian institutions a war objective, but we cannot 'pull our punches' because some of them may get killed."[22] He did confide to reporters once that the AAF could bomb to destroy a city "as well as anybody else" and did sometimes do "pattern bombing," which could be used to break morale, though that was really not a preferred AAF objective.[23]

To support his desire for a postwar independent air service Arnold wanted to avoid alienating the public with an improper image, but he also needed impressive results to prove the effectiveness of airpower. Though he was not really involved in running day-to-day theater combat operations, his authority to relieve field commanders gave him leverage to influence their actions. Poor health limited his effectiveness late in the war. After he suffered his fourth heart attack in January 1945 his involvement in key decisions became especially limited.[24] But his pressure for more raids despite bad weather led to increased use of less accurate radar-directed bombardments in Europe, and his demand for increased efficiency in Japan inspired the resort to fire raids. His main goal was to make the largest possible contribution to winning the war and to ensure that the AAF received credit for it through proper publicity.

There seemed to be little consideration for ethics in Arnold's decisions, but he did espouse the traditional moral position of airpower theory that bombing would cost fewer lives than land warfare and end the war quickly. Like other air leaders, he had a sincere belief that the decisive power of modern aerial technology could prevent a repeat of the deadlocked carnage of World War I and achieve swift, and relatively bloodless, victory. He told his commanders that "when used with the proper degree of understanding," the bomber "becomes, in effect, the most humane of all weapons." He also realized the political costs of indiscriminate bombardment, writing in 1943 that "Careless inaccurate bombing intensifies and spreads those hates which will be stumbling blocks to international amity for years after the war is over."[25] Yet as the war continued and he pushed more and more for decisive results to support his dream of an independent air service, considerations of humanity were never a priority with Arnold.

In contrast, at least one leader in Washington, Secretary of War Henry L. Stimson, did consistently oppose the intentional killing or terrorizing of enemy noncombatants. He was repulsed by the barbarism of indiscriminate attacks on civilians. He had been instrumental in U.S. government protests against such raids during the 1930s and tried to keep a close watch on American strategic air operations during World War II. Stimson's diary is filled with references to atrocities and war crimes, and occasionally concerns for enemy civilians. He was convinced that the Nazi leaders and secret police, not the German people, caused the war. The same sentiment motivated those critics of strategic bombing who concluded that workers in Berlin were no more evil than the airmen ordered to bomb them.[26] Stimson complained that only General George Marshall supported him in that view: "It is singular that the man who had charge of the Department which did the killing in the war, should be the only one who seemed to have any mercy for the other side." The secretary of war felt that, in general, army officers had a better sense of justice on the issue of "responsibility of peoples" than civilians.[27]

Though Stimson called the Japanese "barbarians" in speeches, he did work to restrain "the feeling of war passion and hysteria which seizes hold of a nation like ours in prosecution of such a bitter war." Reports of the fire raids against Japan evoked a strong reaction. Stimson felt he had been misled by Robert Lovett, assistant secretary of war for air, and AAF leaders who had promised to restrict operations there to "the precision bombing which it (the AAF) has done so well in Europe." Stimson explained, "I am told it is possible and adequate. The reputation of the United States for fair play and humanitarianism is the world's biggest asset for peace in the coming decades."[28] Discussing the topic later with President Truman, the secretary of war realized the validity of air force arguments that the omnipresence of dispersed Japanese industry made it difficult to prevent area bombing, but he "did not want to have the United States get the reputation of outdoing Hitler in atrocities." He often agonized over sanctioning bombing raids and wondered about the lack of public protest. Robert Oppenheimer recalled that Stimson thought it was "appalling" that no one protested the heavy loss of life caused by the air raids against Japan. "He didn't say that the air strikes shouldn't be carried on, but he did think there was something wrong with a country where no one questioned that."[29]

Historian Ronald Schaffer is especially critical of Stimson for not being more effective. He points out that Stimson's protest of the fire raids came almost two months after they started and wonders why he did not inquire more into the bombing of Japan and Dresden. Schaffer speculates that Stimson might have been too old and ill, misinformed, or just did not really want to know what the AAF was doing.[30] Stimson was suffering from poor health and often could not work full time. He was also not kept informed on day-to-day operations, but that was not his role as secretary of war. He was more concerned with administrative matters than campaign strategy, and as the war went on his diary deals more and more with the problems of manning and supplying his forces, as the sources of recruits and replacements dried up and the enthusiasm of industry and the public for the war began to wane. The AAF responded when Stimson showed strong interest in a subject, such as the sparing of Kyoto from the atomic bomb or Norwegian complaints about stray bombs from raids on heavy water plants, but they did not feel obligated to brief him on operations. Stimson remarked once of Lovett that "his youngsters have run away with the ball without apparently attracting his attention," but that is the way the military treated the civilians in the war department.[31] Stimson probably learned more about specific operations from the newspapers than he did from soldiers in his department. The war was planned and directed by the Joint Chiefs of Staff (JCS) and fought by the operational- and tactical-level commanders in the field (see map 8.1).

One field commander who was effective in restraining indiscriminate bombardment was Lt. Gen. Carl Spaatz, commander of the United States Strategic Air Forces (USSTAF) in Europe. Many historians credit him with continuing to raise the moral issue in opposition to British attempts to enlist American participation in terror attacks and deviations from precision bombing. Russell Weigley calls him "a pillar of common sense," whom ground commanders could always talk to.

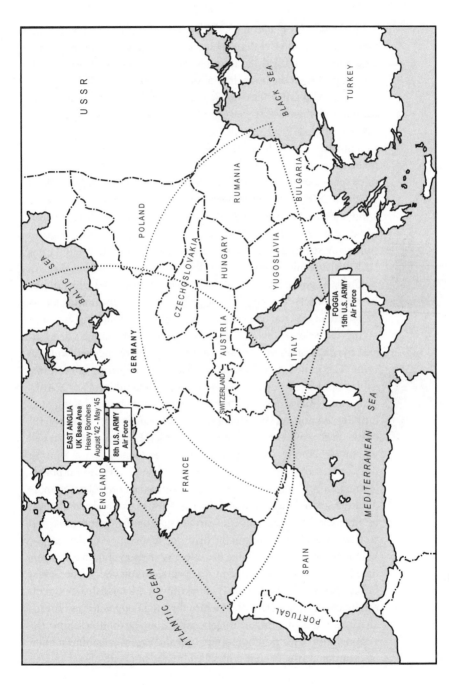

Map 8.1. U.S. Air Offensive against Germany, 1942–1945

While Spaatz felt that "we have proven the precision bombing principle in this war," he realized that with the limits of technology "our precision . . . is in a relative not a literal sense" and continued to strive for "pickle barrel accuracy."[32] Intense German defenses also made accuracy hard to achieve; though by the end of the war, the level of performance had exceeded prewar expectations.[33] Still, in the words of my colleague, Williamson Murray, in the next chapter, as a military tool precision aerial bombardment remained more of a "sledgehammer than a rapier."

Weigley also claims that "Spaatz was an airman genuinely troubled over the moral questions raised by aerial bombardment." The USSTAF commander wrote in his diary after the bombing of Hiroshima, "When the atomic bomb was first discussed with me in Washington I was not in favor of it just as I have never favored the destruction of cities as such with all inhabitants being killed."[34] Spaatz had helped develop precision-bombing doctrine and pursued it doggedly in Europe. While he did emphasize the efficiency of such tactics, he also continually expressed concern over civilian casualties caused by bombing.

Spaatz's primary objective was to make the maximum contribution to winning the war in Europe, and while he cooperated with the ground effort he believed that the precision bombing of economic targets, especially oil, was the best way to use his bombers. His subordinate commanders supported his goals and AAF doctrine, though their attitudes demonstrated varying degrees of concern for morality, efficiency, and public opinion depending on their background and training. Lt. Gen. Jimmy Doolittle, commander of the Eighth Air Force in 1944–1945, was probably the closest to Spaatz in his concern for morality in strategic bombing. A famous air racer and aeronautical engineer before the war, Doolittle was not a career military man like the rest of the major AAF commanders. Wartime biographers emphasized "his superb sense of fair play and his constant observation of the rules of human decency." He restricted his objectives to purely military targets during his famous Tokyo raid and carefully avoided religious shrines in his 1943 bombings of Rome. Attacking enemy capitals was the ultimate aerial *chevauchée*, designed to force the enemy to commit his air force in defense, embarrass his government by demonstrating the vulnerability of his most important city, and cause economic attrition by destroying key objectives. Doolittle wanted to be the first to bomb

Berlin too, but he supported Spaatz in resisting obliteration attacks on that city.[35] In his autobiography, Doolittle remarked that, in his opinion, the Americans who supported daylight precision bombing over the night area attacks used by the British did so not because pinpoint methods were significantly more effective than RAF tactics but because "to us, it was the most ethical way to go."[36]

Achieving an independent air force was paramount in importance to Lt. Gen. Ira Eaker, who commanded both the Eighth and Mediterranean Allied Air Forces at different times during the war and eventually became Arnold's deputy. Favorable public opinion was essential for this goal, and Eaker was deeply concerned about the AAF image, both current and future. He warned the assistant chief of air staff for intelligence to keep criticism of operations out of official correspondence because "We have a mass of historians at both ends watching all this correspondence and these things cannot but creep into the official documents unless we are all on guard."[37] He supported Arnold's drive for publicity about the contributions of airpower to victory, promising that "We are making certain that every American newspaperman we can get our hands on has these facts hammered home to him."[38]

Eaker was extremely intelligent, had a journalism degree, and had even taken some law courses at Columbia. He was the closest to being a true public relations expert of any AAF leader. After serving as the records custodian for Brig. Gen. Billy Mitchell's court-martial, he saw the dangers of confrontation and "deliberately set out to become army air's most persuasive spokesman." He worked hard to develop his writing and speaking skills. Arnold also often sent Eaker to make presentations to the Joint Chiefs of Staff for the AAF. He had written books and articles with Arnold, and the AAF's commanding general often asked his editorial advice.[39]

His comments to Arnold and other sources reveal that Eaker was not as committed to precision bombing as Spaatz was. He advised Arnold to state in a prewar *Saturday Evening Post* article that it was "probably uneconomical to bomb civil populations unless in extreme cases such as London or Paris, where it would be done for the morale effect in the hope for a short war." He admitted in a 1972 interview that he was not "completely sold" on daylight precision bombing when he took over the Eighth Air Force in England in 1942 and viewed his operations as a test of the concept, though he felt Arnold and Marshall were "relying on him to make it work." If he had failed to save daylight precision bombardment at the Casablanca Conference in January 1943, he was prepared to shift his forces to night bombing in three to six months after installing flame dampers, taking out unnecessary machine guns, and retraining crews.[40] Eaker was very impressed with the results of Operation Gomorrah, the RAF firestorm in Hamburg in July 1943, and wanted to exploit the situation with similar attacks on Berlin. Albert Speer was so alarmed by the dislocation caused in Hamburg that he warned Hitler that six more such attacks would "bring Germany's armaments production to a halt." However, because of the unique bombing concentration and weather conditions, the success of Gomorrah could not be repeated until the Dresden raid in 1945, though Eaker remained convinced that civilian morale might be a viable target. When in late 1944 General Spaatz criticized diversions of Eaker's Fifteenth Air Force from the oil campaign, the latter advocated dispersed attacks to destroy German morale. He did also offer that such tactics might pull defenses away from oil targets. When Eaker did come out against terror attacks in early 1945, it was based on his fears about the political and historical ramifications of "throwing the strategic bomber at the man in the street" for the AAF's reputation, especially when the war seemed almost won.[41]

Curtis LeMay, the key shaper of strategic bombing against Japan, was also not wholly committed to precision bombing. He had little interest in theory or strategy, and he claimed that he had learned little about it from any of his formal Air Corps instruction. He was the most innovative air commander of the war, however, and was known for being the AAF's premier problem solver. In Europe, he had developed staggered formations to increase defensive firepower, designed the non-evasive-action bomb run to improve accuracy, and trained selected lead crews to specialize in important targets. He had also experimented with incendiaries and bombing cities. Known to his men as "Iron Ass," he was tough but fair and insisted upon going on missions to share the risks. He had great respect and admiration for his men and hated to lose them, a trait shared by all these air commanders.[42]

The attitudes of American leaders like Spaatz who were dedicated to daylight precision bombing were bound to clash with those of their RAF counterparts, who were dedicated to "dehousing" German workers and obliterating whole cities with night area raids. From early in the war, U.S. military attachés in England had been sending reports criticizing the inaccuracy of night bombing, yet AAF personnel were sympathetic to the reasons for RAF tactics. They knew that aircraft capabilities and German countermeasures made early British daylight precision attacks unprofitable, but public pressure demanded that the RAF strike back at Germany. Night raids on urban areas seemed the only viable alternative. If the British had possessed the long-range escort fighters that eventually made daylight bombing really possible their campaign might have developed differently. But by 1942, AAF leaders realized that British aircraft, with their heavy bomb loads, inaccurate bombsights, and sparse defensive armament, were primarily adapted to night attacks, while the heavily armed American planes, with smaller bomb loads, good bombsights, and no flame dampers, were primarily suited to day operations.[43]

American leaders discouraged any public criticism of their ally that could assist German propaganda. In private, however, sharp differences often existed over the bombing of civilians. In 1943, there was considerable debate between the Allies over the "political" effects of aerial bombardment. The Combined Chiefs of Staff (CCS) gave responsibility for such matters in occupied Europe to the British Air Ministry, and in late 1942 that agency established a double standard that allowed great targeting leeway for operations against Germany but limited objectives in occupied countries to military targets located far from populated areas, thus excluding many key factories. The British wanted to avoid antagonizing French or Belgian civilians and were conducting their primary air operations against German cities anyway. The Eighth Air Force, now under Eaker, was very unhappy with restrictions that limited attacks against lucrative targets in occupied countries. Such objectives were much closer to British bases, not as heavily defended as targets in Germany, and provided better opportunities to perfect daylight bombing techniques with less risk. Eaker, with Arnold's backing, argued with Sir Charles Portal, Britain's chief of Air Staff and CCS agent for the combined bomber offensive, about the limitations. The Americans stressed that although the Allies had to avoid unnecessary civilian casualties and should bomb only key strategic targets, all civilians employed "willingly or otherwise" in Axis industry were assisting the enemy and should accept the risks "which must be the lot of any individual who participates directly in the war effort of a belligerent nation."[44] This policy applied to German workers as well as French and showed a consistency in thought independent of political considerations. Axis employees at work were no longer viewed as noncombatants, an important step in the escalation to total war. Yet it must be noted that this combatant status applied only to workers in factories being bombed; the AAF strategic campaign, unlike that of the RAF, did not target laborers in their homes. While the British were basically prepared to bomb any German citizen anywhere, whether military or civilian, the Americans were ready to target any Axis worker on the job, whether German or French.

In the meantime, Spaatz, commander of Eisenhower's Northwest African Air Forces, was involved in a different dispute with Portal. In July 1943, Doolittle led a decisive air attack on Rome that was notable not only for its fine planning and precision execution but also for its political effects, which contributed to the fall of Mussolini and surrender of Italy. The British then developed plans to cause similar collapses in Germany's Balkan satellites by blasting capitals like Bucharest and Sofia. While Spaatz would risk civilian casualties by bombing marshaling yards in those cities, he resisted conducting indiscriminate attacks targeting morale, and he eventually recruited Ambassador John Winant to persuade FDR to get Portal to stop directing such missions. Winant was successful in obtaining support from the president and the CCS to stop such terror raids by arguing that they were militarily unsound, created ill will against Americans, and assisted the Russians politically.[45]

When Spaatz returned to England to command the newly created United States Strategic Air Forces, he continued Eaker's policies about bombing factories in occupied Europe. He did object strongly, however, to the civilian casualties he predicted would result from the "Transportation Plan" designed to cripple European rail networks before D-Day. While he did believe that his own campaign against German oil would limit Axis mobility more effectively, he also had sincere concern that the Transportation Plan would "jeopardize the good will of the French and Belgian people by the resultant loss of civilian lives in the attack of rail centers in populated areas and all for a very slight effect."[46] Eisenhower chose the plan because it promised more immediate results than the oil campaign, and Spaatz had to content himself with trying to limit noncombatant casualties with extra care and training. Despite his best efforts, civilians in occupied Europe often felt caught between errant Allied bombers trying to free them and brutal Axis measures claiming to defend them. A prayer often heard in France, Belgium, and the Netherlands went "Lord, liberate me from my protectors, and protect me from my liberators."[47]

Once the Allies were safely ashore, strategic air operations focused on the best way to bring Germany to her knees through airpower. Even the basic American plan in 1941 that shaped precision bombing in Europe, called AWPD/1, allowed for a one-time diversion to bombing cities if it became apparent that "the proper psychological conditions exist" for completely collapsing civil morale.[48] While the RAF and AAF continued their respective city-busting and oil campaigns, both developed plans for victory through one decisive air blow. The British concept involved massive attacks on a few German cities, especially Berlin. Spaatz was violently opposed to it, and it even caused consternation in Washington. Lt. Gen. Laurence Kuter, of Arnold's staff, wrote that such strikes against civilians would bring some of the "onus" of night bombing on the AAF, could not affect national will in a police state anyway, and were "contrary to our national ideals."[49] American bomber crewmen in the European theater also were critical of missions against German cities, especially the long and dangerous raids on Berlin. Typical complaints in a 1944 survey were that the city "is not a military target" and that it was bombed mainly for "headlines," and "I don't believe in spite bombing." Indiscriminate attacks on cities with no clear objectives seemed wasteful, brought unnecessary risks, and violated the precision-bombing doctrine airmen had been taught and believed in.[50]

Despite AAF misgivings, Eisenhower approved the operation in September, explaining, "While I have always insisted that U.S. Strategic Forces be directed against precision targets, I am always prepared to take part in anything that gives real promise to ending the war quickly."[51] Ground commanders were often the most avid supporters of massive air operations that made their jobs easier and casualties lower. After the Battle of the Bulge, General Omar Bradley and his staff began pushing for an aerial deathblow, and even George Marshall, concerned about American staying power for the war with Japan still ahead, began "pressing for any and every plan to bring increased effort against the German forces for the purpose of quickly ending the war." Arnold acknowledged that these pressures were causing him to stress "some very marginal projects," but "we will not know just where the breaking point may be." Like the reluctant rowers of the first Athenian dispatch-trireme to Mytilene, Spaatz and Doolittle dragged their feet and delayed, but the British plan was eventually conducted in 1945 under the name "Thunderclap." Predicting that such terror attacks would be ineffective because the citizens of Berlin were used to bombing and lamenting that the raids violated "the basic American principle of precision bombing of targets of military significance," Doolittle managed to redefine American targets over Berlin to some degree, but his 3 February mission still killed an estimated twenty-five thousand civilians.[52]

American bombers also participated in the destructive attacks on Dresden later in the month, but most of the thirty-five thousand or more civilian deaths there were caused by British ordnance. AAF bombs aimed at the city's marshaling yard did spill over onto residential areas though since smoke from the fires of RAF incendiaries obscured most of the target area. The best studies dealing with this raid lay much of the blame on Winston Churchill and the confusion over Russian desires for support. At the Yalta Conference on 4 February, General Antonov and Marshal Stalin asked for Allied attacks on communication centers to prevent the shifting of German reinforcements to the Russian front. On 8 February, Supreme Headquarters Allied Expeditionary Forces (SHAEF) instructed RAF Bomber Command and USSTAF to prepare to bomb Dresden to interdict military movements. Contrary to later reports, the city did contain important industrial and transportation targets worth destroying. Nevertheless, Doolittle was quite disturbed about the devastation from the 14–15 February mission, telling assembled SHAEF air commanders with the "greatest reticence" that smoke from the burning city rose to fifteen thousand feet.[53]

The targeting of Dresden fueled two controversies, one involving SHAEF, USSTAF, and AAF headquarters before the actual attack and another that included the media and the War Department afterward. Allied air leaders meeting at Malta had anticipated Russian requests and revised bombing directives on 30 January. Second priority behind oil became "Berlin, Leipzig, Dresden, and associated cities where heavy attack will cause confusion in civilian evacuation from the east and hamper reinforcements."[54] The wording of the directive troubled

Kuter, an architect of precision doctrine, who inspired queries from Washington to USSTAF concerning the high priority given the bombing of cities. Spaatz replied that the new directions really reflected RAF Bomber Command's capabilities, and USSTAF continued with business as usual. Arnold was satisfied with the answer, emphasizing that he would not accept "the promiscuous bombing of German cities for the purpose of causing civilian confusion."[55] The AAF commanding general's misgivings were reinforced with Spaatz by Brig. Gen. George McDonald, the USSTAF director of intelligence, who was afraid that the new directive would link them "to indiscriminate homicide and destruction."[56]

Arnold's concern intensified even more when, as the result of a press conference after the Dresden attacks, nationwide headlines appeared such as "Terror Bombing Gets Allied Approval as Step to Speed Victory." Howard Cowan, an Associated Press reporter, based his story on a briefing in Paris by Air Commodore C. M. Grierson of the SHAEF Air Staff. Grierson did not mention morale attacks by name but pointed out that recent heavy-bomber attacks on population centers had caused great need for relief supplies and strained the economic system. Arnold feared a public relations disaster at home and immediately demanded an explanation from USSTAF. Maj. Gen. Frederick Anderson, deputy commander for operations, replied that the report had exaggerated the briefing officer's statements and had never been cleared by censors. He reiterated that the USSTAF's mission remained to destroy Germany's ability to wage war and that attacks on transportation centers were not terror attacks. Eisenhower also confirmed that the briefer had gone beyond his knowledge and authority.[57] By 20 February Arnold was satisfied that the matter was under control, but then two weeks later the secretary of war read an account of Grierson's briefing in the press and asked for an investigation of Dresden, noting "an account of it has come out of Germany which makes the destruction seem on its face terrible and probably unnecessary." Typically, Stimson had not been informed about the raid or its aftermath by any of his subordinates. An exasperated Arnold, recuperating in Florida from a heart attack, scrawled the following on a message from his headquarters concerning Stimson's request: "We must not get soft. War must be destructive and to a certain extent inhuman and ruthless." But the resulting AAF report by his staff was not so callous and correctly blamed RAF incendiary bombs for most of the Dresden damage. Trustful of his military advisers, Stimson let the matter drop. The whole controversy caused Arnold considerable strains and contributed to his health problems.[58]

Spaatz also developed his own concept for an aerial deathblow that resembled FDR's earlier ideas, but there were competing plans within his command. Most were generated by his deputy director for intelligence, Col. Lowell Weicker. Typical of these proposals was one called Operation Shatter that was submitted three weeks after the Normandy landings. It aimed to break military and civilian morale by bombing one hundred German cities in one day. Heavy bombers would make attacks on government buildings, transportation facilities, or minor industries "to free such an operation from the stigma of being merely retaliatory terror bombing." Psychological warfare through leaflets and broadcasts would also be used to emphasize the defenselessness of the Reich to air attack.[59]

In July, Weicker became embroiled in a debate over plans like Shatter, and the exchange reveals much about the conflicting attitudes about efficiency and humanity that American airmen could hold. His main antagonist was Col. Richard Hughes, chief of the USSTAF's Target Section. Hughes was a former British army officer who became an American citizen in the 1930s. He has been described by a subordinate as "one of those selfless men, of high intelligence, integrity, and dedication, who play major roles in great enterprises but, operating at a middle level of authority, leave little trace in the formal records of history." Hughes argued that Weicker based his proposals on questionable assumptions and that his plan pursued the same "Will of the Wisp" of morale that had been sought so long in the Balkans, deviated from fundamentally sound doctrine, and diverted resources from more important objectives. He also devoted great attention to morality: "Hypocritically sometimes, Polly Anna-ishly frequently, but none the less fundamentally rightly, America has represented in world thought an urge toward decency and better treatment of man by man. Japs may order our prisoners to be shot, but we do not order the shooting of theirs. Hot blood is one thing—reason and the long view is another. As Mr. Lovett stated very strongly the other day, silly as it may seem to some of us realists here, there is definite and very genuine concern in both the Senate, Congress, and the country about the inhumanity of indiscriminate area bombing, as such."[60]

Weicker replied that Hughes had "a closed mind and a prejudiced point of view." The deputy director for intelligence thought the target selection was based on an orderly system of military requirements and necessity. He agreed that Americans wanted to use "Marquis of Queensberry's rules" to protect civilians, but this approach was not feasible against the brutal Nazi regime. His program was not a new way to kill women and children, he contended, but a method to press home fundamental ideas to the German people about their defenselessness that could end the war. He did argue, however, that if his concept saved a few Allied lives, any price paid by the enemy should "not be a factor of sober and practical consideration." This same kind of ethical calculus would be a factor in the use of fire raids and the atomic bomb against Japan to avoid an invasion. When Col. Charles Taylor, USSTAF's deputy director for plans, saw Weicker's plan and the attached arguments, he agreed with Hughes, adding that the operation went against his own perceptions of General Arnold's desires as well. Taylor's superiors concurred, and he penned "Never sent, Thank God!" on the proposal that was to be submitted to SHAEF. One week later, he killed another psychological warfare plan that proposed to destroy "Nationally Famous Monuments of Industry" to sap morale and degrade the power and transportation infrastructure in 116 cities. His comments, reflecting his growing irritation with such plans, noted that the proposal "leaves the door open for civilian bombing and the needless destruction of industrial monuments." If the "industrial monument" was "a major factor in keeping Germany in the war," it would be destroyed anyway as part of the strategic bombing campaign. He concluded testily that if the target was not that important, "then to hell with it. Let's get on with the war."[61]

Spaatz's own concept, designated Operation Clarion, came to fruition during the Dresden controversy. He initially planned to attack scattered targets throughout Germany to impress the whole country with the invincibility of Allied airpower and break civil morale. He did not want to kill German civilians, just convince them of the hopelessness of further resistance. Even though Spaatz believed his plan was much more humane than Thunderclap and Arnold endorsed it, one of Eaker's staff called it "the same old baby-killing plan dressed up in a new kimono."[62] Eaker and Doolittle also protested against it, as did Lt. Gen. Nathan Twining, now commanding the Fifteenth Air Force. He expressed concern not only about low-altitude attacks by heavy bombers that were risky and unsound but also with "how the enemy and our own people will react to our attacking these types of targets and the resultant heavy loss to the civilian populace."[63] After listening to these complaints and seeing the results of the deadly February raid on Berlin, Spaatz lost faith in chasing the "chimera" of the aerial death-blow. Clarion became just another mission in the campaign against transportation that was a decisive factor in collapsing the German economy.[64] As the war went on, however, the increased American emphasis on attacks of transportation objectives like marshaling yards such as the one in Dresden showed less concern for collateral damage since the larger the urban target, the more widespread bomb spillover would be. But with the diminishing number of good strategic targets, the large number of available bombers, and the constant pressure for missions from ground forces, such a shift was inevitable. Nevertheless, Spaatz and his USSTAF did resist the temptation to attack morale directly and to kill civilians to attain that end. Eventually, the lack of targets, the reaction to Dresden, and imminent German collapse brought an end to strategic bombing over Europe.

Air force advocates like Arnold still had one chance left to show the potential of independent airpower. But by the end of 1944, Twentieth Air Force strategic operations against Japan had achieved dismal results (see map 8.2). Problems with the new B-29s and crew training, logistical problems with remote Chinese bases, incomplete facilities in the Mariana Islands, dispersed Japanese industry, and especially weather at high altitudes made precision bombing nearly impossible. When Brig. Gen. Haywood Hansell, one of the key developers of precision doctrine and commander of the main force of B-29s, Twenty-first Bomber Command in the Marianas, proved unwilling or unable to find more effective methods, Arnold brought LeMay in from China as a replacement and consolidated all B-29s in the Marianas. After retraining crews, finishing bases, and revising maintenance procedures, LeMay still had poor success with high-altitude precision bombing. With American casualties mounting in the theater and the invasion of Japan approaching, there was immense pressure on LeMay from Arnold and others, including MacArthur, Nimitz, and Mountbatten, to produce decisive results from the costly Very Heavy Bomber Program. Grim intelligence estimates predicted that 200,000 regular troops and 575,000 reservists would defend Kyushu, and Japanese reinforcements might be able to overcome planned American local superiority. Added to these influences was a sense of growing war weariness at home. Many American leaders feared that the public could not sustain its war fervor much longer and became particularly apprehensive as V-E Day approached. Admiral Earnest King typified the attitude of the Joint Chiefs of Staff when he told reporters privately that he was afraid "the American people will tire of it quickly, and that pressure at home will force a negotiated peace, before the Japs are really licked."[65]

On his own initiative, LeMay adopted low-level night attacks with incendiaries. The B-29s could carry more bombs, the flight was easier on their engines, lower attacks avoided the jet stream winds at higher altitudes and exploited weaknesses in enemy air defenses, and the fires in districts surrounding factories would hopefully be intense enough to leap the firebreaks around key targets. The primary focus of the devastatingly effective raids was industrial objectives, but eventually the campaign also incorporated psychological warfare by dropping warning leaflets that motivated more than six million civilians to flee from Japanese cities. In LeMay's defense, it must be noted that he sincerely believed the warnings to be a humane gesture that would "convince the Japanese people and certain articulate minority groups of our own people that our Air Force policy is aimed at destruction of the war-making industrial capacity of Japan and not the Japanese people." However, the use of such tactics made the generation of terror a formal, though secondary, objective of the fire raids. The incendiary campaign burned out over 180 square miles of 67 cities and killed or wounded at least seven hundred thousand people. LeMay's air attacks were also one of the key components of the series of shocks that induced Japanese surrender. Racism was not a factor in the development of the new bombing strategy, though it might have facilitated public acceptance of reports of the conflagrations consuming enemy cities. Even Stimson became resigned to the incendiary campaign, though one of his rationalizations for using the atomic bomb was that "it stopped the fire raids."[66] In the Pacific, the pursuit of efficiency had overridden most concerns for humanity.

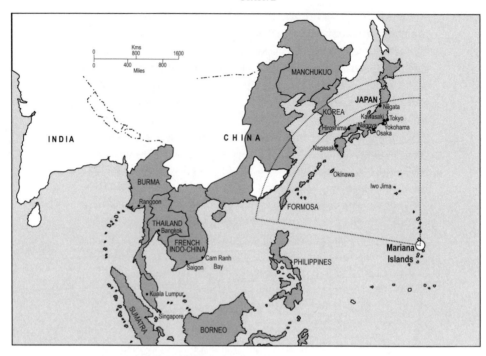

Map 8.2. Strategic Air Offensive against Japan

Stimson's reticence differed markedly from the reaction of the rest of key leaders in Washington. Arnold, for instance, commended LeMay on his proven ability "to destroy whole industrial cities."[67] The Twenty-first Bomber Command expected to wipe out all Japanese industrial capacity by October 1945, and LeMay believed that neither an invasion nor the atomic bomb was necessary. Less optimistic leaders wanted to use gas against defending forces and wipe out the Japanese rice crop with chemicals. As has been noted earlier, Spaatz also was against the use of atomic weapons, but for more humanitarian reasons. As the newly designated commander of United States Army Strategic Air Forces, he had arrived in the Pacific in July with the intent and mandate to change the focus of the strategic air war to transportation and munitions. Instead, he found that momentum, training, and ammunition stocks had fully committed the Twentieth Air Force to the firebombing of Japanese cities.[68]

The escalation that Spaatz had successfully resisted in the European theater had occurred in the Pacific, though no one wanted to admit that the AAF was now engaged in an RAF-style city-busting campaign. At a press conference to discuss Hiroshima, Stimson and Arnold presented a photograph showing the aiming point for the atomic bomb, hoping "that the accuracy with which this bomb was placed may counter a thought that the Centerboard [A-bomb] project involves wanton, indiscriminate bombing."[69] Yet, technology, combat conditions, and the attitudes of theater air commanders had produced two different American air campaigns. Both aimed to break the enemy's will to resist by destroying key industrial and military objectives. However, one considered noncombatant casualties as an undesirable side effect of bombing operations, while the other aimed to exploit civilian distress to magnify the effects of the campaign.

The lessons from both campaigns influenced American precision-bombing doctrine at the beginning of the nuclear age. Air planners realized that area attacks on urban industrial concentrations were another method to destroy an enemy's war-making capacity. Two targeting approaches emerged as to how best to exploit Soviet vulnerabilities, a "vertical" school focused on eliminating key systems such as electric power or transportation and a "horizontal" school that wanted to take advantage of the mass of suitable military and economic targets in cities. The two methods complemented each other in postwar JCS general war plans. Though the avowed purpose of such operations was "to destroy the will of the USSR to resist"—a vague joint strategic concept that gave all services a role—the mission of the Air Force was always "to initiate a powerful U.S. air offensive against selected vital elements of Soviet war-making capacity." Civilian morale was not a target, a fact that appalled Rand Corporation analysts like Bernard Brodie. In 1949, he began to focus on the best way to exploit the psychological aspects of the threat of nuclear strikes, and he worked to educate the Air Force leadership about the utility of terror. And when the Rand Social Science Division did a detailed study that year on the psychological warfare involved in "The Warning of Target Populations in Air War," the first example they looked at was LeMay's leaflet campaign against Japan.[70]

Both American strategic air campaigns in World War II contributed to final victory, but each left a very different legacy. While the Air Force trumpets its commitment to the principles of precision bombing, lurking in our collective memories are the visions of Tokyo and Hiroshima.

The impact of this dual legacy was very evident during the recent NATO bombing campaign to protect Kosovo. While American air commanders favored attacking a broad spectrum of targets throughout Yugoslavia with waves of precision strikes, European allies, remembering Hamburg and Dresden, feared collateral damage and civilian casualties. The gradual escalation that resulted from political compromise failed to achieve any of the initial objectives described by President Clinton to justify the bombing, and after thousands of Kosovars were slaughtered or displaced and NATO frustration mounted, American airmen eventually got their wish. Whatever success the air campaign achieved was not due to relatively ineffective attacks on Serbian ground forces, but instead resulted from an assault on Yugoslavia's economic and social infrastructure that would have been familiar to Army Air Corps planners of the 1930s. The most important raids took out the Yugoslav power grid, disabling everything from the air defense command-and-control network to the country's banking system, hospitals, and water-pumping stations. Petroleum-refining facilities were completely eliminated. Seventy percent of road and fifty percent of rail bridges across the Danube were destroyed. Though bombing accuracy has improved to an extraordinary degree since World War II, the term *surgical air strike* remains an oxymoron. Mistakes and collateral damage still occurred during the Balkan air campaign, contributing to the bombing of the Chinese embassy and the death of as many as fifteen hundred civilians. Though Operation Allied Force did degrade Yugoslav war-making capacity in keeping with traditional precision-bombing doctrine, a Pentagon spokesman speculated that the main factor in Slobodan Milosevic's acceptance of NATO terms was "the increasing inconveniences that the bombing campaign was causing in Belgrade and other cities."[71]

As the 1943 memorandum quoted earlier in this essay forewarned, the recent conflict over Kosovo has demonstrated how aggressive belligerents with the right aerial technology can inflict massive destruction at low cost to themselves. Instead of heading for the sort of future envisioned by contemporary airpower theorists like John Warden, when paralyzing attacks on military structures will end conflicts with relatively little impact on the civilian sphere, we may be headed for that predicted by Giulio Douhet, when new weapons will decide wars by inflicting the maximum amount of distress on the civilian population.[72] Civilian will does appear to be more vulnerable to the destructive power of modern technology than military capability, especially when quick results are desired. As one journalist wrote after concluding that the attacks on Yugoslav civilians were the key to ending the Kosovo conflict, "that may produce an uncomfortable lesson for the politicians who call the shots during the next war: the most merciful way to conduct a war may be to end it swiftly and violently."[73] Curtis LeMay would have approved.

Notes

Much of the material in this essay comes from Conrad C. Crane, *Bombs, Cities, and Civilians: American Airpower Strategy in World War II* (Lawrence KS, 1993). It is used with permission of the publisher. The views expressed herein are those of the author and do not purport to reflect the positions of the United States Army War College, Department of the Army, or Department of Defense.

1. Jean de Bloch, *The Future of War in Its Technical, Economic, and Political Relations* (Boston, 1914), reprinted in 1989 by the Combat Studies Institute, U.S. Army Command and General Staff College, Fort Leavenworth, Kansas. Bloch's translator altered his name to "Jean de Bloch."

2. Martin Gilbert, *The First World War: A Complete History* (New York, 1994), 256 n.

3. Lee Kennett, *A History of Strategic Bombing* (New York, 1982), 50–53; Sir Charles Webster and Noble Frankland, *The Strategic Air Offensive against Germany, 1939–1945* (London, 1961), 4:66–67.

4. Kennett, *A History of Strategic Bombing*, 56; Giulio Douhet, *The Command of the Air*, trans. Dino Ferrari (1942; reprint, New York, 1972), 57–61, 69, 188.

5. "Suggested Reply to Letters Questioning Humanitarian Aspects of Air Force," Humanitarian Aspects of Airpower Binder, Box 9A, Frederick L. Anderson Papers, Hoover Institution on War, Revolution and Peace, Stanford University, Stanford, California.

6. Thomas H. Greer, *The Development of Air Doctrine in the Army Air Arm, 1917–1941* (Maxwell AFB, 1955), 57–58; Haywood S. Hansell Jr., "Harold L. George: Apostle of Air Power," in *Makers of the United States Air Force*, ed. John L. Frisbee (Washington DC, 1987), 77–78.

7. Robert Frank Futrell, "Commentary," in *Command and Commanders in Modern Warfare*, ed. Lt. Col. William Geffen (Colorado Springs, 1969), 313; P. W. Wilson, "Are Laws of War Scraps of Paper?" *New York Times*, 3 October 1937, section 4E, p. 1; Associated Press, *World War II: A Fiftieth Anniversary* (New York, 1989), 49; "Horrors of War" cards made by Gum, Inc. in 1938, reprinted by Card Collectors Co., New York.

8. For American dreams about the airplane, see Joseph J. Corn, *The Winged Gospel: America's Romance with Aviation, 1900–1950* (New York, 1983).

9. Lesson Plan, "Conference on Air Operations against National Structures," 11 April 1939, p. 14, File 248.2020A-25, Air Force Historical Research Agency (AFHRA), Maxwell AFB AL

10. Dept. of Civil and Military Engineering Organizational History/Program of Instruction Files, Academic Year 1938–1939, Box 2, USMA Archives, West Point NY; Hilton P. Goss, *Civilian Morale under Aerial Bombardment 1914–1939* (Maxwell AFB, 1948), 253.

11. Hadley Cantril and Mildred Strunk, eds., *Public Opinion, 1935–1946* (Princeton NJ, 1951), 1067–69.

12. George E. Hopkins, "Bombing and the American Conscience during World War II," *Historian* 28 (May 1966): 467–71.

13. Michael Howard, *The Causes of War and Other Essays*, 2d ed. (Cambridge, 1984), 104.

14. *Foreign Relations of the United States, Diplomatic Papers 1939* (Washington DC, 1956), 1:541–42.

15. *Foreign Relations of the United States*, 542–53; Cordell Hull, *The Memoirs of Cordell Hull* (New York, 1948), 1:671–72.

16. Henry Morgenthau, *The Presidential Diaries of Henry Morgenthau, 1938–1945* (microfilm edition, Frederick MD, 1981), book 4:952.

17. Michael Sherry, *The Rise of American Airpower: The Creation of Armageddon* (New Haven CT, 1987), 78–79.

18. Letter, Laurence Kuter to Frederick Anderson, 8 August 1944, File 145. 161–67, April 1944 May 1945, Misc. Correspondence of Anderson and Kuter, AFHRA.

19. Maj. Gen. H. H. Arnold and Col. Ira Eaker, *Winged Warfare* (New York, 1941), 133–34.

20. Arnold, *Global Mission* (New York, 1949), 227; diary of trip to England, April 1941, Box 271, Arnold Papers, Library of Congress (hereafter LC).

21. Arnold, "Precision Blows for Victory: A Report to the Nation," text of planned speech scheduled for Soldiers Field, Chicago, on 16 May 1943, Box 9A, Anderson Papers. This wording was typical of Arnold's public rhetoric.

22. Memo, T. J. Hanley Jr. to Assistant Chiefs of Air Staff, Personnel, et al.,

"Protest against Killing Civilians in Bombing Raids," 30 April 1943, File 385, Box 114, Arnold Papers.

23. War Dept. transcript of extemporaneous remarks by Arnold at a Pentagon news conference, 18 October 1943, Box 14, Carl Spaatz Papers, LC.

24. Thomas M. Coffey, HAP: *The Story of the U.S. Air Force and the Man Who Built It* (New York, 1982), 358–75.

25. Memo from Arnold to all air force commanders in combat zones, "Evaluation of Bombing Methods and Purposes," 10 June 1943, Box 121, Nathan Twining Papers, LC.

26. See, for example, Dwight Macdonald, *Memoirs of a Revolutionist* (New York, 1957), 76–77.

27. Henry L. Stimson Diary, 5 September 1944, Yale University Library, microfilm edition.

28. Stimson Diary, 3 January 1945, 2 July 1945, 6 May 1945.

29. Stimson Diary, 6 June 1945; Noam Chomsky, *American Power and the New Mandarins* (New York, 1969), 167; Len Giovannitti and Fred Freed, *The Decision to Drop the Bomb* (New York, 1965), 36.

30. Ronald Schaffer, *Wings of Judgment: American Bombing in World War II* (New York, 1985), 180.

31. Letter, Stimson to Arnold with reply by Eaker, 11 June 1945, Secretary of War File, Box 46, Arnold Papers; for more on Kyoto, see Schaffer, *Wings of Judgment*, 143–46; letter, Stimson to Secretary of State, 11 January 1944, Box 114, Arnold Papers; Stimson Diary, 11 October 1944.

32. Russell Weigley, *Eisenhower's Lieutenants* (Bloomington IN, 1981), 104; letter, Spaatz to Arnold, 19 November 1944, Box 16, Spaatz Papers.

33. Compare predicted figures of notes on accuracy of bombing in A-2 (Intelligence Staff) Report, 6 October 1942, Box 10, Spaatz Papers, with results summarized in Philip Kaplan and Rex Alan Smith, *One Last Look* (New York, 1983), 193–97.

34. Weigley, *Eisenhower's Lieutenants*, 59; entry for 11 August 1945, Personal Diary, Box 21, Spaatz Papers.

35. Carl Mann, *Lightning in the Sky* (New York, 1943), 244–45, 252–55; Lowell Thomas and Edward Jablonsky, *Doolittle, a Biography* (New York, 1976), 173–74, 245–46, 294; Wesley Frank Craven and James Lea Cate, eds., *The Army Air Forces in World War II* (Chicago, 1951), 2:463–65; 3:638–39, 725.

36. General James H. Doolittle with Carol Glines, *I Could Never Be So Lucky Again* (New York, 1991), 376.

37. Schaffer, "American Military Ethics in World War II: The Bombing of German Civilians," *Journal of American History* 67 (September 1980): 324.

38. Letter, Eaker to Arnold, 5 January 1945, Box 22, Ira Eaker Papers, LC.

39. James Parton, *"Air Force Spoken Here": General Ira Eaker and Command of the Air* (Bethesda MD, 1986), 24–25, 41–42, 46–47, 216–28.

40. Memo, Eaker to Arnold, 25 August 1939, Box 3, Arnold Papers; 1972 Eaker interview by Joe Green, Ira C. Eaker Papers, U.S. Army Military History Institute, Carlisle Barracks PA.

41. Letter, Eaker to Robert Lovett, 9 August 1943, Box 17, Eaker Papers, LC; Williamson Murray, *Strategy for Defeat: The Luftwaffe, 1933–1945* (Maxwell AFB, 1983), 169; minutes of USSTAF Air Commanders' Conference, 15 October 1944, Box 16, and letter, Eaker to Spaatz, 1 January 1945, Box 20, Spaatz Papers. For more on Hamburg, see Martin Middlebrook, *The Battle of Hamburg* (New York, 1980). That air raid was the deadliest of the war in Europe, incinerating an estimated forty-five thousand people.

42. Coffey, *Iron Eagle* (New York, 1986), 4, 34–38, 50, 56, 69, 139, 243.

43. See attached reports in G-2 Regional File, Great Britain, 1933–1944, 9600–9670, Box 1620, War Dept. General and Special Staffs, Record Group (RG) 165, Modern Military Field Branch, National Archives II, College Park MD; Report by Anderson, 5 January 1942, Box 2, Anderson Papers; memo, Eaker to Spaatz, "Night Bombing," 8 October 1942, Box 10, Spaatz Papers.

44. Directive C.S.15803 on bombardment policy from Air Vice Marshal Slessor, 29 October 1942, File 519.318–1, 1942–1945, Combined Bomber Offensive (CBO) Policy Directives, AFHRA; Bruce Hopper, memo on USSTAF history preparation, 22 September 1944, Box 287, Spaatz Papers; letter, Eaker to Air Marshal N. H. Bottomley, 9 April 1943, Box 19, Eaker Papers, LC; letter, Sir Charles Portal to Eaker, 21 April 1943, Box 41, Arnold Papers; draft of letter, Arnold to Portal, Box 9A, Anderson Papers.

45. Craven and Cate, *Army Air Forces in World War II*, 2:464–65; Ernest R. May, *Lessons of the Past* (New York, 1973), 128; J.P.(43)346, 15 October 1943, "Air Attack on the Balkans," File 512.3171–1, AFHRA; letter, Spaatz to Arnold, 6 March 1944, Box 14, Spaatz Papers; CCS 626, 20 July 1944, with enclosures including Winant note to FDR, ABC 384.5 (25 May 1944), RG 319, Modern Military Headquarters Branch, National Archives (NA), Washington DC.

46. Weigley, *Eisenhower's Lieutenants*, 58–64; "Review of Oil and Transportation Target Systems," 6 June 1944, File 168.7026–6, January-June 1944, Charles Cabell Papers, AFHRA.

47. Minutes of meeting in General Wilson's headquarters, 30 April 1944, Box 14, Spaatz Papers; comment from audience at Siena Conference on World War II, 4 June 1993, Siena NY.

48. "Army and Navy Estimate of United States Overall Production Requirements," 11 September 1941, AWPD/1, tab 2, section 2, pt. 3, appendix 2, p. 6, Joint

Army-Navy Board File 355, Serial 707, RG 225, National Archives, Washington DC.

49. Memo, Kuter to Arnold, "Attack on German Civilian Morale," 9 August 1944; letter, Kuter to Anderson, 15 August 1944, Thunderclap File, Box 153, Spaatz Papers.

50. Research Division, Special Service Division, Headquarters, European Theater of Operations, June 1944, "Survey of Combat Crews in Heavy Bombardment Groups in ETO," 11, Box 18, Spaatz Papers.

51. Memo, Spaatz to D. D. Eisenhower, 24 August 1944, with 28 August return endorsement, Box 18; diary entry, 9 September 1944, Box 16, Spaatz Papers.

52. Letter, Arnold to Spaatz, 30 December 1944, Box 20, and message, Anderson to Spaatz, 1 February 1945, Clarion File, Box 170, Spaatz Papers; diary entry, 29 January 1945, Box 1, Hoyt Vandenberg Papers, LC; message CS93JD, Doolittle to Spaatz, 30 January 1945, File 520.422, AFHRA; Craven and Cate, *Army Air Forces in World War II*, 3:725–26.

53. See maps of damage in Gotz Bergander, *Dresden im Luftkrieg* (Cologne, 1977); Melden E. Smith Jr., "The Bombing of Dresden Reconsidered: A Study in Wartime Decision Making" (Ph.D. diss., Boston University, 1971), 208–9, 237–47; Joseph W. Angell, "Historical Analysis of the 14–15 February 1945 Bombing of Dresden," 11–15, File K239.046–38, AFHRA; USSTAF Air Intelligence Summary 68, RG 334, NA II, College Park MD; notes from Allied Air Commanders Conference, 15 February 1945, File K239.046–38, AFHRA.

54. Craven and Cate, *Army Air Forces in World War II*, 3:640, 653, 724–25.

55. Message Cricket 38, Kuter to Giles, 1 February 1945, Box 316; message, Giles to Spaatz, 17 February 1945 and message UA64462, Spaatz to Arnold, 18 February 1945, Box 20, Spaatz Papers.

56. Memorandum from McDonald, 21 February 1945, Anderson's Diary, Anderson Papers.

57. Smith, "Bombing of Dresden Reconsidered," 70–78; memo, Anderson to Spaatz, 19 February 1945, with messages SC64462, W39222, UA64470, W39730, UA64471, W39722, File K239.046–38, AFHRA.

58. Message UA 64555, Spaatz to Eaker, 20 February 1945, Box 23, Spaatz Papers; Stimson Diary, 5 March 1945; Schaffer, *Wings*, 99–103; "Report of Air Attacks on Targets in Dresden," File 523–6, AFHRA.

59. Memo, Captain John Harris to Brig. Gen. George McDonald, "Operation Shatter," 27 June 1944, File 519.322–1, AFHRA.

60. W. W. Rostow, *Pre-Invasion Bombing Strategy* (Austin TX, 1981), 17; memo from Richard Hughes, 5 July 1944, Pointblank Folder, File 519.4511–14, AFHRA.

61. Memo, Lowell Weicker to McDonald, 6 July 1944; undated memo, Charles Taylor to Charles Williamson; Taylor comments on proposed memo, Frederick Anderson to Sir Arthur Tedder, 8 July 1944, draft of psychological warfare plan with handwritten note from Taylor to Williamson, 16 July 1944, Pointblank Folder, AFHRA.

62. "General Plan for Maximum Effort Attack against Transportation Objectives," 17 December 1944, with Charles Cabell's written comments, File 168. 7026–9, AFHRA.

63. Memo, Doolittle to Spaatz, 27 December 1944, File 519.430A, AFHRA; memo, Eaker to Spaatz, 1 January 1945 and memo, Nathan Twining to Eaker, 4 January 1945, Box 20, Spaatz Papers.

64. Letter, Spaatz to Arnold, 5 February 1945, Box 20, Spaatz Papers; Albert C. Mierzejewski, *The Collapse of the German War Economy, 1944–1945* (Chapel Hill NC, 1988), 184; for more on Clarion, see Conrad C. Crane, *Bombs, Cities, and Civilians: American Airpower Strategy in World War II* (Lawrence KS, 1993), 108–13.

65. Craven and Cate, *Army Air Forces in World War II*, 5:551–76; Crane, *Bombs, Cities, and Civilians*, 129; "Amendment No. 1 to G-2 Estimate of the Enemy Situation with Respect to Kyushu," 29 July 1945, Quintin S. Lander Papers, U.S. Army Military History Institute; Charles F. Brower IV, "The Joint Chiefs of Staff and National Policy: American Strategy and the War with Japan, 1943–1945" (Ph.D. diss., University of Pennsylvania, 1987), 209–10.

66. Foreword to Twenty-first Bomber Command Tactical Mission Report, Mission No. 40, 10 March 1945, prepared 15 April 1945, Box 26, Curtis LeMay Papers, LC; Robert Gleason, "Psychological Operations and Air Power," *Air University Review* 22 (March April 1971): 36–37; Wartime History, Twentieth Air Force, File 760.01, AFHRA; John D. Chappell, *Before the Bomb: How America Approached the End of the Pacific War* (Lexington KY, 1997), 194 n. 86; Henry Stimson and McGeorge Bundy, *On Active Service in Peace and War* (New York, 1948), 632–33.

67. Letter, Arnold to LeMay, 21 March 1945, Box B-11, LeMay Papers.

68. Journal, "Trip to Pacific, June 6, 1945 to June 24, 1945," 13 June entry, Box 272, Arnold Papers; directive, Eaker to Commanding General, U.S. Army Strategic Air Forces, 26 July 1945, Box 13, LeMay Papers. For more on the possible use of gas and chemicals against Japan, as well as Spaatz's attempts to limit the fire raids, see Crane, *Bombs, Cities, and Civilians*, 137–40.

69. Message 082328Z, Lauris Norstad to Spaatz, 8 August 1945, Box 21, Spaatz Papers.

70. Air University lecture by Dan Dyer, "Horizontal Approach to Target Analysis," 12 December 1951, File K239.716251–55, AFHRA. For a typical war

plan, see Plan Bushwacker in volume 8 of Steven T. Ross and David Alan Rosenberg, eds., *America's Plans for War against the Soviet Union, 1945–1950* (New York, 1989), 15 vols.; Bernard Brodie, "The Morale Factor in STRAP Planning," 5 August 1949, Rand paper, Papers of Bernard Brodie, Special Collections, The University of California at Los Angeles; Fred Kaplan, *The Wizards of Armageddon* (New York, 1983), 38–49, 204–5; Barry Steiner, *Bernard Brodie and the Foundations of American Nuclear Strategy* (Lawrence KS, 1991), 46–77; and Rand Corporation Social Sciences Division Research Memorandum 275, *The Warning of Target Populations in Air War: An Appendix of Working Papers* (Santa Monica CA, November 1949)—appendices A and B deal with Japan; the main report is still classified. For more on the legacy of World War II bombing approaches and their application in the Korean War, see Conrad Crane, *American Airpower Strategy in Korea, 1950–1953* (Lawrence KS, 2000).

71. Michael Ignatieff, "The Virtual Commander: How NATO Invented a New Kind of War," *New Yorker* (2 August 1999): 32–35; Steven Lee Myers, "Damage to Serb Military Less Than Expected," *New York Times*, 28 June 1999, p. 1; Rebecca Grant, *The Kosovo Campaign: Aerospace Power Made It Work* (Arlington VA, 1999), 22; Michael Dobbs, "Post-Mortem on NATO's Bombing Campaign," *Washington Post (National Weekly Edition)*, 19–26 July 1999, p. 23. For the stated objectives of the bombing campaign, see R. W. Apple, "A Fresh Set of U.S. Goals," *New York Times*, 25 March 1999, p. A1; see also the text of President Clinton's speech, p. A15.

72. Warden's ideas are expressed in his book, *The Air Campaign: Planning for Combat* (New York, 1989). The best critique of his theories is Lieutenant David S. Fadok, "John Boyd and John Warden: Airpower's Quest for Strategic Paralysis," in *The Paths of Heaven: The Evolution of Airpower Theory*, ed. Col. Phillip S. Meilinger (Maxwell AFB, 1997).

73. Richard J. Newman, "The Bombs That Failed in Kosovo," *U.S. News and World Report* 127 (20 September 1999): 28–30.

Not Enough Collateral Damage

Moral Ambiguities in the Gulf War

Williamson Murray

As in previous twentieth-century conflicts, the Gulf War against Iraq in 1991 raised fundamental issues about the nature, contribution, and morality of using air power in war. Since its inception, air power has played to the "American way of war," one in which war represents an exercise in engineering expertise, thereby removing the warrior from the results of his actions. At the same time, certain segments of American society are profoundly disturbed by the destruction thus unleashed on civilians and military forces alike, even if they are the enemy. Having devoted two years of my life to the study of the 1991 air war, this author is no closer to resolving the ambiguities posed by the inherent tension between expediency, morality, and humanity in the study of aerial war.[1] This essay, then, will discuss those ambiguities that, once again, appeared in full bloom in the Gulf War.

Two events had a considerable impact on the way American airmen of the postwar years viewed the lessons of World War II. The first was the dropping of the atomic bomb on Japan. The nuclear weapon provided new justification for the arguments of prewar air power thinkers and seemingly rendered obsolete the lessons that one might otherwise have derived from the far more problematic conventional bombing campaigns of 1942–1945. Second, the Cold War soon created an atmosphere of crisis and war preparation that was not conducive to a thoroughgoing examination of the last war. Admittedly, U.S. airmen, in the process of gaining status as an independent service, commissioned the *Strategic Bombing Survey*. Significantly, however, that study's terms of reference limited its purview to the *economic* impact of bombing, not the wider questions of military utility or the effect the bombing had on German morale. As a result, the survey failed to address a number of essential questions.

Whatever the weaknesses of the survey, it is doubtful whether air force leaders bothered to read such a long and complicated set of documents anyway. Their focus was on "strategic" air war—but in this case "strategic" now meant nuclear war against the Soviet Union. Within that focus, there was neither an underlying conception of morality *nor any significant attempt to come to terms with the operational parameters of nuclear war*. Instead, U.S. nuclear strategy emphasized the hurling of large numbers of nuclear weapons—as many as the United States possessed at a given time—as quickly as possible, then waiting, if anyone survived, to see what would turn up.[2] There is little evidence that the agonized theorizing about nuclear war that occurred in the academic community ever had a serious impact on the thinking in Omaha. In the end, the United States Air Force did not have to fight a great nuclear war against the Soviet Union, and one can argue that the threat posed by U.S. nuclear capabilities played a crucial role in deterring World War III.

Nevertheless, the United States Air Force did have to fight two major conventional air wars during the Cold War: the first in Korea from 1950 to 1953 and the second in Vietnam from 1965 to 1972. In neither case was it prepared conceptually or operationally for what occurred. In both wars, American airmen instinctively assumed the pre–World War II paradigm that "strategic" bombing would relatively easily translate into a collapse of the enemy's will to fight. At the beginning of the Korean conflict, Far Eastern Air Forces, flying out of Japan, launched their B-29s in attacks against North Korean industry in the belief that such attacks would lead to the collapse of the enemy's ability to wage war. But the intervention of the Chinese communists so changed the war's parameters that it soon became apparent that attacks aimed at North Korea's political will could have no impact on Chinese attitudes.

Vietnam brought even more frustration to air force commanders. Ironically, considering the arguments that took place, the political calculations of generals and politicians alike coincided in their estimate of enemy willpower. Policymakers in the White House believed that surgical strikes, escalated in carefully measured doses, would eventually persuade the North Vietnamese to halt their aggression in the south.[3] There was not much that was either measured or surgical about

Curt LeMay's "bomb them back into the Stone Age" approach. But both sides in the policy debate believed that air power in one form or another would dissuade the North Vietnamese from their course. How the American leadership believed that it could intimidate Ho Chi Minh—an individual who had helped found the French Communist Party and survived both Stalin and Mao—is one of the great mysteries of the period.[4] The result of the American disagreements was the disastrously ineffective and mismanaged "Rolling Thunder" air campaign against North Vietnam. Despite considerable cost in blood and treasure that effort failed to achieve any results and eventually whimpered to a halt in summer 1968.[5]

In 1972, Nixon resumed the bombing of North Vietnam. In this second campaign, he sent B-52s directly into the heart of enemy air defenses surrounding Hanoi. The testimony of American prisoners of war in the north indicates that the bombing had appreciable impact on the morale of the North Vietnamese.[6] And at least the bombing did force the North Vietnamese to make peace, albeit on terms wholly favorable to themselves and their prospects for renewing the war. The bombing never forced them to accept conditions that undermined their long-range policies. In the end, they moved not one iota from their fundamental aim to unify all of Vietnam under a ferocious Marxist-nationalist dictatorship.

One notes in the conduct of the air war against North Vietnam a number of the assumptions that had lain at the heart of air power from its earliest decades. Even when the war was over, American airmen persisted in believing that it was their government's restrictions on the application air power in "Rolling Thunder" that had prevented victory in the Vietnam War.[7] But American airmen now also confronted the fact that changes in technology, politics, and the canons of journalism were making the visual results of assault from the air—always far messier than expected—available to an American population whose concerns for humane behavior were not always reconcilable with the visual results of their government's conduct of military operations.[8]

Some fifteen years later, in summer 1990, Saddam Hussein launched his forces into Kuwait. Even by the demanding standards of the region, Iraq possessed a ruthless, murderous government motivated by a ferocious ideology and an ambitious, utterly unscrupulous tyrant at the helm.[9] Washington responded for motives that remain unclear, but the response did address force with force. Because of the distances to the theater, much of the military power that the United States brought to the Middle East in summer and fall 1991 had to be air power. From the first, that curious, confused mixture in the American mind of expediency, humane behavior, and morality entered into the discussions of senior commanders and planners who had to address the problem of Iraqi power in political and military terms. Confronting a threatening situation on the ground, one exacerbated by U.S. intelligence services' overestimates of Iraqi military power, the theater commander, General Norman Schwarzkopf, turned to the air staff for help.[10] A special staff in the Pentagon, "Checkmate," under Colonel John Warden, was already working on a plan that aimed to "deconstruct" Iraq's military capabilities.[11] Some of the major assumptions of the plan suggest much of the same pattern that has characterized air power thinking since before World War II and is therefore worth examining in some detail.

The plan's chief architect, Warden, had emerged as one of the few senior officers in the air force interested in the application of air power at the operational level of war.[12] Warden and his staff from "Checkmate" briefed Schwarzkopf on their concept for an air campaign in mid-August.[13] The code name for the plan, "Instant Thunder," underlined the planners' rejection of the approach that had undergirded "Rolling Thunder"; there would be no measured application of air power to the war against Iraq. The plans and commanders involved in this war bent over backward to ensure that they did not repeat the mistakes American leadership had made in the Vietnam War by underestimating the enemy. And in some respects, the planning on the operational level represented a brilliant piece of military thinking, perhaps even a conceptual revolution for the air force.[14]

But as with so much of air power thinking, those who planned the air war misjudged the staying power and ruthless control that Saddam's Baᶜthist regime exercised over Iraq. The initial plans suggested that a massive attack on the first night could "decapitate" the Iraqi leadership.[15] In later briefings, the planners eventually settled on the assumption that an air campaign of sufficient strength would lead to an Iraqi collapse within a short period of time. As they argued, the direct result of an orchestrated air campaign would be either Saddam's abdication or a coup by the Iraqi military that would remove him from office.[16] By early September, much of Warden's conception had been folded into the plans of CENTAF (a component of Central Command), and as the operations order of that month stated, "When taken in total, the result of Phase I [the initial attack on Iraq] will be a progressive and systematic collapse of Saddam Hussein's entire war machine and regime."[17]

Those involved in the planning process did go to great lengths to shield Iraq's population from the collateral damage that an air campaign against the Iraqi military and the Baᶜthist regime might cause. This was partly motivated by the planners' sense of what the American people would tolerate, particularly given the prewar uncertainties of many Americans. Shortly after assuming his position in late August 1990, Brig. Gen. Buster Glosson, the air war's chief planner, noted in his diary that the American people "would never stand for another Dresden."[18] Both the general guidance and specific objectives for the campaign emphasized this fundamental concern in Riyadh and Washington.[19] As CENTAF's operations order underlined, "Anything which could be considered as terror attacks or attacks on the Iraqi people will be avoided."[20] Thus, a major concern from the start of the planning processes was the prevention of attacks on civilians. Part of this was undoubtedly due to fears that heavy civilian casualties would result in a public relations disaster and that pictures of Iraqi civilian dead might persuade Americans to end the air campaign before it achieved its objectives.

Operational plans for the air offensive against Iraq aimed to take the Iraqi air defenses apart from the inside out rather than the more traditional approach of rolling the enemy's air defenses back. There were good military reasons for the choice, but the approach also allowed attacking air forces to keep Iraqi civilian casualties to a minimum. The military objectives of the campaign were, first, to wreck the Iraqi air defense system; second, to impair the enemy's command- and-control capabilities, political as well as military; third, to damage to the greatest extent possible Saddam's special weapons programs; and, finally, to destroy Iraq's ground forces both to ease the way for the coalition's ground offensive and to diminish Iraq's threat to its neighbors in the long run. But beyond these objectives one senses in the prewar planning efforts a belief that air power could win the war by defeating Iraq's military power and toppling Saddam Hussein before a ground war would be required.[21]

255

In earlier air campaigns there had been considerable tension in the minds of planners between the need to destroy certain military targets and the danger of collateral damage. In 1944, for example, Churchill had strongly opposed using Bomber Command to attack French transportation targets in order to prepare the way for the Normandy invasion. He had feared that collateral damage by such attacks would permanently poison Anglo-French relations in the post–World War II era.[22] Admittedly, Churchill had good reason to worry, given the past performance of Bomber Command. Fortunately for the invasion, he changed his mind, and indeed British bombers proved that they could hit their targets with surprising accuracy. But intended or not, civilian casualties have always been a result of "strategic" bombing. Until the early 1980s, the air weapon resembled a sledgehammer far more than a rapier.

But by 1990 the technological framework within which air war operates had changed in significant ways. First, "stealth" aircraft allowed the attacker to operate deep within the enemy's air defense system without detection, which would have an obvious impact on the attention that crews could devote to placing their bombs accurately on targets. Second, precision-guided munitions (PGMs) allowed aircrews to achieve unheard-of accuracy. F-117s could attack the heart of the enemy's defenses without being seen and consequently would prove virtually invulnerable. In addition to "stealth" aircraft, the Americans possessed cruise missiles that could hit targets in Iraq with great precision. The initial targets of the "stealth" aircraft were military in nature: the command-and-control nodes of the Iraqi military. These attacks were stunningly successful. Planners in Riyadh, watching CNN (the American cable news network) from Baghdad, were delighted to see the reporters go off the air at 0300 local time, precisely the moment when the first F-117 was slated to drop its bomb on the main communications center in Baghdad.

To reinforce the attack on the Iraqi command-and-control systems and the air defense network, cruise missiles attacked the main electric power centers in Iraq.[23] Air planners hoped to avoid the generator halls of such facilities since damage to them would do substantial long-term harm to Iraq.[24] The rationale was not necessarily humanitarian, but stemmed primarily from the belief that coalition military action would soon eventuate in Saddam's elimination from power. For that reason, one wanted to put the new government in the best position to rebuild Iraq when the war was over. The attacks on the electrical system relied on a special warhead that detonated within the enclosure of the main transformer stations in Iraq. By throwing out fine carbon-fiber wires, the cruise missiles managed to short-circuit much of Iraq's electrical system.[25] The results must have been spectacular. Over succeeding days, however, U.S. intelligence found it difficult to access the damage. Consequently, retargeting of electrical power stations occurred throughout the war, and air attacks eventually did serious damage to the generating capacity of the Iraqi electrical system (see map 9.1).

The attacks on the first night achieved their objectives at minimal cost to the coalition, with only one F/A-18C/D lost during the attack on Baghdad. Casualties among the Iraqi civil population appear to have been minimal. The fact that Saddam's regime failed to highlight such casualties suggests two possibilities: either there was little collateral damage and few casualties in civilian areas, or the Iraqi leadership had no desire to point out to either its own population or the world the success (even at killing Iraqis) that coalition air attacks had achieved in the first night's attacks. The general inability of the Iraqis to produce evidence of serious collateral damage to civilian targets or civilians themselves underlines the level of accuracy that coalition PGMs achieved throughout the war. In the end, the accuracy of the air attacks reduced the Iraqis to dragging coalition newsmen around to structures that displayed signs in English—undoubtedly for the edification of Iraqi workers—declaiming the existence of "baby food" factories.[26]

On the third day, coalition planners changed the pattern of attacks on Baghdad—F-117s at night and cruise missiles during the day, with several strike packages of F-16s. The thought was to bring the capabilities of non-PGM aircraft to bear on the larger Iraqi military and police headquarters in downtown Baghdad. Such strikes, planners hoped, would achieve two objectives: first, the quicker destruction of major targets, such as the security police headquarters, than would be the case if one had to rely on individual attacks by F-117s, and, second, the considerable effect on morale that the appearances of strike packages in the skies over their capital might exert upon the Iraqi people and regime.[27]

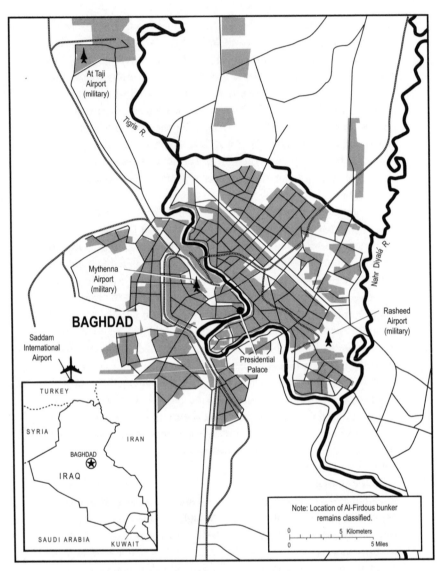

At Taji
Airport
(military)

Tigris R.

Mythenna
Airport
(military)

Nahr Diyala R.

BAGHDAD

Rasheed
Airport
(military)

Saddam
International
Airport

Presidential
Palace

TURKEY

SYRIA

IRAN

BAGHDAD

IRAQ

SAUDI ARABIA

KUWAIT

Note: Location of Al-Firdous bunker
remains classified.

0   5   Kilometers

0   5 Miles

Map 9.1 Baghdad and Vicinity, 1991

The new conception did not work. The first two strike packages against downtown Baghdad were canceled because of the weather. The third package, with seventy-two F-16s, did attack the Iraqi capital, and though it did run into bad weather, it encountered other problems as well. The planning of the raid laid down a pattern that left the most dangerous missions for last, when the Iraqis were at full alert; and the "Weasels" that supported the mission by suppressing enemy air defense systems either ran out of fuel or HARM antiradar missiles. The end result was that a group of F-16s found themselves over downtown Baghdad with fuel, bombs, and drop tanks on board, while radar-guided surface-to-air missiles tracked them.[28] The F-16s' only chance to survive was to shed their loads and take wild evasive action. In two cases even that was not enough; the aircraft were lost. Nevertheless, neither the jettisoned bomb loads nor the aircraft that went down appear to have hit populated parts of Baghdad—at least the Iraqis reported no significant incident.

Interestingly, the response of the air commanders was quite different from that of American commanders in previous wars. The tactic of attacking downtown Baghdad with large strike packages of F-16s ceased immediately. One reason was the fear of losing more aircraft.[29] But the other was that coalition air commanders and planners recognized that exposing conventional aircraft to enemy defenses over Baghdad would significantly increase the chance of a major incident that would kill or injure large numbers of civilians. Such an incident would have an immediate and probably disastrous impact on the politics of the war.[30] Some planners—worried about the possibility that pictures of Iraqi civilian casualties might affect the conduct of the war—suggested interfering with CNN's ability to pass pictures out of Baghdad. But with the widespread breakdown of air force intelligence, the air component commander, Lt. Gen. Chuck Horner, regarded CNN from Baghdad as one of his best intelligence sources. He therefore vetoed the suggestion.

For the first three weeks of the air campaign, coalition aircraft attacked a wide variety of targets, most of which entailed little possibility of collateral damage to civilians or civilian targets. By firing SCUD missiles at both Israel and Saudi Arabia, the Iraqis displayed the same callousness toward civilian casualties that had previously led them to use mustard gas against their own Kurdish population. However, the general inaccuracy of the scuds as well as the considerable efforts made by coalition aircraft to suppress their mobile launchers allowed the coalition to avoid using harsher measures against the Iraqis.[31] The emphasis of air attacks during this period fell on Iraqi airfields and the "hardened" aircraft shelters that protected Saddam's air force. In the first week of February, a sizable number of the F-111Fs that dropped PGMs shifted to attacks upon Iraqi armor and military equipment in the Kuwaiti theater of operations (KTO). The "strategic" air campaign now consisted almost entirely of F-117s, and a wide number of "strategic" targets, particularly in Saddam's special weapons programs (nuclear, chemical, and biological), had yet to be attacked.[32]

By mid-February, with the end of the war in sight, the planners moved to attack once more both the command and control centers and the headquarters of the political and police bureaucracies by which the Baʿthist regime controlled the Iraqi population. The intent was clear: to break Iraq apart politically as well as militarily. The target lists for the night of 12–13 February represented a return to a conception that had surfaced as early as the previous August: a belief that air power could cause the collapse of Saddam's tyrannical regime by attacks on leadership targets. On this night, F-117s were to strike the Iraqi air defense headquarters, the ministry of defense, the headquarters of Saddam's intelligence service, the Baʿthist Party headquarters, the Directorate of General Internal Security, the Directorate of Military Intelligence, the Iraqi intelligence service headquarters, the presidential bunker, and a number of communication sites and bunkers that ran various aspects of the regime's military and political control bureaucracies. This was to be the first night in a series of attacks aimed at disrupting the ability of the regime to control Iraq's political situation.

One of the night's targets was the Al Firdos bunker, which had just emerged as an active command post.[33] Two bombs from an F-117 obliterated the target. Unknown to intelligence, and therefore to the planners, was the fact that the Iraqis were also utilizing Al Firdos as a shelter for dependent family members of senior Baʿthist Party and government officials. The resulting pictures of hundreds of dead, broadcast in lurid detail by television cameras, horrified everyone: pilots, planners, and air commanders as well as the American population. The result was an immediate cessation of such attacks on the political and military headquarters and command bunkers that littered downtown Baghdad.

The Al Firdos bunker incident raises a number of interesting questions about the capacity of the United States to utilize technological weapons in a confusing and ambiguous world, particularly one in which the coin of international relations continues to be military power and the ability to use that power. Saddam's regime did not provide shelters for the great majority of the population in Baghdad. In fact, it provided shelters and access to those shelters only for a small group of Ba'thist elite and their families.

Ironically, at the same time that Al Firdos was occurring the coalition was waging a ruthless, determined campaign to break the Iraqi army in the KTO. That campaign had begun on the first day of the war and continued to the end. Except for the elite Republican Guards, the Iraqi army in the theater consisted mainly of poor, downtrodden, and reluctant conscripts whom Saddam and his regime had dragooned into military service. In many cases, these soldiers were opponents of the regime—ordinary men struggling to survive a vicious and degrading tyranny.[34] To be sure, the bombing of these soldiers was a necessity: after all, Saddam's military had shown great capacity to force even the most unwilling to fight to the end in the war against Iran. But there is surely some irony in the fact that these hapless conscripts were bombed relentlessly, while attacks on critical targets in downtown Baghdad ceased, merely because the policies of the Iraqi government had put the families of its own elite in an operating headquarters.

In fact, the allied campaign that had placed such high hopes on causing the political collapse of the Ba'thist regime exerted virtually no pressure on the population to bring about such a turn of events. Reports of Iraqis who lived through Baghdad during the war indicate that living conditions remained relatively easy, certainly compared to those of the Germans, the Japanese, or even the North Vietnamese, under the bombs.[35] The diary of an Iraqi woman during the bombing suggests how far removed from the war were most Iraqis:

DAY ONE. I woke up at three a.m. to exploding bombs and Salvador Dali, my dog, frantically chasing around the house, barking furiously. I went out on the balcony. Salvador was already there, staring up at a sky lit by the most extraordinary fireworks display. The noise was beyond description. . . .

DAY FOUR. Suha is experimenting with a recipe for basturma. The meat in our freezers is thawing so it's a good thing the weather is cold. In the evening we cook potatoes in the fireplace. . . . I make a dynamite punch with Aquavit, vodka, and fresh orange juice.

DAY FIVE. . . . Apparently people take off for the countryside with their freezers loaded on their pickup trucks and barbecue the food as it defrosts. Only Iraqis would escape from a war carrying freezers full of goodies.

DAY SEVEN. . . . The worst has happened: we have to drink warm beer. I cleaned out the freezer and removed a ton of different kinds of bread. . . . We have to eat everything that will spoil. This means we all shit so much more, all in the garden. . . . I finished Mundher's painting and we had a little party to celebrate its unveiling. We opened a bottle of champagne and ate *meloukhia* and a million other things. I wish that our stock of food would finish so that we could eat a little less.

DAY TEN. . . . Everyone talks endlessly about food. While eating lunch the conversation is about what we are having for dinner. We have cooked up all the meat we had. . . .

DAY ELEVEN. I had great hopes for my birthday. Lots of people were invited, and they all came and more. Drinks flowed in buckets. . . .

DAY THIRTEEN. The peasant's life that we now lead is very hard, and the work never stops. I get up, come downstairs, collect the firewood, clean the grate, and make up the evening fire. I clean the kitchen and boil water for coffee. Suha and Amal cook the meals. Ma makes the bread and cakes. I do the soups and salads. . . .

DAY FIFTEEN. The holes in the Jumhuriya Bridge were neat and precise, with a lot of metal hanging underneath. The bridge was packed with people looking through the holes. A siren was sounding but nobody moved. . . .

DAY TWENTY. It has now been three weeks. Forty-four thousand air raids. I have another leak in the water system. I will have to check the whole house. . . .

DAY TWENTY-TWO. There is a sameness about the days now. I saw the Jumhuriya Bridge today; it's incredibly sad to see a bombed bridge — a murderous action, for it destroys a link. The sight affects everyone that sees it; many people cry. Children play in the street without traffic. They have never had it so good. . . .

DAY THIRTY-FOUR. Tim brought faxes from Sol, Dood, and Charlie, our first contacts with family and friends—a break in our isolation. We had a super barbecue lunch today, a lovely day but quite noisy.[36]

There is no doubt, however, that the air campaign reached directly into the minds of the Iraqi soldiers and destroyed whatever willingness they might have had to fight even before the bombing began.[37] Given the nature of Saddam's tyranny, the only way for the coalition to cause a revolution was either through direct attacks on the population—never considered and, with American attitudes, not a possible approach—or through a systematic attack on the regime and its control system.

The incident at the Al Firdos bunker ended all attempts to destroy Saddam's command-and-control mechanisms for maintaining his tyranny. Where military defeat in the KTO undermined Saddam's political and military structure, the result was revolution that came close to toppling the tyranny. But the political system remained functioning in the heart of Iraq. As a result, even after the disastrous defeat of its armed forces, by late February 1991 it was able to deploy its remaining military strength to quash revolutions in Basra and the north.[38] That system continued to function for one simple reason: the cessation of coalition air attacks on the command-and-control centers required for it to function.

To fully account for the inability of U.S. air power to attack the psychological underpinnings of the Iraqi regime, one must note the role played by military lawyers in targeting—not exactly their normal area of responsibility. One, of course, cannot be surprised that lawyers, in a nation plagued by a legal profession gone haywire, would eventually become involved in the targeting process. In early February, shortly before Al Firdos, the campaign planners selected for destruction a number of Saddam's monuments, including his great statue and the gigantic arc formed by arms (for which his own arms had provided the model) holding crossed swords. However, attorneys for Tactical Air Command, having got wind of the proposal, demanded that such targets be taken off the lists because they were "cultural monuments." As a result, the coalition failed to attack both the political symbols and the control mechanisms of the Iraqi regime. Not surprisingly then, the

Desert Storm air campaign utterly failed to damage the political basis of the Iraqi regime. If the assumptions of airmen on the efficacy
of air attacks proved too optimistic, the inhibitions and confusions
about what constituted humane behavior prevented the United States
from taking full advantage of its capabilities and situation in the Gulf
War. Thus, Saddam's regime still remains damaged but unbowed in the
wreckage of its move into Kuwait.[39]

We have addressed the frame of reference through which Anglo-
American airmen attempted to address the questions raised by air war.
As with military leaders throughout the ages, they heavily emphasized
an approach based on expediency. They claimed for air power the capability to reach across continents into the heart of an enemy nation to
achieve results that could otherwise be gained only by immense sacrifices of blood and treasure on the ground. In other words, air power
provided a simple, cost-efficient solution to the problems raised by war
in the twentieth century.

Besides a continuing willingness to underestimate potential enemy
opposition to air attacks, airmen also regarded (and continue to regard) their weapon as a rapier rather than a sledgehammer. The employment of the air weapon from World War II through to the Gulf
War, however, suggests that a sledgehammer is the more apt analogy.
The planners responsible for the air campaign against Iraq did not
underestimate the capabilities of the enemy's military. On the contrary, they overestimated Iraq's army by a considerable margin. But
like those who embraced the gospel of air power in other wars of
this century, they underestimated the political stability of the enemy's
regime. To those who assessed Iraq, it appeared that the allied coalition confronted a formidable military organization but also a brittle
polity that could not withstand the strain of major air attacks for any
significant time.

Throughout its relatively short history, air war has more often than
not undermined the morale of its opponents. But to do so it has struck
the spectrum of civilian life with little regard to age, sex, or occupation. Yet the actual declines in morale have rarely translated into direct effects: a demoralized population generally has no more power
to influence its government than a spirited one. In the Gulf War, with
rare exceptions, the planners avoided collateral damage. In the KTO,
however, air power bludgeoned poor, unwilling conscripts to such an

extent that they were not only eager to surrender to coalition soldiers but also to remotely piloted vehicles and even Italian newsmen. There were no CNN correspondents in the desert, but there were in Baghdad.[40] In fact, the Iraqi regime, like Stalin's "workers' and peasants' paradise" of 1941, possessed enormous political staying power and relatively little military capacity. As a result, the air campaign dismantled Iraqi air defenses within hours and reduced Iraq's military structure to a paraplegic wreck. But it completely failed in its bid to undermine the regime's political capabilities.

Could it have done so? In counterfactual history, there can be no definitive answers. Nevertheless, the point here is that the American confusion between humane behavior and moral behavior ensured that it could not undo Saddam's tyranny. The United States spared much of Iraq for fear of incurring civilian casualties.[41] Precision-guided munitions did allow attacks on targets in the center of Iraq's cities with little collateral damage. But the mere appearance of civilian dead on CNN screens after Al Firdos sufficed to end whatever chance existed to break the controls that held the tyranny together. Americans should not misunderstand the consequences of their weaknesses. As Winston Churchill remarked in a different but relevant context, "we have sustained a defeat . . . the consequences of which will travel far with us along our road."[42] Saddam's regime has survived. Its ruthless and murderous suppression of the Shiʿite rebellion in southern Iraq and the Kurdish rebellion in northern Iraq in the immediate aftermath of the Gulf War amply demonstrated the moral nature of what has survived. And with Iraq's considerable oil reserves, the world has not heard the last of Saddam Hussein.

Notes

1. No author has more clearly elucidated these issues than Thucydides in his *History of the Peloponnesian War*, trans. Rex Warner (New York, 1954).

2. This author attended a secret briefing on the SIOP (Single Integrated Operational Plan) in 1986 while at the Naval War College. There appeared to be, at least to the author, no operational concept beyond the mere destruction of targets. Those whom I have known who have had more detailed connection with the SIOP have confirmed my impression.

3. For the views in the White House in 1963 and 1964, see *The Pentagon Papers* (New York, 1971), 342, 372, 377, 390, 396, 420, 425.

4. And it is worth noting that a most sophisticated analysis of the North Vietnamese leadership already existed: see Bernard Fall, *The Two Viet-Nams, A Political and Military Analysis* (New York, 1963).

5. As to how badly "Rolling Thunder" was mismanaged by air force leaders, see particularly Barry D. Watts, "Unreported History and Unit Effectiveness," *Journal of Strategic Studies*, March 1989.

6. Scott Blakey, *Prisoner of War, The Survival of Commander Richard A. Straton* (Garden City NY, 1978), 286–94; and the personal testimony of Gen. Charles Boyd to the author, Maxwell AL, February 1991.

7. For a view of how badly the air war was run from the perspective of the air force alone, see Jack Broughton, *Thud Ridge* (New York, 1969).

8. This is in no way meant to subscribe to the myth that the American military "won" the war in Vietnam; it did not. But the point here is that had television cameras been on the scene at Antietam or certainly the Wilderness, it is very unlikely that the North would have continued the terrible struggle that broke the South and ended slavery.

9. All this should have been clear with the publication of a careful study of the political philosophy and nature of Iraq's tyranny by one of those few individuals, Kannan Makiya, who can cross with dispassion the intellectual gulf between the politics of the West and those of Islam. Writing under the pen name Samir Al-Khalil, Makiya laid bare the vicious combinations that Saddam's regime had drawn from both sources. The book made little impression until a review by happenstance appeared in the *Times Literary Supplement* shortly after the invasion of Kuwait. See Samir al-Khalil, *Republic of Fear, The Politics of Modern Iraq* (Berkeley, 1989).

10. General Norman H. Schwarzkopf, *The Autobiography, It Doesn't Take a Hero* (New York, 1992), 318.

11. Oral interview with Lt. Col. David Deptula, Arlington VA, 20–21 December 1991.

12. In fact, while a student at National War College, Warden had written an extended study of how one might best think about using air power to achieve operational objectives in war. The study was eventually published: John A. Warden, *The Air Campaign, Planning for Combat* (Washington DC, 1988).

13. Schwarzkopf, *The Autobiography*, 318.

14. As this author has suggested elsewhere, the first night's attack on a fully operating Iraqi air defense system—an attack that entirely shattered Iraq's capacity to defend itself in one night—represented a far more impressive example of the operational art than did the ground forces' sweep through the shattered remains of Iraq's ground forces in the KTO. See Williamson Murray, *Operations*, vol. 2, pt. 1, *The Gulf War Air Power Survey* (Washington DC, 1994).

15. One of the initial briefings for the "strategic" air campaign against Iraq presented the following on a briefing slide: "psychological operations critical element in the campaign; separate regime from the support of the military and the people." Warden Briefing, 11 August 1990, "Instant Thunder," Gulf War Air Power Survey, Folder #15.

16. "'Instant Thunder,' Proposed Strategic Air Campaign," Checkmate Briefing, 13 August 1990, 2300 hrs., Gulf War Air Power Survey Archive, chaps. 35–36.

17. Quoted in Thomas Keaney and Eliot A. Cohen, *Summary Report, Gulf War Air Power Survey* (Washington DC, 1994), 45.

18. Glosson journal, August 1990; interview, Maj. Gen. Buster Glosson with Gulf War Air Power personnel (Williamson Murray, Barry Watts, and Thomas Keaney), Pentagon, 9 April 1992.

19. Murray, *Operations*, vol. 2, pt. 1, *Gulf War Air Power Survey*, chap. 2.

20. Keaney and Cohen, *Summary Report, Gulf War Air Power Survey*, 46.

21. Interview, Maj. Gen. Buster Glosson with Gulf War Air Power Survey personnel, 9 April 1992.

22. Williamson Murray, *Luftwaffe* (Baltimore, 1985), 251.

23. David A. Fulghum, "Secret Carbon-Fiber Warheads Blinded Iraqi Air Defenses," *Aviation Week & Space Technology*, 27 April 1992, 18–19.

24. Interview, Maj. Gen. Buster Glosson with Gulf War Air Power Survey personnel, 9 April 1992.

25. Fulghum, "Secret Carbon-Fiber Warheads Blinded Iraqi Air Defenses," 18–19.

26. Since the "baby food" factory had no discernible machinery, it is difficult to say what the target actually was. But United Nations inspections since the war have made it clear that the Iraqis are extraordinarily good at moving embarrassing evidence out of the neighborhood in short periods of time.

27. Interview, Lt. Col. David Deptula with Gulf War Air Power Survey personnel (Williamson Murray and Barry Watts), Pentagon, 21 December 1991.

28. Interview, Major John Nichols with Gulf War Air Power Survey personnel (Williamson Murray and Barry Watts), Pentagon, 20 July 1992.

29. Again, the contrast with previous wars is instructive. The proud boast of the U.S. Army Air Forces in World War II was that no mission had ever turned back in the face of enemy defenses, no matter how heavy the casualties. The two raids against Schweinfurt in 1943 certainly back up that claim. Nevertheless, the chief planner and air division commander of the fighter wings, Brig. Gen. Buster Glosson, went out to the squadrons and explicitly stated that *no* target was worth the loss of a single coalition aircraft. Interview, Maj. Gen. Buster Glosson with Gulf War Air Power Survey personnel, 9 April 1992, and

interview, Maj. John Nichols with Gulf War Air Power Survey personnel, 20 July 1992.

30. Interview, Lt. Col. David Deptula with Gulf War Air Power Survey personnel, 20 December 1991; and interview, Maj. Gen. Buster Glosson with Gulf War Air Power Survey personnel, 9 April 1992.

31. There was considerable fear that the Iraqis might use chemicals with their scuds. The coalition's political leaders, including President George Bush, made clear that such action would result in severe countermeasures—although never spelled out—by their aircraft. The Iraqis did not use chemicals with their scuds, but the reason may have been technical problems rather than the effectiveness of deterrence threats.

32. Murray, *Operations*, 2, pt. 1, *Gulf War Air Power Survey*.

33. The Iraqis had a number of redundant command posts in the Baghdad area, and the Al Firdos bunker was one such site. Early in February, U.S. intelligence indicated that the Iraqis had activated the bunker and were using it as a command post. It was therefore a legitimate military target. Keaney and Cohen, *Summary Report, Gulf War Air Power Survey*, 68–69.

34. For the nature of that tyranny, see al-Khalil, *The Republic of Fear and Cruelty*.

35. See Earl R. Beck, *Under the Bombs, the German Home Front 1942–1945* (Lexington KY, 1986).

36. Nuha Al-Radi, "Baghdad Diary," *Granta* 42 (1992): 209–29. One is not sure whether the editors of *Granta* published Al-Radi's diary for its ironic value or because they wanted to underline the sufferings of the Iraqi people.

37. While working on the Gulf War Air Power Survey, this author had the opportunity to examine many of the thousands of pow reports that the coalition forces gathered in debriefing the Iraqi soldiers captured at the end of the war.

38. See al-Khalil, *Republic of Fear*, for particularly graphic descriptions of the ferocity with which the Ba'thist regime eliminated its opponents in the post–Gulf War period.

39. Given the inclinations of the United Nations and the capacity of American statesmen to regard anything that happened more than a year ago as ancient history, we will undoubtedly soon see the sanctions against Iraq lifted. Moreover, given the unfortunately large amounts of oil the Iraqis possess, they will soon be out on the world's arms bazaars re-creating what we destroyed in 1991. One suspects that they will not move next time until they have acquired nuclear weapons, but given the collapse of the Soviet Union and the amounts of weapons-grade uranium sloshing around the world, that also should not represent a great problem.

40. Immediately after the war, American peace activists visited Iraq in a major effort to prove that once again the United States had been guilty of unspeakable crimes. Instead of the massive wreckage they expected in Baghdad, they discovered "a city whose homes and offices were almost entirely intact, where electricity was coming back on and the water was running." John G. Heidenrich, "The Gulf War: How Many Iraqis Died?" *Foreign Affairs* (spring 1993): 118.

41. And even some in the American polity actually suggested after the war that there was something *wrong* in the fact that we inflicted disproportionately heavy casualties compared with our own. None of these critics were, however, close to the battle lines.

42. Winston Churchill, *The Gathering Storm* (London, 1948), 322–27.

CONTRIBUTORS

TRUMAN ANDERSON received his doctorate in history from the University of Chicago in 1995. He is a former lecturer in international history at the London School of Economics and the author of several articles on the German occupation of Ukraine during World War II. He is presently the executive director of the Stuart Family Foundation in Lake Forest, Illinois.

T. C. W. BLANNING is a professor of modern European history at the University of Cambridge and a fellow of Sidney Sussex College; he is also a fellow of the British Academy. He has published numerous books on the French Revolution and the Napoleonic period. His most recent work is *The Culture of Power and the Power of Culture: Old Regime Europe 1660–1789* (Oxford University Press, 2001).

CONRAD C. CRANE is Research Professor of Military Strategy at the Strategic Studies Institute of the United States Army War College. Previously he was a professor of history at the United States Military Academy. He is the author of *Bombs, Cities, and Civilians: American Airpower Strategy in World War II* (University Press of Kansas, 1993) and *American Airpower Strategy in Korea, 1950–1953* (University Press of Kansas, 2000).

MARK GRIMSLEY is an associate professor of history at the Ohio State University. He is the author or editor of several books, including *The Hard Hand of War: Union Military Policy toward Southern Civilians, 1861–1865* (Cambridge University Press, 1995) and *The Collapse of the Confederacy* (University of Nebraska Press, 2001).

HOLGER H. HERWIG is a professor of history at the Centre for Military and Strategic Studies at the University of Calgary. His most recent publications include *The First World War: Germany and Austria-Hungary 1914–1918* (Arnold, 1997) and, with William F. Sater, *The Grand Illusion: The Prussianization of the Chilean Army* (University of Nebraska Pres, 1999).

JOHN A. LYNN is a professor of history at the University of Illinois at Urbana-Champaign and adjunct professor of history at the Ohio State

University. His works include *The Wars of Louis XIV, 1667–1714* (Longmans, 1999), *Giant of the Grand Siècle: The French Army, 1610–1715* (Cambridge University Press, 1997), and *The Bayonets of the Republic: Motivation and Tactics in the Army of Revolutionary France, 1791–94* (Westview Press, 1996).

WILLIAMSON MURRAY, a professor emeritus of history at the Ohio State University, is currently a senior fellow at the Institute for Defense Analyses in Alexandria, Virginia. His many publications include *Luftwaffe* (Nautical and Aviation, 1985), *Air War in the Persian Gulf* (Nautical and Aviation, 1994), and *A War to Be Won: Fighting the Second World War*, coauthored with Allan R. Millett (Harvard University Press, 2000).

PAUL A. RAHE is Jay P. Walker Professor of History at the University of Tulsa. His book *Republics Ancient and Modern: Classical Republicanism and the American Revolution* (1992) is available in a three-volume paperback edition from the University of North Carolina Press.

CLIFFORD J. ROGERS is an associate professor of history at the United States Military Academy. His publications include *The Military Revolution Debate: Readings on the Military Transformation of Early Modern Europe* (Westview Press, 1995), *The Wars of Edward III: Sources and Interpretations* (Boydell Press, 1999), and *War Cruel and Sharp: English Strategy under Edward III, 1327–1360* (Boydell Press, 2000).

INDEX

Aachen, 114

Aegospotami, 1

Albigensian Crusade, xvii, xxv n.2

Albret, Bernard-Ezii, sire de, 36, 53

Alcibiades, 23–24

Alcidas, 13

Alexandre, Charles-Alexis, 122

Al Firdos bunker, xxiv, 260–61, 263, 265, 268 n.33

Alfred P. Murrah federal office building, x

Alsace, 80, 88–89, 92, 100, 125

American Civil War, xii, xv, xx–xxi, 137–55, 266 n.8

American Revolution, 154

American Indians. *See* Native Americans

Anderson, Frederick, 235

Anjou, 50

Ankre Knee, 170

anti-semitism, 129, 178–85, 193–94

Antonov, General, 234

appatis, 47, 49, 50, 56, 58–59. *See also* contributions

Arabic, 169

Archidamus, 9, 15–16

area bombing. *See* bombing

Arnold, Henry "Hap," 223, 229, 231, 233, 235–38, 240–41

Athens, xii, xiv, 1–32, 184

Atlanta, 138, 141–42

atomic weapons. *See* nuclear and atomic weapons

Auberchicourt, Eustache de, 50, 55

Auxerre, 46

AWPD/1, 233

Baden, 79

Baghdad, 256–65

Baker, Edward M., 141

Baltic states, 171–72

banditry, 128–29. *See also* free companies

Barfleur, 45

Barnwell, 137–38

Basin, Thomas, 33

Basra, 263

Bauer, Max, 171

Bavaria, 81, 88

Bear River, 151

Beauvais, 34, 45, 47, 49

Bebel, August, 165

Beck, Ludwig, 176

Belfort, 93

Belgium, 112, 130, 166–67

Belgrade, 242

bellum hostile, 54, 62

Benedict XII, 40

Berlin, 229, 230, 233–34, 238

Bernhardi, Friedrich von, 166, 172–73

Bethmann Hollweg, Theobald von, 164–65

Béthune, 46

Bezuhlivka, 200–201, 203

Big Hole, Battle of the, 143

billeting. *See* quartering of troops

Binasco, 127

Bingen, 85

Bismarck, Otto von, 163–64, 166, 170, 184

Black Prince. *See* Edward of Woodstock

"blinkered professionalism," 164, 169–70, 173, 176–77, 185

Blitz (bombing of London), 224

Bloch, Ivan ("Jean de"), 219

blockades, naval, 219–20

Blomberg, Werner von, 173, 176

Bock, Fedor von, 181

bombing: area, fire, or terror, xiii, xxi–xxiii, 219–26, 230–37, 239–41, 255. *See also* devastation; precision bombing

Bonaparte, Napoléon, 127, 130

Bonet, Honoré, 54

Bonn, 121, 125

Boufflers, Louis François, 80, 95

Bourges, 37

273

attrition," xx, xxiii, 57–58, 62, 144, 147–48, 220, 225, 228, 230, 235, 238, 240, 252; to hinder enemy logistics, xix, 68 n.47, 83, 88, 91–92, 145, 150, 170–71, 173; as impediment to future peace or inspiration for continued resistance, 34, 56, 79, 87–88, 129, 131, 143–44, 220–21, 224–26, 232; as incentive to surrender or pressure government to surrender, xiii, xviii–xix, xxii, 54, 63, 101, 146, 220, 224, 229, 233, 236, 240, 264; as provocation to battle, xii, 56–57, 62, 228; for supply, pay, or profit of troops, xii–xiii, xv, xix–xx, 56–60, 119, 122, 144–46, 150 (see also *appatis*; contributions; "tax of violence"). *See also* bombing

Diodotus, 5–8, 24–25

Dönitz, Karl, 185

Doolittle, James, xxiii, 228–29, 232, 234, 238

"double effect" principle, 142

Douhet, Giulio, 220–21, 243

Dresden, xxiii, 226, 230, 234–35, 238, 242, 255

Duras, Henri de Durfort, Duke of, 80, 85, 95–96, 98–99

Dutch War (1672–78), 88

Eaker, Ira C., 223, 229–32, 238

écorcheurs, 47, 61. See also *routiers*

Edict of Fraternity, 112–13, 115

Edward III of England, xviii, xix, 34, 36, 45, 54, 184

Edward of Woodstock (the Black Prince), 35, 37, 45–46, 57

Eichmann, Adolf, 182

Eisenhower, Dwight, 232, 235

Emancipation Proclamation, 144

Esslingen, 83, 94

Ethiopia, 221

Eugene of Savoy, 88

executions of citizen-soldiers, 182

expedience vs. morality, xvi, 4–12, 22, 180, 184, 221–22, 225, 228, 233, 236–37, 239, 251, 254, 263–65. *See also* collateral damage; "double effect" principle

Falkenhayn, Erich von, 168, 175

Fastolf, John, xv

Fedorov, A. F., 196–207, 210–11

"feedfights," 150

Ferguson, Ronald, 94, 97

fire bombing. *See* bombing

Firmond, Georg Ludwig, 125

Foix, Gaston Phoebus, Comte de, 56

forced labor, 53, 85, 124–25, 167–68, 171, 210

Fra Diavolo. *See* Pezza

François II de Bonne, Marquis of Créquy, 98

Francs-tireurs. See partisans

Frankenthal, 80

Frankfurt, 96, 126

free companies: distinguished from *routiers*, 59. See also *routiers*

French Revolution, xix–xx, 111–32

Freytag-Loringhoven, Axel von, 166

Friderici, Erich, 194, 196, 209

Friedrichsburg, 79

Fritsch, Werner von, 176

Furet, François, 113

Fürstenberg, Egon von, 89, 91

garrison forces, 47–48, 53, 56, 59–60

gas warfare, 168, 173, 175, 220, 240, 259

Geneva Conventions, 181, 192

Genoa, 101

genocide, 101, 152–53, 170, 176, 178

Ghent, 126

Gibbon, John, 143

Glosson, Buster, 255

Goebbels, Joseph, 182–83, 185

Gomel, 207–8

Grant, Ulysses, 145

Grierson, C. M., 235

Groener, Wilhelm, 174

Guderian, Heinz, 180

guerillas. *See* partisans

Guienne, 60

Gulf War, xiv, xxiv, 251–65

Hague Conventions of 1899 and 1907, 168, 175, 181, 192, 213 n.2

Hainaut, 166

Halder, Franz, 175, 177, 180

In *Studies in War, Society, and the Military*

Military Migration and State Formation
The British Military Community in Seventeenth-Century Sweden
Mary Elizabeth Ailes

The Rise of the National Guard
The Evolution of the American Militia, 1865–1920
Jerry Cooper

In the Service of the Emperor
Essays on the Imperial Japanese Army
Edward J. Drea

You Can't Fight Tanks with Bayonets
Psychological Warfare against the Japanese Army in the Southwest Pacific
Allison B. Gilmore

Civilians in the Path of War
Edited by Mark Grimsley and Clifford J. Rogers

Soldiers as Citizens
Former German Officers in the Federal Republic of Germany, 1945–1955
Jay Lockenour

The Grand Illusion
The Prussianization of the Chilean Army
William F. Sater and Holger H. Herwig

The Challenge of Change
Military Institutions and New Realities, 1918–1941
Edited by Harold R. Winton and David R. Mets